Social Science Research and Government

This collection of original essays considers the relationship between social science research and government during the last 30 years in Britain and the United States. Increasingly social science is drawn on by governments to frame economic and social policies. What sorts of social science research are available and how are they used? How has the use of the social sciences grown and with what consequences? What is the role of such expertise in the democratic political process? These are some of the questions which the book seeks to answer by a detailed comparison of the two leading Western nations in social science. Twenty authoritative contributors, most of whom work or have worked in government, review the general features of government–social science interaction, and examine in detail the institutions and methodology by means of which such knowledge-use is fostered. A final section considers the consequences of policies towards social science of the Reagan and Thatcher governments during the 1980s. This is a unique collection, of general interest both to social science staff and graduate students and to policy-makers working inside government.

Social Science Research and Government

Comparative Essays on Britain and the United States

edited by

MARTIN BULMER

Senior Lecturer in Social Administration
London School of Economics and Political
Science

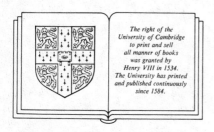

The right of the
University of Cambridge
to print and sell
all manner of books
was granted by
Henry VIII in 1534.
The University has printed
and published continuously
since 1584.

CAMBRIDGE UNIVERSITY PRESS

Cambridge
London   New York   New Rochelle
Melbourne   Sydney

Published by the Press Syndicate of the University of Cambridge
The Pitt Building, Trumpington Street, Cambridge CB2 1RP
32 East 57th Street, New York, NY 10022, USA
10 Stamford Road, Oakleigh, Melbourne 3166, Australia

First published 1987

Printed in Great Britain at the University Press, Cambridge

British Library cataloguing in publication data

Social science research and government:
comparative essays on Britain and the
United States.
1. Social sciences – Research – Great
Britain – Government policy – History –
20th century. 2. Social sciences –
Research – United States – Government
policy – History – 20th century
I. Bulmer, Martin
300'.72041   H62.5.G7

Library of Congress cataloguing in publication data

Social science research and government.
Includes index.
1. Policy sciences – Research. 2. Social scientists
in government – Great Britain. 3. Social scientists in
government – United States. I. Bulmer, Martin.
H97.S637 1987   361.6'1   86-17542

ISBN 0 521 32350 9

CE

Contents

II METHODOLOGIES FOR POLICY RESEARCH

Preface

This collection of original essays reflects a long-standing interest which I have had in the influence on and permeation of government by social science research. Comparing the situation today with that 50 years ago, the governments of industrial countries accept greater use of social science research to inform themselves about the state of society, the causes of social conditions and the impacts and effects of policies. The history of government involvement in empirical social research, of course, goes much further back, but between the 1930s and today there has been a qualitative change in the scale of government involvement. The governments of industrial countries now use social scientists as consultants and advisers, employ them both 'in-house' and 'out-house' to conduct research, and fund basic and applied social science outside government on a scale unimaginable before World War Two.

This expansion in policy-oriented social science has not been without its problems, which it is one purpose of this collection to examine. These problems stem in part from the intellectual status of the social sciences and the status of the knowledge which they offer. Are the social sciences sciences in the same sense as the natural sciences? How well founded and tested are the general theories which they use? How well proven are the hypotheses and generalisations about social and economic behaviour which they offer? What type of expertise do they contribute to the multi-faceted process of policy-making? These problems also stem from the institutional arrangements for the conduct of policy-oriented social research. How is such research to be commissioned and where is it carried out? How does it get done, and how do its results feed into the policy-making process? What are some of the obstacles which hinder its effective utilisation?

The present collection focuses upon the relation between social science research and government in Britain and the United States, the two societies where there are the longest traditions of an effective relationship between social science and policy-making. Its themes are three: consideration of general features of the interaction between government and social science; detailed examination of the institutional arrangements by which social science research is carried out; and discussion of methodological issues in policy research. It is hoped that the range of essays here will be of interest to social scientists and some policy-makers in both societies and elsewhere, in illuminating the character and features of what has rightly been termed an 'uneasy relationship' between government and social science research.

A particular focus of the book is to attempt a preliminary comparison between the situations in Britain and the United States. The collection has been conceived of as a comparative exercise, though a loose rather than a tight comparison. Its purpose is to try to throw light on some of these similarities and differences, focusing particularly upon intellectual, organisational and methodological dimensions of difference and similarity. Less explicit attention is paid to a detailed political comparison of the two systems (itself a subject for an essay in comparative government) or to a detailed study of the policy-making process in each society. A mixture of British and American contributors permits a balance to be struck between experience in each society to bring out salient parallels and differences. Such differences have often been remarked upon, and the attempt is made here to spell out some of the parallels and contrasts more fully.

The focus of this collection is deliberately Anglo-centric, and may be criticised on that account. Even within the English-speaking world it narrows down to two societies. The justification is to gain some depth of perspective, and its conclusions may not be without wider significance particularly to the extent that the United States in particular exercises some wider influence upon the international community of social scientists. Its exploratory character should be underlined. The papers presented here do not constitute a definitive comparison, or even a comprehensive account of the government–social science relationship in each society. They do, however, highlight key salient issues. One particular emphasis (or lack of it) should be mentioned. The focus here is not primarily upon the *process* of policy-making nor upon a comparative politics of the two societies. To some extent a degree of background knowledge is taken for granted on the part of the reader. Some salient differences in the systems of government are sketched in the editorial chapters, but this collection is not primarily intended as a symposium on comparative politics as such.

No-one interested in the relation between social science and government can ignore the change in climate which has occurred in both countries in the 1980s, with the advent of governments less predisposed to large-scale financial support for social science. The implications of these changes are discussed in detail in the last three chapters of the book. To anticipate an argument which I develop there, while these changes are certainly important, it is possible to exaggerate the damage done to social science research. Social scientists have shown themselves capable of effective public self-justification (particularly in the United States), and there has been some success in limiting the extent of budget cuts. In the large, plural, multi-funded research environment of the last quarter of the twentieth century, there is no question of government putting the clock back to the *status quo ante*. It is possible to exaggerate the changes which have been made in recent years, to misinterpret somewhat the malevolence of the Reagan and Thatcher governments towards social science, and neglect the fact that applied social science is a fairly strongly entrenched, if small, sector of knowledge production in contemporary industrial societies.

My own interest in these subjects goes back at least a decade, to a year spent working in the Office of Population Censuses and Surveys in London. Since then I have pursued these interests in various publications, especially *The Uses of Social Research* (Allen & Unwin, 1982) and *Social Science and Social Policy* (Allen & Unwin, 1986). I welcome the opportunity to bring together a varied and distinguished group of contributors here, who have much of interest to say about the general theme. It is a particular pleasure that so many are present or past active participants in government, as opposed to academic observers. Of the latter here, all either have (like myself) themselves worked in government, or have established very close links in the course of first-hand empirical inquiries which they have made. They speak with some authority, even if the total picture of government in the two societies provided here is necessarily a selective one. The responsibility for the selection of contributors, the themes of their chapters, and their arrangement in the book lies with me as editor. My principal debt in preparing the book is to the contributors themselves, for agreeing to write a chapter, for bearing patiently with the editorial process, and for a common desire to explicate some of the excitement, puzzlement and frustration which the social science researcher in the orbit of government comes to experience.

November 1985 MARTIN BULMER
*London School of Economics
and Political Science*

Contributors

MARTIN BULMER (editor) is Senior Lecturer in Social Administration at the London School of Economics and Political Science. Previously he was Lecturer in Sociology at the University of Durham and, for one year in the mid 1970s, a member of the UK Government Statistical Service while working as a statistician at the Office of Population Censuses and Surveys, London. While there he helped to found an informal 'Social Scientists in Government' group. His main teaching interests are in the methodology of social research, the application of social research in public policy-making and the sociology of race relations. His research interests include the utilisation of social science research, the sociology of informal social care, the sociology of privacy and the history of the social sciences. His recent publications include *The Chicago School of Sociology* (1984), *Neighbours: the work of Philip Abrams* (1986), *Social Science and Social Policy* (1986) and (editor) *Essays on the History of British Sociological Research* (1985). He is currently vice-chairman of the Research Resources and Methods Committee of the (UK) Economic and Social Research Council.

STUART BLUME is Professor of Science Dynamics (Wetenschapsdynamica) at the University of Amsterdam, the Netherlands. From 1969 to 1971 he was on the secretariat of the Council for Scientific Policy in the Department of Education and Science, London; from 1975 to 1977 he was a member of the Social Research Co-ordinating Unit in the UK Cabinet Office; and from 1977 to 1980 he was scientific secretary of the 'Black Committee' on inequalities in health. Professor Blume has served as a consultant to (among other organisations) the OECD, Unesco, the National Science Foundation (Washington), the Council for Planning and Co-ordination of Research (Stockholm) and the Science Policy

Advisory Council (The Hague). Among his publications are *Towards a Political Sociology of Science* (Free Press, 1974); *The Commissioning of Social Research by Central Government* (SSRC, 1982); and various articles on the sociology of science, university research policy, and the relations between the social sciences and government.

ROBERT F. BORUCH is Professor of Psychology and Education and Director of the Center for Statistics and Probability at Northwestern University, Evanston, Illinois. He is author of over eighty journal articles on evaluation methods and policy, and co-author of books on the topic, including *Social Experimentation* (1974), *Experimental Testing of Public Policy* (1975), *Reanalyzing Program Evaluations* (1981), *Assuring the Confidentiality of Social Research Data* (1979), and *Solutions to Ethical and Legal Problems in Social Research* (1983). Boruch has served as member and chairman of a variety of committees for the National Academy of Sciences and the Social Science Research Council, on issues ranging from noise impact of the Concorde airplane to evaluation of government sponsored research in chemistry, education, and engineering. His international work spans both industrialised and developing countries including China, Colombia, Nicaragua, Germany, Sweden, the UK, India and Malaysia. The relevant papers appear in professional journals as well as edited monographs published by UNESCO.

JOHN BYNNER is Professor of Education and until recently Dean of the School of Education at the Open University. He was previously a Senior Survey Research Officer in the Social Survey Division of what is now the Office of Population Censuses and Surveys (OPCS), London. His principal present research interests are in the fields of adolescent values, the organisation and practice of distance education and the application of multivariate statistical modelling techniques in education and social-policy research. He has worked previously on follow-up research to the research done for the Plowden Committee and on children's smoking, and is currently co-ordinating the ESRC 15–19 initiative. Besides many OU teaching texts on research methods, publications include *The Young Smoker*, *Parents' Attitudes to Smoking*, and articles and papers on 'Experimental Research Strategy and the Evaluation of Research Designs', 'Self Esteem and Delinquency Revisited', 'Advanced Project Work in Distance Education', 'LISREL for Beginners', and 'Collaborative Schemes and the Ethos of Distance Teaching'.

COLIN CAMPBELL S.J. is university professor in the Martin Chair of Philosophy and Politics at Georgetown University in Washington, D.C.

Previously he was professor and coordinator in the Public Policy and Administration Program at York University in Toronto, Canada. He currently serves as the co-chairman of the International Political Science Association Study Group on the Structure and Organization of Government. His present research, involving a study of the presidential advisory system under Jimmy Carter and Ronald Reagan, will be published under the title *In Search of Executive Harmony*. Campbell's other books include *The Canadian Senate: A Lobby From Within* (1978), *The Superbureaucrats: Structure and Behavior in Central Agencies* (1979), and *Governments Under Stress: Political Executives and Key Bureaucrats in Washington, London and Ottawa* (1983). He has coedited two scholarly collections and published numerous articles in learned journals and books.

RONALD V. CLARKE was until recently Head of the UK Home Office Research and Planning Unit, and is now Professor of Criminal Justice, Temple University, Philadelphia. His research interests include crime prevention, policing, criminological theory, the ecology of crime, evaluation methodology and the treatment of delinquency. He is joint editor of the following books: *Varieties of Residential Experience* (1975); *The Effectiveness of Policing* (1980); *Designing Out Crime* (1980); *Crime Control in Britain* (1983); *Coping with Burglary* (1984); and *The Reasoning Criminal* (in press).

DEREK B. CORNISH is Lecturer in Psychology in the Department of Social Science and Administration, London School of Economics and Political Science. He previously worked at the Home Office Research Unit. His present research interests are in the fields of penal-treatment evaluation, criminal decision-making, and policy-relevant social research. His main publications are: *The Controlled Trial in Penal Research* (1972); and *Residential Treatment and Its Effects on Delinquency* (1975) (both with R. V. G. Clarke); *Gambling* (1978); *Crime Control in Britain* (1983) (with R. V. G. Clarke) and *The Reasoning Criminal* (in press) (also with R. V. G. Clarke).

PAUL FLATHER is currently researching modern Indian politics at Balliol College, Oxford and represents Tooting on the Inner London Education Authority. He has worked for the BBC, and from 1980 to 1984 he was the social science and arts correspondent on the *Times Higher Education Supplement*, covering the Rothschild inquiry. He has worked for a number of MPs and written for a number of British newspapers and weekly magazines.

BARRY HEDGES is Deputy Director of Social and Community Planning Research (SCPR). His substantive research interests during the fifteen years he has spent with the Institute have been in a variety of fields including housing, environment, recreation, transport and, particularly in recent years, employment. His interest in the methodological aspects of surveys was recognised by a Social Science Research Council three-year programme grant that was the precursor of the award of Designated Centre status to SCPR's Survey Methods Centre. His publications include many research reports in the above fields, papers on survey methodology, and contributions to a number of edited volumes.

DENIS F. JOHNSTON is on the faculty of the School of Business Administration, Georgetown University, Washington, D.C. Since his retirement from federal government service in 1981 (latterly in the Office of Federal Statistical Policy and Standards, U.S. Department of Commerce) he has been a private consultant for such organisations as UNESCO, ESCAP (Bangkok), and the U.S. National Research Council and National Center for Education Statistics. He has also lectured at the Development Academy of the Philippines and at the Chinese Academy of Social Sciences (Beijing). Prior to his retirement, he was responsible for the preparation of the last two U.S. national social indicator reports, *Social Indicators 1976* and *Social Indicators III* (1979). He has published numerous articles on social indicators and social forecasting. He holds the degree of Ph.D. in sociology.

LISL KLEIN is a Senior Social Scientist at the Tavistock Institute of Human Relations, London. Since graduating she has alternated between work in industry and research and consultancy on aspects of industrial organisation. Her early research includes work on the human implications of work study and on the behavioural effects of management control systems: consultancy assignments have been on problems of organisation and on the design of jobs and work organisation. Recent assignments include work with the German government's programme to 'Humanise Life at Work' and on the human aspects of plant design. In all her work, the framework has been the use and application of social science. From 1965–70 she was Social Sciences Adviser to Esso Petroleum Co. Ltd. Having written an account of that role, she is currently engaged on research into other attempts to make use of social science in organisations. Her publications include *Multiproducts Ltd: A Case Study in the Social Effects of Rationalised Production* (HMSO, 1964), *New Forms of Work Organisation* (1976) and *A Social Scientist in Industry* (1976).

AUBREY MCKENNELL is Professor (Emeritus) of Survey Methods at the University of Southampton. He was Senior and Principal Research Officer at the (then) UK Government Social Survey (now OPCS Social Survey Division) for seven years ending in 1967, where he directed many surveys including pioneering studies of aircraft-noise annoyance and smoking behaviour and attitudes. He has published *Surveying Attitude Structures* (1974) and many journal articles and book chapters on this topic (for example, in O'Muircheartaigh and Payne's *The Analysis of Survey Data* (1977)). As a Visiting Professor he has spent several periods at survey-research centres in North America including particularly ISR, University of Michigan, beginning with fifteen months secondment there in 1972–3. Collaborative work on the ISR subjective social indicator programme has been reported in book chapters and in journal articles in *Social Indicators Research* and the *Journal of Community Psychology*. Currently McKennell is Co-ordinator for the ESRC Survey Link Scheme described in Chapter 13 and is also directing a major survey of the needs of the visually handicapped for the Royal National Institute for the Blind.

ROBERTA BALSTAD MILLER is the Director of the Division of Social and Economic Science at the U.S. National Science Foundation (NSF). Previously she was the founding Executive Director of the Consortium of Social Science Associations (COSSA) and remained in that position for three years. She has also been Staff Associate at the Social Science Research Council (SSRC). She has taught at Catholic University, the University of Minnesota, Oberlin College and Hiram College. Dr Miller received the Ph.D. from the University of Minnesota in history. She is the author of *City and Hinterland: A Case Study of Urban Growth and Regional Development* (1979) and co-editor (with H. Zuckerman) of *Science Indicators: Implications for Research and Policy* (1980). She has published numerous articles, most recently 'Social Policy Experimentation: Some Comments and Caveats', *Evaluation Review* (1985); 'Research Support and Intellectual Advance in the Social Sciences', and (with F. Juster) 'The Role of Technological Change in Social Science', *Items* (1983) and *Transaction/SOCIETY* (1984); and 'The Social Sciences and the Politics of Science: The 1940's', *The American Sociologist* (1982). A member of the editorial boards of several scholarly journals, she has also been a member of the Board of Directors of the National Council on Public History.

DONALD NAULLS teaches political science at St Mary's University, Halifax, Nova Scotia. He is engaged in a comparative study of accountability among senior civil servants in the U.S., UK and Canada. He has coauthored 'Policy Makers and Facilitators: The Boundaries Between Two Bureaucratic Roles', *International Yearbook for Studies of Leaders and Leadership* (in press).

RAY C. RIST is currently the Deputy Director of the Program Evaluation and Methodology Division, United States General Accounting Office. Prior to coming to the GAO in Washington D.C. in 1981, Rist was a professor at Cornell University. He also has been a senior Fulbright Fellow at the Max Planck Institute in West Berlin. His previous government experience was as Associate Director of the National Institute of Education (1974–6). He has authored or edited thirteen books, the most recent of which are *Policy Studies Review Annual*, Vol. 6 (1982); Vol. 7 (1985); and Vol. 8 (1986). He has also recently published *Finding Work: Cross National Perspectives on Employment and Training* (1986). Rist has served as a consultant to a number of international organisations, has written more than 100 articles and lectured in more than twenty countries.

THEDA SKOCPOL is Professor of Sociology at Harvard University. From 1981 to 1985 she taught at the University of Chicago. A comparative-historical sociologist, Skocpol is the author of the prizewinning book *States and Social Revolutions* (1979) and has edited and contributed to *Vision and Method in Historical Sociology* (1984) and *Bringing the State Back In* (1985). Skocpol's current research focuses on the development of public social policies in the United States from the nineteenth century to the present, with comparisons to Britain, Sweden and other nations. Her interest in social knowledge and public policy-making grows out of this broader research. As Co-Chair of the Social Science Research Council's Committee on States and Social Structures, Skocpol is helping to initiate collaborative scholarly investigations of the relationships between governmental policy-making and the development and application of the modern social sciences.

CYRIL S. SMITH recently retired after ten years as the Secretary of the British Economic and Social Research Council (ESRC), formerly the Social Science Research Council (SSRC). He was previously Director of Studies in Social Policy at the Civil Service College. He now runs a research consultancy advising on research strategies and funding. He is also completing a book at Nuffield College, Oxford, for which this chapter is a preliminary sketch. His publications are mainly in the field of youth and leisure. From 1972 to 1974 he was chairman of the Executive Committee of the British Sociological Association.

PATRICIA THOMAS is Deputy Director of the Nuffield Foundation. She previously worked at the Social Science Research Council as Committee Secretary. She recently served as a member of the Lord Chancellor's Legal Aid Advisory Committee. Her book, *The Aims of Outcomes of Social Policy Research*, was published in 1985.

ROBERT WALKER is Research Fellow in the Social Policy Research Unit, University of York. He was formerly Senior Lecturer in Social Policy at the Civil Service College (where he had a remit covering research-officer training), and Principal Research Officer in the Department of the Environment. His books include: *Housing Benefit: the Experience of Implementation* (1985), *Applied Qualitative Research* (ed., 1985), *Responses to Poverty: Lessons from Europe* (with R. Lawson and P. Townsend, 1984), and *Taxation and Social Policy* (with C. Sandford and C. Pond, 1980). He is currently editing a volume on income inequality and writing a book on the analysis of Social Security.

CAROL H. WEISS is on the staff of the Harvard University Graduate School of Education. She has done a series of studies on the influence of social science research on public policy-making, and recently completed a study of the reporting of social science in the media. In 1983 she was the American Sociological Association's first Congressional Fellow, serving with the Senate Subcommittee on Education. It was there that she undertook the inquiry that led to the paper in this volume. She has been consultant to the U.S. General Accounting Office since 1975 and to the Departments of Education, Health and Human Services and Labor, to the National Science Foundation, and other public and private agencies. She is also the author of *Social Science Research and Decision-Making* (1980), *Making Bureaucracies Work* (with A. H. Barton, 1980), *Using Social Research in Public Policy Making* (1977), *Evaluation Research* (1972), *Evaluating Action Programs* (1972), and scores of papers in professional journals.

CHAPTER 1

Governments and social science: patterns of mutual influence

MARTIN BULMER

Governments in Western Europe and North America have, during the last twenty-five to thirty years, made increasing use of social science research. Looking further back to a time fifty or sixty years ago, governments supported almost no social science research and made very little use of the results of such research produced with support from other sources. Even the pioneering social indicator work of President Herbert Hoover's Committee on Recent Social Trends, which published *Recent Social Trends* in 1933 (paid for by the Rockefeller Foundation) had relatively little impact because by then Hoover had been succeeded by a new President, Franklin D. Roosevelt. The last half century has seen a progressive growth in the scale and scope of social science research carried out for and used by government. The first major impulse came during the second world war, which stimulated social survey research in particular, both in the United States and Britain. In the two decades after 1945, modest growth occurred, faster in the United States than Britain. In the two decades since the mid-1960s the interest of governments in social science research has accelerated, expanding both their expenditure on social science research and their use of its products in policy-making and administration.

Such growth has not been without its problems, reflected in titles of books such as *The Uneasy Partnership: social science and the federal government in the twentieth century* (Lyons, 1969) and *Knowledge and Policy: the uncertain connection* (Lynn, 1978). Unrealistic expectations on both sides (cf. Sharpe, 1978), as well as structural problems in feeding expert knowledge into the policy-making process (Bulmer, 1986, ch. 1) have rendered the relationship far from smooth. In the early 1980s, conservative governments in both Washington and London questioned more fundamentally the place of the social sciences, and sought to reduce

1

their funding by government. This political antipathy to social science is considered more fully in the final section of the book. A few academic commentators, too, like R. Scott and A. Shore in *Why Sociology Does Not Apply* (1979), have questioned whether academic-policy research links are as healthy for particular disciplines as is sometimes assumed. In examining the connections between government and social science knowledge, the links must not be taken for granted, even though they have grown in the last twenty years to considerable proportions.

If one compares developments in Britain and the United States in the immediate post-war period all the running was made by the United States. In Britain, the academic base for the social sciences was a very narrow one. The Clapham Report of 1946 provided for some modest expansion, but even in the early 1960s, there were as many sociologists teaching in universities throughout the country as there were historians teaching in Oxford alone. Inside government, social science research was limited. The Government Social Survey, founded in 1941, had survived a period of austerity in the early 1950s (Whitehead, 1985). A few industrial psychologists worked in personnel selection. Even economists were relatively sparse. Before the election of the Wilson Labour government in 1964, there were fewer than 50 professional economists in central government, most of those in the Treasury (Balogh, 1980).

In the United States, the academic base was broader. Disciplines like economics, political science, sociology, anthropology and psychology had been established in many leading American universities before 1914 and in the inter-war period consolidated their position as independent fields of study. Early philanthropic support on a considerable scale for social science came from the Laura Spelman Rockefeller Memorial in the 1920s (Bulmer and Bulmer, 1981) and then from the Rockefeller Foundation and the Carnegie Corporation. Much of this work was directed to finding solutions to national and social problems, rather than purely the development of academic disciplines, though much of the research was conducted by university staff. The second world war saw the expansion of 'in-house' government research, for example Rensis Likert's group in the Department of Agriculture and Samuel Stouffer's team in the Army Department, but at the war's end its leaders returned to academic life. The next substantial initiative was the behavioural science programme launched by the Ford Foundation between 1951 and 1956, which supported both basic scientific developments and their application to the solution of social problems.

When the National Science Foundation was established in 1946, the social sciences were deliberately excluded from its scope by Congress (Lyons, 1969, pp. 126–36). However, discussions and lobbying in the following year led in 1958 to the creation within NSF of an Office of Social Sciences, converted a year later into a division. The social science budget was $750,000 in 1958 out of a total NSF expenditure of $50 million. By 1960 this had risen to $2 million and by 1965 to $10 million out of a total budget in the latter year of almost $500 million (Lyons, 1969, p. 274). This rapid growth owed much to the push given to American science by the 'sputnik' launch in 1957 and the race to make up deficiencies in America's provision for science. It was this, too, which launched the modern phase of social indicators work, whose course in the 1970s is discussed by Denis Johnston in Chapter 15 (cf. Bauer, 1966). A further impetus came from the election as President in 1960 of John F. Kennedy, who drew into senior levels of science policy people more sympathetic to social science. A panel of the President's Science Advisory Committee produced a report on *Strengthening the Behavioral Sciences* in 1962, and shortly afterwards the National Research Council expanded its Division of Anthropology and Psychology into a Division of Behavioral Sciences.

In contrast to Britain, and although the system was not centrally co-ordinated, federal government funding has reached a considerable level.

> By the mid 1960's, federal support for the social sciences was, in effect, highly decentralised and scattered through a variety of agencies, having developed in response to operating needs and a general growth of research funding. Research expenditures now totalled more than $300 million. There had been changes in the pattern of spending with the government's increasing interest in domestic affairs such as health, education and welfare and a general levelling off in the areas of defence and national security. The pluralism of the system was not unlike the pluralism in the system of support for research in the physical and biological sciences. There were, however, several critical differences. The level of support was significantly lower in the social sciences and the social science programs were not linked together by a network of consultative mechanisms, by agencies for central review like those institutionalised in the office of the President's Science Adviser, or by built-in congressional interests that had emerged in other fields of science, most notably the biomedical sciences. (Lyons, 1969, pp. 288–9)

The take-off of the social sciences in Britain into self-sustaining growth can be dated around 1964, at a time when American social science was already substantial and still growing rapidly. The key events in Britain for academic take-off were the Committee on Higher Education of 1963, chaired by LSE Economics Professor Lord Robbins, and the 1965 Report of the Heyworth Committee on Social Studies. Robbins came down in favour of large-scale expansion of university places, and laid the groundwork for the rapid expansion of social science teaching in universities and polytechnics in the following years. Heyworth recommended the rapid expansion of social science research, with appropriate government support, and led to the establishment of the Social Science Research Council, both to fund research and to support postgraduate students to obtain suitable training. The British SSRC resembled less its American namesake than the social science arm of the National Science Foundation.

In the world of government the change was slightly less dramatic but none the less clear. During the 1960s, social expenditure on housing, education, personal social services, health and social security all increased rapidly. There was more demand for information about disadvantaged groups such as the poor, handicapped and unemployed, as well as ethnic minorities. There was growing interest in the *impact* of social and economic policies upon individuals and groups. Such questions as whether services were reaching those for whom they were intended or how far equity was being achieved required research to answer them.

Robbins was a watershed in more than one sense. The extensive statistical research undertaken for it by Claus Moser underpinned the persuasive arguments for expansion. It showed that rigorous and carefully conducted research could contribute to the determination of a major issue of public policy. Thereafter, royal commissions were much more predisposed to use social research as an aid to their deliberations.

There was some crossing over and mutual influence between the two spheres of academia and government. Robbins and Moser, for example, both moved easily between the two realms, Moser becoming head of the Government Statistical Service in 1967. There was limited movement into the civil service, particularly of academic economists after the change of government in 1964. Expanding jobs in the non-academic research sector were filled by new social science graduates. Government expenditure on social science research increased steadily, although to nothing like American proportions. It is estimated, for example, that by 1976-7 approximately £50 million per annum was being spent on social research in Britain, half in universities, one quarter on 'in-house' government research, and the rest in independent research units and institutes (Social Research Association, 1980). In the same year, the total budget of the Social Science Research Council, including postgraduate training, was £11.7 million, part of which is included in the £50 million total (SSRC, 1977, pp. 27–31). In chapter 5, Cyril Smith makes a well-informed estimate that by the mid-1980s social science research funding from all sources in Britain has risen to £100 million.

In the United States, the rapid growth in expenditure on the social sciences was sustained through the later 1960s and into the 1970s. In 1966 and 1967 Congress considered a proposal for the creation of a National Social Science Foundation, but this was not acted upon. The social sciences became gradually more visible within the National Academy of Sciences. In 1968 its Advisory Committee on Government Programs in the Behavioral Sciences reported (National Academy of Sciences, 1968) emphasising the usefulness of social science research but raising key questions. Could the knowledge and methods of the social sciences contribute effectively to the formation of public policy? Should social scientists seek federal support for the development of their disciplines? Did involvement in government and federal support entail loss of scientific independence and autonomy? The committee recognised that public support required that 'usefulness' be demonstrated, and suggested a pluralistic system of support and grant administration to protect scholarly independence.

During the later 1960s, particularly during the Johnson Presidency, a burst of social programmes to deal with problems of poverty, educational disadvantage, housing and urban blight, and racial discrimination, gave a further boost to social science research. Major initiatives such has the Great Society programme, Head Start, and Negative Income Tax proposals spawned major federally-funded initiatives on a scale unheard of in Britain. The New Jersey–Pennsylvania Negative Income Tax Experiment alone, for example, cost some $8 million between 1968 and 1974 (Ferber and Hirsch, 1982, pp. 57–8). Although funding levelled off in the early 1970s, the scale of American provision remains staggeringly large by European standards. One estimate put US federal spending on social research and development in 1976 at $1.8 billions. To this must be added the considerable funding available from foundations and from other sources. The sum is not strictly comparable to the £50 million for Britain quoted earlier, since the American figure includes statistical services not included in the British figure, as well as demonstrations and experiments to which there are few British equivalents. The order of magnitude of difference is however, comparable to that quoted by Cunningham in 1971 (Cunningham, 1971). The precise order of difference is difficult to calculate, but it appears that the United States, with four times Britain's population, spends between ten and twenty times as much on social research. Proportionate to population, America spends between two and a half and five times as much.

The mutual relationship in America between the social sciences and government is a close and deepening one.

> The relations between social science and the federal government have by now become so complex that they cannot be untangled. Over the

years social science has developed a capacity for measuring, evaluating and predicting social change – though there are still large areas of uncertainty and doubt. At the same time the federal govenment has shown a growing commitment to serve as a positive force in social change ... These developments, whatever their limits, have drawn social science and the federal government together into a working partnership that will almost certainly grow closer as time goes on. (Lyons, 1969, p. 308)

The differences of the scale of funding of social science are a symptom rather than a cause of the striking differences observable between the two societies and their systems of government. As L. J. Sharpe has observed, '(i)t is difficult to pin down this kind of broad difference between the two countries with any precision, but no British social scientist who has visited the United States can have failed to be aware that he was in a milieu that took his calling seriously. The nearest analogy is perhaps that of an English chef visiting Paris' (Sharpe, 1978, p. 303).

One dimension of difference is the place of rational knowledge in the political system. As Gene Lyons has observed, 'there are, in American culture, elements of rationalism and progress which give strength to the application of reason to governing' (1969, p. 310). These can be traced back to the American Revolution and the determination to found the new political system upon the idea that the people had the right, by rational and empirical processes, to build their governmental institutions to suit themselves. As James Bryce observed, America was also the only country in the world which had no great capital. Even New York could not assume the central role of creating and sustaining a national public culture such as that centred upon London. As a consequence, intellectual life in the United States tended in the later nineteenth and early twentieth century to take on a heavily academic and relentlessly special-ised character. More than in Britain, serious social thought became concentrated within academic disciplinary communities. If the cost was a relatively impoverished public culture and a less stimulating general setting for the discussion of social ideas, the gain was a greater readiness to harness scientific and scholarly expertise to the business of govern-ment (Bender 1984: 100–1).

A related feature of the American scene is a greater willingness to harness the latest technique to assist in the decision-making process – tending almost at times to a belief in the technological fix. America, for example, pioneered the opinion poll, and American politicians and the media today make much more extensive use of poll findings than in most Western European counterparts. Similarly, academic social scientists are much more likely to be called upon to serve and advise government, since they are perceived as having knowledge relevant to the operations of the state. One example, without European parallel, was the development of rural sociology in the land-grant colleges at an early date to assist in agricultural planning and management.

In Britain, the political culture is completely different. It is centred upon London, heart of the tightly-knit national culture. The unwritten constitution is hallowed by tradition and bolstered by an evolving common law. Universities are an important training ground for prospective elite members, but are much less likely to be seen as a source of useful knowledge, let alone social science knowledge. As L. J. Sharpe has acutely observed, the British political tradition:

> gives much greater weight to knowledge as accumulated experience – *he who does knows* – and in its extreme form sees practical experience as the only legitimate source of knowledge . . . This elevation of practice over commentary, exposition and theory is also reflected among other things in the extent to which so many of the professions in Britain, not least those which play a large part in government, still conduct their education and training outside the ambit of the universities. (1978, pp. 304–5)

Thus there is no real counterpart in Britain to the American law school, least of all as a training ground for public service, and graduate schools of public policy are few and far between. Indeed the idea of a graduate school for professional or academic training is rather unusual, outside a few departments of economics.

William James made a distinction between 'knowledge about', based on reading, theorising, rational thought, and 'acquaintance with', learned first-hand in the manner of the apprentice. In the British system much more value attaches to 'acquaintance with'.

> The epitome of the government's response to a policy problem in the United States is to select the professor with the highest reputation in the field, give him a generous research budget and put him on a contract. The epitome in Britain is to set up a committee of inquiry made up largely of distinguished practitioners in the chosen policy field with a token academic who may or may not be invited by his colleagues to organise research. (Sharpe, 1978, p. 305)

One illustration of the difference may be taken from the legal traditions of the two countries. The British civil and criminal law takes virtually no cognisance of social science, other than evidence as to individual states of mind in criminal cases, and judges and jurists are in general unreceptive to arguments which adduce social science evidence. Social science research into aspects of judicial administration has also received an extremely cool response from the legal profession. There is no parallel in Britain to that tradition in American law, associated particularly with the names of Brandeis and Frankfurter, which accords a place both to social considerations and social science research evidence. For example, it is inconceivable that social science could play a role in a British legal case analogous to the role it played in the notable Supreme Court racial desegration case of 1954, *Brown v Board of Education of Topeka*. Nor are social scientists in Britain usually called to give evidence as expert witnesses in court as they are in the United States.

Differences in the legal system are parallelled by differences in the political system. These are considered more fully in the next chapter, but deserve mention. The American civil service is more politicised than the British with considerable change in its upper echelons with a change of administration (Heclo, 1977). Partly as a consequence, the permanent civil service is a less attractive career for the very able, and there is more incentive for politicians to turn to outsiders, including academic social scientists, for supplementary advice. This is related to a general characteristic of the American system, that it is much more open structurally, less secretive and more permeable, and so more open to inputs from outside than the British. In the British system, the senior echelons of the civil service are filled by cadres recruited in their 20s and socialised into a closed and fairly secretive world of an executive composed of civil servants and ministers. With a few exceptions, there is little mobility between the civil service and academic life, and even fewer opportunities for outsiders to be brought in. The calibre of senior British civil servants, who are trained as generalists, is very high, but they tend to share the characteristics of their political masters in relying upon experience (their knowledge of the working of the government machine and of the state) and not rating expertise, particularly of social scientists, highly (Bulmer, 1983a).

David Donnison, former professor of social administration at LSE and Director of the Centre for Environmental Studies became Head of the British Supplementary Benefits Commission in October 1975, which administers means-tested welfare benefits to a sizeable minority of the British population. Donnison told his senior officials that he wanted to run as a source of advice to him.

> a regular seminar to which we would invite administrators and research-
> ers – outsiders along with insiders from various other departments. 'I
> hope you do not mean this seriously, chairman', said our Chief Adviser
> (the senior permanent official). 'Who on earth would come? How could
> hard-pressed officials take on such a burden? Confidential thinking
> would be leaked and we would all be made fools of'. I suggested some of
> the people who might attend: insiders such as ... (the) head of the
> Social Research Division at the Department of the Environment ...
> one of the top economic advisers at the Treasury, (the person) in charge

of social statistics at the Cabinet Office and their colleagues. The Commission's officials appeared to know none of them. As for academics and other outsiders – they were regarded as a menace. (1982, p.30)

Donnison successfully overcame his officials' objections and ran a successful seminar, but the case is symptomatic of the distrust with which experts are viewed.

There are differences too among politicians. The typical career paths of British and American politicians are different due to the separation of powers, but this does not entirely account for observed differences. Congressmen have far larger staffs than their counterparts in the House of Commons and as Carol Weiss shows in Chapter 7, these staff play a very active role in interpreting knowledge about political problems to those whom they serve. Moreover, the system of open Congressional hearings on proposals from the executive exposes permanent officials to far closer public scrutiny than they ever receive in Britain, and an opportunity for Congressional staff to deploy social science expertise in examining Presidential and executive action. Moreover, many Congressmen maintain links with academics in their home states, which can act as brains-trusts or sources of informal advice to the legislator. '(T)he whole ethos and style of American politics is strongly impregnated with the tradition of drawing upon the outsider as a vital element in policy-making' (Sharpe, 1978, p. 307).

The typical Member of the British House of Commons is unlikely to employ more than a secretary and possibly a personal or research assistant. British politicians have to develop a sense of self-sufficiency, and if they look for outside advice, are more likely to seek it from civil servants than from academics. There is a surprisingly high degree of contact between British officials and MPs (cf. Campbell, 1983, pp. 288–90). One other feature of the British system is relevant. Because of the prestige of a political career within the relatively small and closed world of national policy-making, the intellectual quality of senior politicians has been higher than their equivalents in Washington. Among leading Labour ministers, for example, Harold Wilson, Anthony Crosland and Richard Crossman were all ex-academics, while on the Conservative benches Sir Edward Boyle left politics to become a university Vice-Chancellor and Sir Keith Joseph was formerly a Fellow of All Souls College, Oxford. Enoch Powell was a professor of Greek at the age of 25. When such politicians become ministers, if they regard social science as relevant to their tasks they are as likely to be their own social scientist as to rely on outside experts.

Some of these structural differences will be pursued further in the next chapter. Several other general features of the two systems are relevant. In the United States, the scale of the demand for social science from the executive arm and from Congress, as well as the funding available from the National Science Foundation, other federally supported institutes, private foundations and other sources, means that the scale of applied social science research activity has something of a self-generating effect. There is a much greater readiness to contemplate new extensions of research activity, such as that of the General Accounting Office, into evaluation, described by Ray Rist in Chapter 16. The readiness of American agencies to fund expensive, large-scale social experiments is another sign of this expansiveness (cf. Ferber and Hirsch, 1982, pp. 80–1). Academic social scientists have much greater opportunities to do applied work in various roles, enhancing the respect with which such work is held. Media reporting of social science in America, for all its limitations, is fuller and more serious than in Britain. There has also developed the considerable sector of independent research institutes, some for profit and some not, explicitly geared to serve government and to respond quickly to funding opportunities. Bodies like Abt, Mathematica, Westat or SRI have very few imitators in Western Europe. The general optimism about the potential for social science, in a context where many different types of application flourish, make it possible to sustain a high rate of growth and, when political scepticism appears, to defend the ground already occupied with effect, as Roberta Miller shows in Chaper 20.

The character of American compared to British higher education is also significant. The United States contains more of the academically distinguished universities in the world than any other country, and the size and wealth of its system gives that part of it devoted to the social sciences a firm base on which to rest. It is not just the great size of the system relative to population which is important. It is also the history and ethos of American higher education. When the modern, research-based, Ph.D.-granting, science-oriented leading American universities developed in the late nineteenth century, they did so in competition with each other and without a clear hierarchy or pecking order among the leading institutions (Shils, 1979). America was still a highly regionalised society, so that a new university like the University of Chicago, which was able to make its mark comparatively quickly, served a different part of the country to that of the older institutions on the east coast (Bulmer, 1984). This competitiveness and striving after leadership persists, so that although the pre-eminence of Harvard is recognised in many fields, it is continually looking over its shoulder not only at Columbia University or the University of Chicago but also at some of the great state universities like the University of California or the University of Texas or the University of Wisconsin.

The vitality which this competitiveness on an affluent base imparts is evident in the openness of the system, mobility within it, and the entrepreneurial attitude to social research which exist. The pool from which potential academic policy researchers may be drawn is both larger and much more receptive than in Britain. In Britain, with a smaller and more hierarchical university system, without the same competitiveness, the links between leading universities and political elites may be quite close, but they are of a different kind (cf. Donnison, 1972). Ralph Turner's distinction between sponsored and contest mobility (1961) is also of relevance here. There is a much less entrepreneurial attitude to research, university finances are not locked into grant overheads, and as Cornish and Clarke suggest in Chapter 10, there may not be all that much incentive for academics to engage in outside research. In short, the general academic climate in Britain does less to foster applied social science research.

There are, however, disciplinary differences between different sides of the Atlantic which also go some way to explain existing differences. The social sciences in the United States have a considerably longer history as distinct empirical disciplines, stretching back to the period around World War One (cf. Ross, 1979). In the last forty years, several disciplines in American social science, political science and sociology in particular, have been much more empirically oriented in the United States than in Western Europe. This is apparent in the much greater sophistication of American social survey research, and the association of leading political scientists and sociologists with centres such as the Michigan ISR and NORC in Chicago, a point developed by McKennell in Chapter 13. These differences extend quite deep. Taking political science as an example, while many American political scientists believe their subject can achieve the status of a science, in Europe the subject is more often regarded as an arts subject, with close affinities to history and philosophy. American scholars are more geared to comparison, system-building and testing general propositions, as well as with the development of insights which are practically useful. European scholars are less interested in building a science than in pursuing scholarship for its own sake. It remains a relatively cloistered and academic activity, and this is consciously chosen by those who pursue it.

These differences are reflected in methodology. In America, traditional historical and institutional analyses using documentary sources have been supplemented by interviews, survey research and participant observation, coupled with the aim of testing propositions and building general theory. Most European students of government resist such methods, whether on philosophical arguments, distrust of scientism or resistance to involvement in practical problems. 'As a consequence, the central tendency in European political-science methodology is conservative rather than innovational; the dominant preoccupations are history, law, political structure and political institutions. An interest in political theory is also prominent. And documentary research continues to be the normal means of gathering professional data' (Ward, 1964, p. 30).

It would be misleading to suggest that similar types of political science research are not found on both sides of the Atlantic, but as a broad characterisation of disciplinary difference the above is accurate. Similar differences exist if, for example, one compares British and American sociology (cf. Abrams et al., 1981; Bulmer and Burgess, 1981). The markedly more pragmatic and application-oriented character of American social science scholarship contributes to the intellectual climate in which applied social research flourishes.

These contrasts between American and European styles should not be overdrawn. In terms of intellectual interests and scholarly networks and exchanges, there are strong links between American and European scholars. The ties are particularly strong between the English-speaking countries, but there are strong nuclei of German, Scandinavian and Dutch social scientists with good knowledge of and sympathy with American trends. In terms of common methodology, social survey research is widely used on both sides of the Atlantic with, as McKennell shows, commensurate interest in technical problems of design and execution. Moreover recent political scepticism about the value of social science, examined by Paul Flather and Roberta Miller in Chapters 19 and 20, shows that these countries have even more in common in the need and capacity to defend the social sciences against their critics.

Certain broader similarities may be brought out by considering different models of the relationship between knowledge and policy and different roles which the social scientist contributing to government in Britain and the United States can play. This can highlight the common elements in application despite some of the considerable differences which divide American and European experience. There is now a considerable literature upon the most appropriate models by which to characterise the way in which social science is used (cf. Janowitz, 1970; Caplan et al., 1975; Weiss, 1977; Lindblom and Cohen, 1979; Bulmer, 1982, 1986). Two broad types of model can be distinguished, one problem-centred, instrumental, control-oriented, the other more open-ended, providing a general orientation, and one input among many to the policy-making process. The first may be called an 'engineering' approach, the second the 'enlightenment' or 'limestone' model. In the 'engineering' model a social problem is defined usually by government. Missing knowledge needed to tackle the problem is identified, and a contractor found to carry out the study. The social scientist then designs the study, collects data, analyses the results and finally produces a report related to the problem solution. Finally, the policy-maker arrives at their chosen course of action, on the basis of the study. Such a linear sequence is assumed to hold. Knowledge presses towards its development. The specific skills of the social science researcher lie in the design and analysis of investigations to answer specific questions.

The most important version of the 'engineering' model in Britain has been Lord Rothschild's enunciation of the 'customer–contractor principle'. Carried out in 1971 as a review of the organisation of government R & D, Rothschild specifically exempted the social sciences from his recommendations. But as Blume shows in Chapter 6, this did not stop central government departments from applying Rothschild's principles to social science research, typically drawn under the umbrella of the Office of the Chief Scientiest (a natural scientist). The report made a central distinction between basic, fundamental or pure research and applied research, that is research with a practical application as its objective. In applied research, '(t)he customer says what he wants; the contractor does it (if he can); and the customer pays' (Rothschild, 1971, p. 3). This principle puts the applied researcher at the service of the person or department commissioning the research, providing them with technical expertise to produce the necessary knowledge for government.

A number of limitations have been pointed out in this conception of research (cf. Weiss, 1978), and an alternative model which posits a less sharp distinction between pure and applied research and a more diffuse process of knowledge-dissemination put forward. This 'enlightenment' or 'limestone' model is discussed by Patricia Thomas in Chapter 4. In this model, the influence of social science research upon policy is not direct but longer-term, like water entering and gradually trickling down through limestone strata, without the observer being sure where or when the water will emerge. In the process the rock is imperceptibly worn away, but it is a very gradual process, and not one when any single point of impact can be identified. Such an outcome of applied research is less easy to justify to policy-makers on utilitarian grounds, but is arguably closer to the ways in which a good deal of social science impacts upon public policy.

There is a need to go beyond these two contrasted general models and spell out the varieties of approach within each. For example, the randomised experiments discussed by Robert Boruch in Chapter 17 represent a means of achieving scientific control through rigorous causal inference. The type of social survey discussed by Barry Hedges in Chapter 14 typically produces reliable and soundly established factual information which gives the policy-maker a sense of the outlines and parameters of the problem. Similarly, the 'gadfly' and 'insider' roles which Patricia Thomas identifies represent different forms of enlightenment, while certain types of 'insider' may act in terms of the 'engineering' model. The uses of analysis by congressional staff described by Carol Weiss are very much in the 'enlightenment' mould. Weiss advances the discussion by relating her analysis to the process by which political decisions are taken and policies evolve. Adequate consideration of different models of social science use requires more extended consideration of decision-making processes, and this is examined more fully elsewhere (cf. Weiss, 1980, 1982; Bulmer, 1986). The point to be made here is that the common experience of applying social science in both America and Britain may reveal similarities in terms of cognitive impact and outcome despite dissimilar structural conditions which would on the face of it suggest more effective use in the United States.

Common elements may also be highlighted if one approaches the knowledge–policy connection in terms of the various roles that social scientists can play in the policy-making process. One has to recognise that in playing these roles social scientists will offer different kinds of knowledge. They will include general ideas, to make sense of particular patterns of behaviour, for example the hypothesis about transmitted deprivation which led to a major programme of British research in the 1970s (Brown and Madge, 1982). They will offer substantive knowledge, in the production of which the various methodologies discussed in Part II of this book play an important part. And they can, in more politically sensitive areas, offer an analysis of the implications of alternative courses of action both for social behaviour and for the political objectives of the policy-makers.

The first clearly identifiable role is that of the social science researcher carrying out a piece of research for government. This may be done 'in-house', by a staff member of a department research division or a central facility such as the Bureau of the Census or OPCS. Or it may be done in a research firm, a non-profit institute or a university by a social scientist not in government employ but under contract. This is probably what most people think of when 'applied research' or 'policy research' is mentioned. It is indeed the central role played by the applied social scientist, though not the only one. The situation of 'in-house' and 'out-house' researchers differs quite markedly. Rist describes in Chapter 16 the new developments in evaluation research within the U.S. General

Accounting Office, which reports to Congress. Some of the problems facing the 'in-house' researcher in Britain are discussed by Walker and by Cornish and Clarke in Chapters 9 and 10. 'Out-house' researchers are more distant from policy-makers, though perhaps no more likely to feel that their services are not appreciated than their 'in-house' counterparts. In this role, the social science researcher has technical expertise and the opportunity to deliver a product to the policy-maker. Given adequate professional standards, scientifically respectable studies using methodologies of different types (cf. Bulmer, 1986) will be carried out. Problems with this type of research commonly relate to the communication, dissemination and outcome of the research, over which the research is unlikely to have any control. Research findings are fed to policy-makers, but the ensuing results are unpredictable in part because of the complexities of the policy-making process and the many inputs into it.

A second distinct role for the social scientist in government is that of the outsider brought in as consultant or expert to advise on a particular policy problem. Perhaps the most typical way in which this is done is by setting up a commission or committee. A special case of this type of inquiry was the review of the Social Science Research Council discussed by Paul Flather in Chapter 19. Lord Rothschild, as a distinguished science administrator and former head of the Central Policy Review Staff, was judged well qualified to provide an objective view, which he did. One-man or woman commissions tend to have been favoured by the Thatcher government. The historically more common pattern, in a number of countries, is the multi-member commission one or two of whom may be social scientists. Lisl Klein in Chapter 11 discusses the example of a major German commission. The social scientist members then try to influence the work of the commission and initiate research before its policy recommendations are framed (cf. Bulmer (ed.), 1980; American Behavioral Scientist, 1983).

Government departments also make extensive use of outside academic advisers in a number of roles, some of whom are social scientists. For example, they may provide advice on specific policy problems, or sit as scientific assessors on departmental committees or advise on the department's research budget. The U.K. Department of Health and Social Security, for example, has an elaborate advisory commitee structure of Research Liaison Groups in determining research priorities (Kogan and Henkel, 1983). The characteristic of this type of advice is that it is offered in an objective and non-partisan manner by outsiders, who have an arm's length relationship to government. Commissions, for example (by contrast to parliamentary select committees), commonly display a desire to produce unanimous reports and to iron out internal differences to make their work more effective. Moreover, members of some recent British commissions have worried about the lack of action by government to implement their recommendations and have made some effort after publication to argue the case for implementation (cf. Bulmer, 1983b). The adviser, however, is not simply a researcher, marshalling data within an implicit or explicit theoretical framework. He or she is offering analysis and recommendations for action based on that analysis which goes beyond that of the discoverer of new knowledge.

The same is true of the third role played by social scientists in government, the 'in-house' adviser who works within government. Such advice can take several forms. All government bureaucracies employ cadres of professional experts such as statisticians, architects, accountants and natural scientists. In recent years this has extended to the social sciences. In British central government the economists play this role most effectively, within the Government Economic Service, where the main career grade carries the title 'Economic Adviser'. Those in the service both conduct applied economic research for government and offer advice to line administrators on economic aspects of current policy problems. In the Treasury, members of the service work alongside administrative grades in the management of the economy. No other group of social scientists has a comparable position. Applied psychologists are used in certain personnel functions, but in a more technical role. Social science research staff are members of a loose-knit, disparate group, which lacks clear professional identity (although particular units in which they work, like the Home Office Research and Planning Unit are cohesive). Only a very few social scientists are employed in a strictly advisory as opposed to a research role, for example in the Overseas Development Administration.

A different use of social science expertise is in central policy planning units in central government. A British case in point was the Central Policy Review Staff, set up by Edward Heath in 1970 to advise the Prime Minister and Cabinet on priorities, consider options that would be ruled out on conventional terms, break down obstacles to co-ordination between departments and look to the longer-term (cf. Plowden, 1981). (CPRS was wound up in 1983.) It could advise ministers directly and its head and his deputy could attend any Cabinet committee which wished (Campbell, 1983, p. 65). Its main role has been to assess particularly contentious policy issues in terms of their strategic consequences for the government of the day. The small staff of about sixteen were drawn half from serving civil servants and half from outsiders. The latter have included over time several social scientists. Their work as members of

CPRS has, however, been very different from that of social science researchers. They must adapt to being a generalist tackling a very wide range of policy areas and issues. As one former member wrote:

> The first time I attended (a weekly) meeting in the CPRS I was dumbfounded by the enormous range of subjects that came up for discussion, including nuclear reactors, heating bills for the elderly, oil depletion policy, civil service cuts and loans for postgraduate students. (Blackstone, 1980, p. 9)

Members were required to be versatile and not put off by their own lack of knowledge. Their own expertise was of secondary importance. In the service of current policy advice they were expected to be something of a dillettante. It also required the ability to work to tight time scales and to be prepared to reach conclusions and recommendations on the basis of less than complete evidence. Thus the staff of such a central planning body have to have the ability to summarise and synthesise and apply their insights to the dissection of pressing policy problems. Rarely could new research be mounted. Their skills consisted in marshalling what evidence was available, from a variety of sources, and reaching concise policy recommendations to be presented to ministers.

In the United States, advice of the second and third types to the Executive and Congress is frequent and intensive. As D. P. Moynihan has observed:

> there is no place on earth where the professor reigns or has done up until very recently, as in the United States. For the past 30 years in a society the intellectuals – the professors – have had influence almost without precedence in history. The economists primarily (I am leaving aside the whole phenomena of the physical sciences), but increasingly also the softer social scientists, the sociologists. (Moynihan, quoted in Sharpe, 1978, p. 307)

Moynihan's own career in government before he entered the Senate, might be said to represent another form of providing expert advice, as a social scientist working within government at a senior level.

The acme of influence on government, in some people's eyes, lies with a fourth role, those social scientists brought in as political advisers or appointees. Again, America differs markedly from Britain. 'Another dramatic reflection of the very different attitudes of the governments of the two countries to the role of social scientists in government is the extraordinary extent, by British standards, to which university social scientists have been brought directly into the Federal Government over the past decade and a half. Professor Kissinger . . . as Secretary of State for Foreign Affairs . . . was only the most celebrated example in a long line' (Sharpe, 1978, p. 306). The opportunity is of course much greater in the divided American system, but it is also facilitated by the larger academic system, with a greater capacity to reabsorb ex-academics when they leave government service.

In Britain, apart from the unusual cases of young academics who make full-time careers in politics, the most obvious way of doing this has been as special advisers either to the Prime Minister or other ministers. The role has perhaps been filled most comfortably by economists, from Nicholas Kaldor and Thomas Balogh in the Wilson government to Alan Walters in the early years of the Thatcher government. Other prominent figures include sociologist A. H. Halsey as special adviser to Anthony Crosland at DES, Brian Abel-Smith advising on health policy at DHSS, and political scientist Bernard Donoghue heading the Prime Minister's Policy Unit at 10 Downing Street under James Callaghan. Such social scientists have combined analysis with a degree of political commitment to the party with which they were identified. All had to have finely-adjusted political antennae, but were in the business of bringing social science research to bear on policy. Accounts of their experience as special advisers by several participants (Balogh, 1980; Peston, 1980; Abel-Smith, 1980) have emphasised several features. First was the value to a social scientist of obtaining a first-hand, inside, view of the policy-making process in action. The second is the extent to which some of the work was of a directly political kind – writing ministers' speeches, advising them on the political implications of particular policy options, meeting people whom the minister is unable to meet on political business. Thirdly, given the unpredictability and uncertainty of the policy-making process, providing an independent source of advice to ministers was far from superfluous. Official departmental advice might tend to follow certain traditional lines; the adviser could provide a fresh perspective. A good example is provided by David Donnison's experience in advising Richard Crossman on rent legislation in the mid-1960s (Donnison, 1972; Crossman, 1975, pp. 24ff.).

Often special advisers have known senior politicians, and have been recruited, through common membership of quasi-political intellectual groups and think tanks, which constitute a fifth channel of influence. All the major parties have such groups, the Fabian Society loosely linked to the Labour Party (cf. Donnison, 1972), the Bow Group linked to the Conservative Party and the Tawney Society to the SDP. Other groups of this kind in Britain include the Institute of Economic Affairs and its offshoot the Social Affairs Unit discussed by Cyril Smith in Chapter 5; the Socialist Society on the left; and the right-wing Centre for Policy Studies, created by Sir Keith Joseph. The problems which face academics in these bodies is that of separating their analysis from their presuppositions, and providing objective warrant for the partisan conclusions which they reach. The Centre for Policy Studies, for example, favours Sir Keith Joseph's anti-statist views which Paul Flather mentions in Chapter 19. In Washington, partisan think-tanks more to the right of the political spectrum include the Heritage Foundation and the American Enterprise Institute, with more lavish funding than their British counterparts. In both countries, an analytic approach to policy problems and partisan commitment are not seen as incompatible. In Britain, for instance, the Fabian Society adopts a social-democratic egalitarian approach to social welfare, so that it could be said of the Fabian poverty researchers around Richard Titmuss in the 1960s that '(t)heir research was explicitly political; they were setting out to reshape policy-makers' interpretation of their environment' (Banting, 1979, pp. 69–70). Not all academic social scientists feel comfortable in such an *engagé* role, but both the Labour Party in Britain and the Democratic Party in the United States have found a more than ample number of academics willing to advise them and to join government to do so.

A sixth role which the social scientist may play is by exercising influence through pressure groups and the media, at arm's length from government. This is the way, par excellence, that the illumination of opinion or the trickling down through limestone occurs. Short shrift may be given to the expert in public life – in Britain no epithet is more damning for a politician than 'clever' – but politicians and civil servants alike pay great attention to the media and pressure groups. Press reporting and filtering of the results of social science is read carefully. Pressure groups mount and use research to press home their case. This is particularly so in the fragmented and decentralised American system, where organised lobbying is much more developed than in Britain, but it also occurs in the more tightly-knit British context, where ministers and officials listen carefully to the messages which pressure groups bring them. Social policy groups like Help the Aged and the Child Poverty Action Group have been able to make effective use of research results in pressing their case.

These six different channels of influence provide different inputs to government. From some, particularly the first, comes substantive knowledge. From others, such as the second, general ideas, frameworks and concepts in terms of which to make sense of policy choices are provided. The relative absence in the British system of social science insiders offering policy advice from within government, the third role, has meant that influence has come to bear more indirectly, through the sixth avenue, or more politically, through the fourth and fifth. The discussion of different roles brings out the extent to which social science research can be used variously as a means of conceptualisation, as a way of providing political ammunition, or as a contribution to the interactive process of policy-making which characterises policy-making within the British and American governments.

This collection of papers does not provide a conclusive summary of all aspects of the relationship between social science research and government. Rather it focuses upon certain aspects of that relationship and provides a report of the present state of play. For the future, the need is less for new theoretical typologies and schemes, and more for the careful analytic examination of empirical cases. Carol Weiss's account in Chapter 7 of Congressional staff use of social science is a good example of the type of illuminating study of which more are needed. Other recent studies in this vein include Kogan and Henkel's study of DHSS research commissioning (1983), Thomas's (1985) study of the outcomes of 12 academic projects with policy relevance, and Weiss and Bucuvalas's study of the use of social science by American mental health administrators (1980). The considerable difficulties of penetrating behind the wall of confidentiality which governments erect should not be underestimated, but given ingenuity and perseverance a great deal can be discovered, particularly by interviewing present and retired elite members (cf. Moyser and Wagstaffe, 1987 for the methods and Banting, 1979 for one example).

A different though related strategy is to tackle the significance of social knowledge producing institutions historically and comparatively (cf. Evans et al., 1985). Theda Skocpol's call in Chapter 3 for further comparative and historical research on the relationship between the development of the social sciences and the structures and activities of modern nation states points the way forward for work of this kind. This collection may be criticised for a certain English-speaking parochialism, and within the English-speaking world, for concentrating on the two most important countries. Experience elsewhere is also highly relevant, if it can be studied systematically, and a bow is taken in that direction by including Chapter 11 by Lisl Klein on West Germany. Particular interest in general attaches to continental European experience in countries such as France, West Germany, Sweden, the Netherlands, Poland and Hungary. Blume provides a fascinating comparison in one respect between Britain and Holland in Chapter 6. Much more extensive systematic comparison is needed. (For an interesting step in this direction, see Wagner and Wollman, 1985.)

The social sciences are more, rather than less, likely to be drawn on by governments in the future (despite certain pessimistic conclusions to be drawn from the final section). Adequate understanding of how and in what ways they exert such influence as they do remains an important task. The chapters which follow in this book are intended to enlarge understanding of the role which they play, focusing upon Britain and the United States. Despite doubts and criticisms, the influence of each upon the other has been and is a reciprocal one, if not of functional inter-dependence, at least of uneasy coexistence and a degree of mutual tolerance. In that respect the last half century has indeed seen a very considerable transformation.

REFERENCES

Abel-Smith, B. (1980), 'Don't have a go at romantic fiction if you know nothing about sex', *Times Higher Education Supplement*, June 27, p. 10.
Abrams, P. *et al.* (eds.) (1981), *Practice and Progress: British Sociology 1950–1980*, London, Allen & Unwin.
American Behavioral Scientist (1983), 'Social Science and Policymaking: the use of research by governmental commissions', special issue, Vol. 26, no. 5 (May), pp. 555–680.
Balogh, T. (1980), 'Time for bold decisions on decision-making', *Times Higher Education Supplement*, June 13, p. 11.
Banting, K. (1979), *Poverty, Politics and Policy*, London, Macmillan.
Bauer, R. (ed.) (1966), *Social Indicators*, Cambridge, Mass., M.I.T. Press.
Bender, T. (1984), 'The Erosion of Public Culture: Cities, Discourses and Professional Disciplines', in Haskell, T. L. (ed.), *The Authority of Experts: studies in history and theory* (Bloomington, Indiana: Indiana University Press), pp. 84–106.
Blackstone, T. (1980), 'The voices that drown in the think-tank', *Times Higher Education Supplement*, August 15, p. 9.
Brown, M. and Madge, N. (1982), *Despite the Welfare State: a report on the SSRC/DHSS programme of research into transmitted deprivation*, London, Heinemann.
Bulmer, M. (ed.) (1978), *Social Policy Research*, London, Macmillan.
Bulmer, M. (ed.) (1980), *Social Research and Royal Commissions*, London, Allen & Unwin.
Bulmer, M. (1982), *The Uses of Social Research: social investigation in public policy-making*, London, Allen & Unwin.
Bulmer, M. (1983a), 'Using social science research in policy-making: Why are the obstacles so formidable?', *Public Administration Bulletin* 43 (December), pp. 37–48.
Bulmer, M. (1983b), *Royal Commissions and Departmental Committees of Inquiry: The Lessons of Experience*, London, Royal Institute of Public Administration.
Bulmer, M. (1984), *The Chicago School and Sociology: institutionalisation, diversity and the rise of sociological research*, Chicago, University of Chicago Press.
Bulmer, M. (ed.) (1985), *Essays on the History of British Sociological Research*, Cambridge, Cambridge University Press.

Bulmer, M. (1986), *Social Science and Social Policy*, London, Allen & Unwin.
Bulmer, M. and Bulmer, J. (1981), 'Philanthropy and social science in the 1920s: the case of Beardsley Ruml and the Laura Spelman Rockefeller Memorial 1922–1929', *Minerva* 19(3), pp. 347–407.
Bulmer, M. and Burgess, R. G. (eds.) (1981), 'The Teaching of Research Methodology', special issue of *Sociology* 15(4) (November), pp. 477–602.
Campbell, C. (1983), *Governments Under Stress: political executives and key bureaucrats in Washington, London and Ottawa*, Toronto, University of Toronto Press.
Caplan, N. *et al.*, (1975), *The Use of Social Science Knowledge in Policy Decisions at the National Level*, Ann Arbor, Michigan, Institute for Social Research.
Clapham Report (1946), *Report of the Committee on Provision for Social and Economic Research*, Chairman Sir John Clapham, Cmd 6868, London: HMSO.
Crossman, R. H. S. (1975), *The Diaries of a Cabinet Minister*. Volume 1, *Minister of Housing, 1964–1966*, London, H. Hamilton and J. Cape.
Cunningham, C. (1971), 'Research Funding in the United States', *SSRC Newsletter* Special issue on 'Politics in the Social Sciences' (September) pp. 19–21.
Donnison, D. V. (1972), 'Research for policy', *Minerva* (104), (reprinted in Bulmer (ed.) (1978), pp. 44–66).
Donnison, D. V. (1982), *The Politics of Poverty*, Oxford, Martin Robertson.
Evans, P. B., Rueschemeyer, D. and Skocpol, T. (eds.) (1985) *Bringing The State Back In*, Cambridge, Cambridge University Press.
Ferber, R. and Hirsch, W. Z. (1982), *Social Experimentation and Economic Policy*, Cambridge, Cambridge University Press.
Heclo, H. (1977), *A Government of Strangers: executive politics in Washington*, Washington, D. C., Brookings Institution.
Heyworth Report (1965), *Report of the Committee on Social Studies* (Chairman Lord Heyworth), Cmnd 2660, London: HMSO.
Janowitz, M. (1970), 'Sociological models and social policy', in *Political Conflict: essays in political sociology* by M. Janowitz (Chicago: Quadrangle Books), pp. 243–59.
Kogan, M. and Henkel, M. (1983), *Government and Research: the Rothschild experiment in a government department*, London, Heinemann.
Lindblom, C. and Cohen, D. K. (1979), *Usable Knowledge*, New Haven, Conn., Yale University Press.
Lynn, L. Jr. (ed.) (1978), *Knowledge and policy: the uncertain connection*, Washington D.C., National Academy of Sciences.
Lyons, G. M. (1969), *The Uneasy Partnership: social science and the federal government in the twentieth century*, New York, Russell Sage.
Moyser, G. & Wagstaffe, M. (eds.) (1987), *Research Methods for Elite Studies*, London, Allen & Unwin
National Academy of Sciences (1968), *The Behavioral Sciences and the Federal Government*, Report of the Advisory Committee on Government Programs in the Behavioral Sciences, Washington D.C., National Academy of Sciences – National Research Council Publication 1680.
Peston, M. (1980), 'A professional on a political tightrope', *Times Higher Education Supplement*, July 11, pp. 10–11.

Plowden, W. (1981), 'The British Central Policy Review Staff', in *Policy Analysis and Policy Innovation: patterns, problems and potentials*, ed. P. R. Baehr and B. Wittrock, London, Sage, pp. 61–91.

Robbins Committee (1983), *Higher Education: Report of the Committee appointed by the Prime Minister under the Chairmanship of Lord Robbins 1961–63*, Cmnd 2154, London: HMSO.

Rothschild, Lord (1971), 'The organisation and management of government research and development', in *A Framework of Government Research and Development*, Cmnd 4814, London: HMSO.

Scott, R. A. and Shore, A. M. (1979), *Why Sociology Does Not Apply: a study of the use of sociology in public policy*, New York: Elsevier.

Sharpe, L. J. (1978), 'The social scientist and policy-making in Britain and America: a comparison', in Bulmer (ed.) (1978), pp. 302–12 (being pp. 10–18 of L. J. Sharpe, 'The social scientist and policy-making', *Policy & Politics* 4(2) (1975), pp. 7–34).

Shils, E. (1979), 'The order of learning in the United States: The Ascendancy of the University', in *The Organisation of Knowledge in Modern America 1860–1920*, eds. A. Oleson and J. Voss, Baltimore, Md., Johns Hopkins University Press, pp. 19–47.

Social Research Association (1980), *Terms and Conditions of Social Research Funding in Britain: Report of the Working Group*, London: Social Research Association.

SSRC (1977), *Social Science Research Council Annual Report*, House of Commons Paper No. 487, Session 1976–77, London, HMSO.

Turner, R. H. (1961), 'Modes of ascent through education: sponsored and contest mobility', in *Education, Economy and Society* ed. A. H. Halsey, J. Floud and C. A. Anderson (New York: Free Press), pp. 121–39.

Wagner, P. and Wollman, H. (1985), 'Determinants, restrictions, and patterns of engagement of social scientists in policy-consulting – a cross-national analysis', Paper presented to the XIIIth World Congress of the International Political Science Association, Paris, July 1985 (Berlin: Wissenschaftcentrum, mimeo)

Ward, R. E. (1964), 'The research environment', in *Studying Politics Abroad: field research in developing areas* ed. R. E. Ward (Boston: Little, Brown), pp. 26–32.

Weiss, C. H. (ed.) (1977), *Using Social Research in Public Policy Making*, Lexington, Mass., D. C. Heath.

Weiss, C. H. (1980), 'Knowledge creep and decision accretion', *Knowledge: Creation, Diffusion, Utilization* 1(3), pp. 381–404.

Weiss, C. H. (1982), 'Policy research in the context of diffuse decision making', *Journal of Higher Education* 53(6), pp. 619–39.

Whitehead, F. (1985), 'The Government Social Survey', in Bulmer (ed.) (1985), pp. 83–100.

1 Research in the context of policy-making

CHAPTER 2

The governmental context: interaction between structure and influence

MARTIN BULMER

The ways in which social science and government inter-relate are mediated by the institutional arrangements of governance. This is so obvious a truism that the differences discussed in the previous chapter between Britain and the U.S. in the scope of applied social science are often either simply attributed to differences between the two systems of government or explained in terms of American exceptionality. The purpose of the present section is to go behind such trite observations to explore how and in what ways the structure, culture and organisation of social science within government vary between the two countries. The aim of this chapter is not to summarise the contributions which follow, but to sketch in a little background within which the individual chapters may be set.

The political structures of the United States and Britain do differ significantly. The separation of powers in the U.S. between judiciary, executive and legislature has no parallel in the unified British system where governments are formed from among members of the legislature, served by a permanent civil service (without political appointees), while the judiciary see their role as interpreting the Common Law as modified by the will of Parliament. Reference was made earlier to differences between the American and British legal systems in their receptivity to social science. This is a whole subject in itself, and will not be pursued further here. Rather attention will focus upon the executive and legislature in both countries.

Structurally, the British system is unified and the American fragmented. With its system of Cabinet government and the doctrine of ministerial responsibility, British politicians holding ministerial office enjoy their position by virtue of the Prime Minister's patronage, are served by permanent officials in the department which they head, and remain members of the legislature, the House of Commons. Though they must remain effective parliamentary performers, they do not face particularly searching challenges from parliamentary committees, whose inquiries they can limit if they choose. The communications between ministers and civil servants are confidential and largely secret. Much of the background work of government is therefore conducted out of the public eye.

In the American system, on the other hand, the President heads the executive branch of government while the legislature, Congress, is elected separately and pursues its own priorities in legislation. The strict party discipline which binds together the British system is absent in Washington, and indeed the party of the President may lack a majority in the House of Representatives or the Senate. An incoming President appoints Cabinet members, heads of departments, senior officials and the White House and Presidential staff, so that with each change of administration there is a considerable turnover in the executive branch. Unlike the British system, this extends to the upper echelons of the civil service, where a significant proportion of positions are held by political appointees (Heclo, 1977). Unlike the British system of collective responsibility, the American president shoulders responsibility individually for the executive decisions of his administration. He heads an extensive system which appears to command substantial support. 'On the face of it, any new president may call upon resources far beyond those provided to chief decision-makers in the United Kingdom ... In fact, one finds it difficult to describe the constellation of offices dedicated to various corners of presidential activity without turning the exercise into a litany' (Campbell, 1983, p. 30). Yet in practice cabinet co-ordination and cabinet responsibility is weak, staff of the White House and the Executive Office of the President tend to be preoccupied with political issues rather than strategic co-ordination of government, and the far-flung federal agencies leavened with newcomers at the top are difficult to co-ordinate. Patrick Moynihan has referred to 'the warring principalities that are sometimes known as the Federal government' (1969, p. xv). Hugh Heclo describes the introduction of staff units into operating agencies as constituting 'yet another force for partitioning an already deeply divided public authority into more self-contained technical and organisational specialities' (1977, p. 61). The Executive Branch initiate legislation, but in doing so the President and his staff have Congress to deal with.

Congress, for its part, is an independent force constrained by the President and linked by political ties, but able to initiate action itself and on occasion thwart the President. The weak party system and the

Congressional committee structure devolves considerable power upon senior Congressmen who occupy committee chairs. As Carol Weiss shows in Chapter 7, sizeable staffs are employed by Congressional committees and by individual Congressmen, which act as an independent source of information and advice, in marked contrast to the lack of aides employed by British MPs. Moreover, the American Congress works in the blaze of publicity, both in its debates but also in its important committee hearings, which play a much more searching part in the process of government than British parliamentary select committees, enter territory which in Britain would be barred to them, and have powers to summon executive officials and cross-question them about departmental or agency matters. The Freedom of Information Act is a further element in the openness of government in Washington.

One implication of this contrast is that in the free-wheeling, complex, compartmentalised system in Washington, there may be more scope for the academic expert to carve his or her niche and make some impact than in the tightly-knit centralised world of Westminster and Whitehall, access to which is confined to certain well-defined paths. Within the legislature, for example, there are far more opportunities for academic influence to make itself felt in Washington than at Westminster. More staff of congressmen and of congressional committees have social science backgrounds, and whether they do or not, make it their business to be acquainted with research findings, as Carol Weiss shows. Members of Congress have their own academic links in their home states. Academic advisers may be brought in to advise congressional committees, and frequently to give public evidence to them. Perhaps the most interesting recent development is the growth of the evaluation capability in the General Accounting Office at the behest of Congress, described in Chapter 16 by Ray Rist. Here a systematic attempt is made to assess the effects of legislation, the results of which are fed back to and used by Congress.

To be sure, in these various channels, social science inputs have to compete fiercely with a whole range of other sources of advice from constituents, pressure groups and lobbies and the media, as well as the very real constraints imposed by day to day political manoeuvring and longer-term political considerations. On many occasions social science inputs may be pushed to one side. This contrasts, however, with the picture at Westminster where Members of Parliament keep their own counsel to a much greater degree. Staff assistance is slight, and social science input negligible apart from the few MPs who themselves have a social science background. In recent years there has been some trend toward using individual social scientists as expert advisers to parliamentary select committees, where they have on occasion had some impact. Academics give evidence less frequently to such committees than do their congressional counterparts, and when they do so their contribution receives little or no media coverage.

Some differences between American and British legislators were outlined in the first chapter. The structural difference to note is that whereas the American Congressman may expect as a matter of course to use academic social science expertise to make sense of what is happening and suggest the direction in which to go – albeit only one input among many – his British counterpart is much less likely to do so. In part this is a function of the different position and standing of American legislators, with much more real influence than British party MPs constrained by the Whip system. In part it is a function of the scale of assistance thought appropriate for a national legislator. In part it is a function of the academic backgrounds of those who work as Congressional staff members.

In Congress, however, information overload is ever present and a marginal addition of social science is not likely to make a significant impact. A greater structural difference between Washington and London lies in the pattern of political appointments to executive leadership and the opportunities this provides to bring in social scientists. In Britain, it is extremely unusual to appoint ministers at any level from outside the House of Commons or existing members of the House of Lords. Very occasionally, the Prime Minister may make an outsider a Life Peer and appoint them to ministerial office. One instance involving a social scientist was that of Lord Crowther-Hunt in the 1970s, an Oxford politics don who had been a member of the Fulton Committee on the Civil Service. The most noticeable pattern of social science influence has been when ministers, like Crosland and Crossman, had prior academic backgrounds, and contacts and interest in social science. In the United States, presidential appointment of leading academics to senior government appointments, either as departmental heads or senior advisers, is a feature of each change of administration. There is no equivalent in Britain to the political careers of the likes of Arthur Schlesinger Jr., J. K. Galbraith, W. W. Rostow, McGeorge Bundy, Adam Yarmolinsky, Henry Kissinger or D. P. Moynihan. The point is not that these scholars were social scientists in action – they became executive advisers, administrators or diplomats as the post demanded – but that in those posts they brought a social science background to bear and were aware of the potential contribution which social science could make, which filtered down through the departments which they headed. There is plenty of scope for argument about the policy consequences of their interventions (cf. Aaron, 1978; Rainwater and Pittman, 1967), but there is no doubt that they represented a significant infusion of social science into American government.

Turning to officials in both countries, the contrasts are sharp and pointed. The scope for British ministers to bring in outside advisers is severely circumscribed by convention and structure. As indicated in the previous chapter, small numbers of political appointees, a few of them social scientists, have been attached to No. 10 Downing Street or other ministerial private offices. In the first Harold Wilson government a considerable number of academic economists were brought in as temporary civil servants, but this has come to an end with the expansion of the Government Economic Service. The usual pattern is for ministers to work with permanent officials whose career commitment is to the civil service, and whose key characteristics are political neutrality in a party-political sense and generalist administrative skills. Administrative civil servants have working with them professional colleagues with subject expertise, of whom the most relevant here are economists. Economists in Whitehall are well integrated into the system of government and do inject a social science perspective into national economic management. A recent assessment concludes that 'economists relate well to specific policy units while keeping in sight of macroeconomic policy as a seamless fabric' (Campbell, 1983, p. 139). These economists, however, are career civil servants.

In Washington, the upper echelons of the civil service are much more open, being filled by a mix of political appointees and permanent officials. The actual structure is a complex one, and the changes of personnel not quite as clear cut as might appear (cf. Heclo, 1977). For example, some political appointees have previously served in Washington and include career civil servants who move over to political appointments. The net outcome, however, is a much more open structure with much greater turnover of personnel between one administration and the next. In recent years there has been a growth of senior and middle level appointments (so called 'grade-creep'), the upward push of specialisation in management and increasing layers of technocratic political appointees (Heclo, 1977, pp. 61–4, 82). This turnover of staff and increase in staff layers within departments and agencies has tended to compartmentalise and fragment executive departments in Washington compared to the British civil service. In economic policy-making, for example, several central agencies share key leadership responsibilities. The principal department, the Treasury, is large and complex, but it does not manage the budget (the role of the Office of Management and Budget (OMB)) nor does it do forecasting (carried out by the Council of

Economic Advisers within the Executive Office of the President). '(N)o US central agency enjoys dominance in economic and fiscal policy' (Campbell, 1983, p. 106) as the Treasury under the Chancellor of the Exchequer does in Britain.

The differing roles played by the social sciences in British and American government owe something to these structural differences between the two civil services. The compact and tightly-knit world of Whitehall – what Heclo and Wildavsky call 'village life in civil service society' (1974, Chs. 1–3) – is different from the larger, more impersonal and changing official world of Washington, what Heclo calls 'a government of strangers' (1977). In the latter there is scope for social science research and advice to be fitted in to an expanding and ramified structure, part of a plural system which within the executive arm alone is divided between the White House, the Executive Office of the President, and operational departments and agencies.

There may also be differences in orientation of civil servants on opposite sides of the Atlantic. Aberbach, Putnam and Rockman have outlined four ideal types of relationship between politicians and bureaucrats. The first conforms to the Weberian ideal type. The second recognises that both politicians and bureaucrats participate in making policy, but bureaucrats bring facts and knowledge, politicians interests and values to bear on the process. In the third image, both sides engage in policy-making and both are concerned with politics. As Richard Rose notes, '(i)n theory, ministers are meant to communicate the ends of policy to civil servants, who then devise administrative means to carry out the wishes of their minister. In this formulation [the first ideal type], the roles of politician and civil servant are separate and complementary. In practice, policy-making usually develops dialectically; both politicians and civil servants review political and administrative implications of a major policy' (1974, pp. 418–19). The fourth image, that of a pure hybrid, is the result of pushing the convergence between the two roles to its logical conclusion, a politicisation of bureaucracy and a bureaucratisation of politics. Heclo and Wildavsky (1974) speak loosely of 'political administrators', without differentiating between ex-ministers and civil servants among those they interviewed. It may be hypothesised that the neutralist and generalist senior British civil servant is still closer to the second type, whereas senior officials in Washington (particularly those which Campbell calls 'politicos' and 'amphibians') display more of the characteristics of the third and even the fourth types.

Reference was made in the first chapter to partisan intellectual groups and 'think-tanks', but it is also pertinent to ask what intellectual back-up is available to government from non-partisan, scholarly sources in the immediate environment of government. Here a comparison between American and British experience is again instructive in throwing light on receptivity to insights and analysis from social science. The Brookings Institution in Washington and Political and Economic Planning in London were both established to provide policy analysis for government, the former being reconstituted in 1927, the latter founded in 1931. Businessmen played an important part in the foundation of both, but the differences between them were more striking than the similarities. Brookings was conceived as a research institute focusing upon economics and government administration whose staff were non-partisan and committed to greater efficiency. The small staff of 25–30 economists and political scientists who worked at Brookings under Harold Moulton between 1927 and 1952 saw themselves as professional social scientists, pursuing research of their own choosing. They were dealing with applied topics, but in as scholarly and objective a manner as possible. As a recent study of the history of Brookings is subtitled, they saw themselves providing expertise in the public interest (Critchlow, 1985). Since the 1950s, Brookings has added expertise in foreign policy to its concerns, and become much larger, providing a setting where former senior members of the Executive branch may engage in analysis and reflection on medium to long-term policies. On occasion dubbed a 'government in exile', Brookings has produced in the period since the mid-1950s Keynesian growth and social-policy oriented analyses which were hard-headed yet concerned with fairness – 'liberal' in the particularly American sense of that term. It is today a large research institute, including among its staff a smaller number of former senior members of the Executive branch.

Political and Economic Planning, set up in 1931, was by contrast much more the product of a small group of enthusiasts drawn from business, Parliament, the civil service, the professions and universities, but with the latter far from predominant. Even bearing in mind the absence of much social science in British universities before the war, PEP was not conceived as an expert 'think-tank' in the same way as Brookings. If Brookings was organised on the model of an academic department, PEP was run much more through committees of enthusiasts who produced collective analyses of the direction policy should take. These were scholarly, independent and broadly impartial, but not always backed by the same depth of research as the products of Brookings. From the outset, two general objectives were greater efficiency in government, and more fairness and harmony in society. Non-partisanship was insisted upon and maintained. In its early years, PEP acted as 'ginger group' within the British establishment, linking together back-bench politicians,

officials, and outsiders with strong policy interests (Pinder, 1981). It
formed an influential network of the kind which, as Cyril Smith suggests
in Chapter 5, has been so characteristic of the British 'establishment' in
absorbing outside influences.

In the post-war period, when its role as a centre of research expanded,
the influence of social science was not as marked as might have been
expected. A good deal of its work on social policy, for example, consisted
of fact-finding surveys, often of an illuminating kind, which lacked any
grounding in theory. This characteristic British empiricism is one of the
features which has handicapped the advancement of the social sciences
(cf. Bulmer, 1982). The view that 'the facts speak for themselves' is an
appealing one to practical people but one which relegates social science
to merely technical expertise in the efficient execution of research. One
commentator (Isserlis, 1981) perceived a tendency of younger research
staff in recent years to withdraw into their own particular interests,
disciplines and techniques, but this could also be taken as evidence of
growing professionalisation in research. Certainly PEP got a new lease of
life with its merger in 1979 with the Centre for Studies in Social Policy,
and their joint re-emergence as the Policy Studies Institute (PSI).

PSI, however, is still a very different animal from Brookings, even
though its reconstitution as PSI owed something to pressure for a British
Brookings in the late 1970s. Although maintaining close links with
Whitehall and Westminster, and briefly headed by an ex-civil servant,
D. J. Derx, it does not provide a refuge for those out of office in the way
that Brookings does. Nor does it interchange staff with government, and
is thus short on those with practical experience of government. It is an
effective, modest, centre for social research, with comparatively weak
links to academic social science. Its works are written up in the media and
quite widely disseminated, but it probably lacks the authority within
government which Brookings enjoys. The contrast between the two
institutions was well brought out symbolically by their respective heads
of state. Celebrating Brookings's fiftieth anniversary in 1966, President
Johnson declared: 'You are a national institution, so important to, at
least the Executive branch – and I think the Congress of the country –
that if you did not exist we would have to ask someone to create you'
(Critchlow, 1985, p. 5). When PSI was formed in 1979, the new Institute
was formally opened by Prime Minister James Callaghan, who used the
opportunity to make some rather equivocal remarks about the value of
'think-tanks' and outside policy advice for government. Some academic
observers (e.g. Dror 1984) have also questioned their value.

The rather technocratic orientation of Brookings is certainly not
apparent in the Policy Studies Institute, and may reflect more general

differences between the two systems. A recent American student of British policy analysis has suggested that there is a connection between ambivalence about analysis and the closed and secret character of British government.

> There is little or no demand for policy analysis; indeed, not only is there ministerial disinterest in policy analysis but also intolerance of it. This view is reflected in Parliament where members and select committees have virtually no staffs. Under the circumstances, as one civil servant put it; 'The civil service comes to feel that analysis is not quite the thing a gentleman should do.' In the case of the top mandarins ... the problem is not only lack of knowledge of hard-edged policy analysis but the absence of competition ... The monopoly of ministers and top mandarins in the decision-making process diminishes the rigor of challenge and scrutiny. There is no competition to show up preconceptions and poor ideas or encourage fresh thinking. (Williams 1983: 22)

Economics comes closest to making a technocratic contribution, but even there the tendency has been for the most effective government economists to be able to put ideas into lay terms.

Differences in intellectual culture were discussed in the last chapter, and will be briefly alluded to here. The education of civil servants in the two societies differs markedly. The typical British pattern is to enter the civil service straight from an undergraduate course at Oxford or Cambridge, in which history, classics or Oxford PPE figure largely. This is considered a suitable preparation for a generalist career, with little social science input, a lack not made up at the Civil Service College (which provides 'inhouse' courses) except for economics. Indeed, so strong are the doctrines of political neutrality that social and political theory are not taught at the college because they are considered controversial subjects (Bulmer, 1983a, p. 47). Campbell's data (1983) show that a higher proportion of American government officials have studied social science, particularly at graduate school. If political appointees are excluded, the proportion is higher still, with a marked concentration on political science (rarely studied by British members of his sample). Career officials had also studied economics in some numbers. Perhaps the most striking finding is the high relevance which political science and public administration are perceived to have in America for public service, and their low salience in Britain. This is also reflected in the existence in American universities of schools of public policy on a considerable scale, and of institutions like the Kennedy School of Government at Harvard, which have no British equivalent. Nuffield College, Oxford, elects visiting fellows from among people in public life, but their direct involvement in the institution is marginal.

There are interesting differences also in where senior officials turn for information and advice outside of government. British officials consulted outsiders less frequently than their American counterparts, and such consultations were much more likely to be indirect than direct in London compared to Washington (Campbell, 1983). The most striking finding was the much greater reliance of British than American officials upon the media, no doubt reflecting the quality of British newspapers and television, but also their role in the political system as a source of information and orientation. The main sources after the media for British officials were business and union leaders, friends and acquaintances, politicians, local government officials, and public opinion polls. Academic sources came well down the list, below pressure groups. The American officials ranked business leaders first, the media second, friends and acquaintances third, and state officials and academics fourth equal. Excluding political appointees, American career officials cited academics as the second most important group with whom they would consult (Campbell, 1983, pp. 290–4).

Such data lead back to the considerations of political culture raised in the previous chapter. There is certainly evidence in Britain of consistent and continuing resistance among senior officials to social science inputs other than from economics. In part this is due to some of the structural features discussed above, in part to certain features of British social science itself, such as its endemic empiricism and certain tendencies in subjects like sociology to politicisation (Bulmer, 1983a). It is also due in Britain to the bureaucratic marginality of social science within government. This feature is brought out very clearly by Robert Walker in Chapter 9. Arguably this structural problem is more acute within a tightly knit bureaucratic system controlled by generalists, without alternative bases for the deployment of expertise in the legislature or among the personal staffs of politicians.

A common contrast made between London and Washington is to draw attention to the close-knit political and intellectual ties within London and in the London–Oxford–Cambridge triangle. Oversimplifying somewhat in Britain, it has proved difficult for social scientists to become insiders, either as civil servants or as advisers, compared to the more fluid and open system in Washington. Of the three groups which Cyril Smith discusses in Chapter 5, the Titmuss group gained an entrée largely because of their political contacts, and this was also true to some extent of the Oxford industrial relations school. Only the Keynesian economists established unblemished credentials, as non-partisan experts, and economics is an exception to several of the generalisations about Britain offered here. Even where academic social scientists have become insiders at a high level – such as David Donnison, A. H. Halsey, Brian

Abel-Smith and others – this has not advanced the cause of social science researchers of more junior status, since there is such a wide gap between these lower echelons and the top (cf. Table 9.3, p. 149). There are very few social science research posts even as high as Assistant Secretary level in the Civil Service, as Walker makes clear, a powerful obstacle both to influence on policy and to recruitment of the ablest talent. 'Insiders', as Patricia Thomas suggests in Chapter 4, may be particularly effective, but in the British system it is a comparatively unusual social scientist who achieves such impact. In the American system there are much greater opportunities for potential policy relevant contributions to be made, both through research and as an adviser, the social sciences are more respected, more visible, and more an accepted part of the system of government. It does not follow, however, that their influence is vastly greater than in Britain. The American system of government is a complex one, with plural sources of power, and balancing elements both within legislature and executive and between the two. The contribution of social science has to compete with a variety of other voices – many of them more effective or more vociferous – so that the presence of social science, and even a belief among policy-makers in the efficacy of social science does not necessarily mean that its contribution is highly effective in all cases.

The aim of this discussion has been to set the scene for the chapters which follow and for the comparisons which are implicit in them when juxtaposed to each other. Some of the chapters, such as those of Theda Skocpol and Patricia Thomas, are general in orientation. Other authors, like Cyril Smith, look at the affinities between particular social science disciplines and a policy orientation. Stuart Blume, Colin Campbell and Carol Weiss examine the use and impact of social science in particular governmental settings. Robert Walker and Derek Cornish and Ronald Clarke examine the particular problems of in-house research in British government. The use of governmental commissions is a device for gaining policy advice at arm's length from government, often involving social scientists and social science research, though not unattended by strain (cf. Popper, 1970; Komarovsky, 1975; Bulmer, 1980, 1983; American Behavioral Scientist, 1983). Lisl Klein's chapter is a case study of the use of social science by a very considerable West German governmental commission, drawing an implicit comparison with the more modest and pragmatic manner, relying less on expertise, in which British government uses the skills of social scientists. There are also interesting parallels to pursue between this German commission and Swedish governmental commissions (cf. Premfors, 1983), which act not only as outside bodies to deliberate upon contentious policy issues, but also as forums for negotiation between conflicting interests in order to attempt to achieve a political solution to policy problems.

This German case is also a salutary reminder that large-scale social science research is not confined to the United States. The editor may be criticised for including a chapter which strictly speaking is outside the remit of the collection. Its inclusion, however, is deliberate to underline the points made at the end of the introduction and by Theda Skocpol in Chapter 3, about the potential value of more systematic comparative research on these issues. The other eight chapters which follow in this section are intended to permit better-documented comparisons between Britain and the United States. They represent the beginnings rather than the end-product of such an historical and contemporary inquiry into the interrelations between social science and the state.

REFERENCES

Aaron, H. (1978), *Politics and the Professors*, Washington D.C., Brookings Institute.

Alberbach, J. D., Putnam, R. D. and Rockman, B. A. (1981), *Bureaucrats and Politicians in Western Democracies*, Cambridge, Mass., Harvard University Press.

American Behavioral Scientist (1983), 'Social Science and Policymaking: the use of research by governmental commissions', Special issue Vol. 26, no. 5 (May), pp. 555–680.

Bulmer, M. (ed.) (1978), *Social Policy Research*, London, Macmillan.

Bulmer, M. (ed.) (1980), *Social Research and Royal Commissions*, London, Allen & Unwin.

Bulmer, M. (1982), *The Uses of Social Research: social investigation in public policy-making*, London, Allen & Unwin.

Bulmer, M. (1983a), 'Using social science research in policy-making: why are the obstacles so formidable?', *Public Administration Bulletin* 43 (December), pp. 37–48.

Bulmer, M. (1983b), *Royal Commissions and Departmental Committees of Inquiry: the lessons of experience*, London, Royal Institute of Public Administration.

Campbell, C. (1983), *Government Under Stress: political executives and key bureaucrats in Washington, London and Ottawa*, Toronto, University of Toronto Press.

Critchlow, D. T. (1985), *The Brookings Institution, 1916–1952: expertise and the public interest in a democratic society*, De Kalb, Ill., Northern Illinois University Press.

Dror, Y. (1984) 'Required breakthroughs in Think Tanks', *Policy Sciences* 16, pp. 199–225.

Heclo, H. (1977), *A Government of Strangers: executive politics in Washington*, Washington D.C., Brookings Institution.

Heclo, H. and Wildavsky, A. (1974), *The Private Government of Public Money: community and policy inside British politics*, London, Macmillan. (2nd edition with a new Preface, 1981.)

Isserlis, S. (1981), 'Plus ça change. . . . .' in Pinder (1981), pp. 162–70.

Komarovsky, M. (ed.) (1975), *Sociology and Public Policy: the case of the Presidential Commissions*, New York, Elsevier.

Moynihan, D. P. (1969), *Maximum Feasible Misunderstanding: community action in the war on poverty*, New York, Free Press.

Pinder, J. (ed.) (1981), *Fifty Years of Political and Economic Planning: Looking Forward 1931–1981*, London, Heinemann.

Popper, F. (1970), *The President's Commissions*, New York, Twentieth Century Fund.

Premfors, R. (1983), 'Governmental commissions in Sweden', *American Behavioral Scientist* 26 (5), pp. 623–42.

Rainwater, L. and Yancey, W. L. (eds.) (1967), *The Moynihan Report and the Politics of Controversy*, Cambridge, Mass., M.I.T. Press.

Rose, R. (1974), *The Problem of Party Government*, New York, Free Press.

Williams, W. (1983), 'British policy analysts: some preliminary observations from the U.S.', in A. Gray and W. I. Jenkins (eds.), *Policy Analysis and Education in British Government*, London, Royal Institute of Public Administration, pp. 17–24.

CHAPTER 3

Governmental structures, social science, and the development of economic and social policies*

THEDA SKOCPOL

'Social scientists', the eminent physicist Edward Teller once exclaimed to a group of undergraduate students at Michigan State University, 'are no more scientists than *Christian* scientists!' Such a crude put-down calls forth both a defensive wince and a will to do righteous battle, especially among those U.S. social scientists who have spent the last several decades trying to persuade their natural science counterparts at the National Science Foundation of their true scientific credentials (Riecken, 1983). Yet, of course, the modern social sciences have always been not only quests for evidence and theoretical understanding of human affairs, but also value-laden endeavors based on faith in the contributions that applied social knowledge might make to social progress. Consequently, the social sciences have been inescapably affected by – and implicated in – the vagaries of public policy-making on openly contested social issues.

Nineteenth-century social scientists were very aware and open about the ways in which their efforts married value-commitments and new kinds of systematic social research. Were all of us taken back through time to a meeting about a century ago of the American Social Science Association, we would find ourselves amidst the elite progenitors of U.S. social science disciplines, many of them self-conscious social Christians who believed that the empirical discovery and analysis of social facts was an enterprise intrinsically tied to the advocacy and active pursuit of social reforms (Haskell, 1977). Although many were involved in voluntary private efforts at 'social betterment', the early American social scientists also hoped that governments at city, state, and (even the) national levels might implement appropriate reform measures once social problems

* This is a revision of remarks presented at the Social Science Research Council Symposium on Studies of Science and Technology, held at the Halloran House in New York City on June 11, 1984.

were diagnosed through research. In this, they echoed in less promising American political conditions the still stronger faith that nineteenth-century British investigators, from utilitarians to social Christians, held about the capacity of their government to act wisely to cope with social ills or disturbances of economic equilibria once these were discovered and measured through official questionnaires or privately-sponsored social surveys (Abrams, 1968).

The modern state and demands for social knowledge

Indeed, as this look backward can remind us, the modern, research-oriented social sciences and the socioeconomic interventions of modern national states – 'welfare states', as we now label them – emerged and grew up together. In very general terms, there are several reasons for this interconnection. States necessarily concern themselves with social order and with at least the external conditions for the smooth functioning of markets and production processes. Their needs to act on these issues in increasingly complex socioeconomic settings create growing demands both for general theories of how economies or societies function and for reliable and apparently impersonal statistical data on particular issues that seem problematic (such as the living conditions and likely behavioral responses of the lower classes). Public officials themselves may both demand – and develop their own intra-governmental capacities to supply – social theories and statistical data. But demands and supply also come from economic enterprises and politically active social groups.

Indeed, liberal-democratic societies are almost certainly the most hungry for social knowledge, and the most congenial to the growth and political application of the social sciences. For the rise of the modern 'public sphere', in which voluntary groups propose ameliorative measures in the collective interest or in their own interest, fuels the search for information and analysis about social problems. Such information and analysis, in turn, encourages demands for governmental interventions – or abstentions! – to improve social welfare. The government's interventions and abstentions themselves generate more problems and, directly or indirectly, more needs for social knowledge to help officials and politically active groups set things right. Things are never set entirely right, of course, so the process goes on and on.

General points such as these can be spun out to make overall sense of the interconnections between the rise of the modern social sciences and the increasing scope and depth of interventions by modern states in the realms of economic and social life. Beyond that, the contemporary literature on social science and public policy tends to ask non-historical questions which take for granted an optimistically progressive view of social science in relation to politics: are social scientists getting sufficient resources for their endeavors, and from whom? Are public policymakers or the general politically engaged public getting the best, the most up-to-date, theoretically powerful and technically accurate research results, and are they willing and able to act upon this 'information'? If not, what explanations can we draw from organization theories or political sociology to explain where the 'irrational' blockages lie? These have been some of the favorite questions pursued in the available literature on social science and public policy (for good overviews of the literature, see Rich, 1981a; Rein, 1983: ch. 13), and no one would gainsay that studies such as Robert F. Rich's *Social Science Information and Public Policymaking* (1981b) have contributed important answers to such questions.

Nevertheless, equally important questions and answers about the interrelations of social knowledge and governmental structures and policies are to be found at a level of analysis 'in between' grand overviews of the joint growth of social sciences and the modern state, on the one hand, and detailed studies of the policy utilization (or non-utilization) of social scientific findings, on the other. Fresh insights are to be found through historical and comparative investigations that ask about the *various* ways in which governmental structures and activities have affected the intellectual development and social organization of the social sciences themselves, as well as their policy applications.

I can briefly illustrate some of the issues that might be pursued through wide-ranging comparative and historical studies, by discussing some of what we already know (or have begun to understand) about the relations between the social sciences and public policy-making in the United States, Britain, and Sweden. Historical and comparative studies make it clear that governments and their activities have profoundly affected the emergence and social organization of social science disciplines, as well as their intellectual orientations. In turn, variously organized and oriented social sciences have subsequently influenced the overall shape and content of governmental interventions for economic and social-welfare purposes.

The formation of social science professions in the United States and Britain

Why, for example, have 'agricultural economics' and 'rural sociology' long been separately organized in many American universities, especially in public land-grant institutions? A major part of the explanation lies in the early prominence within America's generally weak and decentralized public administration of the U.S. Department of Agriculture and the federal-state extension services. From the late nineteenth century through the 1920s, these government agencies provided the resources – and inspiration – for partially distinct disciplines oriented to accumulating appropriate, policy-relevant social knowledge through empirical research on farmers and farm conditions (and there were parallel development in the natural sciences) (Gaus and Wolcott, 1940; Rossiter, 1979).

By the time of the New Deal, moreover, social scientists who had been educated at, and had pursued careers within, the highly policy- and practice-oriented disciplines of agricultural economics and rural sociology were better prepared than any other knowledge-bearing professions – except certain lawyers (Irons, 1982) and the labor economists of the state of Wisconsin (Schlabach, 1969) – to fashion new federal government interventions (Kirkendall, 1966; Rowley, 1970; Skocpol and Finegold, 1982). Their ideas and their career experiences alike bridged the realms of academic scholarship, grass-roots public administration, and the interest politics of various farmers' lobbies. Once the New Deal gave them opportunities, such people fashioned an entire array of federal agricultural programs that were politically and administratively institutionalized for several decades, providing economic protections and incentives and a kind of social welfare to commercial farmers in America. Yet, because their expertise rarely stretched beyond the economic problems of commercial agriculture and farmers as such, these unusually policy-relevant American social scientists (whatever their individual hopes) also helped to create policy barriers to more fully national macroeconomic policies and to social-welfare measures that might have redistributed resources to poorer rural and urban Americans alike.

Moving to another example, we can see that government interventionism does not always straightforwardly stimulate corresponding academic disciplines – especially not disciplines with autonomous orientations toward theoretical and methodological innovation. British historians of social science such as the late Philip Abrams (1968) and Martin Bulmer (1978) have argued that the consolidation of a coherent discipline and profession of British sociology was historically *discouraged* not only by the uncongenial academic environments of Oxford and Cambridge, but also by the ready interventionism of the nineteenth- and early twentieth-century British state. The British national state was 'permeable', or readily open to educated British reformers interested in researching the facts of immediate social problems and acting upon them through ethically justified modifications of existing parliamentary programs or administrative measures. Hence (argue Abrams and Bulmer) potential sociologists were drawn into politics and public administration, not left to carve out space in the elite universities for a new scientific discipline to compete with moral and political philosophy. Theories of society were not developed in close conjunction with empirical social research, and a less prestigious and more narrowly practical discipline of 'social administration' made greater headway in British academia until after World War II.

In contrast to the retardation of the professionalization of the academic social sciences in Britain, the United States became between the 1880s and the 1920s the preeminent home of a full array of university-based social science disciplines, including major disciplines committed to 'pure' theories and 'basic' research using increasingly sophisticated quantitative methods (Bulmer, 1984; Haskell, 1977; Ross, 1979). There were, of course, various facilitating conditions. The sheer size and cultural diversity of the United States, along with its federal-democratic political structure, laid the basis for the eventual emergence of a remarkably competitive and decentralized system of national universities (Vesey, 1965; Shils, 1979). And during the 1920s private foundations provided crucial resources to support the development of facilities for social research (Bulmer and Bulmer, 1981; Grossman, 1982; Robinson, 1983: 35). But, ironically, the *retardation* until the 1930s of the emergence of nation-wide U.S. social provision may also have been an important condition for luxuriant and early academic professionalization in the social sciences. Certainly, this retardation can help us to understand why American sociology developed from its turn-of-the-century normative preoccupations with practical reforms directed at specific urban social problems toward a more theoretically oriented set of discourses and a more statistically based set of research endeavors aimed at understanding 'society' as a whole. The University of Chicago in the pivotal 1920s was the pre-eminent and most telling site of this transition, which came only *after* university-based scholars were frustrated by the limits of Progressive Era social reforms and by failures of struggles to restructure Chicago city government and Illinois state government (Bulmer, 1984; Diner, 1980; Karl, 1974).

American academics and public policy-making

American social scientists have been by international standards unusually 'academic', or university-based, professions, free to innovate theoretically and methodologically in relative isolation from the immediate policy interests of government. Normatively speaking, modern American social scientists place great value on 'non-applied' academic careers and intellectual achievements, and (more than their British and Continental European counterparts) they fear the distractions and even 'corruptions' of too close an involvement in partisan politics or in governmental practicalities. Nevertheless, as the historian Robert Church has shown in a fine essay (1975) on the formative years of academic economists in the United States, modern American social scientists no sooner extricated themselves from nineteenth-century reform activities and ensconced themselves in the relatively insulated universities, than they began to act in new ways on enduring concerns for policy-relevance. They looked for arms-length ways to have their 'objective' ideas and findings achieve beneficial effects through politics – either via the enlightenment of the educated public of active citizens, or by offering 'expert' advice to strategically situated policy elites (see also Furner, 1975). By the 1920s, Herbert Hoover's nationally prestigious research conferences, and his officially encouraged overviews of 'Recent Economic Trends' or 'Recent Social Trends' seemingly allowed U.S. academic social scientists to be 'policy-relevant' while remaining true to their own academic standards and continuing to anchor their careers in the universities (Karl, 1969). Similar opportunities were also provided to academics when they served temporarily on advisory or regulatory commissions without permanent commitment to civil service careers.

Yet when it comes to whether to relate any more directly than in these arms-length ways to politics and public policymaking, a profound *hesitance* is built into the basic role definition of the social science professional in the United States. There are good historical and experiential reasons why this should be so. We have already noted that academic social science disciplines have flourished in the United States in part because there were no nation-wide social policies before the 1930s, and also because – in contrast to the situation in Britain – U.S. governmental careers have always been unbeckoning as alternatives to university life for social scientists. Equally important, perhaps, have been the lessons taught by experiences at watershed such as the New Deal and the Great Society, when prestigious academic social scientists have plunged enthusiastically into politics, attempting to guide major policy innovations to their envisaged ends according to the best theoretical and technical ideas available. On those occasions the frequent result for both individuals and social science communities has been frustration. I am thinking of such examples as: the drubbings administered by Congress to the ideas of public administration reformers and advocates of national planning during the New Deal (Clawson, 1981; Karl, 1974: chs. 12–13; Polenberg,

1966); the similar political defeats suffered by the Harvard-Tufts 'stag-nationist Keynesians' of the 1938 to 1946 period (Collins, 1981: chs. 1–2; Weir and Skocpol, 1985); and the frustration of Daniel Patrick Moynihan's much more recent efforts to fashion comprehensive welfare reform and public measures to deal with the manifold crises of the black family (Moynihan, 1973; Rainwater and Yancey, 1967).

American in contrast to Swedish patterns

In all of these instances, prestigious academic social scientists attempted to do in U.S. national policymaking what Swedish social scientists have again and again done through participation on major investigatory and policy-planning commissions: use the best available theories and the most up-to-date research techniques and findings of their disciplines as a basis for proposing fundamental policy innovations, which self-consciously build upon and correct previous policies whose effects have been analyzed. Yet in Sweden, social scientists operate in a context where elite civil servants themselves engage continuously in policy monitoring and policy innovation, where a single political party, the Social Democrats, has (with but brief interruption) governed according to relatively consistent principles for decades, and where normal processes of policy planning simultaneously entail consulting conflicting interests and building up the political support necessary for both legislative success and consistent administration thereafter (Anton, 1969; Meijer, 1969). In these circumstances, academic social scientists, ranging from Ph.D. dissertation writers to internationally acclaimed figures such as Alva and Gunnar Myrdal, can successfully deploy the highest theoretical and technical skills in designing truly holistic national policies.

These are not the conditions that U.S. social scientists have experienced at the centers of national politics. American government is inherently fragmented and adversarial, and administrative continuity happens at best for individual, specialized programs. Thus it is not surprising that those academic social scientists who have tried to operate in Washington as if it were Stockholm have neither succeeded nor escaped without setting off bitter political controversies.

Swedish and British observers of U.S. social scientific studies of poverty – a highly policy-relevant literature launched from the time of the Great Society anti-poverty efforts of the 1960s – have highlighted the strengths and weaknesses of the American work in contrast to its counterpart in their native countries (Bulmer, 1983; Korpi, 1980). American scholarship, these observers agree, is extraordinarily methodologically sophisticated and pursues many creative analytic approaches, especially when it comes to evaluating policy failures or assessing pilot experiments. But the more practical-policy-oriented the research, the more specialized it becomes, and the less inclined to use concepts or theories to criticize the premises of existing lines of public action. Poverty studies, like U.S. policies toward the poor, have tended to remain isolated from macroeconomic ideas and from analyses of unemployment. And these studies have remained wedded to income-based definitions of poverty and notions of how to ameliorate it, even though European social scientists have developed more theoretically justifiable social measures of relative impoverishment. In the picture painted by these British and Swedish observers, it is as if the specialized virtuosity of American research on this obviously policy-relevant issue mirrored the programmatic fragmentation and stigmatizing orientations toward the poor of the American welfare state itself.

But to leave it at this would be misleading. In Sweden, perhaps, social scientists – especially those willing to work from normative points of view congruent with Swedish Social Democracy's programs and self-image as a class-based political movement – may have found unusual opportunities to combine policy relevance with the pursuit of large-scale empirical studies and the elaboration of macroscopic social and economic theories. Yet even Walter Korpi (1980), a foremost practitioner and celebrant of this frankly Social-Democratic-oriented social science, praises the technical innovativeness and the intellectual open-endedness of U.S. poverty research, despite his sense of its theoretical narrowness. And what may happen in Sweden if the social conditions and political certainties sustaining the long-established Social Democratic welfare state come to a fundamental watershed? How free and able will the Swedish social sciences be to hypothesize about and do relevant research on the new situation?

In the American case, it is clear that social scientists have had no satisfying opportunities at all to be philosopher kings and queens within a comprehensive modern welfare state. Even so, the normal pursuit of unusually flourishing academic disciplines has given rise to telling ideas and research findings that have facilitated new public interventions for the social good. Public policies towards race relations are a good case in point. From the late 1940s, Robert Merton (1949) and other scholars drawing on academic work within the structural functionalist theoretical tradition disseminated a conceptual distinction between 'prejudice' and 'discrimination' – a distinction that made it easier for many educated people, including some public officials, to understand how legal or administrative changes at variance with consciously felt social attitudes might nevertheless promote racial changes by, first, modifying behaviors and practices regardless of attitudes. Subsequently, psychological experiments on children's self images by Kenneth Clark and others helped to support the 1954 decision of the Supreme Court justices to outlaw school segregation. In this case, empirical research findings deployed at a strategic location and moment in America's adversarial polity, helped to buttress basically normative arguments in favor of the use of public judicial power to spur forward one of America's most momentous social changes.

Since the courts have arguably always been the most authoritative organs of public power in America, perhaps it is not surprising that social science should have gained important leverage through this modality. Similarly, opportunities to draw upon ongoing research or theorizing to affect legislative changes or administrative improvements have often appeared in particular cities or states within America's decentralized federal system. This was true during the Progressive Era of the early twentieth century, when most social policy innovations occurred at those levels of government. And in the present period, as the federal government pulls back from some of its domestic interventions, the cities and states may again become the most vital arenas of policy experimentation for social scientists scattered throughout America's decentralized and competitive university system.

Conclusion

This has been but a brief and speculative look at the social sciences in relation to the distinctive patterns of American government, with sideways glances to Britain and Sweden. The purpose has simply been to illustrate some of the complex interconnections between the development of the social sciences and the structures and activities of modern national states – patterns that certainly must be unravelled more fully by further comparative and historical research.

In the final analysis, it may be that each national array of social sciences – an array that emerged historically in relation to a particular government and its activities – has its own distinctive modalities for becoming relevant to politics and public policymaking. If so, further studies of the long-term development of modern national states in relation to the social sciences should help us to see more clearly what the alternative creative possibilities for the social sciences have been – and might be – in different times and places.

REFERENCES

Abrams, Philip (1968), *The Origins of British Sociology*, Chicago, University of Chicago Press.

Anton, Thomas J. (1969), 'Policy-making and political culture in Sweden', *Scandinavian Political Studies* 4, 88–102.

Bulmer, Martin (1978), 'Social science research and policy-making in Britain', in *Social Policy Research*, edited by Martin Bulmer, pp. 3–43, London, Macmillan.

Bulmer, Martin (1983), 'Science, theory, and values in social science research on poverty: the United States and Britain', *Comparative Social Research* 6, 353–69.

Bulmer, Martin (1984), *The Chicago School of Sociology: Institutionalisation, Diversity, and the Rise of Sociological Research*, Chicago, University of Chicago Press.

Bulmer, Martin, and Bulmer, Joan (1981), 'Philanthropy and social science in the 1920s: the case of Beardsley Ruml and the Laura Spelman Rockefeller Memorial, 1922–1929', *Minerva* 19: 347–407.

Church, Robert L. (1975), 'Economists as experts: the rise of an academic profession in the United States, 1870–1920', in *The University in Society*, ed. Lawrence Stone, vol. II, pp. 571–609, Princeton, New Jersey, Princeton University Press.

Clawson, Marion (1981), *New Deal Planning: The National Resources Planning Board*, Baltimore, Maryland, The Johns Hopkins University Press.

Collins, Robert M. (1981), *The Business Response to Keynes*, New York, Columbia University Press.

Diner, Stephen J. (1980), *A City and Its Universities: Public Policy in Chicago, 1892–1919*, Chapel Hill, University of North Carolina Press.

Furner, Mary O. (1975), *Advocacy and Objectivity: A Crisis in the Professionalization of American Social Science, 1865–1905*, Lexington, University of Kentucky Press.

Gaus, John M., and Wolcott, L. M. (1940), *Public Administration and the United States Department of Agriculture*, Chicago Public Administration Service.

Grossman, David M. (1982), 'American foundations and the support of economic research, 1913–1929', *Minerva* 20: 59–82.

Haskell, Thomas (1977), *The Emergence of Professional Social Science: The American Social Science Association and the Nineteenth-Century Crisis of Authority*, Urbana, University of Illinois Press.

Irons, Peter H. (1982), *The New Deal Lawyers*, Princeton, New Jersey, Princeton University Press.

Karl, Barry D. (1969), 'Presidential planning and social science research: Mr. Hoover's experts', *Perspectives in American History* 3: 347–409.

Karl, Barry D. (1974), *Charles E. Merriam and the Study of Politics*, Chicago, University of Chicago Press.

Kirkendall, Richard S. (1966), *Social Scientists and Farm Politics in the Age of Roosevelt*, Columbia, University of Missouri Press.

Korpi, Walter (1980), 'Approaches to the study of poverty in the United States: critical notes from a European perspective', in *Poverty and Public Policy: An Evaluation of Social Science Research*, ed. Vincent T. Covello, pp. 287–314, Cambridge, Massachusetts, Schenkman.

Meijer, Hans (1969), 'Bureaucracy and policy formation in Sweden', *Scandinavian Political Studies* 4: 103–16.

Merton, Robert K. (1949), 'Discrimination and the American creed', in *Discrimination and National Welfare*, ed. R. M. MacIver, New York, Harper and Brothers.

Moynihan, Daniel P. (1973), *The Politics of a Guaranteed Income: The Nixon Administration and the Family Assistance Plan*, New York, Vintage Books, 1973.

Polenberg, Richard F. (1966), *Reorganizing Roosevelt's Government, 1936–1939: The Controversy Over Executive Reorganization*, Cambridge, Mass., Harvard University Press.

Rainwater, Lee, and Yancey, William L. (1967), *The Moynihan Report and the Politics of Controversy*, Cambridge, Mass., The M.I.T. Press.

Rein, Martin (1983), *From Policy to Practice*, Armonk, N.Y., M. E. Sharpe.

Rich, Robert F. (1981a), *The Knowledge Cycle*, Beverly Hills, California, Sage Publications.

Rich, Robert F. (1981b), *Social Science Information and Public Policymaking: The Interaction between Bureaucratic Politics and the Use of Survey Data*, San Francisco, Jossey-Bass.

Riecken, Henry R. (1983), 'The National Science Foundation and the social sciences', *Items* (Newsletter of the Social Science Research Council, New York City) 37(2–3): 39–42.

Robinson, Marshall (1983), 'The role of the private foundations', *Items* 37(2–3): 35–9.

Ross, Dorothy (1979), 'The development of the social sciences', in *The Organization of Knowledge in Modern America, 1860–1920*, ed. Alexandra Oleson and John Voss, pp. 107–38, Baltimore, Maryland, The Johns Hopkins University Press.

Rossiter, Margaret W. (1979), 'The organization of the agricultural sciences', in *The Organization of Knowledge in Modern America, 1860–1920*, ed. Alexandra Oleson and John Voss, pp. 211–48, Baltimore, Maryland, The Johns Hopkins University Press.

Rowley, William D. (1970), *M. L. Wilson and the Campaign for Domestic Allotment*, Lincoln: University of Nebraska Press.

Schlabach, Theron F. (1969), *Edwin E. Witte: Cautious Reformer*, Madison, State Historical Society of Wisconsin.

Shils, Edward (1979), 'The order of learning in the United States: the ascendancy of the university', in *The Organization of Knowledge in Modern America, 1860–1920*, ed. Alexandra Oleson and John Voss, pp. 19–47, Baltimore, Maryland, The Johns Hopkins University Press.

Skocpol, Theda, and Kenneth Finegold (1982), 'State capacity and economic intervention in the early New Deal', *Political Science Quarterly* 97(2): 255–78.

Vesey, Laurence R. (1965), *The Emergence of the American University*, Chicago, University of Chicago Press.

Weir, Margaret, and Skocpol, Theda (1985), 'State structures and the possibilities for "Keynesian" responses to the Great Depression in Sweden, Britain, and the United States', in *Bringing the State Back In*, ed. Peter B. Evans, Dietrich Rueschemeyer, and Theda Skocpol, Cambridge, England and New York, Cambridge University Press.

CHAPTER 4

The use of social research: myths and models

PATRICIA THOMAS

Social research permeates our everyday lives. It is the stuff of journalism, advertising and market research. When events bring a subject to the forefront of our consciousness – football violence, the price of North Sea oil, famine in Ethiopia – there are always social scientists who have carried out related research and are prepared to tell the radio listener or newspaper reader about it for a brief spell before returning to the normal tasks of addressing their peers and their students.

It is surprising, then, that social science (and still more sociology with which it is sometimes confused) enjoys such low public esteem. The findings of social scientists are often dismissed as too obvious to be worth stating or too obviously incorrect – contrary to currently accepted truths – to be taken seriously. Yet a very proper role for social science is to explain society to itself, to gather information by close observation or scientifically based surveys, to analyse it rigorously and, on the basis of it, offer new insights to the reader.

I will argue that the expectations of the parties concerned with social research and its use are largely to blame for its unpopularity. The expectations of those who are involved in social policy research seem to me to be especially prone to these problems. Ten years ago a little over half the 1,830 social science investigators asked who they were trying to influence mentioned policy- or decision-makers as the major audience.[1] Now that acute spending cuts have made the pursuit of relevance even more important, the proportion of social scientists trying to influence policy-makers is unlikely to have diminished. The pursuit of relevance, and the paths along which it has been pursued, have to my mind lessened rather than increased the actual utilisation of social research. If I am right, the problem lies not so much with the choice of subject as with the view taken about the relationship between research and policy. The

51

parties to the research/policy process look to different models of research use: the fact that the models so seldom interact results in disappointment and frustration for the social policy researcher.

An excellent typology of the uses to which research may be put has been produced by Carol Weiss in her book, *Using Social Research in Public Policy Making.*[2] One of the models which she dismisses as irrelevant to social research is the decision-driven model: the social problem is defined, the missing knowledge needed to solve it is identified and social science techniques are then employed to supply and interpret the knowledge required, the whole process culminating in policy choice. She argues that the policy-making process is political, attempting to reconcile interests rather than implementing logic and truth. In the political process, research does not play a large part. Should we expect governments to base policy decisions on social research rather than on party manifestoes and the realities of everyday life? Most reasonable people reflecting on the problems of making policy would say no.

The myths

There is, however, a time when all the parties concerned with social policy research and its potential use seem happy to subscribe to the myth that research on matters of social policy will, if properly conducted, find its results incorporated into policy. This is at the time when the research is being considered for funding. The researcher couches the application in terms of its relevance to policy, the funding body considers it in the same light, and the government department concerned, if consulted, reacts as though the research is of potential use in the policy-making process. This suspension of disbelief for the moment is prevalent within government departments when the 'customer' or policy division asks for research about a controversial subject but nowhere is the gulf between aspiration and practice so wide as in a body outside central government control, a research council or a private foundation or trust.

It is difficult not to succumb to the temptation to conduct, or fund, or ask for, research on topics of current interest, especially if they are the subject of political debate. Ironically, the more closely such research is geared to policy, the less use will be made of it. The reasons are not hard to find: the normal life of a research project is about three years with perhaps six months for writing up the results. Within that time the agenda for action will have changed, so that, even if the research results are known about in Whitehall and in Westminster, interest is unlikely to have been sustained over this period. If interest has been sustained and the results known – to pile improbability on improbability – the research results will have to compete not only with other research findings but also with the many components of the policy-making process, most of them overtly political. The likely result is that the research will have no direct impact on the policy-making process. One might expect such an outcome to lower the spirits of the actors in the drama; in fact the researcher will probably by now have moved on to another project, the funding body will have revised its research agenda and the policy-makers will be attending to the business in hand. A feature of the fantasy about the close relationship between research and policy is that it is transient, seldom lasting beyond the point when a grant is made. It is a sad truism of social research that, however interesting, relevant and well argued it is at the time an appliction is made for its funding, it loses most of its appeal when it appears as a report. Responsible funding bodies insist on receiving, and reviewing, final reports but do so with more diligence than zeal. As a result myth succeeds myth and fantasy gives way to fantasy, giving some satisfaction to all parties.

At worst the emphasis on research as a problem-solver can backfire: a radical social scientist may draw a gloomy portrait of present-day society and recommend solutions that entail heavy public expenditure, and therefore be unpopular with the present administration. At best it leaves policy research – and by extension social science in general – vulnerable to the charge of failing to deliver what it promises. If it were possible to compare the aspirations of all policy researchers as set out in their applications for grants with the final outcome *in terms of social change* the results would no doubt be depressing.[3] Judged solely in those terms the exercise would seem to have failed.

Funding bodies

The organisations which fund research are largely responsible for the style of research supported. Whether passive or active in the role they give their constituents some idea of their requirements. The prudent applicant finds out as much about the funding body as he can, selecting the one which most closely mirrors his own research preferences. (He might even change the emphasis in subtle ways to make it acceptable.) There are three major sources of funds for social policy research in Britain. By far the largest (despite cutbacks) are government departments; next in size is the Economic and Social Research Council (ESRC). The foundations and trusts run a poor third, but their independence of government makes them a significant force.

Government departments

Most government departments fund research. It may be undertaken in-house, commissioned from the universities, polytechnics and research institutes or – less often these days – funded in response to requests from outside the department. Most of the research is, naturally enough, geared to the work in the department itself. It is far more likely to be policy-oriented than theoretical or fundamental research. Most departments have a fairly sophisticated machinery for assessing 'research needs' and for ensuring that the results become known to the policy division which originally asked for it. However well-run the system, it cannot ensure that senior officials or Ministers read, take note of, or act upon any advice that may be embodied in the research. If the research was begun three years before, the chances of it being of equal interest at this later stage are remote, as mentioned above, and the research has in any case to compete with a variety of other influences on the policy-making process. Nevertheless the conditions for successful policy research use are better within a government department than they can possibly be if the research is undertaken independently of it. Most government departments believe they can look after their own research needs, so that little attention is given to seeking out the results of externally funded research. That is not to say that such research findings are not read within a department – they obviously will be of some interest – but they will seldom play an important part in decision-making.

The Economic and Social Research Council (ESRC)

The ESRC – until 1984 the SSRC – has been in existence for twenty years. Its Charter requires the Council, inter alia, 'to encourage and support by any means research in the social sciences by any other person or body'. Before it came into being the foundations and trusts had largely been responsible for providing social science research except for what was then called applied research and undertaken in or for government departments for their own use. In a sense the SSRC usurped the role of both the voluntary and the statutory sector, as it soon became the largest patron of fundamental and methodological research while striving in a variety of ways to be useful to society. In the Council's early days the desire to be useful was not always translated into a wish to influence policy, though at least one large programme of research, the Educational Priority Area Programme of action research funded in 1968 by the SSRC and the Department of Education and Science, was aimed very precisely at government policy. Writing in the SSRC Newsletter in 1968 Michael Young, the then Chairman, said:

> The Council has also joined with a Government Department – the Department of Education and Science – in promoting some 'action research' designed to show what are some of the best ways of giving support to children and their families in six Educational Priority Areas, in Dundee, Sunderland, Liverpool, the West Riding, Birmingham and London. The experiment could be a model in a double sense – a model for what, if all went well, might be included in general educational policy in the 1970s; and a model for what might be done in many other sectors of public policy. It is certainly high time that when major policy changes are made they should where possible be tried out on a small scale and properly assessed before there is a final decision to plump for them. A lot of mistakes could be avoided that way.[4]

Dr Young's intention was to make educational policy better informed. He did not in the article claim that research should be prescriptive or problem-solving, but that it should have an educational function.

More recently Michael Young's successors, especially Michael Posner and the current Chairman, Sir Douglas Hague, have attempted to make ESRC research even more directly helpful to Government. The dominant theme of ESRC research at the moment is 'What is wrong with Britain?' and Hague has expressed the hope that social scientists, by pursuing this theme, will be able to demonstrate their potential contribution to solving the economic problems of the country.

But despite the pursuit of relevance, there is little evidence that ESRC research has more direct impact on government policy-making than, say, that of foundations and trusts (who are less committed to influencing government in a direct way). It has better contacts, more machinery formal and informal, government representation on Council and committees. It is powerless, however, if there is no will on the part of Whitehall or Westminster to listen and act on what they have heard. When there is a willingness to act on the basis of research, the research selected is more likely to be the visible, government-funded, study than one supported by a research council.

Foundations and trusts

In the social sciences these no longer cut a dash as they did in the days before the research councils, when they were the main source of social science funding outside government. Nevertheless, the Leverhulme Trust, the Joseph Rowntree Memorial Trust and the Nuffield Foundation together spend several millions of pounds annually on social research and so form an important third force with government and the

ESRC in supporting social science research. Each trust is of course constrained by the policy of its trustees. Tax relief also imposes an obligation to fund projects which are in the public interest. None of these trusts is interested in social research, or indeed in research, to the exclusion of other forms of support.

The Leverhulme Trust is primarily concerned with education, interpreted quite widely. It supports research in many fields, awards scholarships and fellowships and facilitates academic exchanges. Its emphasis is on academic excellence rather than topicality of subject matter. Its interests lie primarily in matters which will promote the creation of wealth and efficiency in the British economy. Leverhulme is less likely than either of the other two trusts to support projects in social welfare.

Rowntree is committed to the improvement of social conditions and does so through research and experiment. Its funding is concentrated in housing, social care and employment. It makes a substantial contribution each year towards the running costs of the Policy Studies Institute. Rowntree follows through its research projects more intensively and more consistently than Leverhulme or Nuffield. A major project is usually overseen by an Advisory Committee. Rowntree also commissioned a report which examined the outcome of its projects, *To Investigate and to Publish*.[5] This report looked particularly at the influence which the research had had on practice. Whereas Leverhulme, with its emphasis on academic excellence, has no need to be concerned about the practical results of its research, Rowntree, with the interest in the product of the research, is as concerned about the aftermath of research as about the research itself.

Nuffield's funding is neither so academic as Leverhulme's nor so concerned with outcome as Rowntree. Traditionally Nuffield has been preoccupied with academic projects in science, medicine, education and social science, but recently the emphasis has shifted towards the practical. It has never been as consistent as Rowntree at monitoring research or its outcome. Nuffield does not support 'policy-relevant' research, but it is interested in research which looks critically at statutory arrangements and current practice. Such research might throw light on the unintended consequences of a current policy or suggest ways in which a practice or provision might be improved.

The attitude of trusts towards government has a bearing on the kind of research they support and the impact it has. Nothing raises the collective blood pressures of foundation officials so much as being advised – as they often are – by representatives of government of an appropriate role for them to play. They see their independence of government as a valuable asset and even co-operating with a friendly government department does not come easily. Their resources dwarfed by those of government and the research councils, they relish the part of David to government's Goliath. Research which is likely to yield results critical of current policies therefore has some appeal for foundations. To say so is to oversimplify foundations' policies and selection procedures but at least one would not expect them to be looking out for projects likely to be directly helpful to Ministerial decision-making.

Government departments, the Economic and Social Research Council and the foundations fund most of the social research in the United Kingdom. (A significant amount is, of course, unfunded work which does not require a grant.) All three are trying to exert influence according to their different styles, though the influence may be quite diffuse. To try to influence government policy-makers in a direct way is, we have argued, in general misguided, except for researchers funded by government – and in such cases the government has set, or selected, the research question. There are nevertheless ways of being influential which have little to do with the research itself. Two of the three described entail the employment of skills quite different from those of the assiduous researcher.

The limestone model[6]

This is the model to which most policy research most closely conforms. (Very often research originally intended to have a direct bearing on policy falls into this category.) It relies on indirect or cumulative interest and requires no action other than the research itself and the presentation of the findings in a readable way. If circumstances permit (and the researcher has no control over many of them) the work may, in combination with other work with a similar theme and message, seep into the public consciousness. If this happens, people's views are subtly altered and the parameters within which the public and the policy-makers conduct debates on or discussions of the issues are changed. The research may draw attention to an issue or situation which was not hitherto seriously considered. Although much social research is of this kind, whether or not it succeeds in seeping through the limestone, it is not the model to which policy research is *expected* to conform. Social research not concerned with policy may also conform to this model. If social researchers had a monopoly on social comment, this limestone research would be extremely influential. But this is not the case. Journalists and broadcasters are also vying for the public's attention on the same or similar issues. Though social research may be more authoritative than a journalist's work, it may also be less accessible and less easily read. To say this is not to denigrate or in any way detract from the usefulness of limestone research, but there is more permeating the limestone than research.

The gadfly model

It has been argued that government, left to its own devices, is impermeable to outside research. But there are ways of penetrating the carapace. Two different models are relevant here and the first we have called the gadfly model.

The gadfly needs a thorough knowledge of the government machine, its strengths and weaknesses. He or she knows administrators at several levels and possibly Ministers too. The successful gadfly is of some use to these people. As the name implies, the gadfly is regarded with some irritation but is tolerated because he is knowledgeable and able to get things done. He sees research as a necessary part of social change, but one which is subordinate to the change itself. If an important change comes about, it is seldom attributed to him, but a diligent observer of the scene would notice a consonance, over time, between the courses of action he was promoting and the changes taking place.

Those who are hostile to the gadfly attack his work on methodological grounds (and there are few social scientists whose work cannot be faulted on points of detail). His research is unlikely to be supported by government as he cherishes his freedom to criticise policy and practice. The foundations are the most appropriate source of support, being wholly independent of government themselves. Many social scientists are aspiring gadflies but the task is time-consuming and can be frustrating. The necessary qualities – enthusiasm, diligence, and understanding of bureaucratic procedures – are not always found in combination. As a result, the successful gadfly is a rarity.

The insider

The insider shares some of the attributes of the gadfly. Like the gadfly, he knows government officials and probably Ministers. He, too, has a mission to reform but his horizons may be larger. He is more likely to compromise, where necessary, and will work with administrators to make their job easier as well as his own. He may have worked in government at some stage, either full-time or as a consultant or adviser.

He may also act as facilitator or broker for other people's research. Like the gadfly, he regards the research as an instrument, rather than an end, so that the source of the research is immaterial. His own research may well be government funded, though everyone wants to sponsor the insider because he is known to be influential. Because a process of negotiation may be helpful to both parties, he may welcome a research contract, especially if this facilitates access to data.

It is, of course, possible to combine the roles of insider and gadfly, though the models in their pure form imply different personalities and methods of work. Elements of each model may exist within the same person. The researcher who conforms more closely to the pure limestone model is unlikely to play the part of the gadfly or insider from time to time. His expectations are different. On the other hand, as I mentioned earlier, there are many researchers who intended to bring about policy change and who, by default, have taken the more indirect route of the limestone model.

Social research is influential, far more so than its critics suppose. The funding of social research is, however, a costly activity on which central government alone is estimated to have spent about £35 million in 1979–80. Much of this lies unread in dusty corners of Whitehall. Millions will also have been spent on research which failed to live up to the promise implied at the time it was funded. It will have signally failed to make a direct impact on policy-making because the parties involved in its inception – researcher, funding body and government department – too readily subscribed to the myth that research, by its very existence, can influence policy. They will have paid too little attention to the means by which research influences policy and will not have considered the models of research use. And they will, alas, spend little time mourning the failure to achieve the desired end before falling enthusiastically upon the next 'policy-relevant' research project which is looking for research funds. Thus the myth sustains and perpetuates itself. If the same money were spent with more thought for the outcome of the studies, we might understand our own society and others' better than we do. And the three parties to the process of policy research would have time and enthusiasm to engage in the difficult business of ensuring that usable research is indeed used.

NOTES

1 Norman Perry, *The Organisation of Social Science Research in the United Kingdom*, Occasional Paper No. 6, SSRC Survey Unit, p. 68, Table 22.
2 C. H. Weiss, *Using Social Research in Public Policy-Making*, Teakfield, 1978.
3 The author carried out an exercise of this kind for her book, *The Aims and Outcomes of Social Policy Research*, Croom Helm, 1985. She selected projects funded by the SSRC and the Foundations between 1968 and 1970 which

seemed likely to yield prescriptive results. After reading the publications arising from the grants, she talked first to the investigators; then to officials in research divisions within the relevant government departments and, finally, to senior administrative civil servants who had been in the policy divisions to which the research was addressed at the time the publications emerged. The aim was to discover the views of these three groups of people about the individual projects and, more generally, about the research/policy relationship.

4 SSRC Newsletter 4 (1968), p. 3.
5 J. A. Heady, *To Investigate and to Publish*, Joseph Rowntree Memorial Trust, 1977.
6 The author is indebted to Robin Guthrie, Director of the Joseph Rowntree Memorial Trust, for the term. He describes the effect of this kind of research as like 'the action of water through limestone'. You may know where the water falls on the limestone, but there is no means of knowing what route it will take down the various levels or where it will emerge through unexpected fissures. 'Research and Social Policy', paper delivered at the Conference of Researchers on Violence in Marriage, Bristol, September 1979.

CHAPTER 5

Networks of influence: the social sciences in Britain since the war

CYRIL S. SMITH

It is a common observation about British political life that it works through who knows who. The very term 'Establishment' was coined in Britain to describe it, and it includes not only the connections carried over from school days ('the old boy network') and those made at Oxford and Cambridge, but also the lifetime connections of men's clubs, the City and large Corporations.[1] The Labour Party is not without its own networks, nor are the Trades Unions – Ruskin College for example. This 'people culture' is also strong in the intellectual life of the country, and ideas have always been regarded with suspicion. There has been a certain congruence therefore in the political and intellectual life of the country, and it is in this context that the political influence of the social sciences has to be understood. The state has powerful weapons at its disposal to maintain this understanding and to shape the work of intellectuals; patronage, honours, and the resources which social scientists increasingly need for their work. This paper is about one aspect of the mutual influence which government and the social sciences have had on each other since the War.

To somebody like myself who has worked in government, the literature on research and policy making is peculiarly arid. The conceptual framework seems to contain a world occupied by ghosts rather than real people engaged in mutual influence and negotiating advantage for competing interests and ideas. The approach to be adopted in this chapter might be termed a 'social organisation' approach since it aims to analyse the structure of informal social relations which develop between social scientists and those who make decisions, and how this has been affected by the more formal relations of large-scale activity in the social sciences. The history of relations between the social sciences and policy-making in Britain since the second world war falls roughly into two overlapping phases: the first which lasted until the late sixties was a period in which social scientists were actively seeking from the outside to influence government, but where the influence they had was of an ad hoc kind. The social sciences were still on a small scale, dominated by certain individuals and monopolised by certain schools of thought. The intellectual consensus they represented corresponded in large measure with the political consensus, especially with respect to the management of the economy and the need for a Welfare State. The second phase, by contrast, was marked by a considerable expansion of the social sciences, first in their teaching in universities and polytechnics, and later in the growth of research funding by government, and the employment of social scientists in the bureaucracies. This incorporation of the social sciences into the business of government on a regular basis has coincided with the breakdown of the previous intellectual and political consensus. This has created considerable conflict and tension between the new political masters and the 'establishment' of the social sciences: politics has been changing faster than the social sciences.

In 1938 there were only 212 university teachers in the social sciences in the whole country whereas today there are over 7,000.[2] There are nearly as many again in the Polytechnics. In 1938 there was almost no funding of empirical research on a regular basis. From time to time charitable foundations or government committees commissioned particular pieces of research ad hoc. Even as late as 1962/3 the total research funding from all sources was only £5m. Today despite the cutbacks of the late 1970s and early 1980s it is over £100m. Moreover, there are many thousands of social scientists employed as such in government, business and industry. It must not be forgotten either that the social sciences have become increasingly an international activity. Against this background of expansion both inside and outside higher education, it is not surprising that only a few of this number are known personally to the political and administrative elite. Indeed even within the scientific communities it is no longer the case that everybody knows everybody. It would be wrong to conclude from this however that personal contacts in the social organisation of the social sciences have ceased to be important.

If one examines the influence of the social sciences in the period after the War there are three outstanding examples of success, all reaching their peak of influence in the 1960s; the Cambridge Keynesians; the Titmuss School of Social Administration; and the Oxford School of Industrial Relations. By contrast the sociologists of whatever persuasion, and the psychologists, had only the most marginal influence on public affairs. There is an obvious reason for this since all three successful groups were working on problems central to the political agenda during this period – the management of the economy and the role of the trade unions, and the imperfect working of the Welfare State, but that is only part of the story of why they were listened to and others were not.

To start with the most influential social scientist Britain has known, Lord Keynes had a long association with politics and with City finance before he published *The General Theory of Employment* in 1936.[3] When it appeared it was not immediately accepted, and indeed as Austin Robinson has written 'it came as a shock to the outside world'. But its claim to offer an answer to the problem of unemployment generated a considerable moral commitment from Keynes's fellow economists in Cambridge and elsewhere. Again as Robinson has written 'subsequent discussion was conducted very much in the atmosphere of the revivalist meeting' and 'the following years provided a most illuminating example of the processes and psychology of conversion'.[4]

The acceptance of Keynes' ideas of demand management proceeded by several stages of which the 'revivalist' stage was one. The second stage was to convert these general ideas into tools which could be used by government, and this needed a whole apparatus of national statistics which did not then exist. A third, and parallel stage, was the elaboration, testing and dissemination of his ideas to his fellow economists. To achieve this third stage some control over intellectual resources – in the universities, the research institutes, and the learned societies – was essential. A fourth stage which assumed a willingness on the part of the Civil Servants, was to place in government those people who were sympathetic to these ideas and to deploy them in ways useful to government. Something more needs to be said about each of these stages.

The second stage was accomplished during the war with the establishment of national income accounting by Sir Richard Stone and Sir James Meade. Its completion was also assisted by the work of the National Institute of Economic and Social Research, an institute created in 1938 to help find an answer to unemployment.[5] The NIESR was to become an important staging post between Cambridge and the Treasury, and many Cambridge Keynesians spent a period working there. In the 1950s NIESR was asked by Sir Robert Hall (later Lord Roberthall) at the Treasury to set up the first programme of economic forecasting in the U.K. as he was convinced that the research resources of the Treasury were not equal to the demands being made upon in the management of the economy.

The third stage was easier to accomplish since there was virtually no intellectual opposition to Keynes and his circle in Cambridge or elsewhere in the UK (Hayek was one important exception at the LSE). One significant step forward in establishing macro-economics firmly as a subject was the establishment of the Department of Applied Economics at Cambridge in 1945 by Sir Richard Stone. By 1954 nearly 30% of chairs in economics in British universities were filled by economists who had studied in Cambridge, and Oxford which shared similar views of the subject supplied another 20%.[6] NIESR maintained its monopoly of macro-economic modelling until the 1960s and continued to have a central role until quite recently. Its quarterly review was particularly influential in monitoring government management.

The groundwork carried out in the early stages contributed to success of the fourth stage which was completed in the mid 1960s.[7] Although the Cambridge Keynesians did not penetrate Whitehall in any number before the Labour Government came to power in 1964 a commitment to demand management had already been made by the previous Conservative government in 1961, for example in setting up the National Economic Development Council. However, it was the Treasury and the Civil Service which saw the need for economists, not the politicians. Very few of the Cambridge Keynesians had a specific party affiliation (Keynes had been a Liberal).

The Cambridge Keynesians of the period from 1945 to 1965 not only shared common ideas, they were also bound together in a social network. This network radiated out from the Cambridge colleges into the City, the Treasury, the NIESR and other universities. Its members not only shared the Cambridge culture but they were connected by the life of other institutions which they helped to manage. Many of them received public honours and these include peerages to Kaldor and Balogh; knighthoods to Cairncross, Berrill, Hopkin, and Stone. They continued their influence well into the 1970s but as we shall see later, in a very different social framework and political climate.

Richard Titmuss, the second example of success for social sciences, lacked the social pedigree of Keynes, and his department at the LSE lacked the cachet of the Faculty of Economics in Cambridge.[8] Titmuss had never studied at a university and most of his working life before taking up the chair of social administration at the LSE in 1950 had been spent working in insurance. His reputation at that stage rested on a book published in the same year – his official history of social policy in wartime. His professional background had been in statistics and although he associated himself for a time with sociology in the late 1950s, he eventually created his own subject, that of social administration. In the space of about fifteen years his department became the source of much of the Labour party's thinking about pensions, the health service, and housing. Many of his students and staff went off to head new departments in other universities.

Titmuss gave leadership to his department in two ways: intellectual and moral. Intellectually his greatest contribution was made by his essay 'The Social Division of Welfare' published in 1956. This widened thinking about social security from the narrow perspective of the Welfare State to include the benefits to be derived from the fiscal system and from occupational pensions. This approach, which still maintains a certain vitality, opened up a whole new range of problems to be studied, and in particular the way in which the middle classes benefitted from public expenditure on welfare. Among the many academics who have taken this idea forward are Brian Abel-Smith, Peter Townsend and David Donnison. Not surprisingly, the message had great significance for those who wished to defend the Welfare State, not least the Labour Party which claimed its parentage.

Titmuss also offered a moral leadership which was perhaps as important as his ideas in his lifetime, and in particular during those long years the Labour Party was out of power (1951–64). His passionate commitment to equity and the simplicity of his own life style attracted a great many talented young people to work with him. However, it also created problems for him in coming to terms with the counter-culture of students in the 1960s, and radical students were particularly critical of his role as Deputy Chairman of the Supplementary Benefits Commission.

The real influence of the Titmuss circle came to be seen in the Labour governments of the 1960s and 1970s but it is difficult to isolate one particular change for which they were responsible. They had certainly put the issue of poverty back on the map, and in particular family poverty, but the device of clawback (recovering the benefit through adjustment of taxation) invented to reduce the costs of increasing family allowances universally, came from elsewhere; from the fertile mind of Lord Kaldor. The Bill for the National Superannuation scheme, largely drafted by Titmuss and his colleagues, failed for lack of parliamentary time when the Labour Government left office in 1970.[9] Nonetheless three Ministers were advised by members of this circle: Crossman at the Ministry of Housing and Local Government, and later the DHSS; Crosland at the Department of the Environment; and Barbara Castle also at the DHSS. Titmuss was rewarded by a CBE in 1966. Not all of Titmuss' followers were as patient as he in accepting the lack of action on poverty. Townsend and a number of other academics founded the Child Poverty Action Group in 1965 which became a persistent source of criticism of official policy.[10]

By contrast with the Cambridge Keynesians the 'Social Administra-

tionists' exerted their influence through a political party and through
ministers. They never achieved the same penetration of the bureaucracy
although a number acted as ministerial advisers. Their intellectual
backgrounds were diverse; some coming from economics, some from
sociology, and some from social work, but the attempt to weld these
together has not achieved any more coherence than the original Titmuss-
ian paradigm. The Social Administration Association with its *Journal of
Social Policy* has provided the forum for those who research and teach in
these fields. As with the Keynesians, influence of Social Administration
had waned by the second half of the 1970s with the ending of the post-war
consensus.

   The third success story is that of the Oxford School of Industrial
Relations. This school which reached its high point of influence with the
Royal Commission on Industrial Relations (the Donovan Commission)
from 1965 to 1968, had no single dominating figure but perhaps the best
known is Hugh Clegg. The school had its roots back in a group based in
Nuffield College in the 1950s. One slightly sour critic wrote of it in the
following way. 'The "Oxford Line" might be described as combining an
industrious extension of established avenues of enquiry (and particularly
a meticulous pursuit of institutional detail), a preference for the short-
term rule of thumb over the broader generalisation, a rather low
awareness of those disciplines – in ascending order, of sociology,
statistics and economics – which may illuminate the field with normative
observations, and a variety of propagandist mini-reformism which consists partly in leading people boldly in the direction they appear to be
going anyway. This approach was clearly influential in the Commission:
it dominated the Research Papers. In large measure, both their many
virtues and their deficiencies thus derive from a specific academic point
of view.'[11] Hugh Clegg was a member of the Commission and Bill
MacCarthy, another member of the 'Nuffield Group', was its Research
Director.

   The group was given some public profile in 1968 by an article in *New
Society*. This sought to identify membership of the group and to assess its
influence over thinking in the Industrial Relations field. 'A group of a
half-dozen or so share among them rather more than half the achievements and much more than half the influence of their profession.'[12] To
some degree its influence was a result of command over intellectual
resources. As Clegg put it 'If five years ago there were 40 Industrial
Relations specialists in the whole country, ten at least would have been at
Oxford.' Significantly there was no Department at Oxford although the
group did have a base at Nuffield College. Elsewhere there had been
departments for some considerable time (at Cardiff and Leeds for

example) but none offered serious intellectual competition to Oxford. The British Universities Industrial Relations Association was dominated by the Oxford group although the journal established in 1968 was published elsewhere (from the LSE).

The great advantage of the Oxford Group in exercising influence on public affairs was that they represented a repository of useable knowledge. The group had considerable expertise in the fields of trade union government, procedures, agreements, and wages. This could be tapped readily by the Government bodies and commissions set up by the Labour Government. More than that they had been communicating their ideas to trade unionists through Ruskin College and the Extra Mural Delegacy of the University throughout the 1950s. Some of their brighter students had gone on to read degrees in the University. They also had good contacts with the leaders of some of the large unions. What was noticeable given their common sympathy with the Labour movement and the Labour Party was that, with one exception, their influence was not directly on the political leadership. It is worth remembering that they were not seen as partisan and their ideas were part of the political consensus.

When one considers other established social science disciplines in this first period, it is surprising that mainstream sociology and psychology achieved so little impact. The London School of Economics was in a strategic position in the late 1940s to influence the whole course of development of sociology in Britain and indeed many of its students went off to staff the new departments elsewhere, particularly to Liverpool and Leicester, but with little help from their professors.[13] They did not take an LSE view of the subject with them, for the senior staff of the department were deeply divided, with Morris Ginsberg, David Glass and Edward Shils all offering different views of the subject. Glass, of the three, was the one with the clearest policy interests – family planning and population policy – but these interests inevitably took him in the direction of the Third World, rather than to domestic policies. However, his interest in social mobility in Britain stimulated his colleagues and students to study educational opportunity, and the most well known of these, A. H. Halsey, advised Crosland on educational policy in the 1960s. However, social policy research at the LSE was for the most part left to the Department of Social Science and Administration (or the Department of Applied Virtue as it was known contemptuously by the sociologists).

Psychology in the UK in the 1940s presented an altogether different picture.[14] Here one department, that in Cambridge, was dominant, and that department was dominated by one man, Sir Frederick Bartlett, with a very personal view of the subject. The struggle for recognition by psychology in Cambridge had been won by Bartlett, Rivers and Myers in the 1920s but, discouraged by the lack of progress, Myers went off in 1938 to found the National Institute of Industrial Psychology. Bartlett was left the pre-eminent figure locally and nationally although Sir Cyril Burt was pursuing his own line in psychology at University College, London. Bartlett's view of the subject showed a great breadth of interest and a concern for real life problems. It showed a distaste for statistics, and although it became known as Experimental Psychology he had no interest in experimentation on animals. It achieved some importance during the War in helping the Royal Air Force, and in 1944 his research programme was given the status of a Medical Research Council unit. Bartlett was knighted in 1948. The importance of his view of psychology can be seen from the fact that in 1957 (five years after Bartlett retired) 10 of the 16 chairs in the subject were occupied by his students. However, it has since been overwhelmed by the trends towards professionalisation and experimentation. Even the NIIP which promised much after the war in its researches on productivity, collapsed in the early seventies and its place has not yet been filled.

To summarise, the first phase of social science and policy-making was characterised by small-scale activity and by the domination of a few individuals, often with idiosyncratic views of their subjects, as seen from an international perspective. Where social science was most influential it both shaped and responded to a national political agenda. The second phase which began in the early seventies took on a very different complexion. The scale of activity was much greater and the work was organised differently. Moreover the political consensus was beginning to break down.

The new situation was most clearly seen in economics.[15] By 1970 there were now several thousand economists most of whom had no connection with Cambridge even though many still shared Cambridge ideas about demand management. Their working life, whether in higher education or in business, required a more specialised expertise. Even in the field of macro-economics it required a new level of sophistication in mathematics and statistics. A large number found themselves in Whitehall but addressing a different kind of economic problem, such as transport investment decisions. There was a new consciousness of belonging to a profession which expressed itself in the growth of professional associations such as the Society of Business Economists. Moreover, small groups of political activists appeared on the right and left fringes of the subject, analysing and contributing to the break-up of the Keynesian consensus.

Throughout the late 1960s and the early 1970s as the number of economists grew, more of them were incorporated into the state bureaucracy – some of them as career civil servants, and others as advisers. Still others were recruited to run public bodies such as the NEDC and the SSRC. The bureaucracies absorbed these experts in a systematic and orderly way. They were recruited into a specialist class on the basis of their professional qualifications and given conditions of service devised for civil servants and therefore unlike their professional colleagues in the universities. They became members of a hierarchy which in most departments ended below the top of the department (see Table 9.3, p. 149). They usually worked to generalists of a higher rank than themselves and only the most senior worked directly to Ministers. They were required more and more to specialise in an area of policy.

Such incorporation into the public bureaucracy has inevitably defined the scope of the role which economists are expected to perform. It constrains their choice of problems for study, the way they tackle them, and what they do with the results. Problems now become of a middle order of importance and of medium term departmental interest. The necessary skills in manipulating information were very much those of a statistician. So far the tradition of free publication of Government Economic Service reports which had been established in the 1960s seems to have been maintained.

As the scale of economic research has grown it has become more and more dependent upon state funding and the chosen channel for such funding has been the research council. In this way the academic economists could help ration resources and get the best work done. By 1982 the number of economic models supported by the SSRC had grown so numerous (accounting for nearly half of all expenditure on all types of economics research) that it was felt necessary to rationalise expenditure. It was also an opportunity for the Treasury and the SSRC to ensure that the range of models supported more accurately represented the new political reality. Some like the DAE at Cambridge had their grants reduced and some like the monetarists at Liverpool University had them increased. In the process the grant to NIESR was substantially cut.

The process of incorporating economists into the public bureaucracies was one important factor in determining the role of economists, another was more internal to the discipline, that of professionalisation and specialisation. The characteristic form of association among academic economists has been the Royal Economic Society but unlike other learned societies it had a large number of members who were not economists, and it did not hold conferences. Its basic function was to publish *The Economic Journal*.[16] Although there have been moves to establish associations for professionals, so far there is no single body. Different sectors have their own groupings: the Association for University Teachers of Economics, the APTE for those in polytechnics, the Society for Business Economists, and so on. In so far as economists have needed to organise to protect their interests they have looked to the relevant trade unions.

The loosening of the hold of the Cambridge Keynesians has happened not only because of the expansion of the subject and the new ways in which it is organised. It is also because of the break up of the old consensus. The crisis in Keynesian economics was debated in the economic journals at the end of the sixties, long before the political consensus on management of the economy had broken down. In terms of the shift in political opinion the source of the change can be confidently located with the influence of one institution – the Institute of Economic Affairs (IEA). Founded in 1957, IEA began publishing papers which explored the market approach to issues of the day. By 1981 nearly 90 papers had been published on subjects ranging from pensions to trade unions. The general approach was to challenge state intervention in economic and social policy. Again they were responsible for introducing the work of the Chicago monetarist Milton Friedman to politicians. In the volume published in 1981 to celebrate the 25th anniversary of its founding, it was possible for a past head of the Civil Service to speak of the changes they had wrought in the thinking of the Civil Service. It 'has never been great but . . . it is far more significant than it was'.[17]

Other organisations with more explicit political objectives have followed in the footsteps of the IEA, among them the Centre for Policy Studies and the Adam Smith Institute, on the right, and at the same time a critique has developed from the left. The Conference of Socialist Economists, which publishes *Capital and Class*, has been particularly influential in criticising the mistakes of the Labour Governments of the 1960s, and especially the incomes policies which had become a necessary part of the practice of demand management.

No other social science achieved quite the same success as economics in the post war period but in the second phase the influence of sociology became relatively more important. However, at the same time, the influence of social administration waned and the influence of psychology remained negligible. In the field of social policy, sociology achieved its greatest impact with medical sociology, but its influence was also felt in other areas such as housing, education, and penal policy alongside other disciplines.[18]

All branches of applied knowledge have been subject to the processes of specialisation and professionalisation but in psychology they were much more pronounced. The increasing use of psychologists in the health service, in education, in vocational guidance, and in the prisons have increased the pressures within the learned society, the British Psychological Society, to become a professional body concerned with accreditation of competence to perform a relatively narrow technical role, and these in turn have encouraged university psychology departments to engage in professional training. At the same time those concerned with the scientific development of the discipline went off into the opposite direction, that of experimentation in the laboratory, but both developments took the subject away from the issues relevant to policy making. Sociology by comparison resisted strongly the notion of professionalisation.[19]

In examining the areas of social policy where the influence of the social sciences was felt in the second stage it is useful to return to Social Administration and its declining influence. Titmuss died in 1973 and his personal charisma was greatly missed. His followers went off in two directions. Some became incorporated into the system and were provided with substantial resources by the DHSS for the study of poverty and social welfare. The others became increasingly alienated from the Labour Party and turned their attention to the study of inequality. Some much further to the left were attracted to new forms of Marxism. Interestingly, when one considers other areas of policy, there has been little sign of a right wing critique. The IEA has given birth to the Social Affairs Unit but as yet it has been no match for those who write in support of the Welfare State. The political commitment of the present government to carry out a radical review of social security policy has so far had to rely upon the evidence and the cool assessment provided by the civil servants. No particular intellectual circle has captured the government's thinking in the way that Titmuss and his colleagues did.

Despite the early interest shown by Titmuss and Abel-Smith in the National Health Service, the main developments in the study of health in the second phase came from elsewhere and particularly out of sociology and economics. Medical sociology, perhaps the largest specialism in sociological research, was mainly financed by government departments and research councils (over 70% according to Field *et al.*),[20] and the recipients of this funding had few connections with LSE and Social Administration. In the register of research published in 1982 it is clear that the 274 projects listed are spread thinly over a wide range of health needs and problems, but the study of the professions, and particularly of GPs and nurses, are one area of concentration. The implications of such research are perhaps more visible in the circulars issued by the DHSS than in the statements of politicians or political parties. Although a number of competing paradigms have been developed in medical sociology, no one is dominant.

Although educational research was one of the largest sectors of social science research in the 1960s no particular network controlled the funding and influenced policy.[21] There were individuals who acted as advisers to the Department and to Ministers and they knew each other, but they were not a network which shared a single view of educational policy, except perhaps on the issue of Comprehensive Schools. Educational research has continued at a high level of activity up to the present day but much of it is now concerned with the curriculum and with educational performance. Departmental funding is concentrated at a number of centres, such as the National Foundation for Educational Research which have no particular political profile, and there is strikingly little in the way of policy research. The challenge to the conventional wisdom of education has tended to come from outside the educational establishment, and from outside of higher education. The University of Buckingham, as an idea which originated from the IEA, has successfully challenged the monopoly of state funded universities, but as yet the market inspired views of education, and the idea of vouchers, have made little headway. Progress in thinking about training has come from the Manpower Services Commission rather than the Department of Education and Science.

Until the present government took office, housing research was well supported by the Department of the Environment.[22] That department had its own research division and it supported an extensive programme of research at a number of centres. This has greatly changed. The Centre for Environmental Studies was closed in 1979, and support for other centres has been much curtailed. Research contracts now have to be individually approved by Ministers, and a proportion have to be issued to commercial agencies. The Economic and Social Research Council has to some degree filled the gap with its own centre for housing research at Glasgow University (Donnison, the original director of CES, is one of the directors).

The remaining area of social policy where the social sciences, and particularly sociology, has had influence is that of penal policy. Support for criminological research began early in the UK[23] and was in particular influenced by refugees from Germany. The Home Office Research Unit, set up in 1957, marked a new phase. Since then the Home Office has maintained a dominant position in funding and has chosen to continue to support the Unit and to concentrate support at a few other centres (Cambridge, Oxford, Sheffield and Edinburgh). The ESRC has funded relatively little research on crime and criminal justice until quite recently.

The research community sponsored by the Home Office stands somewhat apart from the more radical ideas held by other parts of the academic community, where the deviance school of the 1960s (the National Deviancy Symposium) has been giving ground to the Marxists. Senior civil servants at the Home Office maintain close contacts with a small number of key academics, and also the established reform groups. This incorporation of possible sources of criticism has undoubtedly softened the attacks on penal policy. By contrast with the civil servants, neither the Labour Party nor the Conservative Party have involved social scientists in shaping their policy documents on crime, at least not since the 1960s.

In the five areas of social policy which have been examined there has been a significant social science presence since the late 1960s but for the most part it has been successfully incorporated on terms acceptable to the civil servants. However, in many of these areas the political status quo is no longer stable. The control of public expenditure has been central to this Government's economic strategy and the pressure for a hard line on Law and Order issues has grown. It is hardly surprising in this situation that the Government is seeking to reduce the influence of the social sciences and trying to build up its own network of sympathetic intellectuals. This conflict came to a head with the attempt to abolish the SSRC in 1982 and the accusation of bias at the SSRC's Industrial Relations Research Unit, discussed in Chapter 19.

This brings us back to consider the Oxford School of Industrial Relations in the second phase. Here too one can see the process of incorporation at work, but also the break up of the old corporatist views on industrial relations. Members of this network were drawn increasingly into the business of arbitrating and conciliating in industrial disputes, and serving on public bodies and committees. The SSRC established an industrial relations research unit at Warwick University in 1970 and its first director was Clegg. His place was taken by George Bain, another member of the group. These two set out a strategy for industrial relations research for Britain in a key article in 1974.[24]

The influence of the Oxford School ran counter to the Government's intentions in 1979 to curb the power of the trade unions and it became a target for criticism. Lord Beloff, previously Professor of Government at Oxford, led this criticism. He wrote to Lord Rothschild when he was conducting his enquiry into the possible abolition of the SSRC that there has been 'so much dissatisfaction with the strong pro-TUC bias of the SSRC Industrial Relations Research Unit at Warwick University that a new Institute of Labour Affairs is being founded by a group of businessmen and academics under the leadership of Sir Leonard Neal'.

Rothschild subsequently recommended in his Report that 'the Chairman of the SSRC should set up an impartial examination, in depth, of this accusation, and ventilate the results'. The Chairman of the SSRC, Michael Posner, invited Sir Kenneth Berrill and two leading academics to carry out this task, and the committee reported in 1983 that 'they found the accusation of bias . . . has not been substantiated'.[25]

The 'Nuffield Group', insofar as it still exists as a network, no longer has an identifiable intellectual standpoint.[26] Allan Flanders died, Alan Fox who wrote for the Donovan Commission soon abandoned his commitment, and MacCarthy entered the House of Lords. New approaches, some Marxist and some sociological, have provided the focus for the debate among academics on industrial relations. Meanwhile the Government has pursued its course in reforming industrial relations using the law as an instrument, and limiting the power of the trade unions, all in the face of the weight of opinion of the academic community. Where the Group still maintains its influence is with senior personnel managers, such as those who belong to the Devonshire House Group.

In the forty years since the Second World War the social sciences in the UK finally came of age. They could no longer be ignored. In the 1960s they reached the peak of their influence in the affairs of the nation, particularly in the management of the economy, the handling of the trade unions, and in policy on social security. It was a happy conjunction of intellectual orthodoxy and political consensus. It was underpinned by a network of supporting relationships and institutions, in which Oxford, Cambridge and the LSE played a leading role. Since the 1970s it has been downhill most of the way. Some of the members of the networks have died and they have not been replaced by younger people. The orthodoxy has been replaced by heterodoxy, and the consensus by conflict.

The Conservative governments since 1979, far from being anti-intellectual as they are often described, are in the business of dismantling the existing intellectual establishment and encouraging new orthodoxies. Given the institutional independence of the universities, and their slowness to change (deaths and desertions are few in number), it will take them some time to get their way. However, given their control of research resources and their patronage they could choose a different route. They might decide to shift the balance of research effort away from the universities either into independent research institutes, or more likely, into commercial or political research organisations. Interestingly, the Civil Service remains committed to the social sciences, and if not to the old orthodoxies, at least to the institutions and people who nourished them. Since no modern government can now live permanently without the social sciences, and the prospects for a new national consensus look slim, we are likely to see future governments encouraging their own brands of social science.

REFERENCES

1 Henry Fairlie popularised the term in *The Spectator* in 1959. See also T. Heald, *Networks*, London, Hodder & Stoughton, 1983 for a recent journalistic account of networks in British society.

2 Cyril S. Smith, 'The research function in the social sciences', in *The Future of Research*, ed. G. Oldham, Guildford, Surrey, Society for Reseach Into Higher Education, 1982, pp. 150–70.

3 See R. Skidelsky, *John Maynard Keynes: a biography*, London, Macmillan, 1983, vol. 1 and R. Skidelsky (ed.), *The End of the Keynesian Era*, London, Macmillan, 1977, esp. Ch. 2 by John Vaizey.

4 E. A. G. Robinson, 'Memoir on Lord Keynes', *Economic Journal* Vol. LVII, March 1947, pp. 1–68.

5 Sir R. Hall (now Lord Roberthall) in the 50th issue of the NIESR's *Economic Review* November 1969.

6 P. Collison, 'The qualifications of academics', *Universities Quarterly*, Vol. 10, No. 3, May 1956.

7 A. W. Coats, *Economists in Government: an international comparative study*, Durham, North Carolina, Duke University Press, 1981. Professor Coats has written many interesting papers on the history and social organisation of British economics.

8 D. Reisman, *Richard Titmuss: Welfare and Society*, London, Heinemann, 1977. The introduction has some useful biographical details. See also M. Gowing, 'Richard Morris Titmuss', *Proceedings of the British Academy*, vol. LXI (1975), p. 29.

9 K. Banting, *Poverty, Politics and Policy: Britain in the 1960s*, London, Macmillan, 1979.

10 P. Seyd, 'The Child Poverty Action Group', *Political Quarterly*, vol. 47, 1976 pp. 189.

11 H. A. Turner, 'The Royal Commission's Research Papers', in the special issue of the *British Journal of Industrial Relations*, vol. VI, 1968, p. 347, reviewing the report of the Royal Commission on Trades Unions and Employers' Associations chaired by Lord Justice Donovan.

12 J. Bugler, 'The New Oxford Group', *New Society*, 15 Feb. 1968.

13 A. H. Halsey, 'Provincials and Professionals: the British Post-War Sociologists', in *Essays On the History of British Sociological Research*, ed. M. Bulmer (Cambridge, Cambridge University Press, 1985), pp. 151–64.

14 C. Crampton, *The Life, Work and Influence of James Ward, W. H. Rivers, C. S. Myers and Sir Frederick Bartlett* (Ph.D. Thesis University of Edinburgh 1978). See also D. Broadbent, 'Bartlett. An appreciation', *Bulletin Br. Psychol. Soc.*, vol. 23, 1970, and E. Belbin, 'The Bartlett Era', *Br. Journ. Psychol.* vol. 70, 1979, p. 187.

15 See A. W. Coats, 'The Royal Economic Society and professionalisation', *Br Journal Sociology*, vol. 21, 1970, and *Economists in Government, op. cit.*
16 *ibid.*
17 A. Seldon, ed. *The Emerging Consensus . . .? essays on the interplay between ideas, interests and circumstances in the first 25 years of the IEA*, London, IEA, 1981.
18 Throughout this section of the paper it is useful to refer to the *Annual Review of Statistics of Research and Development* (HMSO) for information on government spending on the social sciences. See also S. Blume, *The Commissioning of Social Research by Central Government*, London, Social Science Research Council, 1982.
19 J. A. Barnes, 'Professionalism in British Sociology', in P. Abrams, R. Deem, J. Finch & P. Rock (eds)., *Practice & Progress: British Sociology 1950–1980*, London, Allen & Unwin 1981, pp. 13–24.
20 D. Field, B. A. Clarke and N. Goldie, *Medical Sociology in Britain: a register of research and teaching*, British Sociological Association Medical Sociology Group, 1982, p. 149.
21 J. Nisbet and P. Broadfoot, *The Impact of Research on Policy and Practice in Education*, London, SSRC, 1980. L. Cohen *et al.*, *Educational Research and Development in Britain 1970–80*, Windsor, NFER/Nelson, 1982.
22 A. Tinker and M. Ryan, 'The dissemination of research findings with particular reference to housing', *Journal of Social Policy*, vol. 8, Part 1, Jan. 1979, pp. 61–82.
23 I. J. Croft, 'Criminological research in Great Britain', in *Crime and Justice – Annual Review of Research*, vol. 5, ed. M. Tonry and N. Morris, Chicago, University of Chicago Press 1983, pp. 265–80.
24 G. Bain and H. Clegg, 'A strategy for industrial relations research in Great Britain', *British Journal of Industrial Relations*, vol. xii, No. 1, 1974, pp. 91–113.
25 Sir K. Berrill, Sir E. H. Phelps Brown and D. G. T. Williams, *Report of an investigation into certain matters arising from the Rothschild Report on the SSRC*, London, SSRC, 1983.
26 D. Winchester, 'Industrial Relations Research in Britain', *British Journal of Industrial Relations*, vol. xxi, March 1983, p. 100–14.

CHAPTER 6

Social science in Whitehall: two analytical perspectives

STUART S. BLUME

Introduction

A general tendency in contributions to the study of 'social science and government' is to orient discussion towards elucidation of the 'proper' function of the social sciences. Such analyses, which typically proceed from theoretical assumptions as to the nature of policy-making (eg Lindblom and Cohen 1979), or as to the nature of the social sciences (eg Dahlstrom, 1976, 1978), have themselves given rise to the distinction between 'engineering' and 'enlightenment' models, and a typical preference for one or the other (eg Weiss, 1980). A number of authors have gone further, in arguing for some new model (eg Bulmer, 1981) or for some new type of social science (MacRae, 1976). However, this literature shows little concern either with historic change in the implicit model which may have dominated government arrangements or concerns, or with the possibility that variations in culture, policy system or social science traditions may give rise to significant variations between nations. The objective underlying this paper is essentially to open up discussion of these two dimensions of complexity. In the following section the development of British social science arrangements and concerns in Whitehall is discussed, and certain notions by means of which these developments might be understood are proposed. Thereafter, some limited international comparisons of the relations between government and the social sciences are made (largely between Britain and the Netherlands, though with reference also to the situation in a number of other European countries). Such comparisons permit us further to develop our theoretical understanding.

The evolution of social science in Whitehall

With a single exception, Whitehall involvement with (non-economic) social science research is essentially a post-war phenomenon.[1] The important exception is the Government Social Survey (now the Social Survey Division of the Office of Population Censuses and Surveys). The Social Survey had been founded during the war as a means of developing quantitative information on public opinion and morale: funded by the Ministry of Information, but operating under the joint aegis of the LSE and the NIESR (Whitehead, 1985). By 1944, having been reorganised and brought into its parent Ministry, it had carried out more than a hundred surveys in areas of concern to the wartime government. Beyond this, the structure of government administration in Britain showed little evidence of concern with social research, or the social sciences, until the beginning of the 1960s. The Home Office Research Unit, which was to grow to one of the largest social research organisations in Whitehall, was founded to carry out criminological studies in 1958. The Heyworth Committee, writing in 1965, referred to small numbers of economists, psychologists and other social scientists employed in a number of departments, but mostly with principal functions outside research. In addition there was limited funding for academic social science from the Human Sciences Committee of the Department of Scientific and Industrial Research (DSIR), the Medical Research Council, and the Colonial Office (succeeded in 1962 by the Department of Technical Cooperation) (Heyworth, 1965). 'Much of the effort in Government departments', the Heyworth Committee suggests, '*is directed to fact-finding and is not research*' (italics added).

The Clapham Committee, reporting in 1946 (Clapham, 1946), had been asked to consider 'whether additional provision was necessary for research into social and economic questions'. The essential focus of the work, and the report, of this committee was not arrangements in Whitehall, but in the universities. The Committee considered that the chief need at that time was to develop basic competence in social science within the universities: to strengthen university staffs in this area, and to provide for 'routine research'. The Committee made three recommendations, of which two concerned funding of university social science through the Universities Grants Committee. The third recommendation was that a Standing Interdepartmental Committee on Economic and Social Research should be set up to survey and advise upon research work in government departments.

The Interdepartmental Committee was established with, as terms of reference, to

survey and advise upon research work in Government departments and
in particular (a) to bring to the notice of departments the potential value
for research purposes of the material which they collect and to suggest
new methods and areas of collection; (b) to advise on how there could
be made available to research workers information, gathered for their
own purposes by departments, which has potential value as material for
research (quoted in Heyworth, 1965, p. 7).

The emphasis of the Committee, then, enshrined in their terms of
reference, was not the (potential) use of social science in relation to the
departments' policy-making, but the availability to academic researchers
of governmental data. Reporting in 1965, the Heyworth Committee
drew attention to Reports of this Interdepartmental Committee
published in 1948, 1950 and 1956, but went on to point out that by the
time their own inquiries began, the Committee was moribund. Most
government departments had never heard of it, and it had not met since
1960.

   In 1962 the Prime Minister appointed a Committee under the Chairmanship of Sir Burke Trend to consider national arrangements for the
organisation and funding of non-military science research. The Committee reported in October 1963 (Trend, 1963). Reaffirming the principle
established by Lord Haldane in 1918, the Trend Report was adamant
that the 'control of research should be separated from the executive
function of Government': that the Research Councils (through which
civil science should largely be funded) would have guaranteed autonomy. The Trend Report was to reshape the structure of British science,
and to establish the principles upon which science policy would rest for a
decade to come. But though its terms of reference referred to 'civil
scientific research in the various fields concerned', the Trend Committee
had no word to say about the social sciences. In its implicit exclusion of
the social sciences from the scope of science policy Trend established a
principle of post-war science policy which was to prove more durable
than the principle of autonomy which they were at so great pains to
defend.

   However, at about the time the Trend Committee reported, the
Secretary of State for Education and Science established a quite separate
committee, under the Chairmanship of Lord Heyworth:

> To review the research at present being done in the field of social studies
> in Government departments, universities and other institutions and to
> advise whether changes are needed in the arrangements for supporting
> and coordinating this research. (Heyworth, 1965)

Heyworth took a very different view of his task than Clapham had
done. Here central attention is paid to the relations between social
science and policy-making.

> Anyone engaged in administration in central or local government ... is
> engaged in fields which social scientists study. Whether he knows it or
> not, he is using methods and techniques ... that a social scientist would
> recognise. Those he uses may well be years out of date. Of course much
> administration is concerned with day-to-day business, but unless an
> attempt is made to identify long-term problems or penetrate behind the
> curtain of everyday decisions, the decisions taken will be based on
> wrong or inadequate data. That is why research in the social sciences is
> important to the administrator. (Heyworth, 1965, p 5)

If the social sciences were to make their proper contribution to the work
of government departments, Heyworth argued, there were two crucial
needs. First, it was necessary for 'administrators and managers to be
familiar with the scope and value of the social sciences, not only as direct
aids to administration, but as disciplines which are able to limit the
uncertainties within which decisions have to be taken ...'. However,
'Problems in government ... do not usually present themselves to
administrators in a fashion which at once shows how they could be
clarified by research in the social sciences.' Also necessary, therefore, is
that social scientists work 'at points where problems first emerge' so that
they may help 'identify and deal with them'.

Beyond this, the Heyworth Committee, pursuing the same line as had
Trend, argued for the establishment of a Social Science Research
Council, 'to provide support for research, to keep under review the state
of research, to advise the Government on the needs of social science
research, to keep under review the supply of trained research workers
...' This recommendation was accepted by the government, and the new
SSRC received its Royal Charter in 1965. At the same time, it was
considered that interdepartmental machinery within government was
needed, to represent and coordinate Whitehall interests *vis-à-vis* the new
body. Under Treasury auspices a new interdepartmental Committee on
Social Science Research (CSSR) was established, to parallel the (already
functioning) Committee on Economic Research (CER).

These developments, and those which followed, largely reflect and
embody the then dominant beliefs in notions of coordination, planning
and rationalisation of policy. In 1968 the Fulton Committee on the Civil
Service reported, with recommendations many of which embodied a
similar 'rationalist' critique of policy-making procedures (Fulton, 1968).
Drawing attention to the need for long-term planning ('if the problems
of modern government are to be foreseen, and the groundwork for
decisions prepared in good time'), the Fulton Committee proposed the
establishment of departmental planning units, to which policy analysts
trained in the social sciences would make a major contribution. Whilst
this recommendation was rejected, some at least of the philosophy

behind the Committee's work rubbed off. A new Civil Service College was established in the summer of 1970, to provide training for civil servants, much of which was to be based in the social sciences. The College was to carry out research as well (and had been seen by Fulton as an institution wherein research required by the departmental planning units might frequently be carried out). In his first report to the College's Advisory Council, the Principal provided many arguments for the importance of research in their work, and argued that this research would typically consist of 'projects with a longer time span than would ordinarily be undertaken in a department' (Grebenik, 1972).

The view that a more co-ordinated approach at least to the provision of the social services was required, which led to the creation of Crossman's Office of the Secretary of State for Social Services, had important consequences for social sciences in Whitehall. Responsibility for the non-economic social research committee (the CSSR) passed from the Treasury to the new Office, located in the Cabinet Office, and a Social Research Coordinating Unit (SRCU), incorporating some social scientific expertise and research experience, was established as its secretariat at the end of 1969.

With the change of government the following year came somewhat different, but not wholly incompatible, co-ordination and rationalisation initiatives. In 1970 the Heath government established the Central Policy Review Staff, and introduced the output-oriented approach to policy-planning, based on the American PPBS, which became known as Programme Analysis and Review (PAR). These developments have been well discussed elsewhere (Heclo and Wildavsky, 1974; Plowden, 1981). The early seventies were the heyday of this belief in the possibilities of rational policy-making, based on consideration of long-term goals, policy outcomes, and so on, with PAR and the CPRS under Lord Rothschild of considerable importance. The implications for utilisation of the social sciences, however, were not what they might have been. In particular, the fortunes of the attempt at systematic, coordinated deployment of social science in policy (planning), represented by the interdepartmental committee and its secretariat (SRCU), were dominated by other considerations. One of these was its attachment, under the arrangements of the previous government, to the Crossman Coordinating Office. A second, which was to be of continuing importance, was the implementation of the proposals made by Rothschild in 1971 for a new approach to science policy (embodied in a White Paper of 1972). By 1972 the coordinating machinery had ceased to function. Government provision and arrangements for the social sciences were coming to be dominated less by those beliefs about the connection between research and policy which had informed the Heyworth and Fulton Reports than by the new arrangements for research and development (R&D) introduced by Cmnd 5046 (the White Paper *Framework for Government R&D* in which Lord Rothschild's proposals were taken over). Like Trend, Rothschild had not considered the application – or the applicability – of his proposals to government commissioning of social science research. Broadly speaking, the immediate consequences of the new arrangements were as follows. (Further more detailed discussion is to be found in Blume 1982).

Departments with large research budgets, and significantly involved in research *outside* the social sciences (that is, not only the 'industrial' departments, but also the Department of the Environment and the Department of Health and Social Security) rapidly established the formal committee structures, corresponding to the range of their responsibilities, which the White Paper required. In these committees (the DoE's Research Requirements Committees, the DHSS' Research Liaison Groups), representatives of the appropriate policy division, of research management, and of research, were together to formulate needs pertaining to the policy area in question. Other Departments, with more limited research expenditures (Education, Employment, the Home Office, the Civil Service Department included), did not initially establish such machinery, and most of these did not appoint a Chief Scientist (as proposed in the White Paper). Here, research needs in the early years tended to be identified through rather more ad hoc procedures (including, in the case of Employment, an annual 'trawl' of policy divisions), deriving from previous practices. These Departments have tended rather gradually to move to more formalised arrangements. Arrangements for external advice on research programmes also differed. Thus, DHSS included external scientific advisors (some social scientists) as members of RLGs; DoE initially made use of external advisory committees separate from the RRC structure; many departments had recourse to external advice only on an ad hoc basis. The new arrangements represented an increasing 'sectorisation' of government research. The principle, which came to dominate most social research commissioned by government, as well as innovation-oriented and other R&D, was that research had to correspond to specified (and current) policy concerns. Nevertheless, in 1974 arrangements for co-ordination of social science across departments, which in 1972 had become moribund, were again reactivated. A new interdepartmental social research committee was established, and the SRCU reestablished in the Cabinet Office as its secretariat. But once more this initiative failed. The time was not right.

'Rothschild' legitimated strictly departmental approaches, and bilateral arrangements on a purely ad hoc basis. Within science and technology policy generally any attempt at a co-ordinated 'science policy perspective.' was in course of abandonment. The Committee on Economic Research (CER), which had functioned throughout, was soon to be transferred from the Treasury to the Civil Service College, and thereby inevitably weakened. The Joint Approach to Social Policy (JASP), which represented the attempt by the CPRS to develop the longer term and co-ordinated approach to social policy, and which was announced publicly in 1975 (CPRS, 1975), rapidly ran into the ground. At the end of 1977 Cabinet Office arrangements were again dismantled, and the rump of the Social Research Co-ordinating Unit transferred to the Department of Education and Science.

In 1979, in a review of the implementation of Cmnd 5046 (published as *Review of the Framework for Government Research and Development (Cmnd 5046)* in Cmnd. 7499 March 1979), the government announced itself as broadly satisfied with developments over the previous years. Whilst, unusually, the social sciences here received some attention, this was largely within the framework of consideration of the relations between the SSRC and government departments. The Government proposed to establish with the Council 'a "modus vivendi" which will permit the SSRC to perform its function effectively and enable the Departments to secure the social science research which they require for policy purposes' (p. 14). Beyond this, and in particular in its discussions of the way in which research was to be relevant, and of arrangements for co-ordination of research, there was no indication that the social sciences were in any sense different from other sciences. The insights which had informed the Heyworth Report, and the arguments which it had so eloquently deployed, were by now only history. Perhaps their only legacy was the SSRC, whose major tribulations were still to come.

It is not easy to generalise about the place of the social sciences in Whitehall, for variations in attitudes and arrangements between the departments have been substantial for twenty years. It nevertheless seems permissible to hypothesise, on the basis of this brief review, that the social sciences have been in a situation of what one might call *double jeopardy* throughout the two or three decades of their Whitehall history. On the one hand they have been dependent upon attitudes toward rational, co-ordinated social policy (such as indicated by the Heyworth Report and by the JASP). On the other hand their fortunes have also been dependent upon arrangements for co-ordinated – or on the other hand highly sectorised – science and technology policy. But significantly, neither the documents which set out the principles of science policy for the 1960s and the 1970s (Trend, Rothschild), nor the arrangements in which they came to be embodied, paid them any attention. By the end of the 1970s, both co-ordinated social policy and co-ordinated science policy had been superseded.

Whitehall arrangements in international perspective

In the previous section I argued that the arrangements governing the interaction of British government departments with the social sciences could be understood in terms of two sets of beliefs, dispositions. I want now to suggest that not only historical study, but also comparative analysis of social science–government relations in different countries can advance understanding of the contingent nature of these relations. As with the previous historical section, what is offered here is no more than a brief prolegomena to the sort of analysis for which I am arguing.

As pointed out earlier, the tendency in Whitehall over the past few years has been to establish networks of research committees within individual departments, in which scientists and policy makers together seek to identify research needs. Following the customer–contractor principle introduced by Rothschild, the identification of research has tended to flow from the notion that every piece of research must have its own research customer within the policy structure. There has tended to be little systematic planning ahead, or anticipation of the research implications of future developments in policy. In the past two years or so, the application of these notions to research financing in *certain* fields of science has come in for some criticism. Lord Rothschild himself, in a recent inquiry into what was still the SSRC, drew attention to its limitations as applied to the social sciences (Rothschild, 1982). In all countries, where social policy departments commission social scientific research, comparable problems arise of 'how' and 'to what end' this is to be accomplished. In relation to the difficulties involved, a recent French report referred to a 'process of elaboration which consists in adjusting the needs of administration – themselves often difficult to determine – to the real possibilities of social science research': a problem which, in France 'is far from being resolved' (Boudon-Freville, 1979).

In the Netherlands too a central concern of the last decade has been to try to bring about a more effective relationship between research and policy.[2] But in so far as this hope has been translated into an approach to the formulation of research needs, it is very different from the customer-contractor principle. Of course, just as in Britain, the practice of different departments has varied. But in so far as there has been any kind of 'ideal' which has tended to structure discussion of departmental practice, then it has been a notion of 'programming'.

The ideal of programming derived from an expectation that it should be possible simultaneously to improve the quality and the policy-relevance of commissioned social research (Van Hoesel, 1985). The concept subsequently became a matter of debate. Whilst some inclined to a 'minimalist' notion (involving perhaps systematic listing of requirements), others argued that programming must be 'deductive' (and so derive research programmes from fundamental and a priori questions). But the complexity of this debate, and the participation in it of responsible officials who have sought to work with the concept, in itself suggests one conclusion. In the Netherlands, far more than in Britain, administrative discourse has been permeated – informed – by academic studies of the nature of science and of social science. Moreover, whereas in Britain Whitehall discussion was largely restricted to the research needs of policy, at least over the past decade, Dutch officials concerned with the social sciences have had an eye also on the needs of science.

Individual Dutch departments differ in their approach to research programming. Thus, in the department concerned with spatial planning (the Rijks Planologische Dienst, RPD), an attempt was made to generate research *in advance* of policy: to anticipate the requirements of policy. Although this was not altogether successful, the fundamental approach was quite different from that adopted in (say) the housing field, where the research programme has tended to be built up by the research sections on the basis of annual discussions with policy makers. Housing researchers tended to feel that in their area the field of work was clearly delineated, whereas in planning 'what should be the subject of research' is more problematic. In this manner they seek to explain the fundamental difference in approach between the planning researchers' attempts to anticipate and their own to respond to the needs of policy. The Ministry of Education and Sciences had a rather complicated set of arrangements. In 1965, wishing to provide for the growing interest in educational research, and feeling itself ill-equipped to discharge this responsibility, the Ministry established the Foundation for Educational Research, SVO. SVO would distribute funds from the Ministry as an independent research council. By the mid seventies, as the Ministry came to require research relating more specifically to its own policy concerns, SVO had so developed that it became difficult to influence their research programme in line with departmental needs. A second set of funds had to be established. Effectively, though the Ministry's conception of the relations of social research to educational policy had changed, it proved impossible to bring arrangements into line with this new conception. SVO had acquired an independent legitimacy.

Just as in Britain, inter-departmental variations in the Netherlands reflect different conceptions of the function of social research in relation to policy. This seems to be a general phenomenon. The Boudon-Freville report, reflecting on a similar diversity in France, noted that it was reasonable to suggest that 'the great diversity in problems to be studied and in appropriate research environments itself gives rise to a variety of solicitation procedures. But in fact the variety of procedures seems to derive less from considered reflection than from habit' (Boudon-Freville, 1979, p. 47). A general conclusion would thus seem to be that it is on the one hand different notions of what research is to provide, and on the other differences in ministerial traditions and cultures, which largely explains differences in departmental practices.

Dutch ministries carry out less of their social research internally than has typically been the case in Britain, and contract out a greater share of it. In looking for a suitable research contractor, there is a significantly lesser sense that this might be problematic. This is perhaps unsurprising. The expert staffs of departments are large (in relation to the sizes of research programmes, much larger than their British equivalents) and there is a much higher degree of mobility between the civil service and the academic world than in Britain. Relations between the two sectors have tended to be easy, informed, and informal. Whilst this renders the daily business of research contracting unproblematic to the participants, there is another aspect to be considered.

The most common practice of Dutch ministries has been to approach the single institute considered as most appropriate for a given new project, and invite it to submit a proposal. Personal contacts thus play an important role in a selection process which remains largely implicit. Such a procedure has the inherent danger that competition in the scientific community (over conceptual, theoretical and methodological matters) becomes transposed to the level of personal relations. The 'danger' inheres in the fact that intellectual competition (or conflict) may be an essential element in research creativity, in policy-related social science as in theory. The Boudon-Freville Report makes a similar point. Here reference is made to the desirability of 'allowing a small number of research institutes sufficient funds for the development of their work (in a given field) when they have demonstrated their competence and their sensitivity to current problems. It is a question of stimulating groups which are geographically dispersed, or which rely on different disciplines, but which are working on similar themes with compatible methodologies, regularly to confront each others 'work and progress' (Boudon-Freville, 1979, p. 50). Moreover, 'the notion of a programme contract must not lead to the creation of monopolies: wherever possible it is appropriate to develop competing research networks' (p. 52). It can be argued, then, that by comparison with the UK, Dutch ministries are too 'locked in' with a limited number of research institutes. In Britain, shortage of funds and pressures to 'relevance' have forced research managers increasingly to play safe: to return over and again to trusted research performers. Such a tendency to conservatism acts on the Dutch ministries too, though here it may rather be reinforcing established tendencies.

The nature of these relations acquires a different sort of significance when a need for new expertise emerges, perhaps because of a shift in policy concerns. British experience suggests that a ministry can properly take the initiative in seeking to open up a policy field to new perspectives, or to establish research relevant to a new problem of policy. In Britain, the DHSS attempted to do this in relation to research on mental handicap: to attract researchers having other expertise than those who had typically worked in the field. The attempt here was, in fact, not wholly successful. Another example concerns the question of 'women and redundancy'. Here the Department of Employment could find no research group working on this problem which could be offered a research contract. On the basis of detailed discussion with a number of groups having related interests, however, the Department's own research staff was able to convince a number of groups to submit proposals, and to ensure that these were of a high standard. These examples are intended to illustrate how departments, faced with new – or newly pressing – problems, may seek to act on the social science community. In the Netherlands ministries seem rarely to exert this kind of influence on the research world. Though they have become more initiatory in their formulation of problems, the structure of expertise, the existing structure of relations between practical problems and research approaches, has tended to be taken as given.

In the earlier discussion of Whitehall arrangements, attention was paid not only to individual departmental arrangements but also (and indeed rather more) to co-ordination between departments. There is an important reason for this. Social science which addresses itself to the problems of society is not necessarily bound by the concerns, the modes of action, of any one government department. Much of the best social research, with the most fundamental implications for policy, deals with problems having significance for a broad range of policies. Moreover, some of the most challenging issues for social scientific inquiry have potential implications which are not readily identified in advance. For example, studies of social inequalities in health, or rural depopulation, or the impact of microelectronics, may have conclusions relevant to the work of a number of departments. So may the use of certain social science methodologies, as for example the birth cohort study, in which the evolving interaction of wide ranges of variables over many years may be studied. It may convincingly be argued that it is through work of this kind – bounded neither by disciplinary constraints nor by existing administrative perspectives – that social scientists make their most profound contribution to social policy. It follows that provision for research of this kind is essential. How then are demands for such 'transdepartmental' research in practice generated?

The question is partly one of the existence, or not, of bodies whose concern is with setting strategic frameworks for policy development, and with the interactions of policies. In this respect national systems of government differ greatly. In Britain, the CPRS began with such a role, but gradually retreated to the analysis of discrete and unrelated topics (Plowden, 1981), before finally being disbanded. Despite the initiation of the JASP, which was to have been the basis for a more transdepartmental approach to social policy, and despite the presence in the Cabinet Office of the Social Research Co-ordinating Unit, no real demand for transdepartmental research ever emerged. In contrast, in other countries there exist bodies with this strategic responsibility which do function as 'customers' for research of this kind. In France, in 1969, the Commissariat du Plan sought to provide for such research by creating the Comité d'Organisation des Recherches Appliquées sur le Développement Economique et Social (CORDES). This Committee, under the chairmanship of the Commissaire au Plan, initiated a number of research studies on four fundamental themes: changes in international economic relations; restructuring the system of production and its implication for social relations; living conditions and inequalities; and social regulation and changing conditions of economic effectiveness (CORDES, 1977). The committee even began its own journal *Recherches Economiques et Sociales*. However the Committee has now ceased to exist. The Netherlands too has a long tradition of prospective planning of this kind, with the Central Planning Bureau dating from 1947, the Social and Cultural Planning Bureau from 1973, and the Scientific Council for Government Policy (the WRR) from 1972. These bodies have a clear need for studies focusing on the interactions of policies (Baehr, 1981).

A separate aspect of the initiation, or not, of transdepartmental social research relates to departments *jointly* defining and commissioning a study having relevance for their individual responsibilities. This of course is a potentially more pervasive notion of transdepartmentalism, and of the possibilities of 'strategic' social research coming to bear in policy. In both the Netherlands and Britain officials take the view that commissioning of research by individual departments accurately reflects policy needs, and that where a common need is identified ad hoc collaboration will be established. Yet matters do not always proceed in so uncontested a fashion, and disputes between departments may reflect simultaneously striving for control of lavish new programmes *and* for the right to impose a problem-definition. In terms of whose traditional mode of intervention is the problem to be defined? Such questions have saliency both for research and for policy. In Britain the problem of 'urban deprivation' was for some years the subject of just such a definitional contest. Similarly in the Netherlands, when (in 1978) an advisory commission on minorities research (ACOM) was established it was placed under the then Ministry of Culture Recreation and Social Work. When however a policy-co-ordinating body was established in the same area (ICM), it was placed under the aegis of the Ministry of Internal Affairs. These processes of negotiation over the right to define a problem, demarcation disputes, are not unique to government: they occur also in many areas of professional practice (e.g. medicine) and in science itself. In government, given the possibility of either outright victory, or some division of spoils, the possibility of a truly transdepartmental approach to the formulation of research needs carrying the day is remote. In both countries the complacent view of officials is to a degree self-fulfilling. Nevertheless the fact remains that in the Netherlands, but not in Britain, there do exist customers for social research investigating fundamental aspects of social structure and having unpredictable implications for policy, though potentially of major strategic importance. Through the WRR, and the other planning bodies, such research can be brought to bear in policy planning in the Netherlands. In Britain no such institutionalised channels exist.

Conclusions

In this paper I have tried to show that understanding of the contingent nature of government arrangements for the social sciences may be advanced through two complementary analyses: historical and comparative.

Consideration of the changing attention to, and arrangements for, social research in Whitehall, over the post-war period, suggests an awkward situation of double jeopardy. With the rise of the view that rational, 'long term', 'output oriented' co-ordinated social policy was possible, in the mid sixties, government social science developed from limited fact-gathering to something distinctly more ambitious. Even at its most developed, however, social science never enjoyed the connection with policy analysis, with policy planning, envisaged by the Heyworth and Fulton Reports. Subsequently, with the decline of this rationalising spirit, the situation changed. Social science in Whitehall came to be dominated by the departmental concerns – the concerns of specified areas of administration – legitimated by the customer–contractor principle. Government arrangements for social research came to be dominated, in other words, by approaches, structures, developed with the characteristics of the physical and engineering sciences in mind. This was particularly visible in the collapse of the very structures through which a more co-ordinated strategic, long term approach to social science might have been articulated.

When processes obtaining in British ministries are compared with those obtaining in counterpart ministries elsewhere, it becomes apparent that these processes – and the assumptions on which they rest – are determined less by the 'nature of the social sciences' than by the culture of British public administration. Thus, comparison of the relations of British ministries with the social sciences to the relations obtaining in the Netherlands leads to certain further tentative conclusions.

In both countries, as we saw, much effort has been devoted over the past decade to trying to ensure the 'relevance' of government social science to policy. But 'relevance' is a concept open to varying interpretation. The objectives, the intentions, underlying the British customer–contractor principle scarcely correspond to those underlying the Dutch notion of 'programming'. It is hard to avoid the conclusion that Dutch arrangements, and a fortiori the discussion which has surrounded them, reflects a greater appreciation of the ways in which social science differs from technology than has typically been the case in Britain. The 'ideals' of course, are translated into practices which differ substantially between one ministry and another, in both countries. Ministries differ in the dominant objectives behind their commissioning of social research. Emphasis might be put, for example, on the attempt to add to current knowledge of complex social problems (such as mental illness, patterns of saving, or the consequences of unemployment); or on the development of medium term planning (through studies of, for example, local labour markets or the relation between school size and achievement); or the establishment of relevant characteristics of 'client groups' (such as one-parent families, or the long-term unemployed); or on the evaluation of current policy initiatives or arrangements in terms of impact or coverage (Blume, 1982, p. 53). To some degree, these different perceptions of what is to be expected from social research, what role it is to play, condition the different arrangements made by individual departments.

In this context it is interesting to note that, despite the major differences in policy systems, there are certain aspects of similarity between practices in comparable policy areas. For example, in both Britain and the Netherlands, research in the field of criminology/law enforcement tended to be developed internally, within the relevant ministry, to an extent scarcely equalled elsewhere in the administration. This of course may reflect the extent to which research in this area involves sensitive questions of the confidentiality of records and of security. Education is another area of partial convergence. Educational research in both countries stands out as in certain ways different from much other government-funded social research. Special provision has tended to be made for its funding, and just as in the Netherlands a special research foundation (SVO) exists, so too have there been frequent calls for an educational research council in Britain. Funds for educational research have tended to be relatively privileged, perhaps because of long dominant views as to the importance of education. Research is carried out in special institutes, and is generally closely tied to recognised problems of educational policy and practice. Something of the same is true of social work research, and in both countries specialised national institutes have tended to play an important role. Here we seem to be led to a sociological explanation going beyond 'administrative culture', for what characterises these fields (and differentiates them from research on unemployment, or housing) is that they are areas of professional practice. Teachers and social workers, to some degree, have acquired the privileges of professionalism. These social resources are brought to bear on the research process, and come to dominate the weaker social resources which social scientists can generally deploy. Thus, for example, we can begin to understand the dominance of the educational profession over research in the British ministry, where advice has tended to be provided by the educational inspectorate and not by social scientists.

Beyond this there are significant differences between the two systems, and each serves to illuminate the strengths and weaknesses of the other. In the Netherlands, as we have seen, there exists a 'customer' for transdepartmental social research of fundamental and strategic importance for policy which is lacking in Britain. But against this is to be set the fact that in the (larger) British system there seems to exist the possibility of intellectual competition in policy research which may be vital for creativity, and which is largely absent in the more consensual Dutch system.

Ultimately, of course, the focus of this paper has been upon the *study* of the relations of social science and government. And if I cannot justifiably claim to have provided new insights into social science in Whitehall, I hope that I might at least claim to have suggested procedures through which others might accumulate such insights. I hope that this more limited claim will be put to the test.

NOTES

1 Development of the Government Economic Service, and the role of the economist in Whitehall, also largely has its origins in the war, but this is another story. See Winch, 1972 for further discussion.
2 The discussion which follows is closely based upon a study carried out by the author and P van Hoesel on behalf of the Directorate General for Science Policy of the Dutch Ministry of Education and Science. See Blume and van Hoesel, 1982.
   The author would like to express his thanks to Mrs A. K. Jackson, from whom he learned so much of the matters discussed in this paper.

REFERENCES

Baehr, 1981 P. R. Baehr, 'Future studies and policy analysis in the political process: the Netherlands Scientific Council for Government Policy' in P. R. Baehr and B. Wittrock (eds), *Policy Analysis and Policy Innovation*, London and Beverly Hills, Sage Books.

Blume, 1982 S. S. Blume, *The Commissioning of Social Research by Central Government*, London, SSRC.

Blume, and Van Hoesel 1982 S. S. Blume and P. van Hoesel, *Government Commissioning of Social Research: Dutch Experience in Comparative Perspective*, Leiden, LISBON, University of Leiden.

Boudon-Freville, 1979 'Rapport sur la politique contractuelle en sciences sociales', *Le Progrès Scientifique 45* 199–200.

Bulmer, 1981 M. Bulmer, 'Applied social research: a reformulation of "applied" and "enlightenment" models', *Knowledge: Creation Diffusion Utilisation 3*, 187.

Clapham, 1946 *Report of the Committee on the Provision for Social and Economic Research* London, HMSO Cmd 6868.

CORDES, 1977 'Croissance, crise et changement social', *Recherches Economiques et Sociales* Numéro Spécial, June.

CPRS, 1975 Central Policy Review Staff, *A Joint Approach to Social Policy* London, HMSO.

Dahlstrom, 1976 E. Dahlstrom, 'Social scientists and practitioners' (Department of Sociology, Gothenburg, Report no. 38).

Dahlstrom, 1978 E. Dahlstrom, 'Role of social science in working life policy: the case of post-war Sweden' (Department of Sociology, University of Gothenburg, mimeo'd).

Fulton, 1968 *Report of the Committee on the Civil Service 1966–1968* (Chairman Lord Fulton) Cmnd. 3638 London: HMSO.

Grebenik, 1972 *The Civil Service College 1970–1* (First Annual Report by the Principal to the Civil Service College Advisory Council) London HMSO.

Heclo and Wildavsky, 1974. H. Heclo and A. Wildavsky, *The Private Government of Public Money*, London, Macmillan.

Heyworth, 1965 *Report of the Committee on Social Studies*, London, HMSO Cmnd 2660.

Van Hoesel, 1985 P. H. M. van Hoesel, *Het Programmeren van Sociaalbeleidsonderzoek: Analyse en Receptuur* (Dissertation, University of Leiden).

Lindblom and Cohen, 1979 C. Lindblom and D. Cohen, *Usable Knowledge*, New Haven, Conn, Yale University Press.

MacRae, 1976 D. MacRae, *The Social Function of Social Science*, New Haven, Conn., Yale University Press.

Plowden, 1981 W. Plowden 'The British Central Policy Review Staff', in P. Baehr and B. Wittrock (eds), *Policy Analysis and Policy Innovation*, London and Beverly Hills, Sage Books.

Rothschild, 1971 *A Framework for Government Research and Development*, London, HMSO, Cmnd 4814.

Rothschild, 1982 Lord Rothschild, *An Inquiry into the Social Science Research Council* London, HMSO, Cmnd 8554.

Trend, 1963 *Committee of Enquiry into the Organisation of Civil Science*, London, HMSO, Cmnd 2171.

Weiss, 1980 C. H. Weiss, 'Knowledge creep and decision accretion', *Knowledge; Creation Diffusion Utilisation 1*, 381.

Whitehead, 1985 F. Whitehead, 'The Government Social Survey', in M. Bulmer (ed.) *Essays on the History of British Sociological Research*, Cambridge, Cambridge University Press.

Winch, 1972 D. Winch, *Economics and Policy: a historical study*, London, Fontana.

CHAPTER 7

Congressional committee staffs (do, do not) use analysis

CAROL H. WEISS

With the recent growth in the numbers of Congressional staff, Congress should be better equipped to do policy analysis and to make use of the policy research and analysis done by others. It might be expected that Congressional committees and subcommittees[1] would be the locus of such activity, inasmuch as they have the explicit task of formulating policy through legislation. Yet despite the growth in committee staffs, and their increasing specialisation and professionalism (Fox and Hammond, 1977), the amount of formal analysis done in committees is generally low. Even committee staff's *use* of analytic studies done elsewhere – by Congressional support agencies, the executive branch, or by independent scholars in think tanks or universities – tends to be sporadic. Since Congressional committees are remarkably varied on this dimension as on others, there are exceptions to the statement, but few would quarrel with the generalisation. (See Jones, 1976; Dreyfus, 1977; Zweig, 1981.)

This paper examines why Congressional committee staffs have not proved to be major consumers of policy research and analysis and whether there is movement in that direction. Basically, two types of factors interfere. One is the rival forces, such as political ideologies and organised interests, that compete for the hearts and minds of members of Congress and congressional staff. Since the Congress is pre-eminently the institution where contending ideologies and interests are negotiated and reach resolution, these forces tend to outweigh the 'rationality' of analysis. Yet knowledge is by no means irrelevant. Only with good information about current conditions can the prevailing coalition translate their interests and ideologies into a coherent program of legislation. Only with good understanding of cause-effect relationships can they design appropriate mechanisms to bring about the effects they seek. Of

course, Congressional committee staff have many sources of information other than research and analysis – experience, testimony, conversation, commonsense understandings, professional lore, ordinary
everyday assumptions. They do not start with a blank slate but with an
existing stock of knowledge. If analysis is to influence policy, its lessons
have to be assimilated into the stock of knowledge with which members
of Congress and staff already make sense of the policy world.

The second set of factors that impedes the flow and potency of analysis is the structure of the Congress and its committees. Jurisdictions and
boundaries of committees, standard operating procedures, and communication channels make a difference. Among the important structural
elements are recruitment and retention practices not only for members
but more importantly in this regard, for committee staff. The fate of
analysis depends to a considerable degree on who is on the receiving end
of the information. Their receptivity is influenced by the reward and
incentive structures that govern their work, their time pressures, the
other messages that clog their communication channels, the prestige
hierarchies that affect how much respect they accord to analysis as compared to political concerns. Another structural element is the availability of analytic agencies, such as the Congressional Budget Office and
the Congressional Research Service, and the types of messages they
send to congressional receivers.

As Congressional committees and the environment in which they
work have changed in recent years (Smith and Deering, 1984), some of
the traditional resistance to research and analysis has weakened.
Although major obstacles remain, committee staffs are not dead set
against analysis in the ways that they were – or were assumed to have
been – in the past. In fact, a later section of this paper argues that committees staffs increasingly perform an analytic role. They do so *informally* through their intense rounds of communication with other actors in
the policy process. Some of the actors with whom they interact are
direct and indirect transmitters of analytic information. Increasingly,
the discourse of Congressional discussion adopts the language of social
scientific analysis, and in so doing, subsumes many of the concepts and
constructs that social analysis provides.

Preface

By analysis, I mean systematic review of evidence (data, studies,
program records, financial statements, etc.) concerning the nature of
current conditions and the consequences of present or proposed policies. As MacRae writes, 'Policy analysis is the use of reason and evi-

dence to choose better as against worse policies' (quoted in Jones, 1976).

As Malbin has written, 'Congress clearly has been acting over the past decade as if it felt a need for more policy analysis produced on Capitol Hill' (1980, 204). The evidence is the hiring of more and better educated committee staff, fewer of whom hold law degrees than in the past and more with training and experience in substantive specialties. Eight per cent of committee staff professionals in 1976 held Ph.D.s (Fox and Hammond, 1977), and more probably do now. As one veteran staff member said, 'Staff are more likely to be experts than the cronies they replaced' (Frantzich, 1982, 15).

Even more persuasive is the growth in the four Congressional support agencies – the Congressional Budget Office, Congressional Research Service, Office of Technology Assessment, and the General Accounting Office. Each of these agencies performs analytic functions for the Congress. GAO, for example, since 1974 has expanded beyond its role as auditor of the books of executive programs and has entered upon evaluations of the consquences of programs. In 1974 it set up an Institute for Program Evaluation staffed largely by social scientists, which has now been absorbed into the agency as a regular division.

One of the main reasons behind the zeal for increased analytic capacity was Congress' distrust of the information it received from the executive agencies. Congress believed that agencies' information was self-serving, designed to bolster their programmatic proposals and budget requests. Congress wanted its own capacity to amass and review data and to make sense of competing claims.

Committees' fitful hospitality to analysis

Despite the sincerity of the yearning, most committees evidence feeble devotion to analysis.[2] Observers have identified a series of compelling reasons for the general inattention.

Committees have become advocates for the programs in their domain. Armed Forces committees support military expansion, agriculture committees support aid to farmers. Members of Congress seek assignment to committees on which they can serve their constituents, and this generally means channeling additional federal money into ventures that benefit them. Such biased recruitment perpetuates the advocacy stance of the committees (Davidson, 1976). Therefore, committees are not in the market for objective research that might raise questions about proposals to expand services to their constituencies.

Another barrier to impartial analysis derives from tangled committee jurisdictions. Often pieces of a policy issue are parceled out to different committees and subcommittees. Committees wrangle over which one shall have authority over the issue. (In recent years arrangements have been made for joint, sequential, and split referrals of the same bill to different committees [Davidson, 1981].) When a new issue erupts into prominence, as energy did in the 1970s, the existing committee structure finds a dozen or so committees and subcommittees with claims on some piece of the action. When issues are fragmented and shards assigned to different committees, no committee has the authority or the interest to look at analysis of the issue as a whole. Analysis tends to be comprehensive; committee jurisdictions are often segmental.

A perpetual obstacle to the use of analysis in the Congress is the limited time and energy of the members. The House of Representatives has 435 members, the Senate 100, and no increase in staff or growth of computer resources can stretch the total allotment of attention that each member can give to information. Ultimately, each member on a committee and in the chamber has to make up her/his mind on proposed legislation, and there is a limit to how much information each person can absorb (Dreyfus, 1977). Staff have little incentive for adding to the information overload which is endemic in Congress, when they know how brief a span of attention their 'boss' can give to the message.

Staff on Congressional committees are aware of another brake on the consideration of analysis – the hectic pace of legislative activity. In the 96th Congress, senators averaged 10 committee and subcommittee posts, members of the House averaged 5.5 assignments (Davidson, 1981). They have time to spend only a few minutes at hearings or markup sessions before rushing to the next committee room; meanwhile bells keep ringing summoning them to floor votes. A House report indicated that representatives spent 11 minutes a day reading (U.S. House, 1977). The greatest gap between what they identified as very important to do and what they actually did was studying and legislative research (Davidson, 1981, 113). Staff are caught up in the same kind of activity. When several bills come up for consideration before a committee, staff can work far into the night for weeks on end keeping up with the press of work – working out accommodations, drafting language, writing reports, fending off amendments, etc. In this context, analysis looks like a dispensable luxury.

Quite a number of the committee staff whom I interviewed came to their jobs expecting to do analysis. They anticipated that, unlike work in a member's personal office, a committee job would entail examining the merits of legislative provisions. They expected to read research and evaluation reports, look for data, call on the services of the Congressional

support agencies, and spend long stretches of time analysing the
probable effects of alternative proposals. Although this was a prevalent
assumption, it did not survive long after they started work. Both the pace
of work and the incentive system (which rewards very different behavior)
effectively doused the dream.

Furthermore, analysis is alien to the traditional style of the Congress'
collection and processing of information. Members of Congress gather
ideas and perceptions primarily through oral communication – listening
to constituents and interest groups, attending committee hearings, and
talking to their staff and fellow members (Fenno, 1978). They gather
ideas and information through personal interaction, and they take pride
in their ability to 'read people' rather than read reports. They filter the
information in a largely intuitive style and develop their political judgments. Because they are able and experienced politicians, they have faith
in their judgment about the wisdom of alternative policies. They would
not have risen to their present position unless they were skillful in
eliciting and attending to salient information and processing it into
political stands. What they tend to want from analysis is support,
justification, statements from experts and collateral data that confirm
their judgments.

Staff rapidly become aware that, on those issues on which their boss
has taken a position, s/he rarely wants to hear about someone's objective
research – unless it is supportive. Of course, there are many issues before
the Congress on which members have no firm convictions and could be
open to evidence. But the issues that come before the committee are in
their bailiwick. Through specialisation and experience, they are specialists in committee business, and on issues that come before the committee
they are likely to have made firm judgments. Committee staff, therefore,
operate in an environment in which there are few rewards for dispassionate analysis. At a Congressional Research Service seminar attended by
committee staff and analysts, where the identity of speakers was
removed from the written record, one analyst said:

> The attitude most typical of committee staff is "Whose side are you
> on?" If you are not for us, you must be against us. The Hill works in a
> partisan sort of advocacy style. The objective analyst, whose job is to
> illuminate alternatives and not make recommendations, finds a commu-
> nication gulf right away with most committee staff because there is no
> room for neutrality (Schick, 1977b, 117).

Probably the most effective damper of all on committees' use of
analysis is the nature of Congress' mission. Congress is a body whose
mandate is to reconcile divergent interests. In part because the party
system is weak, members have a strong commitment to bargaining and

compromise. They seek to accommodate the multiple competing groups in the society and pass legislation that is at least minimally acceptable to all interests that are mobilized and represented.

Staff work in committees emphasizes building coalitions and negotiating compromises so that bills can be passed. Rewards go to staff who can surmount the roadblocks in the legislative process and shepherd a bill through to passage (Redman, 1973). From early days staff, like members, become promoters of 'their' bill. They do not value analysis that seeks the 'right answer' to the problem – for two rather different reasons. One, analysis might not support the bill that they are committed to pushing through. But the second reason is that 'authoritative answers' are likely to prove counterproductive; they can promote a hardening of positions and lessen the willingness to negotiate with people holding different positions. Thus, in the unlikely event that policy analysis produced firm answers and unambiguous recommendations, such analysis (however desirable on other grounds) would undermine a basic value in the Congress – the necessity for bargaining and compromise.

An additional reason for committees' limited attachment to analysis impressed me when I served as a Congressional Fellow in 1983. It is certainly not as important as many of these other factors, but it has received little attention in print. That is the fragmentation of committee staffs.

Staff fragmentation

The term 'committee staff' suggests coherent organization, but each committee (and subcommittee) actually has two separate staffs – majority and minority. The 1946 Legislative Reorganization Act which authorized committee staffs anticipated nonpartisan staffs, and in the first years that was the norm (Kofmehl, 1962). But by the early 1950s, nonpartisanship had eroded and it survives today in only a few committees. Almost from the start, what was meant to be the staff of the whole committee became the staff of the majority party members and primarily of the chairman (Ripley, 1969). Members of the minority party clamored for staff of their own, and most committees worked out some arrangement. The Legislative Reorganization Act of 1970 increased the size of staffs and formally designated one-third of each committee's professional staff as minority. Although the provisions were not immediately implemented (Malbin, 1980), this is now the prevailing pattern in both houses.

Majority staff are hired by the chairman of the committee or subcommittee, and their loyalty is to him. Minority staff are hired by and owe their allegiance to the ranking minority member. Since Congressional staff have no civil service protections (they can be fired at any time) and serve solely at the discretion of their 'boss', loyalty is no trifling matter. Committee staff often come from the member's home state/district and usually are in sympathy with his/her general political outlook. Whatever their other qualifications for the job, certain commonalities in perspective seem essential. Staff have, or develop on the job, considerable concern with the political fortunes of their member. For one thing, if the member of Congress whom they serve loses his/her seat, they may be out of a job.[3] New chairmen often bring their own people with them. So, many staff tend to look at legislative proposals through bifocal lenses: is it a good provision? *and* how will it look to voters in the home district? While I was a Congressional Fellow, I remember running into the majority staff director in the hall. She complained that she and her staff had been putting in twelve hour days for the past week, keeping a bill alive, and 'we only get about $600,000 out of it'. It took me a few seconds to place the 'we' – it was Vermont, the state that the chairman of the subcommittee represented. Close involvement with the aspirations and interest of their boss comes about through a variety of mechanisms – selective recruitment, the staffer's own self-interest, and the mutuality of outlook on the legislative agenda they want to pursue.

When people talk about a committee or subcommittee staff, they usually mean the majority – the chairman's – staff. The minority staff is a separate entity. It has its own budget, it hires its own people, it responds to the concerns of a member of the other party. Because of the overcrowded office conditions that plague the Congress despite the building boom, the minority staff is often located in offices some distance away from the majority staff, even in a different building.

Nor is that the limit of committee fragmentation. Since the majority staff is the chairman's staff, other members of the committee from the chairman's party have relatively little access to it. The same is true for the minority party. Over the years, junior members became dissatisfied with their limited call on committee resources, and the two chambers responded. The Senate, for example, passed a resolution in 1975 (S. Res, 60) that made budgetary provision for staff (known in charming nineteenth century style as 'clerk-hire') for all members on a committee or subcommittee. For each committee on which a senator serves, he can hire a staff person (or some fraction of a staffer's time) to work on committee business. Staff hired under clerk-hire provisions do not have their desks in the committee offices. They are usually located in the member's personal office. Although they spend their time working on, say, veteran's affairs or education, their primary loyalties rest with the person who hired them, and their daily colleagues are the other staff working for the member on constituent affairs, public relations, and overtly partisan matters.

The fact that 'committee staff' is such an unco-ordinated aggregate of people, hired by and responsible to an array of members, has consequences for their ability to do and use policy analysis. For one thing, majority and minority staff rarely share analytic information. Neither they, nor the staffers of junior members, combine forces for an intellectual attack on a problem. Since each is intent upon promoting the political and substantive concerns of her/his boss, they maintain a polite separateness. Whatever information or analysis they collect, they generally keep to themselves – for whatever political advantage it may provide. Therefore, much work is duplicated in several offices. (It is possible that the members themselves co-operate more readily with other committee members than do the staffs acting as their agents.)

Moreover, since the staffs do have to co-operate in the passage of bills through the committee, they spend a lot of time in contact with each other keeping up with the latest developments. During certain phases of the session, this means an astonishing number of phone calls back and forth for purposes of internal liaison. Outside interest groups and executive agencies that want to influence legislative activity not infrequently make it a point to touch base with majority staff, minority staff, and staff who work on committee business for other sympathetic members. Duplicate series of communications pour in from outside (although the messages may be given a special tilt to appeal to each audience). Thus, requirements for *internal* co-ordination and demands for *external* attentiveness effectively displace analysis as a focus of staff activity. Since I served as Congressional Fellow with a minority staff, I was particularly aware of the separation, duplication of effort, and the fact that analysis made available to one staff rarely traveled beyond its quarters.

Informal analysis

The factors that work against the use of policy analysis in committees make a daunting list. Yet one of my most surprising learnings was that committee staffs know a good deal about relevant research and analysis. They manage to hear about work done by analysts in the support agencies, some work done by executive departments, and even some research done in institutes and universities. The ideas and generalisations that serious analysts produce – some of them, anyway – make their way through the thickets and get a hearing. How this happens and how committee staff judge the validity of the research and analysis they learn about are the subjects of this section.

First, it is well to mention that certain elements are favorable for the use of analysis. Members of Congress recognise the repute in which analysis is held in academic and scholarly circles, and many of them give it at least rhetorical respect. As already noted, they want their own sources of information as a counterweight to the executive branch, they have increased the staffs of the support agencies, they have had computers installed in every office with access to Library of Congress reference files, they expect their staffs to keep them abreast of analytic developments – at the very least, to avoid surprise. Analysis does not face a hostile environment, but rather one whose local practices are out of synch with standard procedures of analytic work.

Nor is policy analysis totally ignored. Even an observer who says that analysis is 'only in the backwaters of policy making' suggests that Congressional 'policy making is 90 percent politics, 10 percent analysis' (anonymous participant in Congressional Research Service Seminar, in Schick, 1977b, 121). Ten percent sounds not insignificant. Congress has mandated evaluations of government programs; it has funded large numbers of studies. Committee reports frequently make reference to research (Boruch & Leviton, 1983). Some Congressional staff have come to their jobs with higher degrees and analytical experience and serve as active links to the research community. The Congressional Research Service supplies 'issue papers', CBO produces reports not only on budgetary and economic issues but on subjects as far afield as math and science education; GAO evaluates existing programs; OTA analyses 'technologies' as diverse as federally supported libraries and industrial innovation. Mass media bring reports of research to the attention of the reading public, including Congressional staff. Kingdon (1984, 57) found that researchers, academics, and consultants were frequently named as important participants in policymaking in the areas he studied, transportation and health. They were not as important as members of Congress, the administration, or interest groups, but in certain policy communities, he found that 'all know and cite by name the leading academicians during their discussions' (Kingdon, 1984, 58).

One of the most strategic channels through which information flows is from interest groups. Congressional committees know and understand interest groups, and they are structured to listen to them. When spokespersons for an interest group present committee staffs with a set of policy claims, they support the claims with arguments and, often, data. Competing interest groups advance their own arguments, with the accompanying research and analytical foundations, to make their own case. Thus committee staffs are exposed to a wide variety of research, analysis, evaluation, and statistics. They hear about them in just the circumstances that motivate them to take the information seriously. This is not neutral, objective data, stuff they 'should' know about to be intellectually respectable. This is information intermeshed with politics, information making the case for different legislative provisions, information directly linked to committee business. It comes from clients and constituents of the committee or their organisational representatives, people whom committee staffs listen to. This is real, not ivory tower.

Of course, information that arrives in this style is not neutral. Congressional staff recognise that there is a substantial component of bias. But Congress is comfortable dealing with self-interested bias. That is the context with which they are most familiar – groups out to advance their own cause.

The information that committees receive from these diverse sources is inconsistent. Since each group highlights its case, they arrive with an array of discrepant and conflicting information. Committee staff become proficient in testing the arguments and analysis that they receive from one party by playing them off against the knowledge and judgments of other parties. Their primary resources is the nexus of telephone contacts which they build up over time, a resource that Zweig (1981, 147) calls 'the heart of the staff information trade'. Their tactic is to ask each group what it thinks of the arguments and data put forward by other groups. If a consumers' group claims that legislative remedy is needed because consumers are bilked in 32 percent of transactions, staff ask the producers' group their estimate of these data, and will usually get not only a rebuttal but a methodological critique of the data source. Iteratively, they will test the producers' arguments with the consumers and with other active parties.

Through such informal strategies, staff continuously test the knowledge claims of each set of actors. Their usual premise is that both sides are exaggerating and that truth lies somewhere in between. They see their task as ferreting out enough about the strengths and weaknesses of each side's arguments to get a good purchase on the actual situation.

Of course, testing of empirical claims is not the central feature of the information exchanges. Staff are particularly interested in what each party wants and how intensely they want it, and as Zweig (1979, 151) notes, they are 'exquisitely sensitive to interest groups, proposals and counterproposals, coalitions, nature of the conflict episodes, and possibilities for conflict resolution'. Probing analytic assumptions and justifications is part of this larger endeavor.

Staff talk to experts, too, people with knowledge and experience in the substantive field. Some experts have become policy advocates, not in service to a client group but on behalf of their own views of the public good (Heclo, 1978). Such people may not wait to be sought out by staff but lobby as actively as any organizational spokesman. Staff call on other experts, from places like the Brookings Institution or their home-town universities, usually people with whom they have developed a relationship of trust over the years. As Andringa (1976, 79) notes, knowledgeable friends may be more influential than nationally recognised authorities. Ongoing conversation is supplemented by newspaper reading, glancing at CRS issue papers or CBO analyses, listening to witness at hearings, reading constituent mail. Staff are constantly processing and screening a wide assortment of information.

Basically, committee staff sit at the nodes of what Heclo (1978) has called 'issue networks'. Through their centrality in the information exchange, they sooner or later hear about much of the research and analysis that is relevant to their work. They sift and filter the information through adversarial interchanges and, of course, through their own political judgment. Therefore, despite their limited interest in formal analysis, they in effect perform a crucial analytic role.

Many of the criteria by which staff judge competing analyses are overtly political, more so in committees with highly politicised jurisdictions, less so in technical and procedural areas. Political criteria rise in importance over time as early ideas and proposals become solidified in bills, to which sponsors and reputations are attached. Given the mission of Congress, its committees and staffs, it is inevitable that political considerations predominate. Nevertheless, staff want to avoid errors and inefficient choices. Therefore, they informally test the empirical as well as the political bases of the arguments advanced by policy partisans, and they filter the truth claims of competing advocates.

The influence of analysis

How much influence does one study have on the direction of a subcommittee's work? Even under favorable circumstances, probably not much. The rare case happens when one study has a direct effect on legislative provisions, but when it does, it seems to be in cases where an issue has been deadlocked. The analysis either strengthens one side and gives it more credibility in the debate (Weiss, 1970) or finds an unexpected way *around* the deadlock, at least minimally satisfying both parties (Hayes, 1982). In other cases, the analysis may be cited, footnoted, and quoted, but the members actually make up their minds on other grounds and use the 'expert's report' as window dressing.

Few observers are concerned that analysis plays too influential a role in

Congressional deliberations. But Malbin (1980) does. He believes that not only does Congress allow staff too much power but it also gives analytic studies too much weight. In the case of natural gas deregulation, 'the imposingly technical material flooded the system, intimidated the members, and beguiled them away from debating some important matters' (p. 232). Furthermore, 'members of Congress seem to prefer using the new quantitative rhetoric of social science to discussing the unquantifiable but more informative assumptions on which the numbers rest' (p. 234).

The important point he makes is that excessive deference to analysis can divert attention from the value premises underlying the arguments, which Congress should be focusing on. Yet even he acknowledges that 'the numbers' probably swayed few minds. Some members 'hid behind the studies; even though they may have made their decisions on other grounds, they felt more comfortable knowing that if something should go wrong, they would be able to say they simply went along with the experts' (p. 233). Since Congress discussed at least half a dozen studies on deregulation which came to widely different conclusions, members of almost any persuasion could find a study to hide behind.

Congressional committees are more apt to use analysis to bolster an already taken position than to select a new position. Much of the work of committees deals with traditional subjects about which members and staff have built up considerable substantive knowledge over the years. They have a body of expertise and experience, ongoing contacts with advocacy organisations and interest groups, and relationships with capable informants. One new study is unlikely to shake their views. Schick has written (1976, 228), 'Congress treats analysis much as it treats gossip, news, constituency mail, the local newspapers, etc. Everything is grist for the Congressional mill, and analysis enjoys no preferred position by virtue of its esteem in intellectual circles.' Although this is an understatement of the legitimating function of analysis, it may be a reasonable estimate of direct impact. The way that research and analysis affect the committee agenda is probably much the way such work influences thinking in executive agencies – through the slow percolation of new concepts, generalisations, and data into people's understanding of how the world works (Weiss, 1980). Over time, the ideas generated by research and analysis alter people's priorities and the types of action that they see as legitimate and effective.

For social scientists who would like to see their work inform legislation, an effort to reach committee staff may be tempting. Staff are relatively accessible. They will listen to social scientists who come with appropriate credentials, academic reputations, or introductions from people they know, especially if the social scientist has something brief and pithy to say. But it is important to reach committee staff early in the process of developing legislation – before too many detailed provisions are drafted and before interests have hardened around them. Much staff work consists of negotiating the specifics of bills, and by that time, it is too late for analysis to have much chance of influence.

To be influential, policy analysis probably needs to get into the pipeline while general approaches to legislation are still being considered. Policy analysts who seek a hearing will want to reach committee staff in the months before specific bills are introduced. They may also want to reach out to other policy activists who draft legislative proposals – advocacy organisations, executive agencies, and the recognised experts and consultants whose advice is widely sought in policy formulation. By the time Congressional committees begin action on specific bills, the determining conceptual premises have usually started to set.

Committees deal in bills. They don't deal in problems, they deal in solutions. They do not analyse current conditions and canvass all possible strategies for improvement. Their currency is legislative proposals. Past laws expire and need to be reauthorised. New bills are introduced by the carload and assigned to committee for processing. Some committees have aggressive and entrepreneurial staffs who seek out issues that their bosses can do something about. In an attempt to put the issue on the agenda, they also scout out a solution that seems to hold promise of headway. Whatever the source of proposal, staff's major job is to work out an acceptable amalgam from the array of existing proposals.

The rational (analytic) model posits a sequence of events that begins with recognition of a problem, then proceeds to development of alternative solutions for dealing with the problem, the weighing of costs and benefits of the alternatives, and ends with selection of the best solution. As March (1978) and others have suggested, such a tidy sequence does not generally characterise organizational decision making. In Congress, the departure from the model is extreme. Solutions (proposals) often come first, preceding any systematic effort to understand the dimensions of the problem (or even whether there is a bona fide problem). Proponents of proposals, whether in Congressional committees, executive agencies, or interest groups, may have done some investigation of the problem and the effectiveness of alternative strategies for coping with it. But most of staff work in committees involves helping members select key proposals for serious attention, and then amend, combine, revise, reconcile, and above all negotiate, so that the bill makes its way through committee, through the chamber, and through conference with the other house.[4]

When committee staffs initiate issues and develop their own proposals, they have more influence on the facet of the issue to address, the remedies to consider, and the selection of plans for action. In these cases, analysis can have more central influence. If researchers want their work to be influential, they have to know who the key actors are, what alternatives they are considering, and when they start the process in motion (Verdier, 1984). Analysis has greater likelihood of impact on the development of new policies than in reauthorisa- tions when players have more interests at stake and more axes to grind.

Can the use of analysis be improved?

If there is one thing all Congress-watchers are agreed upon, it is that Congress doesn't want or need more data, more undigested, unprocessed information. Information, to be useful, should be attached to specific proposals, either supporting or opposing or identifying the need for change in proposed legislation. Where analysts prize objective data, data separated from values, Congressional staff prefer data that *combines* facts with values – and with directions for action. Because Congressional staff have so little time to do or search for analysis on their own, they want it wrapped in a package which includes concrete proposals for action.

Lindblom (1968) and others have suggested that policy analysis that has an effect on policy is *partisan* policy analysis. It is research that accepts the client's ideological assumptions and political preferences. Because it is congenial, policy makers use it to clarify issues and speed the deliberative process along.[5] However, in the Congress a wide spectrum of political preferences is represented. Analysis that appeals to one cluster of committee members is likely to be rejected by others. Less overtly partisan and more objective analysis can serve a broader band of committee members and even provide a forum for discussing and negotiating their differences. Strictly for political reasons, nonpartisan analysis may have greater appeal because it provides a more convincing public rationale for action. Most policy researchers, particularly those in universities, are more comfortable trying to produce analysis that eschews political allegiances and strives for 'truth'. But truth is not the name of the game on the Hill, and people in Congress doubt that analysts are after truth, either. Members and staff are used to claimants calling on the phone, asking for things. They know how to deal with lobbies and interest groups and constituents who want them to vote for a bill or change legislative language. They tend to distrust researchers and analysts who claim that they are interested only in purveying 'innocent' and impartial information. They wonder what these people's game is and what they really want. As a participant in the CRS discussion (Schick, 1977b, 128) said:

> I think all policy analysis is political. The people who do it are political animals and bring a certain set of values to bear on any problem. They have a methodology that they believe is good, and they try to honor it. But very often they honor their values more. Congress knows this. Congress has to know this. It looks at all analysis as being political. I think this is good, but we have been discussing analysis as if it were something that was not political but objective – a tool. Congress does not approach the problem that way at all.

In this sense, Congress is not wrong. Scholars have long recognised that research inevitably contains implicit value assumptions. In the way that questions are framed, the choice of measures, criteria for comparison – in a dozen ways, the researcher's value preferences affect the shape of conclusions. Some of the values that commonly permeate political research are beliefs in efficiency, rationality, and (because we tend to deal with individuals outside of their social settings) individualism. More political values, such as belief in deregulation or in government intervention, are not uncommon in analytic work.

Recently, some writers on policy analysis have suggested a style of analysis that is closer to the cast of mind and style of work of Congressional committees than to traditional research. In this view analysis takes as its starting point not a situation but a policy argument. A policy argument is the 'reasons for the adoption of a policy' (Paris and Reynolds, 1983, 3). The analysis concentrates on testing the premises of the argument, both the empirical and normative premises. The analyst attempts to investigate the extent to which the claims embedded in the argument do, in fact, hold. A result of this mode of analysis would be not one 'truth', but a series of ratings of competing policy arguments as having more or less empirical legitimacy. Paris and Reynolds (1983) describe the endeavor as developing 'rational ideologies'.

Analysts in the Congressional Budget Office have been doing something similar for years. They talk to people involved in a policy community and find the range of arguments in currency. Then they seek evidence that reveals the extent to which each argument is supported or refuted. By being intentionally comparative, this style of analysis gives staff and legislators assessments not only of the strength or weakness of their own positions but also ammunition to use against the arguments of others. If they are considering dropping their own argument, it gives them grounds to choose an alternative. In addition, the analysts can canvass the situation in the policy arena that gave rise to the arguments and describe the parameters of the issue – which often differs from committee members' and staff's perceptions of the problem (Koretz, personal communication, 1984).

Other writers on policy analysis have been urging more overtly value-based analysis (Dunn, 1981; Fisher, 1983; Miller 1984). It has long been recommended that policy analysists make explicit the value assumptions that guide their work, rather than allow value premises to sneak under the tent, unrecognised by client *or* analyst. Some of the newer work suggests further that policy analysts consciously develop a vision of a desirable future and analyse the steps necessary to move toward that future. Miller (1984) calls such an approach 'design science'. When objectives are widely shared (or seem to be), this type of analytic approach has been common practice, e.g. in seeking means to reduce water pollution or trade deficits. What current writers seem to be calling for is policy analysis that self-consciously departs from the mainstream status quo assumptions that have dominated analysis in the past and instead allies itself with efforts at significant social change. They do not want analysis to sacrifice either method or rigor. On the contrary. But they want analysis to widen the range of alternative futures visible to policy makers and to model and test strategies that hold promise of attaining them.

To critics, the call has the ring of ideological arrogance. Who are analysts, either of the left or the right or perched on some altogether different political axis, to determine the ends (as well as the means) of political action? Yet analysis has always had political content, often of liberal intent and conservative effect. Whatever the merits of the various contentions that have recently surged into print, current writing at least represents a serious effort to go beyond the old-style injunctions to 'be politically feasible'. Scholars are trying to adapt the methods and theory of analysis to fit the realities of political decision making. They are trying to integrate normative, empirical, and action components into analysis.

Integration of normative, empirical, and action elements should have intuitive appeal to Congressional staff, and to other decision makers who deal in complex currency. The Congressional committee, in fact, might be a particular good audience, because much more than a bureaucratic agency, it represents a range of political predilections and might well be receptive to an equally wide-ranging analytic menu. When analysis makes values explicit, rigorously analyses good data, and makes clear the implications for action, the results tend to fit the staff's needs for coherent policy packaging.

Members of Congress and Congressional staff probably need to make some adaptations as well. Before the recent budget crisis, their zeal was directed at getting bills through, no matter what their consequences. The need to cut government spending has slowed the tide of legislation, but when the crisis recedes, they may fall into old patterns. It would be well to take this opportunity for reappraisal. The continuing expansion of Congressional oversight responsibilities (Aberbach, 1980) should alert Congress to the endemic shortfalls between what was planned and what resulted from prior legislation. A more ardent concern with consequences could have a healthy effect on staff use of analysis.

The outlook for a more productive mesh of Congressional staff work and policy analysis is by no means bleak. A variety of efforts are under way to shape policy analysis to the political environment. Congressional staff, surrounded as they are by analysts in all the support agencies on the Hill, are growing increasingly familiar with analytic techniques and arguments. But committee staff and analysts have different job descriptions and they will inevitably continue doing different jobs.

NOTES

1 Much of the work of the Congress is done in subcommittees. For the sake of simplicity, I use the word 'committee' to refer to both committees and subcommittees.
2 Select and special committees are a special case. Since few of them have authority to authorize legislation, their influence comes through creating publicity for an issue. In this cause, they may do considerable sophisticated analysis of the scope and dimensions of the issue under their aegis. The Senate Select Committee on Aging is a good example.
3 Salisbury and Shepsle (1981) calculated the frequency of staff turnover when members leave the House and Senate. Turnover of committee staff, while not as high as personal staff, is noticeable.
4 Furthermore, since most laws leave details of implementation to the operating agency and its rules and regulations, much analysis seems extraneous to the legislative project. Staff says 'Let the agency figure that out' (and of course, reap the criticism that accompanies the definition of specifics).
5 This is the exact reason why nonpartisan staff early gave way to separate majority and minority staffs. Members wanted staff who shared their values and political concerns.

REFERENCES

Aberbach, Joel, 'Changes in Congressional Oversight', in Carol H. Weiss and A. H. Barton (eds.), *Making Bureaucracies Work*, Beverly Hills, Sage, 1980, pp. 65–87.
Andringa, Robert C., 'Eleven Factors Influencing Federal Education Legisla-

tion', in *Federalism At the Crossroads: Improving Educational Policymaking*, Washington, D.C., Institute for Educational Leadership, 1976.

Boruch, Robert F. and Laura C. Leviton, 'Contributions of Evaluation to Education Programs and Policy', *Evaluation Review*, vol. 7, No. 5, October 1983, pp. 563–98.

Davidson, Roger H., 'Congressional Committees: The Toughest Customers', *Policy Analysis*, vol. 2 (Spring 1976), pp. 299–323.

Davidson, Roger H., 'Subcommittee Government: New Channels for Policy Making', in T. E. Mann and N. J. Ornstein (eds.), *The New Congress*, Washington, D. C., American Enterprise Institute, 1981, pp. 99–133.

Dreyfus, Daniel A., 'The Limitations of Policy Research in Congressional Decision Making', in Carol H. Weiss (ed.), *Using Social Research in Public Policy Making*, Lexington, MA., D. C. Heath, 1977, pp. 99–108.

Dunn, William N., *Public Policy Analysis: An Introduction*, Englewood Cliffs, N.J., Prentice-Hall, Inc., 1981.

Fenno, Richard F., *Home Style: House Members in their Districts*, Boston, Little Brown, 1978.

Fisher, Frank, 'Methodological Foundations for Public Policy Analysis: A Review Essay', *Policy Studies Journal*, vol. 12, No. 2, December 1983, pp. 399–409.

Fox, Harrison, W. Jr. and Susan W. Hammond, *Congressional Staffs: The Invisible Force in American Lawmaking*, New York, Free Press, 1977.

Hayes, Cheryl D. (ed.), *Making Policies for Children: A Study of the Federal Process*, Washington, D.C., National Academy Press, 1982.

Heclo, Hugh, 'Issue Networks and the Executive Establishment', in Anthony King (ed.), *The New American Political System*, Washington, D.C., American Enterprise Institute, 1978, pp. 87–124.

Hicks, Ronald Lee, 'Sunset Legislation', in F. M. Zweig, *Evaluation in Legislation*, Beverly Hills, Sage, 1979, pp. 17–27.

Jones, Charles O., 'Why Congress Can't Do Policy Analysis (or words to that effect)', *Policy Analysis*, vol. 2, (Spring 1976), pp. 251–64.

Kingdon, John W., *Agendas, Alternatives, and Public Policies*, Boston, Little, Brown, 1984.

Kofmehl, Kenneth, *Professional Staffs of Congress*, West Lafayette, Ind., Purdue University Press, 1962. (Also 1977, 3rd edition.)

Koretz, Daniel (Congressional Budget Office), personal letter, October 9, 1984.

Lindblom, Charles E., *The Policy Making Process*, Englewood Cliffs, New Jersey, Prentice-Hall, 1968.

Malbin, Michael J., *Unelected Representatives: Congressional Staff and the Future of Representative Government*, New York, Basic Books, Inc., 1980.

March, James G., 'Bounded Rationality, Ambiguity, and the Engineering of Choice', *Bell Journal of Economics*, vol. 9, No. 2 (Autumn 1978), pp. 587–608.

Miller, Trudi C., 'Conclusion: A Design Science Perspective', in T. C. Miller (ed.), *Public Sector Performance: A Conceptual Turning Point*, Baltimore, Md., Johns Hopkins Press, 1984, pp. 251–68.

Paris, David C., and James F. Reynolds, *The Logic of Inquiry*, Longman, 1983.

Patterson, Samuel C., 'The Professional Staffs of Congressional Committees', *Administration Science Quarterly*, vol. 15 (March 1970), pp. 22–37.

Redman, Eric, *The Dance of Legislation*, New York, Simon and Schuster, 1973.

112   Carol H. Weiss

Ripley, Randall B., *Power in the Senate*, New York, St Martin's Press, 1969, pp. 201–2.
Salisbury, Robert H., and Kenneth A. Shepsle, 'U.S. Congressman as Enterpise', *Legislative Studies Quarterly*, vol. 6 (November 1981), pp. 559–76.
Schick, Allen, 'The Supply and Demand for Analysis on Capitol Hill', *Policy Analysis*, vol. 2 (Spring 1976), pp. 215–34.
Schick, Allen, 'Complex Policymaking in the United States Senate', in *Policy Analysis on Major Issues*, a compilation of papers prepared for the Commission on the Operation of the Senate, 94th Congress, 2nd session. Washington, D.C., U.S. Government Printing Office, 1977a.
Schick, Allen, 'Environment, Energy, and Economics: A Seminar Conducted by the Congressional Research Service', in *Policy Analysis on Major Issues*, Commission on the Operation of the Senate, 94th Congress, 2nd session. Washington, D.C., U.S. Government Printing Office, 1977b.
Smith, Steven S., and C. J. Deering, *Committees in Congress*, Washington, D.C., Congressional Quarterly Press, 1984.
U.S. House of Representatives, Commission on Administrative Review, *Final Report*, 95th Congress, 1st session, vol. 2, 1977.
Verdier, James M., 'Advising Congressional Decision-Makers', *Journal of Policy Analysis and Management*, vol. 3, no. 3, (1984), pp. 421–438.
Weinberg, Hillel, 'Using Policy Analysis in Congressional Budgeting', in F. M. Zweig (ed.) *Evaluation in Legislation*, Beverly Hills, Sage, 1979, pp. 28–44.
Weiss, Carol H. (with Michael J. Bucuvalas),, *Social Science Research and Decision-Making*, New York, Columbia University Press, 1980.
Weiss, Carol H., *The Consequences of the Study of Federal Student Loan Programs: A Case Study in Research Utilization*, New York, Columbia University, Bureau of Applied Social Research, 1970.
Zweig, Franklin M., 'On Educating the Congress for Evaluation', in F. M. Zweig and K. E. Marvin (eds.), *Educating Policymakers for Evaluation*, Beverly Hills: Sage 1981, pp. 16–36.

CHAPTER 8

Social-science training as related to the policy roles of US career officials and appointees: the decline of analysis

COLIN CAMPBELL and DONALD NAULLS

It has become an old saw that a virtual explosion of interest in the social sciences took place in the 1960s. This was felt more intensely in the U.S. than in any other nations. Undergraduates pursued social science majors much more than in any previous generation. As well, unprecedented proportions of these went on to seek MA and PhD degrees in their chosen specialities. Many of those who completed their advanced work assumed the myriad positions in high schools, colleges and universities freshly created to satisfy burgeoning student demand for social science courses. In that respect, the various disciplines enjoyed through the 1960s breeder expansion. That is, the market for their courses seemed to grow exponentially with the availability of trained personnel.

Such salad days have long since passed. The circumstances surrounding any market for academic credentials would suggest, of course, that a glut of graduates at all levels would eventually develop. In the case of the social sciences, the market became sated by the early 1970s. All of the major professional associations became concerned about the growing surfeit of PhDs. Even the most prestigious departments began to find that all but their very best graduate students were unemployable. Thus, associations and top programs turned by reflex to government as a market for PhDs which might still provide some potential for growth. To be sure, many jobs were found within the public sector at all levels. However, one fact presented itself with unremitting clarity. Government had already greatly expanded its use of social scientists with advanced degrees. In fact, it trailed only slightly behind education in the path towards its saturation point.

Even now that we are well into the 1980s, the impact of the influx of social scientists into government remains unclear. On the numerical level, they have made their presence felt. By the early 1970s, data collected by Aberbach, Putnam and Rockman suggested that in the U.S. around one-third of both career civil servants and political appointees in top posts had earned social science degrees (1981, 52). Campbell reported in 1983 the results of a comparative study of officials working in departments and agencies responsible for government-wide co-ordination and control in the U.S., U.K. and Canada. He found that 51 per cent of his U.S. respondents had received graduate degrees in social science fields as compared to 27 and 37 per cent for, respectively, their British and Canadian opposite numbers (329). The bulk of the American officials had done their advanced work in economics or political science.

In notional terms, the social scientific approach to public issues had for a number of decades appealed to the institution builders who had framed or expanded central agencies such as the Bureau of the Budget (BOB) or co-ordinative units within operational departments. Berman reports that Harold Smith, the director of BOB when it moved from the Department of the Treasury to the Executive Office of the President in 1939, held social scientists in especially high esteem. Smith commented in his diary:

> ... BOB has some 50 vacant positions ... we are having the devil's own time in securing persons with sufficiently broad background and experiences, who at the same time have balanced outlook and judgement concerning governmental problems ... More and more I am impressed with the value of broad training in the social sciences and the development of people with planning types of minds (Berman, 1979, 20).

Heclo has spoken in a similar vein regarding officials working in staff units that report directly to agency heads. These officials, who remain the most enduring legacy of the 1960s Planning, Programming and Budgeting System, pride themselves in intellectual acuity and detachment:

> ... such analysts are often the agency head's only institutional resource for thinking about substantive policy without commitments to the constituents, jurisdictions, and self-interests of existing programs ... Many are likely to identify themselves as "partisans for more rational decisionmaking" or "part of a professional analytic group laying out and evaluating the options" (Heclo, 1977, 151).

Changing times

More than simply the glut of social scientists in government has modified the marketability of their training within the bureaucracy. On the one hand, the era of stringency has substantially altered the nature of policy decisions. On the other, executive-bureaucratic politics both in departments and at the center of government have intensified to the point where many officials find that gamesmanship counts more than analysis in most assessments of options.

The effects of fiscal stringency on the relevance of elaborate analyses have not escaped the attention of those who were skeptical of their practical force within decision processes to begin with. For instance, Aaron Wildavsky makes the point that governments have moved increasingly toward adoption of blunt instruments for controlling public expenditure as the proportion of gross national product. In the process, he maintains, the political leaderships' shift of focus from the 'quality' to 'quantity' of spending puts analysis largely under eclipse (Wildavsky, 1983, 181).

Campbell has cautioned elsewhere that the near demise of analytic budgeting might be greatly exaggerated (Campbell, 1986, in press). That is, the cloud of stringency will lift someday. If, by then, analytic shops have not atrophied completely, political leaders will turn again to rigorously trained policy assessors. They will need expert guidance on how to resolve conflicting claims for new resources which inevitably arise under more robust fiscal circumstances than currently prevail. They will also encounter a sobering irony. Posterity will pay a heavy toll for our current era. That is, the very strain of political leadership which has wailed the loudest about the size of government will leave a state apparatus greatly weakened in its ability to identify and root out inefficiency and ineffectiveness.

The rise of executive-bureaucratic gamesmanship among analysts stems both from the stringent times and a transformation in the very nature of political administration. The first factor concerns the politicisation of agencies; the second centers on individual officials' role socialisation. Both elements interact considerably. To begin, stringent times, as noted by Allen Schick, normally work to erode the neutrality of budget analysis (1980, 94–5). Increasingly, the budget becomes simply a 'decisional' instrument for constraining programmatic choices through broad-stroke imperatives. The analyst becomes more a repository and enforcer of the political will than a clarifier of options.

In the U.S., the movement toward politicisation has become especially acute. Notwithstanding the fact that the American system already provided a very wide berth for political appointees, presidents have increasingly tended to add to the layers of such positions within departments and to base the distribution of these posts on the ideological purity of aspirants. Two Republican presidents, Richard Nixon and Ronald Reagan, adopted these approaches with the greatest singlemindedness (Nathan, 1983). Nixon, of course, simply fueled fears that he sought to imperalise the presidency (Nathan, 1975). Reagan, through a fortuitous combination of personal bonhomie and a swing in the public mood toward conservative policies, managed to receive praise rather than criticism for pursuing – indeed, more energetically and effectively – the same strategy (Newland, 1983 and Moe, 1985).

Very dramatic changes have taken place throughout this century in officials' views of their bureaucratic roles. Writing in the early part of this century, Max Weber fully grasped the degree to which bureaucrats wielded political power (1946 translation, 232). Yet, reformers seemed only to fasten upon Weber's conceptualisation of civil service as a quasi-vocational commitment. In the United Kingdom, the effective dichotomy between bureaucratic and political career routes gave the permanent civil servant an monopoly over the administrative resources of the state (Chapman and Greenaway, 1980, 53, 62; and, Christoph, 1975, 32–6). In the U.S., the founding fathers of public administration as a profession all upheld a similar politics–management dichotomy (Wilson, 1941 reprint, 493–5; Goodnow, 1900, 92–3; Gulick, 1937, 10). By the 1950s, however, cracks began to appear in the wall – at least, in the U.S.. Simon, for instance, allowed that both politicians and bureaucrats involve themselves in policy decisions (1957, 57–8). Public servants, however, try to stick to the factual issues behind the options. Similarly, Shubert maintained that officials distinguish themselves within the policy process in the degree to which they base their assessments on professional and informed analysis (1960).

Strangely, this is precisely the point where our story line begins to thicken. At the very time in which analysis was establishing itself as a distinctive element to decision making, writers began to voice doubts about the neutrality of permanent bureaucracies. Hugh Heclo and Aaron Wildavsky coined the term 'political administrator' in registering their conclusion that Whitehall mandarins partook freely in executive-bureaucratic gamesmanship of the very highest order (1974, 3). Several of the most prominent students of American public administration wrote compellingly of the effects of public-service willfulness in shaping the contours of most policies (Landau, 1962, 10; Holden, 1966, 944; and, Kaufman, 1969, 4–5).

Aberbach, Putnam and Rockman have taken us further than any other authors in pinpointing the consequences of the drift in bureaucrats' perceptions of their roles from strict managerial or analytic foci to political administration (1981, Ch. 1). They employ the term 'Image III' to designate permanent officials who freely associate their functions with policy-making. Such individuals, however, do distinguish themselves from appointees in the form that their involvement in policy normally assumes. They tend to be specialists rather than generalists. Thus, they normally mediate narrower concerns as expressed by formalised groups rather than broad-based representations – some of which would be made by the unorganised. As well, they tend to prize analytic criteria for decisions. Thus, they will normally eschew passionate, partisan, idealistic or ideological approaches to issues.

This chapter looks one step beyond the usual habitat of Image III officials. It examines orientations to policy roles among appointees and career civil servants alike who shoulder special responsibilities toward coordination and control throughout government. Not unrelatedly, these same officials gain entry to work worlds in which they become strongly associated with ultimate executive authority as embodied in the presidency. Many – in particular appointees – take on the aura of personal association with the president. Others can freely invoke the president's name – even without an explicit remit – simply because their agency serves as custodian of his prerogatives.

In either case, 'Image IV' officials – as Aberbach, Putnam and Rockman term them – must take on a wider span of mediation than 'Image III' bureaucrats. Most significantly – for this chapter, even rigorously trained permanent officials working in a milieu dominated by 'Image IV' will become engrossed in the gamesmanship of executive-bureaucratic integration at the center of government. They begin, thus, to value their skills in this enterprise more than analytic detachment.

The data and some theoretical expectations

Our current analysis will focus on central agents' reports of their involvement in two roles, namely policy-making and facilitation. The former of these fits entirely within the compass of Image IV while the latter bridges Images III and IV. Along the way we will ascertain the effects that various blocks of influences have on respondents' association with the two roles. These include 'positional circumstances and activities', 'career orientations', 'career routes', 'education', and 'socio-demographic backgrounds'. This format, thus, allows us to assess the relationships between professional training in the social sciences and officials' association of themselves with policy-making and facilitation within the broader context of other influences on respondents' identification with these approaches.

The interviews from which our data derive concentrated on officials working in the White House Office, the Executive Office of the President – including the Office of Management and Budget, the Department of the Treasury and the Office of Personnel Management. These agencies possess or share the lead in three dimensions to central coordination and control in the U.S. executive branch. These responsibilities include: (1) mapping out administration strategies and assuring that key substantive positions and initiatives taken in operational departments adhere to these; (2) developing and integrating economic and fiscal policies; and (3) allocating and managing physical and human resources. The field work for this study occurred from April to August 1979 during the Carter administration and from November 1982 to June 1983 during Ronald Reagan's first term.

Insofar as the numbers of respondents support statistically separate treatment, we will distinguish in the analysis between five groups. The first of these, taking in 69 officials, were *career* civil servants working in central agencies during the Carter administration. These respondents occupied positions in the first two permanent bureaucratic layers below the levels filled by political appointees. Time and resources did not permit sampling a second career group which would have allowed us to probe differences within this cohort during the Carter and Reagan administrations.

Under Carter, 63 interviews covered political appointees. This group further divides into *amphibians* and *politicos*. The former respondents received their positions by virtue of a mix of the correct ideological coloration, service to the party through involvement in political operations *and* expertise within some substantive issue area. Politicos, on the other hand, claimed no specialised knowledge or experience in a policy field sufficient to play a significant role in their securing an administration appointment. Thirty-eight Carter appointees were amphibians and 25 were politicos. The same breakdown among Reagan appointees yielded 29 amphibians and 31 politicos.

With respect to our theoretical expectations, several propositions suggest themselves. First, we might assume that – as we move from politicos through amphibians to career officials – we will find a decreasing inclination on the part of respondents to claim explicit policy-making roles. When we move in the opposite direction, however, we might find a decreasing level of identification with facilitation. Second, we might anticipate that professional certification in social sciences will manifest itself strongly among clusters of influences operating toward the career group's preference for facilitation. Third, in comparisons between Carter and Reagan appointees, we might detect greater educational effects in the former group. That is, the Reagan administration's relative discipline and ideological homogeneity might have weakened the links between respondents' subject-matter expertise and role perceptions.

Policy-making and facilitation

We tapped several items from our interview schedule in an effort to ascertain the degree to which respondents identify with policymaking and facilitating. Insofar as they see themselves as facilitators, officials will stress the view that their involvement in the policy process centers on attempts to simplify and expedite decisions. On the other hand, respondents who style themselves as policy-makers will render their roles as engaging in substantial ways their personal concerns about the direction of the administration and/or the federal government. Here appointees would refer directly to their attempts to follow through on a president's mandate; and permanent civil servants would acknowledge explicitly the strategies they adopt to safeguard the 'long-term' interests of the presidency and the executive branch.

Two additive variables convey the degree to which respondents described their roles in ways which fit the policymaking or facilitation approaches. With respect to the former, officials received one point each for any of the following types of involvement with policy-making: setting strategic plans for the administration; establishing priorities among substantive policy objectives; and, central co-ordination of expenditure budgeting. In addition, officials gained one point if they specifically characterised themselves as policymakers and one point if they claimed responsibility toward the entire mandate of their agency.

Regarding facilitation, respondents obtained one point for each of 17 possible specialised policy sectors toward which they claimed some co-ordinative responsibilities. Similarly, they were assigned one point for each of six possible characterisations of policy roles which dealt with various dimensions to facilitation. These would include such activities as helping to make sure that the policy process runs smoothly or maintaining lines of communication inside and outside of government. Finally, points were added to respondents' facilitation scores for each mention of responsibilities toward five possible dimensions to their agencies' work short of the entire mandate.

Table 1 summarises the means and standard deviations for career officials, Carter amphibians and politicos, and Reagan amphibians and politicos under the 'policy-maker' and 'facilitator' headings. It becomes clear that officials and the two appointive groups under Carter ascribed to themselves policy-making roles to much the same degree. That is, the average scores of 2.3 attained by amphibians and politicos exceed only slightly the comparable figure for the permanent civil servants which was 2.1. In the case of all three groups, respondents – on average – scored

Table 1 *Policy-making and facilitation indices*

	Carter career	Carter amphibian	Carter politico	Reagan amphibian	Reagan politico
Respondents	69	38	25	29	31
per cent	35.9	19.8	13.0	15.1	16.1
Policy-making index					
Mean	2.1	2.3	2.3	3.4	3.4
Standard Deviation	1.0	1.0	1.2	1.1	1.2
Facilitation index					
Mean	3.3	3.4	3.2	3.6	3.4
Standard Deviation	1.1	1.4	1.2	1.2	1.1

roughly a full point more on the facilitation index. For the Carter group, thus, the expectation that politicos would register stronger orientations to policy-making than would amphibians and career officials, simply does not pertain. As well, a reverse pattern for facilitation – whereby career officials mark the strongest preferences for the role followed by amphibians and then politicos – fails to emerge.

The findings for the two appointive groups under Reagan fall almost entirely in line with those for their Carter opposite numbers regarding orientations toward facilitation. That is, amphibians made on average 3.6 mentions of activities associated with this role whereas politicos volunteered 3.4 references. However, the 3.4 average scores for both Reagan groups on the policy-making index exceed by 1.1 the comparable figures for their counterparts under Carter.

Influences on emphases of policy-making and facilitation

As noted above, we will assess the salience of social scientific education to orientations toward policymaking or facilitation in relation to other factors which might influence adoption of these roles. The entire series of variables includes, thus, those measuring positional circumstances and activities, career orientations, career routes, education and socio-demographic characteristics. Table 2 summarises the profiles of each of our respondent groups according to constituent elements of these five umbrella categories.

Positional factors

Eleven variables allow us to examine the positional elements to officials' role perceptions. Here we take a page from Aberbach, Putnam and Rockman. Essentially, the variables attempt to gauge the extent to which our respondents have gotten themselves into the 'policy net'. If they do business continually with the president, cabinet secretaries, top departmental officials and congressional leaders, officials will tend – Aberbach, Putnam and Rockman maintain – to register relatively strong identification with policymaking (1981, 203). With regards to our central concern – the carryover of social-scientific training to role perceptions, the sheer moment of respondents' engagement in the policy net might override any personal preferences for analytic detachment in the treatment of policy issues (Campbell and Szablowski, 1979, 12–3).

The first of the measures in this section taps the degree to which respondents styled their interactions with the president, and the heads and officials three tiers lower in the hierarchies of their own and other departments as occurring on a regular basis. Officials could receive a total of nine points under this heading. The results from this index suggest that Carter politicos, with an average score of 4.4, adopted the widest compass in regular contacts. They were followed closely by Carter amphibians (3.9). The Carter career group along with both politicos and amphibians under Reagan produced average scores ranging somewhat lower – that is, between 2.8 and 3.0. The Carter respondent groups – with the exception of career officials – performed slightly better than did the Reagan ones with regard to another variable listed under positional circumstances and activities. Carter amphibians and politicos both average 7.2 levels of contact in which most relations concern policy. This contrasts with 6.9 and 6.7 average levels of contact over policy issues acknowledged by, respectively, Reagan amphibians and politicos.

The findings concerning the points at which respondents maintain regular contact and the degree to which such relations concern policy understate, if anything, the extent to which the Reagan groups outstripped their opposite numbers in the Carter administration. Both Reagan politicos and amphibians claim twice the annual frequency of interactions with the president and cabinet-level officials reported by their counterparts under Carter. They more than replicated these performances in their renderings of annual interactions at sub-cabinet levels within departments and agencies. In the case of both of these frequency variables, Reagan politicos apparently enjoyed considerably more access than did amphibians. While politicos benefited from a similar edge under Carter, the margins were narrower. As well, career officials under

Table 2 *Possible influences on roles*

Variables according to blocks	Mean (standard deviation)				
	Carter career	Carter amphibian	Carter politico	Reagan amphibian	Reagan politico
Positional circumstances and activities					
Personal interaction					
regularity (nine	2.8	3.9	4.4	2.8	3.0
possible levels)	(1.8)	(1.7)	(1.5)	(1.8)	(1.6)
Agency-head contact	81.8	221.1	374.4	462.1	796.6
(annual frequency)	(127.0)	(179.2)	(162.7)	(421.8)	(599.9)
Contact on policy	6.2	7.2	7.2	6.9	6.7
(# of levels)	(2.1)	(2.1)	(1.9)	(2.2)	(2.5)
Sub-agency head					
contact	256.1	424.3	450.6	1070.0	1306.5
(annual frequency)	(231.2)	(374.6)	(329.2)	(740.8)	(1248.6)
Quality of Cabinet					
Committee attendance					
Not regular (%)	92.7	86.8	72.0	44.8	51.6
Regular (%)	7.3	13.1	28.0	55.2	48.4
Cabinet Committee					
attendance	2.1	5.8	9.9	3.3	9.4
(frequency)	(7.1)	(12.9)	(18.7)	(9.4)	(20.4)
Interdepartmental					
Committee attendance	2.6	2.9	4.5	4.9	2.7
(# attend regularly)	(1.9)	(2.1)	(3.5)	(3.3)	(3.7)
Quality of					
interdepartmental					
involvement					
Passive (%)	47.8	36.8	24.0	72.4	77.4
Active (%)	52.2	63.2	76.0	27.6	22.6
Legislative contact	26.4	52.7	175.3	92.4	405.1
(annual frequency)	(60.8)	(89.0)	(170.4)	(147.9)	(710.3)
Congressional staff					
contact	29.9	53.0	84.3	32.4	187.4
(annual frequency)	(45.2)	(83.0)	(124.8)	(69.0)	(558.5)
Interest group	3.5	5.5	6.4	3.3	6.5
Sources	(2.3)	(3.2)	(4.0)	(2.8)	(4.2)
Career orientations					
Why they entered					
Idealism	.32	.21	.36	.14	.16
	(.47)	(.47)	(.49)	(.44)	(.37)
Scholastic	.48	.82	.28	1.0	.58
training	(.56)	(.61)	(.46)	(.73)	(.62)
Policy or political	.87	.87	1.2	.97	1.2
commitment	(.64)	(.81)	(.52)	(.68)	(.67)

Table 2 (*Cont.*)

Variables according to blocks	Carter career	Carter amphibian	Carter politico	Reagan amphibian	Reagan politico
			Mean (standard deviation)		
Why They Have Stayed					
Impact	1.35	1.66	1.20	2.10	1.30
	(.99)	(1.15)	(1.10)	(1.20)	(1.50)
Process	1.12	.87	1.12	1.89	1.68
	(.90)	(.91)	(.78)	(1.18)	(1.40)
Personal	1.04	1.34	1.24	1.45	1.90
satisfaction	(.85)	(.99)	(.60)	(1.30)	(1.17)
Career Routes					
Decision to enter					
government					
Before or during					
university (%)	76.8	34.2	64.0	55.2	54.8
Later (%)	23.2	65.8	36.0	44.8	45.2
Number of years in	17.6	6.8	4.6	9.6	7.9
government	(8.9)	(8.4)	(3.8)	(10.6)	(6.4)
Number of government	1.5	1.3	1.0	1.1	1.4
positions	(1.3)	(1.3)	(1.0)	(1.4)	(1.1)
Education					
University education					
undergraduate (%)	10.1	7.9	16.0	24.1	35.5
graduate or					
professional (%)	89.9	92.1	84.9	75.9	64.5
Undergraduate university					
Elite (%)	15.9	18.4	8.0	10.3	9.7
Non-elite (%)	84.1	81.6	92.0	89.7	90.3
Graduate university					
Elite (%)	40.6	44.7	28.0	17.2	19.4
Non-elite (%)	59.4	55.3	72.0	82.8	80.6
Undergraduate fields					
(% of responses)					
Political science	17.8	22.7	42.9	13.9	37.9
Economics	35.6	25.0	3.6	27.8	10.3
Social sciences	8.2	15.9	17.9	8.3	10.3
Other	38.4	36.4	35.7	50.0	41.4
Total number					
of responses	73	44	28	36	29
Graduate fields					
(% of responses)					
Political science	13.8	29.1	29.2	14.3	22.2
Economics	43.6	23.6	8.3	31.0	18.5
Social sciences	2.1	3.6	0.0	0.0	0.0
Other	40.4	43.6	62.5	54.8	59.3

Table 2 (*Cont.*)

Variables according to blocks	Mean (standard deviation)				
	Carter career	Carter amphibian	Carter politico	Reagan amphibian	Reagan politico
Total number of responses	94	55	24	42	27
Socio-demographic characteristics					
Age	46.5	40.3	36.4	46.4	41.8
	(7.7)	(8.4)	(5.2)	(8.1)	(6.8)
Sex					
Male (%)	94.2	78.9	96.0	96.4	87.1
Female (%)	5.8	21.1	4.0	3.4	12.9
Regional roots					
Periphery (%)	59.4	57.9	72.0	82.1	79.3
Core (%)	40.6	42.1	28.0	17.9	20.7
Father's occupation					
Professional (%)	27.7	34.2	33.3	39.3	24.1
Managerial (%)	23.2	28.9	45.8	17.9	48.3
White collar (%)	10.8	13.2	8.3	10.7	6.9
Blue collar (%)	30.8	18.4	12.5	28.6	20.7
Farmer (%)	7.7	5.3	0.0	3.6	0.0
Religious preference					
Roman Catholic (%)	30.4	15.8	16.0	24.1	25.8
Protestant (%)	43.5	36.8	48.0	51.7	61.3
Jewish (%)	15.9	34.2	20.0	10.3	9.7
None (%)	10.1	13.2	16.0	13.8	3.2
Secondary school education					
Public (%)	79.1	78.9	72.0	86.2	80.6
Private (%)	20.9	21.6	28.0	13.8	19.4

Carter fell somewhat short even of amphibians in both variables. For example – with regard to interactions at the presidential and cabinet levels, the average career respondent reported 8.18 contacts per year as against 221.1 for Carter amphibians.

Meetings, of course, provide one of the main forums for officials' engagement in policy nets. Here the peculiarities of the two administrations come to bear (Newland, 1983; Campbell, 1986: in press). The Carter administration minimised the use of exclusive and regularised cabinet-level bodies. It preferred ad hoc groups designed to resolve specific policy issues. On the other hand, the Reagan administration followed in the first term one of the most routinized cabinet committee systems ever to operate in the US.

These differences in the approaches of the two presidents perhaps explain the somewhat contradictory data concerning our respondents' involvement with interdepartmental committees. In response to probes as to whether officials viewed their attendance at cabinet-level bodies as regular, 48 per cent of Reagan as against 28 per cent of Carter politicos answered affirmatively. With the amphibians, the gap widened to 55 per cent under Reagan as compared to 13 per cent under Carter. Yet, both Carter groups yielded higher annual frequencies of attendance at meetings which included cabinet-level officials than did the Reagan groups. As well, they tended much more than did their opposite numbers to characterise their participation in such gatherings as active rather than passive.

In the U.S., of course, policy nets extend beyond the executive-bureaucratic complex. The fragmented nature of the system forces officials to develop especially strong and regularised links with legislators, congressional staff members and interest-group representatives. Scholars have termed the resulting issue communities 'subgovernments', or, in their more rigid variants, 'iron triangles' (Ripley and Franklin, 1980; Rose, 1976: 161; King, 1978, 388–95). In fact, Aberbach and Rockman have discovered strong evidence of convergence in the socialisation of top federal executives and congressmen into a common political entrepreneurship. This stems from shared experiences within policy nets that overlap the executive branch, Congress and interest groups (1977, 23–47).

Among our respondents, it becomes clear that politicos under both administrations maintained stronger ties with legislators and congressional staff than did amphibians. In turn, both amphibian groups reported more frequent interactions at these levels than did career officials. The fact that Reagan politicos appeared considerably more active than even their counterparts under Carter probably reflects the emphasis in the former's White House of 'implementation'. This involved following administration decisions through with intense and concerted congressional liaison. The approach, however, did not entail heightened efforts to sell Reagan administration positions directly to interest groups. It comes as no surprise, thus, that Reagan and Carter politicos took similar compasses for consultation with those outside government. Relatedly, Reagan amphibians proved less expansive about contracts with interest groups than even career officials under Carter.

Career orientations

The variables which probe officials' career orientations derived from two questions. First, what motivated respondents to enter the public service? Second, what did they consider to be their most important accomplishments since entering government? All six variables listed under this heading in Table 2 allowed for the fact that officials might have stressed more than simply one element of the dimensions being tapped.

With respect to their reasons for entering government, all of the respondent groups except Reagan amphibians gave the greatest weight to a desire to influence policy and/or some sort of political commitment from among the three broad motivational categories. The appropriateness of respondents' scholastic training to a public-service career played the next greatest role. Interestingly, both amphibian groups stressed such motives even more than did our career respondents. This finding fits entirely with the criteria employed in the appointment of amphibians. As well, Carter politicos emphasised this factor much less than did their equivalents under Reagan. In the case of all five groups, idealistic goals – such as serving the public – drew relatively little comment.

The responses concerning why officials have stayed in government proved to be more evenly distributed. For instance, both career officials and Carter amphibians gave the nod most to having an impact within a policy field as a major factor behind their desire to continue. Yet, many in both groups acknowledged the relevance of their influence on the governmental process and/or personal benefits – lifestyle or psychic – as reasons for remaining in government. Carter politicos practically gave equal weight to all three factors. Their equivalents under Reagan made the most mention of personal benefits. On the other hand, Reagan amphibians yielded higher proportions than any other group citing their impact on a policy sector and contribution to the decision processes as reasons behind their desire to remain in government.

Career routes

Robert Putnam and Ezra Suleiman have studied public servants in two traditional bureaucratic systems. Respectively, these are Italy and France. In both cases, officials follow sharply defined career routes. Insofar as their experiences have not involved work in strategic and coordinative units – such as the French cabinets, they continue to espouse the dichotomy of policy and administration (Putnam, 1973, 268, 271; Suleiman, 1974, 117).

Obviously U.S. career officials fit the traditional mold much more than do appointees. This fact pertains even to central agents. Our career official group provided the highest proportion claiming that they decided upon their careers before leaving university (76.8 per cent) and yielded the longest average tenure in government service (17.6 years). In keeping with the relative lack of mobility between units and departments within the U.S. bureaucracy (Heclo, 1977, 116–20), our career respondents have served, on average, in only 1.5 previous positions. Among the appointive groups, Reagan amphibians and politicos both decided upon government careers fairly soon and pointed to a relatively large number of years actually in government. Even though they had by 1979 accumulated, on average, 6.8 years of experience, Carter amphibians chose to enter government relatively late in life. Carter politicos, on the other hand, sought careers early on but had only accumulated, on average, 4.6 years actually in place.

Education

Education stands at the heart of this current examination. Our analysis takes in several variables. These concern whether respondents completed graduate or professional school after their undergraduate degrees, whether they attended Ivy League institutions at either level, and their fields of study.

Large majorities of all five groups received graduate or professional degrees. However, the percentages for the Reagan groups – 75.9 per cent for amphibians and 64.5 per cent for politicos – fell somewhat short of those for the others. These latter had ranged between 84.9 and 92.1 per cent. In all groups, fewer respondents than we might expect attended Ivy League schools during their undergraduate years. This was especially the case with Carter politicos and both Reagan groups. Over 40 per cent of both career officials and Carter amphibians did, however, receive graduate or professional degrees from Ivy League universities.

Well over half of respondents in all groups but Reagan amphibians took at least one social science bachelor's degree. The Reagan amphibians split evenly between those who did and did not complete social science undergraduate programs. Regarding specific disciplines, the two politico groups favored economics strongly. Carter amphibians divided almost equally between political science and economics, and Reagan amphibians preferred economics somewhat. Career officials took undergraduate degrees in economics exactly twice as frequently as they did in political science. Only the two Carter appointive groups produced more than 15 per cent citing a major in social science apart from political science or economics.

With respect to graduate and professional studies, all appointive groups except Carter amphibians produced less than 50 per cent with social science degrees. This finding largely owes to the attractiveness of law degrees among appointees (Campbell, 1983, 328–31). The two Carter groups gave the greatest emphasis to political science, although a solid proportion – 23.6 per cent – of amphibians' degrees were in economics. Reagan amphibians stressed economics. Their politico colleagues divided more evenly between political science and economics. Career officials gave a very clear edge to economics.

Socio-demographic characteristics

No bureaucratic elite constitutes a mirror image of the general populace. However, some are more representative than others. As well, an earlier school of thought in administrative behavior maintained that individuals' socio-demographic characteristics influence their adoption of roles within the executive-bureaucratic arena (Long, 1952, 810). This study includes among these background factors, age, sex, regional roots, father's occupation, religious preference and secondary education.

Regarding age, career officials and Reagan amphibians averaged slightly over 46 years. Carter amphibians and Reagan politicos followed at just over 40. True to their youngish image, Carter politicos had an average of 36 years. All of the groups except Carter amphibians contained fewer than 20 per cent women. Indeed, the proportions of women among career officials, Carter politicos and Reagan amphibians proved very small. Over forty per cent of both career officials and Carter amphibians hailed from the north-east U.S. The figures for the other groups – especially, the Reagan appointees – fell considerably short of 40 per cent.

While substantial percentages of all groups classified their father's occupations as professional, Reagan amphibians provided the highest proportion (39) and career officials produced the smallest (28). The over 45 per cent of Carter and Reagan politicos whose fathers worked in managerial positions considerably exceeds that for the other groups. Interestingly, Reagan amphibians almost equalled the 31 per cent of career officials whose fathers had blue-collar jobs. Career officials overrepresented Catholics slightly while the Carter groups fell roughly ten per cent short of the national average and their Reagan opposite numbers came out about on target. Jewish respondents make up a much larger proportion of all groups than obtains in the general populace.

However, this was especially the case with Carter amphibians. Carter politicos drew the largest proportion from private secondary sachools (28 per cent). Reagan amphibians again displayed relatively egalitarian roots with only 14 per cent having attended private high schools.

Regression analyses

Table 3 summarizes the results of analysis of variance for regression of our two dependent variables – namely, 'policy-maker' and 'facilitator' – on the influences discussed in the above section. This analysis assesses the effects of the five blocks of independent variables. The figures under the heading 'zero order' represent the variance in respondents' orientations to a role explained when an influence cluster is entered alone in a regression equation. The results under 'unique effects' account for the variance explained by the cluster when other blocks of independent variables are held constant.

Unfortunately we had to collapse the Carter and Reagan appointive complements in order to conduct this phase of the analysis. Otherwise, the group sizes would not sustain this multivariate approach. The upshot of such pooling leaves us with three reasonably even contingents. That is, we have 69 career officials, 63 Carter appointees and 60 Reagan appointees.

The figure for the regression of 'policy-maker' on the five influence clusters turned out as fairly robust. In each regression, the factors taken together account for over 20 per cent of the variance. Indeed, the total explained variance in the Reagan regression amounts to almost 37 per cent. In the case of permanent officials, career orientations work the strongest zero-order effects (11 per cent). Educational factors and socio-demographic characteristics follow closely, respectively, at nine and eight per cent. An examination of the unique effects, however, widens the gap between career orientations, and the educational and socio-demographic clusters. Also, it uncovers the fact that the positional block wields the most sway when other influences are held constant.

The zero-order regression of 'policy-maker' for the Carter appointees uncovers no influence group that exerts especially strong effects on its own. However, controls for other blocks suggest that socio-demographic (20 per cent), positional (16) and career orientation (14) factors all contribute fairly substantially to the adoption of policymaking roles. This pattern reemerges in the zero-order Reagan regression. In this case, however, the unique effects analysis indicates that the positional (19 per cent) and career orientation (17) blocks stand up the best under controls.

Table 3 *Analysis of variance for regression analysis*

Group of independent variables	Per cent variance explained		
	Carter career	Carter amphibian politico	Reagan amphibian politico
Zero order effects: policy-maker			
Positional circumstances and activities	5.8	2.8	20.3
Career orientation	11.2	6.0	16.0
Career routes	0.4	0.6	0.8
Education	9.0	3.7	8.4
Socio-demographic	8.1	3.4	12.1
Total explained by all variables	20.8	25.6	36.7
Unique effects*: Policy-maker			
Positional circumstances and activities	15.3	15.8	18.7
Career orientation	14.3	13.9	17.3
Career routes	1.2	2.1	5.5
Education	9.3	2.1	0.5
Socio-demographic	5.3	19.6	4.8
Zero order effects: facilitator			
Positional circumstances and activities	2.0	3.1	1.8
Career orientation	1.3	0.3	0.6
Career routes	2.5	2.8	4.9
Education	12.1	25.6	6.3
Socio-demographic	6.4	2.9	10.6
Total explained by all variables	14.0	31.1	17.4
Unique effects*: facilitator			
Positional circumstances and activities	6.3	6.7	14.2
Career orientation	5.3	5.4	16.7
Career routes	3.1	3.4	10.1
Education	6.8	16.4	6.2
Socio-demographic	0.8	3.8	9.4

*Equal to the additional variance explained by each set of variables *after* all other variables are in the equation.

The educational cluster fails to distinguish itself in either the Carter or Reagan regressions.

The regressions of 'facilitator' on the independent variables produced some very strong evidence of educational effects in the career and Carter groups. In fact, the educational block contributes much stronger effects than do the others in zero-order analysis. Among the Carter respondents, it attains clear dominance when we ascertain its unique effects. The Reagan regressions, on the other hand, suggest that the educational cluster finds, at best, a muted role. In fact, the unique-effects analyses underscore positional and career-oriented influences which parallel those which operated on Reagan appointees' association with policy-making roles.

Table 4 presents the effects of each constituent element of the influence clusters on career officials', Carter appointees' and Reagan appointees' adoption of policymaking or facilitating. Standardised co-efficients depict the relative weight of individual variables when 'policy-maker' or 'facilitator' are regressed on each block. In the cases of father's occupation and religion, the indicators which make up the subset of a cluster derive from mutually exclusive categories. According to regres-sion protocol, we therefore, excluded from our equations the category into which the largest proportion of respondents fit. For example, 'blue collar' becomes the 'reference' variable among career officials for the subset 'father's' occupation in the socio-demographic cluster.

With respect to influences on career officials' views of themselves as policymakers, undergraduate training in political science presents itself as the strongest positive influence on our respondents' adoption of the role (the standardised coefficient of .571 is significant at the 0.5 level). As well, permanent officials who cited idealism and specific policy commit-ments as motivating their careers demonstrated significantly greater preferences for policymaking (.369–.05 level – and .343–.05 level, respectively). Those whose fathers worked in managerial occupations similarly tended to opt for the role (.379, .05 level).

On the negative side of the ledger, career officials who did not register a religious affiliation tended to avoid characterisation of themselves as policy-makers (−.298, .05 levels). Most striking of all – especially in light of the theory that involvement in policy nets fosters the role among bureaucrats, the career officials who reported the most frequent contacts with legislators proved to be strongly disinclined towards policymaking (−.651, .05 levels). However, some research does suggest that officials let their interactions in the outer circles of salient policy nets slide when they enjoy especially good links at the very heart of the executive branch (Aberbach, Putnam and Rockman, 1981, 221–2; Campbell and Naulls, 1986, in press). The regressions of 'policy-maker' on the variables clusters for Carter appointees does not offer much guidance beyond what we found in Figure 3. This is with the exception of the very pronounced tendency among the Carter people with graduate degrees in economics to define their roles in policymaking terms (.941, .01 level).

The results from the 'policy-maker' regressions for Reagan appointees

Table 4(a) *Regression analysis for 'policy-maker'*

Independent variable	Carter career	Carter amphibian politico	Reagan amphibian politico
Positional circumstances and activities			
Contact, all categories	.358	.222	.207
Agency-head level contact	−.271	−.228	−.133
Contact on policy	.215	.110	−.265
Sub-agency-head level contact	.014	.355	−.071
Cabinet Committee regular attendance	−.040	.302	−.323*
Interdepartmental Committee attendance	.139	−.053	.386
Interdepartmental involvement	.134	.118	.205
Legislative contact active	−.651*	.237	.385
Congressional staff contact	.009	−.237	−.439
Interest group sources	.037	.004	−.157
Career orientations			
Idealism	.369*	.101	−.494*
Scholastic training	−.169	−.268	−.071
Policy/political commitment	.343*	−.058	−.519*
Impact	−.243	.260	.442*
Process	−.270	−.138	−.258
Personal satisfaction	−.155	.228	.542**
Career routes			
Late decision to enter government	.094	.260	−.025
No. of years in government	−.053	−.326	.164
No. of government positions	−.224	.046	.089
Education			
Undergraduate university education	.181	.432	.436
Elite undergraduate education	−.256	−.035	−.021
Elite graduate education	−.033	.004	.275
Undergraduate fields:			
Political science	.571*	.395	.060
Economics	.407	.089	−.057
Social science	.207	.323	−.025
Other	.002	.162	.023
Graduate fields:			
Political science	.094	.371	.524*
Economics	−.005	.941**	.116
Social science	−.024	none	none
Other	.193	.207	.173
Socio-demographic			
Age	−.127	.039	−.234
Sex	−.024	.160	−.004
Core area	−.054	.060	.142

Table 4(a) (*Cont.*)

Independent variable	Carter career	Carter amphibian politico	Reagan amphibian politico
Father's occupation			
Progressional	.096	−.237	−.063
Managerial	.379	refer.	refer.
White collar	.147	.004	−.099**
Blue collar	refer.	−.080	−.099
Farmer	.039	−.108	.174
Religion			
Roman Catholic	−.189	.147	.096
Protestant	refer.	refer.	refer.
Jewish	−.010	−.153	.054
None	−.298*	−.031	−.254
Private secondary school education	.297	−.142	−.052

* significant at .05
** significant at .01

invite much more comment. With reference to positional variables, a paradox emerges. It appears that policy makers carry heavy loads of interdepartmental committee work (.386) and interactions with legislators (.385). However, they usually do not involve themselves intensely in cabinet-level bodies (−.323, .05 level). The findings for the career-oriented cluster lend themselves to greater consistency. Idealistic Reagan appointees and those with specific policy objectives tend less to style themselves as involved in policymaking per se (−.494–.05 level – and −.519–.05 level, respectively). On the other hand, those who report that having an impact on significant matters plays a part in their staying in government and those who derive personal benefits from their careers both frequently framed their roles with respect to policy-making (.422–.05 level – and .542–.05 level, respectively). Among the educational background variables, graduate work in political science relates very strongly to Reagan appointees' association with policy-making (.524, .05 level). Finally, the offspring of fathers who held white collar occupations short of the professions or managerial posts clearly eschewed policymaking roles (−.449, .01 level).

Turning to the 'facilitator' regressions, those for the career officials turn up a number of interesting results. Consistent with Table 3, educational variables manifest themselves as significant factors. Strangely, the strongest elements seem somewhat contradictory. To be sure, permanent officials who received graduate degrees in political

Table 4(b) *Regression analysis for 'facilitator'*

Independent variable	Carter career	Carter amphibian politico	Reagan amphibian politico
Positional circumstances and activities			
Contact, all categories	−.109	.160	.422*
Agency-head level contact	−.392	−.256	−.214
Contact on policy	−.047	.047	−.168
Sub-agency-head level contact	.573*	−.302	−.333
Cabinet Committee regular attendance	−.011	.120	.099
Interdepartmental Committee attendance	.076	.036	−.025
Interdepartmental involvement active	−.122	−.044	−.126
Legislative contact	.028	−.165	−.227
Congressional staff contact	.357	.156	.705
Interest group sources	.256	.079	.022
Career orientations			
Idealism	−.021	−.310	.563*
Scholastic training	.111	−.061	−.270
Policy/political commitment	−.083	.131	−.061
Impact	.268	.283	−.153
Process	.066	.346*	.397
Personal satisfaction	−.075	−.071	−.302
Career routes			
Late decision to enter government	.110	−.184	.0976
No. of years in government	.467	−.121	−.484
No. of government positions	.043	.193	−.384
Education			
Undergraduate university education	.562**	.254	−.476
Elite undergraduate education	−.048	.244	−.122
Elite graduate education	−.081	−.483*	.099
Undergraduate fields:			
Political science	−.347	−.616*	.493*
Economics	−.129	.080	.633
Social science	−.068	−.559*	−.277
Other	.101	−.599*	.166
Graduate fields:			
Political science	.628**	.229	−.709*
Economics	.422	.009	−.351
Social science	.065	none	none
Other	.055	.181	.115
Socio-demographic			
Age	−.329	−.109	.151
Sex	−.243	.090	−.063
Core Area	−.001	.362	−.201

Table 4(b) (*Cont.*)

Independent variable	Carter career	Carter amphibian politico	Reagan amphibian politico
Father's occupation			
Professional	.235	.177	−.343
Managerial	.256	refer.	refer.
White collar	−.154	.184	.465*
Blue collar	refer.	.162	−.083
Farmer	−.137	−.120	−.305
Religion			
Roman Catholic	.232	−.059	−.458*
Protestant	refer.	refer.	refer.
Jewish	.180	−.172	−.083
None	.039	.034	.206
Private secondary			
school education	.310	−.330	.444*

* significant at .05
** significant at .01

science gravitate toward facilitation (.628, .01 level). Similarly, those who completed advanced work in economics appeared to favor the role somewhat (.422). However, respondents who had only completed undergraduate degrees – independent of field – also tended strongly to fashion their roles as those of facilitators.

The other statistically significant relations from the career regressions occur among the positional factors. Those who center their contacts within the executive-bureaucratic complex at the sub-agency-head level frequently opt for facilitation (.573, .05 level). Interestingly facilitaors in the career group also maintain relatively active relationships with congressional staff members and interest groups (.357 and .256, respectively). In support of the view that the best connected in policy nets tend to let their contacts lower down lapse, career facilitators do not boast very good access at the agency-head level (−.392).

The regressions of 'facilitator' for Carter appointees again uncover educational background as highly salient. Those who took their graduate or professional degree from Ivy League schools (−.483, .05 level), and those who completed their undergraduate work in political science, social sciences other than political science or economics, and non-social-science fields all rated relatively poorly as facilitators (respectively, −.616, −.559 and −.599 – all at the .05 level). In keeping with what we might expect from individuals who identify with facilitation, those who have stayed in government through a continued desire to influence the operation of the policy process reveal a strong inclination toward the role.

The results for 'facilitator' among Reagan respondents suggest that educational background operates in the opposite direction to that effected among Carter appointees. Both those with political science and those with economics undergraduate degrees lean strongly in the direction of facilitation (.493 and .633 respectively – both significant at the .05 level). However, those with political science and economics graduate degrees tend to downplay the role (−.709–.05 level – and −.351, respectively). As for the other clusters, Reagan appointees with an expansive array of interactions in the executive-bureaucratic complex and those who cited idealistic reasons for entering government service prove disproportionately attracted to facilitation (.422 and .563, respectively – both at the .05 level). As well, three socio-demographic variables appear to carry some weight. Respondents whose fathers worked in white-collar occupations and those who attended private secondary schools placed themselves relatively high on the facilitator index (.465 and .444, respectively – both at the .05 level). Meanwhile, Catholics among the Reagan respondents seem to have an aversion to the role (−.485, .05 level).

Conclusion

This chapter has examined the influence of training in the social sciences on senior officials' views of their involvement in the policy process. During the 40s, 50s and 60s, the reformers of central agencies and framers of policy units in operational departments encouraged the influx of social scientists to the federal government. The increased availability of such officials, many believed, held out a great hope for improvement of the analytic base and rationality of decision making. Many of the respondents in this study found themselves the beneficiaries of this era. All of them work in central agencies that shoulder special responsibilities toward coordination and control throughout government. Among them, career officials with social science degrees probably experienced the most direct connection between their possessing advanced credentials and obtaining access to the heart of the executive-bureaucratic complex. Amphibians, however, secured their positions through an amalgam consisting of, one part, the right political experience and coloration and, the other, expertise. Although some politicos had completed advanced work in a social-science field, proven ability in the craft of political operations played the dominant role in their securing a central-agency post.

Three factors have mitigated the effects which we might expect social-scientific training to exert on central agents' views of their work. First, successive fiscal crises during the past decade have sharply limited the salience of policy analysis. That is, governmental efforts to finetune policies increasingly fall victim to overarching macroeconomic imperatives. Second, U.S. central agencies have undergone a significant politicisation. This has taken the form of additional layers of partisan appointees in previously career-oriented, neutral-competence agencies. It also entails the co-optation of analytic resources for the packaging and selling of administration policy stances. Finally, the very nature of the work worlds of central agents has spawned a new image of officialdom. Here even those who uphold analytic criteria for decisions still must engage themselves fully in the political entrepreneurship which determines who wins or loses in the executive-bureaucratic milieu.

We employed regression analysis in order to chart the relevance of social-scientific training among other factors which might influence officials' views of their roles within the policy process. Here we utilised two dependent variables. One measured the degree to which respondents considered themselves policy-makers; the other ascertained the extent to which they tempered their descriptions of involvement in the policy process by emphasising their responsibilities toward facilitating decisions.

The regressions of 'policy-maker' on the various influence clusters for career officials suggest that positional factors play the heaviest roles followed by career orientations and, then, education. A closer examination at specifically which variables in the clusters relate the strongest to policy-making turns up the fact that career officials who interact frequently with legislators tend not to adopt the role. This finding fits squarely with those by Aberbach, Putnam and Rockman to the effect that individuals not involved higher up in issue networks usually do not acclimatise themselves fully to policy-making. With respect to specialised training, we found that only career officials with undergraduate degrees in political science became especially strongly oriented to policy-making. This emphasis of undergraduate training in the softer of the two dominant social sciences might operate behind the tendency for idealistic officials and those with specific policy commitments to favor the role. With respect to the regressions of 'facilitator' for the career group, the educational cluster proved to be the strongest. Here graduate training in economics or political science both related strongly to the role. As if to further confirm Aberbach, Putnam and Rockman, those who spoke relatively modestly of the levels at which their most regularised interactions occur also strongly favored facilitation. The career regressions, thus, do appear to uncover some substantial effects associated with specialised training, and – with reference to positional factors – respondents' location of themselves within policy nets.

In the regression of 'policy maker' for the Carter appointees, the socio-demographic, positional and career-orientation blocks – in that order – work the clearest effects in the analysis of unique effects. However, an examination of the individual variables within all clusters suggest only one strong relationship. Contrary to our theoretical expectations, Carter appointees with graduate degrees in economics claim the strongest associations with policy-making. As with career officials, the unique-effects regressions of 'facilitator' for Carter appointees highlighted the educational cluster. An examination of the individual variables in the educational block fails to establish that advanced work in the social sciences relates especially strongly to facilitation. However, those without Ivy League graduate degrees and those who stay in government in order to influence the operation of the policy process do favor facilitation. Among the Carter appointees, thus, the facilitator role appears to thrive more among the modest – of educational background and desired span of influence – than the professionally credentialed.

Among the Reagan appointees the positional and career-orientation blocks stood out in the 'policy-maker' regression. Those with the most frequent exposure to cabinet-level and interdepartmental bodies revealed the most intense involvement with policy-making. Interestingly – in light of the administration's emphasis of congressional relations, policy-makers under Reagan actually expanded their views of their networks to include legislators. With respect to education, those who completed graduate work in political science strongly prefer the role. This finding contrasts sharply with the tendency among Carter respondents with advanced training in economics to style themselves policy-makers. It suggests, as well, that graduate work in the social sciences does not cause officials to eschew involvement in policy-making.

Clearly, our appointees' commitments to their administration largely overroad any tendency specialists might reveal toward limiting themselves to facilitation. Indeed Reagan appointees with advanced degrees in political science and, to a lesser extent, those with graduate work in economics appear to downplay facilitation. This suggests that, in practice, social scientific credentials serve principally as union cards for many appointees. That is, an advanced degree in any field might only tip those selecting central agents to individuals with proven intellectual acuity. Whether appointees actually engage their specialised skills in analysis becomes an indifferent matter when recruiters principally factor graduate work into their selections as evidence of mental agility.

REFERENCES

Aberbach, Joel D., and Bert A. Rockman (1977), 'The Overlapping Worlds of American Federal Executives', *British Journal of Political Science* 7, 23–47.
Aberbach, Joel D., Robert D. Putnam and Bert A. Rockman (1981), *Bureaucrats and Politicians in Western Democracies*, Cambridge, Mass., Harvard University Press.
Berman, Larry (1979), *The Office of Management and Budget and the Presidency, 1921–1979*, Princeton, N.J., Princeton University Press.
Campbell, Colin and George J. Szablowski (1979), *The Superbureaucrats: Structure and Behavior in Central Agencies*, Toronto, Macmillan.
Campbell, Colin (1983), *Governments Under Stress: Political Executives and Key Bureaucrats in Washington, London and Ottawa*, Toronto, University of Toronto Press.
Campbell, Colin (1986), *Managing The Presidency: Carter, Reagan and The Search for Executive Harmony*, Pittsburgh, University of Pittsburgh Press.
Campbell, Colin and Donald Naulls (1986), 'Policy Makers and Facilitators: The Boundaries Between Two Bureaucratic Roles', *International Yearbook for Studies of Leaders and Leadership* 3, in press.
Chapman, Richard A. and J. R. Greenaway (1980), *The Dynamics of Administrative Reform*, London, Croom Helm.
Christoph, James B. (1975), 'High Civil Servants and the Politics of Consensualism in Great Britain', in *The Mandarins of Western Europe: The Political Role of Top Civil Servants*, ed. Mattei Dogan, New York, Halsted.
Goodnow, Frank, J. (1900), *Politics and Administration*, New York, Macmillan.
Gulick, Luther (1937), 'Science, Values and Public Administration', in *Papers on the Science of Administration*, ed. Luther Gulick and L. Urwick, New York, Institute of Public Administration.
Heclo, Hugh and Aaron Wildavsky (1974), *The Private Government of Public Money: Community and Policy Inside British Politics*, Berkeley, University of California Press.
Heclo, Hugh (1977), *A Government of Strangers: Executive Politics in Washington*, Washington, The Brookings Institution.
Holden, Matthew (1966), '"Imperialism" in Bureaucracy', *American Political Science Review* 60, 943–51.
Kaufman, Herbert (1969), 'Administrative Decentralization and Political Power', *Public Administration Review* 29, 3–15.
King, Anthony (1978), 'The American Polity in the Late 1970s: Building Coalitions in the Sand', in *The New American Political System*, ed. A. King, Washington D.C., American Enterprise Institute.
Landau, Martin (1962), 'The Concept of Decision-Making in the Field of Public Administration', in *Concepts and Issues in Administrative Behavior*, edited by Sidney Mailick and Edward H. Van Ness, Englewood Cliffs, N.J., Prentice-Hall.

Long, Norton C. (1952), 'Bureaucracy and Constitutionalism', *American Political Science Review* 46, 808–18.

Moe, Terry M. (1985), 'The Politicized Presidency', in *The New Direction in American Politics*, edited by John E. Chubb and Paul E. Peterson, Washington D.C., The Brookings Institution.

Nathan, Richard P. (1975), *The Plot That Failed: Nixon and the Administrative Presidency*, New York, Wiley.

Nathan, Richard P. (1983), *The Administrative Presidency*, New York, Wiley.

Newland, Chester A. (1983), 'The Reagan Presidency: Limited Government and Political Administration', *Public Administration Review* 43, 1–21.

Putnam, Robert D. (1973), 'The Political Attitudes of Senior Civil Servants in Western Europe: A Preliminary Report', *British Journal of Political Science* 3, 257–90.

Ripley, Randall B. and Grace A. Franklin (1980), *Congress, the Bureaucracy and Public Policy*, Homewood, Ill., Dorsey.

Rose, Richard (1976), *Managing Presidential Objectives*, New York, Free Press.

Schick, Allen (1980), 'The Problem of Presidential Budgeting', in *The Illusion of Presidential Government*, ed. Hugh Heclo and Lester M. Salamon, Boulder, Col., Westview.

Shubert, Glendon (1960), *The Public Interest*, Glencoe, Il., Free Press.

Simon, Herbert A. (1957), *Administrative Behavior*, New York, Macmillan.

Suleiman, Ezra N. (1974), *Politics, Power, and Bureaucracy in France: The Administrative Elite*, Princeton, Princeton University Press.

Weber, Max (1946 translation), 'Politics as a Vocation'; and 'Bureaucracy', in *From Max Weber: Essays in Sociology*, translated by H. H. Gerth and C. Wright Mills, New York, Oxford University Press.

Wildavsky, Aaron (1983), 'From Chaos Comes Opportunity: The Movement Toward Spending Limits in American and Canadian Budgeting', *Canadian Public Administration* 26, 163–81.

Wilson, Woodrow (1941 reprint), 'The Study of Administration', *Political Science Quarterly* 16, 481–506.

CHAPTER 9

Perhaps Minister: the messy world of 'in-house' social research[1]

ROBERT WALKER

The scale of social research activities in central government is today extensive and yet the obstacles to the use of social science by government remain considerable. Five such obstacles have been identified by Bulmer (1983, 39–45):

1 *Bureaucratic marginality.* ' ... disciplines such as sociology, political science, social anthropology, social psychology and social administration lack acceptance and recognition ... ' ' ... social science has a marginal position within Whitehall, not only in the terms of careers of research staff, but also in the location of research units'.

2 *Specialists and generalists.* 'One factor is clearly the long-running tension in British central administration between generalists and specialists.' An early sign of 'the low perceived relevance of social science' was ' ... the government's immediate rejection of "preference for relevance" in recruitment of fast-stream administrators, suggested by Fulton'.

3 *Endemic empiricism.* 'Absence of social science backgrounds among a majority of political administrators also encourages a particular view of the role of social science research as being to gather "the facts".' 'Fact-gatherers would not presume to offer advice about policy, nor would they be seen as fit persons to do so.'

4 *The politicisation and lack of professionalism of social science.* ' ... the personal political view of social scientists has tended to be left of centre ... ' which ' ... hinders relations between social scientists and administrative civil servants who are suspicious of over-commitment'. 'Lack of rigorous methodological standards weakens the appeal of social science to critical policy-makers.'

5 *Constraints of the policy-making process itself.* 'The academic social

141

scientist frequently fails to appreciate the context in which the policy-maker works as well as on occasion having an exaggerated opinion of his own contribution.' 'Social scientists, particularly academics, are not good at meeting ... deadlines.' 'Time also constrains the type of research which is appropriate.'

To these obstacles should be added the political risks which accompany the commissioning of research by government[2] (see below).

These six obstacles constitute recurring reference points throughout this chapter. However, any list or conceptual framework such as that adopted by Bulmer is apt to convey a degree of order and structure that is generally absent in the real world. Moreover, it may be that this lack of structure, the messiness of practical administration and real-life government, is itself a reason for the failure of social science to make a greater impact on policy development. It is therefore, the aim of this chapter to give a hint of the *process* of social science research in government. In doing so, the chapter focuses on three broad aspects of the research process: the initiation and commissioning of research; factors affecting quality; and procedures for the dissemination of research findings. However, it is necessary first to explain a little about the organisation of government social science research and about the role of social science research officers (SSROs).

Social scientists in government

A few distinctions and definitions are in order. Four service-wide social science specialisms are recognised within the civil service personnel structure: economists, statisticians, psychologists and research officers. The research officer category is further sub-divided into two groups, 'social science' and 'resource and planning.' In some departments, notably the Department of Environment, this distinction reflects a real difference in work content but in others the distinction, even where it formally exists, is often unclear. For completeness, mention should be made of social survey officers found only in the Office of Population Censuses and Surveys. For management purposes social survey officers come under the wing of the social science group of the Research Officer Management Committee although their grading structure is inferior. This chapter is concerned very largely with the activities of Social Science Research Officers (SSROs), for the most part excluding social survey officers.

Estimates of expenditure on social science research undertaken by government departments are given in Table 1. 'In-house research' refers

Table 1 *Estimated expenditure on social science research by home government departments* and the SSRC, 1982–3*

			Thousands £
Department	In-house	External	Total
Health and Social Security	245	13,174	13,419
Environment	250	2,900	3,150
Scottish Office	750	1,850	2,600
Manpower Services Commission	N/A	2,319	2,319
Home Office	1,299	652	1,951
Employment	208	696	904
Other	653	5,453	6,106
Total	3,405	27,044	30,449
Social Science Research Council (Now ESRC)	–	–	8,594**

Source: Cmnd 1982; ESRC 1984; D.H.S.S. 1984
*   Excluding Foreign and Commonwealth Office
** Research units, grants for research and research contracts.

to that undertaken by civil servants, albeit with some contracting-out of fieldwork. In the departments named in Table 1, in-house research would generally be the responsibility of SSROs. In most departments the external research budget exceeds in-house expenditure. External research is undertaken directly for government by outside bodies notably universities, market research agencies and independent research institutes. SSROs may commission and supervise external research but the extent to which they do so varies between departments (see below). Taken overall, government research exceeds the *total* budget of the Economic and Social Research Council (£21 million in 1982/3) by £9 million.

In 1984 325 research officers were employed in government, 102 of them women. Of the total about a third belonged to the social science group. The Home Office and the Employment Group, that is the Department of Employment and the Manpower Services Commission, together probably employed over half of all social science research officers with the Scottish Office, Department of Environment and the Department of Health and Social Security employing the vast majority of the remainder.

Diversity

The work of SSROs, and the nature of their role, vary markedly between departments and also within them. At one extreme, represented perhaps uniquely by the Home Office Research Unit (HORU, incorporated into the Home Office Research and Planning Unit (HORPU) in 1980), research officers may constitute a cadre of experts within a particular specialism. HORU was a centre of excellence in criminology with an output unrivalled in quantity and quality on this side of the Atlantic. Researchers typically worked on substantial pieces of research, often drawing on established theory and in the process developing it. A model of supervision was adopted that was very akin to that found in universities with each researcher being very largely responsible for their own intellectual development and with little day-to-day management intervention. However, it may reasonably be deduced from the 1980 reform of HORU that there was a feeling among influential policy-makers outside the unit that the research was sometimes too academic, and insufficiently addressed to policy issues. As a result of the reforms – which were associated with staff reductions – the unit ceased to report to the Chief Scientist (a post which was abolished) and instead reported to a senior policy-maker at Deputy Secretary level. A significant proportion of research staff were out-stationed with the main customer policy divisions, one consequence of which was that their line managers became policy-makers even though they continued to report professionally to senior researchers in HORPU.

At the other extreme, notably in parts of the Chief Scientist's Office in the Department of Health and Social Security, research officers undertake no research themselves but instead supervise research commissioned externally by the Department and act as a liaison between researchers and policy-makers. Perhaps the more usual situation is for a research officer to undertake research – which may range from a large survey to ad hoc literature searches – while at the same time, depending on grade and experience, supervising a limited number of external projects. In most departments SSROs also play an important brokerage role for social science. They provide a two-way link between government and the research community, feeding research evidence into the policy process, advising on the validity of research findings and the quality of research proposals and drawing attention to the need for, and possibility of, commissioning new research to be undertaken either in-house or externally.

Typically a research officer will not share the disciplinary background of his research colleagues and may not even have graduated in the social sciences. Unfortunately, the potential for multi-disciplinary research, which this situation offers, is rarely realised not least because research officers in a research division will be working on disparate research problems for different policy customers. In practice, research projects are defined within the parameters of a policy problem and have only a limited theoretical content. As a consequence, a lot of the research undertaken by social science research officers is perhaps best char-acterised as 'up-market' market research; up-market in the sense that the research will have had a longer gestation and be informed by a more detailed knowledge of the substantive policy problems than would ordinary market research. A common complaint among research officers is that the most intellectually challenging projects are commissioned externally (although the reverse argument is sometimes made by academics (Bradshaw, 1985)).

The afore-mentioned reorganisation of research in the Home Office reflects a commitment, shared by most departments in the last few years, to effect a closer relationship between researchers and policy-makers. Thus the Social Research Division in the Department of the Environ-ment was disbanded in 1980 and researchers 'bedded-out' in policy divisions (although the strategy has recently been reversed). Even in the Scottish Office – where researchers have traditionally been located in policy divisions, though managed from a central research unit – there has been a rapid increase in the role of administrative customers as commis-sioners of in-house research.

The closer formal relationship with policy-makers impacts on the type of research undertaken by research officers which in turn is also affected by changes in the type of question that politicians and administrators are asking. The trend, commencing in some departments before the arrival of the 1979 Conservative government, has been away from long-term developmental research aimed at providing background information, towards more research on the implementation and evaluation of policies. There has been a particular growth in short-term policy analysis and the collation of evidence from existing research.

Job content is also affected by grade. Senior research staff naturally spend more time on staff management and supervision. However, given that communication between parts of a civil service department normally occurs between persons of the same grade, the low grading of researchers relative to their administrative counterparts (see below) means that the advisory role of researchers is likely to be undertaken largely by senior staff, albeit based on work undertaken by junior staff and often arising out of projects on which the latter are engaged.

The precise workload of any one researcher will therefore depend on many factors including their grade, the department in which they work,

Table 2 *Net central government expenditure on research and development, 1966/7–1983/4*

	1966/7	1970/1	1973/4	1978/9 (A)	1981/2 (B)	1983/4 (A,B)
Social science £M	2.7	7.1	11.6	31.2	52.8	52.6
– ESRC £M	0.6	1.5	2.7	5.7	15.3	17.3
Scientific £M	498.1	598.6	859.7	911.1	3370.7	3787.2
Index of real expenditure (1966/7 = 100)						
Social Science (inc. ESRC)	100	219	279	356	402	348
Scientific	100	183	207	218	260	254
Adjusted index of real expenditure (C) (1966/7 = 100)						
Social Science (inc. ESRC)	100	219	279	356	339	294
Scientific	100	183	207	218	253	247

Source: Cmnd, 1982.
(A) Estimated
(B) Source: Bowles, 1984; expenditure on universities excluded for comparability with earlier years
(C) There is a major unexplained upward revision of expenditure estimates between Bowles, 1982, and Bowles, 1984, which differentially affects social science expenditure. This revision has been statistically removed from the expenditure estimates for 1981/2 and 1983/4

their formal relationship with policy-makers, and the degree of inertia imposed by ongoing research commitments.

Insecurity

Research officers in government are among the best paid social scientists in Britain. For the most part, their terms of service – security of tenure, inflation-proofed pensions, etc., – are next to none. Moreover, they have access to information held by government and to research resources that are the envy of their academic counterparts. But this is only part of the story.

Table 2 shows the very significant increase in social science research undertaken or commissioned directly by government departments between 1966 and 1978/9 and the subsequent decline. A similar pattern is evident in the number of government research staff, plotted in Figure 1 for each year since the research group was created in 1975. However, in

Data for Figure 1 *Numbers of Research Officers, Economists and Statisticians lost, 1975–84*

	Research Officers	Economists	Statisticians
1975	393	331	479
1976	446	397	485
1977	458	389	498
1978	443	381	514
1979	432	393	537
1980	450	399	532
1981	435	374	526
1982	401	364	516
1983	356	360	450
1984	330*		

* Includes estimate of 5 Open Structure staff

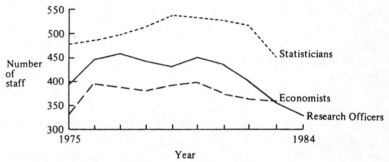

Fig 1 Numbers of Research Officers, Economists and Statisticians Lost, 1975–84

this case, growth was concentrated before 1977 and numbers declined at an accelerating rate from 1980.

It is evident from Figure 1 that in 1977, the peak year for research officer employment, research officers outnumbered economists by almost 1.2 to 1. This is perhaps surprising. Less so is the fact that since 1980 research officers have suffered far more job losses, both in absolute terms and proportionally, than have either economists or statisticians.

There are a number of possible reasons for the decline in the number of research officers some of which relate to the same 'obstacles' as identified by Bulmer. The Conservative government elected in 1979 was committed to a reduction in the role of government and in the size of the Civil Service and saw efficient government as a priority. An end to expansionist government means a reduced demand for fact-finding and research linked to policy development; while the focus on efficiency predicates a concern with assessment and evaluation. (A government committed to policy withdrawal may be less likely to request research on the consequences of its actions.) The impact on the nature of government research has already been noted but this does not in itself explain the differential shedding of research officers.

However, statisticians and economists are more securely embedded in Whitehall than social researchers, both in the centrality of their influence and in organisational terms. While recommending a cutback in the collection of statistics, the Rayner Report on Government Statistical Service (GSS) emphasised the extent to which decision-making in government and industry is dependent on a stream of statistics prepared by the GSS (Rayner, 1980). Statistics are self-evidently relevant to the short-term political calculations which are so all important to ministers. Moreover, professional statisticians are needed to interpret the statistics produced. Researchers, on the other hand, had to scramble to change the style and content of their work in order to meet the new circumstances. In particular, the long-time horizons of research had to be collapsed. At the same time organisational changes were forced on researchers. With departments aware of the need to reduce staffing complements, the way was open for staff cuts.

If anything, economists have an even more vital part to play in government although they have suffered marginally greater job losses than statisticians since 1980 (Figure 1). The economy remains central to the government's intentions and aspirations, even if the professed aim is to leave the economy alone in order for it to respond to the laws of the market. Moreover, terms such as efficiency and cost effectiveness are part of the conceptual language of economics while monetarism – which in 1979 provided the apparently rationalistic underpinning for the Conservative government's ideology – was itself dreamed up by economists. However, as Bulmer stresses, the politicisation of social research is of a different hue. Very many members of Mrs Thatcher's first cabinet were positively antagonistic towards social research and ministers became noticeably more involved in commissioning and vetoing research than had traditionally been the case. As a result, in the early 1980s research staff found themselves underworked and research divisions had few new commissions coming on stream.

As a general rule, research staff are more exposed than statisticians and economists in organisational terms. They are bureaucratically marginal, to adopt Bulmer's terminology. The GSS was established in 1946 and the GES in 1964, 11 years before the research officer group. Economists and statisticians were able to consolidate their position during a time of government expansion. As a result, before the amalgamation of senior professionals into the Open Structure of grading in

Table 3 *Civil Service Career Hierarchies**

Administrative	Economists	Statisticians	Research Officers	Social Survey Officers
Permanent Secretary (1)‡				
Second Permanent Secretary (1A)	Head of the Government Economic Service and Chief Economic Adviser (Treasury)	Head of the Government Statistical Service and Director, Central Statistical Office		
Deputy Secretary (2)	Deputy Chief Economic Adviser (Treasury)	Deputy Director, Central Statistical Office		
Under Secretary (3)	Chief Economic Adviser†	Director of Statistics†		
Assistant Secretary (5)	Senior Economic Adviser	Chief Statistician	Chief Research Officer	Chief Social Survey Officer A
Senior Principal (6)			Senior Principal Research Officer	Chief Social Survey Officer B
Principal (7)	Economic Adviser	Statistician	Principal Research Officer	Principal Social Survey Officer
Senior Executive Officer				Senior Social Survey Officer
			Senior Research Officer	
Higher Executive Officer	Senior Economic Assistant	Senior Assistant Statistician		Social Survey Officer
			Research Officer	
Executive Officer	Economic Assistant	Assistant Statistician		Assistant Social Survey Officer
Clerical Officer				
Clerical Assistant				

Table 3 (*Cont.*)

* Situation prior to 1 January 1984 when posts above Principal equivalent were reorganised into a 6 grade 'Open Structure'. In 1986, the open structure was extended downwards to Grade 7, at Principal level. Position in the table is determined by maximum point on the respective salary scales.
† Titles vary. May be graded under-secretary (grade 3) in open structure.
‡ Numbers in brackets denote grade of all posts at this level in the open structure now operating (1987) in the civil service.
Sources: Civil Service College Library and MPO (1982).

1984, both groups supported staff on salary scales that were roughly equivalent to Deputy Secretary, whereas research posts petered out at Assistant Secretary level (Table 3). Strategic policy decisions can therefore involve statisticians and economists on roughly equal footing with administrators. In contradistinction, there could be no direct support for research at the most senior levels where decisions on manning levels are taken.

In 1977 36 per cent of research officers were women compared with 19 per cent of statisticians, 11 per cent of economists and just 8 per cent of the administrative group above higher executive officer level (CSD, 1978b). Given the entrenched position of men within the senior ranks of the civil service, the relatively large proportion of women researchers may itself contribute to the marginality of research within Whitehall. It may also be a factor in the disproportionate job losses suffered by research staff. 46 per cent of the net losses occurring between 1980 and 1983 involved women and by 1983 the proportion of women had fallen to 31 per cent. 'Natural wastage' may be greater among women than among men since more leave to look after children. However, one would expect to find similar disproportionate losses among female economists and statisticians but these did not occur. On the other hand, it is probable that many of the probationary and short-term contract research posts in the late seventies were held by women and that these were shed first. Also, the very severity of the job losses borne by the research group may itself act to distort official statistics. It may be, for example, that posts 'disappear' while women take maternity leave only to re-appear in a different guise when they return to work.

Although few in number, SSROs constitute a foothold for social science in government. Their position is tenuous and has become more so during the Thatcher administration. What can be achieved is limited but not to be ignored. How it is achieved is the subject of the remainder of this chapter.

Initiation and commissioning of research

When asking why the impact of research or policy-making is limited it is helpful to examine the process by which research is initiated, the loci of policy interest, the reasons why research is undertaken and the resultant constraints which are placed on the design and content. In doing so, it is necessary to separate formal procedures from informal processes and stated objectives from the unstated intentions of the principal actors involved in the initiation process.

The Rothschild formula

The formal procedures for initiating and commissioning social science research in government departments owe much to the influence of the Rothschild report (Cmnd, 1971). This is ironic since Lord Rothschild's recommendations concerned scientific and technical research and made no mention of social science. (Indeed elsewhere Rothschild (Cmnd, 1982) states that social science was explicitly excluded from the 1971 enquiry.) Rothschild drew a distinction between 'basic, fundamental or pure research' and 'applied R&D' (research and development) which has 'practical application as its objective'. The assumption was that government department's should be concerned only to fund the latter kind of research (the former being the preserve of the universities and research councils) and that in doing so they should abide by the 'consumer–contractor' principle: 'the customer says what he wants; the contractor does it (if he can); and the customer pays' (Cmnd 1971, para. 6). Rothschild further proposed that all departments engaged in R&D should have a 'Chief Scientist'. The Chief Scientist was to advise customers on their research needs and was to be part of the customer organisation. A 'Controller R&D' was also to be appointed as executive head of the R&D function which would be provided either through in-house facilities or external commissions.

Rothschild believed that, as a result of following his guidelines, the responsibilites of the consumer and contractor would be clear and that research priorities would become apparent. This view was shared by the government in their response to the Rothschild report:

> Departments as customers, define their requirements; contractors advise on the feasibilty of meeting them and undertake the work; and the arrangements between them must ensure that the objectives remain obtainable within reasonable costs (Cmnd 1972).

To a greater or lesser extent all departments have adopted the consumer–contractor principle though none has implemented a pure version of the Rothschild administrative structure. Moreover, departmental procedures have continued to develop in the post-Rothschild era. Where Chief Scientists have been appointed, as in the Department of Health and Social Security, the Home Office and, formerly, the Department of the Environment, they have in practice fulfilled the role of Controller R&D even though Rothschild stipulated that the two roles should be quite separate. All departments have a committee structure, varying in its degree of formality, which identifies research needs and agrees appropriate work programmes and priorities. The component committees are usually organised by broad policy area and comprise both policy customers and professional interests including researchers, some of whom act as contractors in the Rothschild sense. Committees may sometimes include outside academic advisers and practitioners as is the case with the Research Liaison Committees in the Department of Health and Social Security.

Despite Rothschild

However, the formal administrative structures set up to establish research priorities represent only the most visible part of a more 'organic' system that exists in spite of, and sometimes because of, the commitment to the Rothschild ethos.

Underlying the Rothschild proposals was an assumption that, aided by the Chief Scientist, consumers could readily identify research needs. In practice 'policy-makers have to work hard to identify problems' and to formulate them in ways amenable to research (Kogan and Henkle, 1983, 9). In part this reflects the academic background of administrators and the continued commitment of the civil service to the training of generalists (CSD, 1978a). Twenty-six per cent of the fast-stream recruits appointed between 1980 and 1984 held degrees in social science: a proportion that is marginally greater than for graduates as a whole but which does not match the policy content of their work (CSC, 1985). Moreover, while their training includes modules on statistics and economics there is no input whatsoever on the appreciation and application of social science research.

Equally important, as far as social science is concerned, the Chief Scientist generally does not, and for the most part is unable to, perform the necessary role of research midwife. Social science is likely to be overlooked – constituting as it does only a small part of most departments' R&D – and even where it isn't, the Chief Scientist is likely to be involved only at the stage of evaluating the scientific merit of specific proposals and not when formulating research needs in the language of social science. Where the midwifery role is performed at all, it is performed by in-house researchers who have to overcome the barriers to communication and credibility already discussed. This may involve working lunches to discuss the research requirements of key policy-makers. (Lunches are better than meetings if the aim is to 'sell' research; moreover lunch is often the only time that a policy-maker is prepared to 'give-up' to discuss what he may regard as rather peripheral issues.) Attention is frequently targetted on specific individuals, notably assistant secretaries heading policy divisions. If an assistant secretary can be suitably influenced soon after taking up an appointment, a research division can often count on his support and alliance for the two or more years that he remains in post. To 'foul-up' a relationship with a policy-maker is akin to an advertising agency losing the account of an important client. The rapid turnover of policy personnel however means that the process of influencing customers is a continual one and one which, even if it is later placed on more formal footing, rarely gets much further than stimulating a general awareness of the existence of a research capacity.

The Rothschild model also envisages a research contractor able to negotiate with the consumer about, for example, what research can be done and how. However, the virtual monopoly power of the policy consumer, combined with the need to secure work for in-house researchers in the face of competition from extramural organisations, frequently precludes constructive negotiation. The result is to perpetuate the narrow empiricist mode of research with which administrators are most familiar and which, as Bulmer notes, so limits the potential contribution of social science. The same pressures can lead research divisions to accept impossible briefs (see below).

Rothschild further assumed that policy-makers would appreciate the need for R&D although this is frequently not the case with respect to social science research. As Rothschild noted in his later report on the SSRC:

> The characteristic objective of applied R&D in the natural sciences is to find out whether and if so how something can be done. The main purpose of applied social science research is to be provide the material upon which it is possible to conduct more informed debate and make better decisions (Cmnd 1982, p. 11).

Moreover, as Rothschild acknowledged again in the context of work commissioned by the SSRC, 'much social science research is the stuff of political debate' and that 'all such research might prove subversive to government policies because it attempts to submit such policies to empirical trial, with the risk that the judgement may be adverse' (Cmnd, p. 12). This is a risk taken by all civil servants whenever they commission research. Research may demonstrate that the policy is inadequate. The Department may appear as incompetent. The staff involved in implementation may be shown to be incapable, or worse, which in turn may erode management relations with the trade unions. In all probability too, the research will argue a good case for increased expenditure at a time when departmental priorities may be elsewhere. To avoid the public embarrassment of ministers restrictions may be placed on publication, but this strategy has the attendant risk that the findings may be leaked and the Department accused of a 'cover-up'. (It also serves further to undermine the tenuous position of researchers within the Department. See below.)

On the other hand, it may not be at all clear what the policy-maker stands to gain from research. Research is very unlikely to provide a black and white, definitive answer to a complex policy problem. Rather it may help to elucidate the myriad shades of grey and thereby to enrich understanding, but it rarely makes the taking of decisions any easier. Also, a competent policy-maker is likely to have a quite accurate appreciation of the policy domain in which he operates. This he is apt to label 'common-sense'. When research confirms his 'commonsense' understanding, he may well feel that the research has not taken him very much further. If the research confounds his expectations, then an understandable first response is to feel that it has made his already difficult job more so. It is therefore a brave policy-maker who will take so great a risk for so little apparent and immediate gain.

Researchers as initiators of research

It is not surprising, therefore, that much research is initiated by researchers – 'contractors' in Rothschild terminology – and not by 'customers', although the latter will in practice commission the research. Research officers are the group best able to appreciate the potential of research. Because they move posts less frequently than administrators, they may sometimes act as the Department's collective memory on certain aspects of policy. Moreover, it is very much in their own interests to get and to keep research going.

Where departmental research priorities are drawn up on an annual cycle, there is often a period in the year when research officers can be found frantically 'working-up' research ideas. These are likely to reflect existing research interests and areas of expertise, but kites may be flown if researchers wish to move in to another policy area. In content and presentation the proposals are likely to reflect what research officers feel will appeal to policy customers. There then follows a spell of intense lobbying – outside the formal committee structure – with a view to convincing potential customers of the attractiveness of particular research proposals. Researchers can probably count fellow professionals among their natural allies in this process, but the latter will also have projects up for consideration and a certain amount of sniping is possible which frequently manifests itself as quibbles over methodology.

Within the formal committee structure, research is then selected from a menu of research possibilities with the result that the research programme is determined by the proposals on offer rather than being drawn up in response to a coherent set of research requirements. Details of specific projects will of course be worked out in later discussions with customer divisions but it may still be that the research is not as closely attuned to policy needs as it might be. In very extreme cases policy-makers may feel that they have had the research hoisted upon them which inevitably conditions their response to the ultimate findings. But research divisions also stand to suffer from the accidents of decision-taking. They may be requested to undertake too many or too few projects and rarely have the opportunity to develop a coherent programme of research.

The objectives of research

The vast majority of government research is no doubt under-taken with a view to more informed policy-making (Thomas, 1985). It may feed into any of the many stages in the policy process including system definition, problem formulation, consideration of policy options, evaluation and monitoring (Stokey and Zeckhauser, 1978). In each of these cases the Rothschild vision of a partnership between consumer and contractor, with the former calling on the latter's professional expertise to assess the feasibility and viability of research, to map policy require-ments into a workable research design and competently to undertake research, is a reasonably obtainable goal.

But not all government social research is of this kind. Research may be undertaken simply to shelve an uncomfortable political issue in the hope that it will go away or to give the Department time to formulate a response. The research itself may constitute the Department's policy on a matter, perhaps being the outcome of a ministerial commitment to do *something*. Again research may be commissioned from an outside body simply as a means of extending it government funding or legitimating any subsidy which it already receives. It may on occasion constitute part of a determined effort to influence what such bodies do or say publicly. Research of a defensive nature may be commissioned in order to demonstate that something – perhaps an 'off-the-cuff' ministerial state-ment – is in fact the case or that the existing policy, or a proposed policy change, is the right one. The research may be pre-emptive in the sense that it is aimed to fend off anticipated criticisms. It may have promotional intent – a demonstration project, for example – and be part of the presentational package accompanying a policy. In most of these cases the training and professional ethics of the researcher come to nothing. The Rothschild partnership is devoid of meaning. The research and the research officer are both exploited and devalued.

It would also be wrong to underestimate the individual motives and sub-departmental interests that underpin some government research. In the same way that researchers may initiate research to further their own individual and collective interest so, on occasion, do policy customers.

Within government departments, and indeed in any other bureaucracy, individuals compete for recognition and are engaged in activities designed primarily to foster personal satisfaction (McMahon, Barrett and Hill, 1983; Elmore, 1976). In government, policy ideas are often the currency of personal advancement but policy developments in one part of a Department are likely to have repercussions elsewhere. As a result, policies tend to evolve – in part at least – through a process of conflict and changing alliances between policy divisions in which research is one of the many 'weapons' that are deployed. At times when the departmental impetus is behind policy development, the commissioning of research may in itself be sufficient to fulfil the need to be seen to be doing something. More pointedly, research findings may sometimes be used to undermine the policy interests and credibility of other divisions.

In summary, the customer may not be able to say what research he wants. The research he wants may be methodologically unsound. The research that he gets may not be what he wants and what he wants may have little direct relevance to the evolution of policy. How often this is the case is a matter for conjecture. That it sometimes is, is part of the reason why research has not been more successful in influencing policy.

The quality of research

Other reasons why social research has not had a greater impact on policy relate to the quality of the research produced. Figure 2 lists eight evaluative criteria which may be applied to government research and proposes a number of reasons why some projects may be deficient when assessed against them. It is not intended to suggest that all research projects fail on all counts or even more that most fail on at least one. Rather the diagram illustrates points in the research process at which things may go wrong.

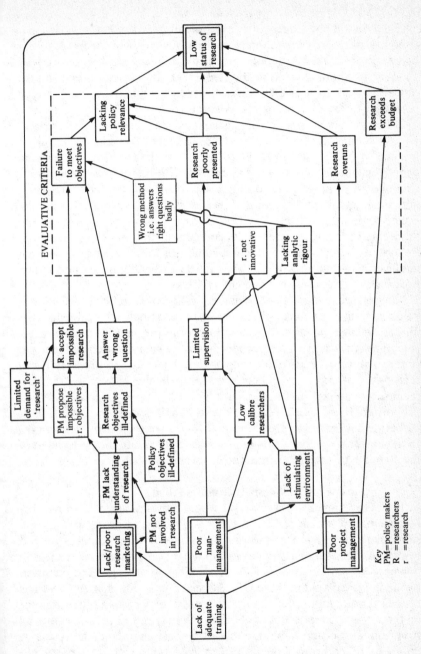

Fig 2 Factors influencing the quality of government research

EVALUATIVE CRITERIA

Low status of research

Lacking policy relevance

Failure to meet objectives

Research poorly presented

Research overruns

Research exceeds budget

Wrong method i.e. answers right questions badly

r. not innovative

Lacking analytic rigour

Limited demand for 'research'

R. accept impossible research

Answer 'wrong' question

Limited supervision

PM propose impossible r. objectives

Research objectives ill-defined

Low calibre researchers

PM lack understanding of research

Policy objectives ill-defined

Lack of stimulating environment

Lack/poor research marketing

PM not involved in research

Poor man-management

Poor project management

Lack of adequate training

Key
PM=policy makers
R =researchers
r =research

Meeting research objectivess

As acknowledged already, not all government research has straightforward research objectives. However, even when a policy-maker has a clear appreciation of the project objectives, they may not be adequately communicated to the researcher. In particular the research officer may not have a full grasp of the policy context, a problem which may be exacerbated when the government researcher is acting as a 'middleman' between policy-maker and external contractor. Researchers, for their part, may seek to avoid what they consider to be 'interference' by policy-makers and to defend their areas of professional competence by not involving the customer in the research process, for example after piloting and during preliminary analysis when decisions are taken that affect the nature of the research project and constrain the policy content of the findings. This problem is again heightened by the differential grading of researchers and administrators – which has even frustrated attempts to bring them together for joint training on research applications – but also reflects the fact that research is among the less pressing things to cross policy-makers' desks.

Much is often made of policy-makers' failure to appreciate the nature, value and limitations of research and the structural problems that militate against the immediate solution of this problem. But equally it is sometimes the case that researchers have over-sold research and that – in order to stave off staff reductions or to enhance the status of research divisions – projects have been undertaken in the knowledge that the results were unlikely to be of much value. At the same time the increased proportion of research officer time which is spent on 'intelligence' gathering has served to erode the skill content of the researcher's work. In the longer term none of these processes can work to the betterment of the standing of research within the government machine.

Appropriateness of analysis and method

Government researchers are sometimes guilty of a 'conveyor-belt mentality' which results in forcing all research problems into the same methodological framework. The 'house style' is usually oriented towards a social survey, but may be limited to 'case studies' or even, as in one case, to postal surveys. The social survey approach is underwritten by the impressive skills of the OPCS Social Survey Division and by their concentration on this mode at the expense of expertise in other areas of methodology. Adoption of the house style may reflect pressures arising from unrealistic time tabling imposed by customers and the resultant failure to 'think through' the project. It may also be simpler to use an old technique rather than to learn a new one. Moreover, over-confidence built on the fact that familiar techniques have worked in the past may conceal a blindness to alternative approaches, a lack of competence in them, and an unwillingness to acquire new skills. This methodological narrowness – which it should be said is a criticism that most government researchers reject – is one aspect of the endemic empiricism of government research with its primacy of method over theory. (Applicants for research officer posts have been known to be asked whether they have come to grips with the prime theory of sociology – the social survey!) It can lead to a failure systematically to explore the patterns found in data and to mammoth projects where 'the opportunity is taken to collect as much information as possible', which in turn leads to turgid reports full of tables describing superficial relationships. Both of these weaknesses are sometimes blamed on policy-makers who are said to despise theory and to be naturally inquisitive but, as things are, only researchers are in a position to insist on the more explicit use of theory (or, at very least, the explicit statement of assumptions) in the execution of government research.

Competition for government posts is intense. (There were 866 applicants for 26 posts in 1984 (CSC, 1985).) Nevertheless, some research officers lack the skills of their craft. This phenomenon is not restricted to research in government but reflects a national problem (e.g. see SRA, 1985). Comparatively few universities offer courses in research methodology and post-graduates normally leave universities with a narrow research perspective conditioned by experience gained from a single project (Clarke, 1981). Graduates recruited into the research class are generally thought able to 'do research' or to be likely to acquire sufficient expertise through experience. Those who receive additional formal training generally seek it out themselves so that researchers who are least aware of their own deficiencies may miss out altogether. Similarly, research management may not always be effective nor the general envirionment conducive to the promotion of excellence. Moreover, for whatever reason – be it the absorbtion of the generalist ethos, complacency or something else – a significant proportion of staff at principal level are very resistant to the idea of further training particularly in methodological issues.

Project management

A related question concerns the endemic failure to meet deadlines and cost targets. This in turn frequently results in valuable data being left unanalysed. Policy-makers invariably require results 'tomorrow' and researchers feel compelled to accept unrealistic targets in order to maintain credibility (only to lose it again when the results are late or bids for additional funding have to be submitted). But more important, researchers are rarely trained in the skills and techniques of project management despite the fact that they are responsible for projects that are often large, expensive and complex even by industrial and commercial standards. Research staff themselves are very largely to blame for failings of this kind although the very irregular pace of the Whitehall machine does not help as a particular project may have high priority one moment and none the next.

While much government research is of the highest standard, some could undoubtedly be improved. Until it is, the quality of research will continue to serve as an explanation – or an excuse – for the marginal impact of research on policy.

Dissemination

In the narrowest interpretation of the Rothschild 'consumer-contractor' principle, dissemination amounts to no more than ensuring that policy customers have access to the research findings. But, as Rothschild noted in his report on the Social Science Research Council, the 'ultimate customer' for social science research is often the 'citizen' or even 'future generations'. The decisions to which applied social science research is devoted in a democratic society: 'are not the sole concern of Ministers or officials. Members of Parliament on both sides of the House, journalists, academics, the public at large – all of these are the beneficiaries of applied social science research.' (Rothschild, 1982, p. 12.) This is arguably the case even for research commissioned by government departments for their own internal purposes.

To focus first on the process of dissemination within government; this is clearly the responsibility of research staff. How far it is the researcher's job to spell out the policy implications of research findings, and how far he is qualified to do so, are mute points and the practice varies from department to department, from time to time and from policy division to division. As a broker for research commissioned externally, the research officer has perhaps a clearer duty to present the research in a way that takes account of the nuances of current policy thinking of which the external researcher cannot be aware. (The external researcher will no doubt feel frustrated that he is not permitted to be privy to this thinking.)

Under ideal circumstances, the policy division will have been kept in touch throughout the project and will have seen and commented on preliminary reports and briefing papers. Few policy-makers above principal level find time to read research reports and will pass them to more junior staff to précis. Moreover, the précis is often 'boned' still further as it proceeds up the administrative hierarchy so that, on the rare occasion when it is presented to ministers, it will rarely consist of more than a page or two or doubled-spaced typescript. With this in mind, the astute researcher will provide a summary of their own (or external) research in the hope that this will provide the basis of the script to be absorbed by policy-makers. On rare occasions, and with enthusiastic policy-makers, oral presentations may be made to Ministers. This is perhaps the only time when all but the most senior researchers have direct access to Ministers.

However, the time scales of research and policy rarely coincide. On many occasions interested policy staff will have moved on before the final report is available and administrative preoccupations may have shifted. In the latter case the researcher's role may be reduced to one of assimilating and storing findings until such time as they assume policy relevance once more. In the former case, and sometimes in the latter too, it falls to the researcher to stimulate new interest, although the routes open to him are surprisingly limited. It is advantageous to be located in a department with a Chief Scientist since research findings may then be circulated through him at a senior level. Elsewhere researchers may once again be disadvantaged by their low status; civil servants are given to evaluating the content of correspondence according to the grading of its signatory. Researchers may therefore have to rely on allegiances that have been built up with sympathetic policy-makers and with the more influential professionals. It is sometimes helpful to have informal contact with the various academics and practitioners who act as advisors to government departments. In DHSS for example, it was originally anticipated that the Research Liaison Groups would decide on the use made of research findings and certain of them have taken quite an active role in dissemination. Sometimes oral presentations of research findings may be organised by researchers but, even with much advanced planning, it is not always possible to ensure that key policy interests are present or that they are represented at sufficiently senior levels. Dissemination is an ongoing process rather than a one-off event and researchers can achieve much through their informal day-to-day contacts with administrators and by demonstrating an informed and constructive commitment to policy development.

One method of generating policy interest is to propose publication. In some departments it is the norm for all research to be published and the Department of Employment and Home Office, for example, have established a series in which research results are published. In others an exceptional case has to be made before research findings are published and even then they may be given no publicity. The difference in departmental attitude extends to research commissioned externally. Some departments maintain the power to veto publication entirely and others put research reports through a process of scrutiny and amendment that is almost as tight as for official departmental statements. The Department of Health and Social Security, on the other hand, takes a more open view of publication and external researchers are free to publish after the Department has been given an opportunity to comment. However, the wording of the standard DHSS research contract has recently been revised, seemingly with the intention of restricting contractors' freedom to publish.

The point about publication is that policy divisions will usually insist on their right to comment on the script in order to ensure that their interests are properly covered and protected. Their comments may be very detailed and vary from points of grammar to substantive issues concerning the interpretation of findings and their presentation. Often comments from different policy divisions are incompatible and research reports may go through several drafts before customers are satisfied. Even after this exhaustive process of consultation, the research will frequently be published with a disclaimer to the effect that the views expressed are those of the author alone and do not necessarily reflect official departmental views. In some departments there has recently been a trend towards commissioning research in-house or from market research firms on the grounds that demands for publication are less and the control greater.

Leaving aside the fundamental justification for publication raised by Lord Rothschild and presaged by the nature of democracy, the dissemination of research findings outside departments is vitally important for in-house government social science research. It provides an invaluable mechanism whereby the quality of research may be judged by outsiders who are free to the sometimes insidious pressures which bear on researchers inside government; pressures to produce quick results consistent with current policy thinking and which serve to numb critical judgement. Similarly, widespread publication offers government researchers an opportunity to reflect on their results in the light of explicit theoretical perspectives and to assess the impact of their own and departmental values on the validity and reliability of the research. Only in this way can high standards be maintained and improved.

Publication also helps to establish the legitimacy of government research outside Whitehall, not only within the academic community, but also among practitioners who may have been the subjects of research, and who will have to implement policies developed on the basis of the findings.

From a more personal viewpoint, government researchers often have two reference groups: the academic community in which they acquired their research skills and which is likely to have significantly influenced their world view, and the department which provides their current livelihood. These two environments also provide research officers with their two main lines of career advancement. A failure to publish seriously curtails the option of researchers to move out of government into the wider research community.

But pressures against publication are considerable and continue to grow. The process of consultation and clearance is slow, time-consuming and often frustrating. From the viewpoint of research management it absorbs staff time that could be better spent on developing new research projects needed to ensure the survival of in-house research. There is an ever present danger that political concern over embarrassing leaks will turn opinion in Whitehall against publication (and perhaps ultimately against research); much research is now undertaken on the understanding that publication is unlikely. The result is to undermine the role of researchers as the gatekeepers of social science in government. The more distanced they become from the social science community, the less well equipped they are to evaluate the research received by government, the less competent is their professional advice to policy-makers and the less able they are to act as emissaries for social science.

Perhaps Minister

This description of the process of in-house research is inevitably one-sided. It is the view of a researcher who has observed research from the inside, from a distance, but never directly from the viewpoint of the policy-maker. Moreover, the description has been slanted in order to address the question 'why has research not been more successful in influencing the formulation of policy?'. The obstacles proposed by Bulmer: the bureaucratic marginality of research and of specialists in general; the endemic empiricism of social science; its politicisation and lack of professionalism; and the constraints of the policy-making process itself – not least the political risks associated with research – provide the basis of a cogent answer. The aim in this chapter has been to show the guises in which these obstacles arise in practice. However, perhaps the severest obstacle of all resides in the complexity of the social world, and in the consequent inability of social science to provide Ministers and policy-makers with unequivocal 'yes' or 'no' answers in relation to the major policy questions of the day.

NOTES

1 I have learnt so much from so many government research officers over the years that it is impossible to thank them all. Most will be unaware of their contribution but some will, I hope, recognise their own experiences in what I have written. Nevertheless, my own view may be an idiosyncratic one and no one else can be held responsible in any way for distortions and omission.
2 Since writing this chapter, I have read the excellent note by Hennessy and Kirby (1984) which identifies two other constraints on the use of research: the great weakness of the British legislature in extracting 'the facts' from the executive arm of government, and the highly partisan envirionment in which any facts extracted are used to score cheap points in debate rather than as any part of reasoned policy analysis.

REFERENCES

Bowles, J. R. (1982), 'Central government expenditure on research and development', *Economic Trends* 346, pp. 82–94.
Bowles, J. R. (1984), 'Research and development in the United Kingdom in 1981', *Economic Trends* 370, pp. 81–9.
Bradshaw, J. (1985), *Priorities for research on supplementary benefit and housing benefit*, Social Policy Research Unit, University of York, Working Paper No. 242.
Bulmer, M. (1983), 'Using social science research in policy-making: why are the obstacles so formidable?', *Public Administration Bulletin* 43 (December), pp. 37–48.
Clarke, R. V. G. (1981), 'The effectiveness of graduate education in sociology: employment in a central government department', *Sociology* 15(4), pp. 525–30.
Cmnd (1971), *The organisation and management of government R&D*, Cmnd 4814, London, HMSO.
Cmnd (1972), *Framework for Government Research and Development*, Cmnd 5406, London, HMSO.
Cmnd (1981), *Government Statistical Services*, Cmnd 4814, London, HMSO.
Cmnd (1982), *An Enquiry Into the Social Science Research Council (Lord Rothschild)*, Cmnd 8554, London, HMSO.
CSC (1985), *Annual Report 1984*, London, for Civil Service Commission.
CSD (1978a), *Fast Stream Training: report of the Administrative Review Committee*, London, Civil Service Department.
CSD (1978b), *Civil Service Statistics 1977*, London, HMSO, for Civil Service Department.
DHSS (1984), *Research and Development Report and Handbook 1983*, London, HMSO for Department of Health & Social Security.
Elmore, R. (1976), 'Organisational models of social program implementation', *Public Policy* 26, p. 215.
ESRC (1984), *Annual Report 1983/4*, London, Economic and Social Research Council.

Hennessy, P. and Kirby, K. (1984), *Conference of Social Science Research Officers, 19–20 January*, London, DHSS Office of the Chief Scientist, mimeo.
HM Treasury (1985), *Civil Service Statistics 1984*, London, HMSO.
Kogan, M. and Henkel, M. (1983), *Government and Research*, London, Heinemann.
McMahon, L., Barrett, H. S. and Hill, M. (1983), 'Power bargaining models in policy analysis', *Public Administration Bulletin* 43 (December), pp. 49–68.
MPO (Management and Personnel Office) (1982), *The Civil Service Yearbook*, London, HMSO.
Rayner, D. (1980), *Review of Government Statistical Services. Report to the Prime Minister*, London, Central Statistical Office.
SRA (1985), *The State of Training in Social Research: report of a Sub-Committee*, London, Social Research Association.
Stokey, E. and Zeckhauser, R. (1978), *A Primer for Policy Analysis*, New York, Norton.
Thomas, P. (1985), *The Aims and Outcomes of Social Policy Research*, London, Croom Helm.

CHAPTER 10

Social science in government: the case of the Home Office Research and Planning Unit

DEREK B. CORNISH AND RONALD V. CLARKE

Introduction

No modern government can function without recourse to social research. At the very least, a variety of social and economic indicators will routinely be required; but on occasion there will be additional needs for *ad hoc* information-generating exercises and for policy-analysis and evaluation. Even the most ideological administrations will sometimes require the services of social research, or make use of its products (Weiss, 1980, 1982) – either for the purposes of smoothing the passage of controversial measures by promising their objective evaluation, or as a means of providing information favourable to a chosen policy.

But the benefits which social research brings to government cannot be purchased without some costs. These costs result from an essential conflict between the aims and values of the political and the scientific processes – a conflict similar in many respects to those identified by Kornhauser and others between science and industry (cf. Cotgrove and Box, 1970). To put the matter baldly, for the politician the starting-point for policies is an ideological position; for the social scientist, however, it should be a consideration of the available (or obtainable) facts. However caricatured this representation of complex realities, the fact that differing perspectives exist makes it inevitable that on occasion the social scientist will undermine policy by the production of unhelpful information or by attacking the basic assumptions which fuel the demand for political action. Thus, governments will always tend to get more than they bargained for, however much they may seek to direct and control the social scientist's work.

It is with the institutional arrangements for managing this conflict and for harnessing social research to the aims of policy that this paper is

166

concerned. We shall proceed by presenting a case study of one such long-standing and, in many respects, successful arrangement – that of the Home Office's Research and Planning Unit. We will then assess the effectiveness of this attempted solution to the fundamental conflict identified above, and consider the likely strengths and weaknesses of alternative arrangements. Although our discussion will focus upon crime-control policies, we have no reason to suppose that the general arguments are not applicable in other fields of social policy.

The Home Office Research and Planning Unit: a case history

The Home Office Research and Planning Unit (formerly the Home Office Research Unit) is a multidisciplinary body of social scientists located in the central government department of England and Wales which is responsible, among other things, for the prison, probation and police services, and for some aspects of the administration of justice. Apart from undertaking its own programme of research, the Unit provides advice to administrative divisions within the Home Office, and also disburses Home Office funds for the undertaking of criminological research by universities and other bodies. The present scientific staff of the Unit number about 40. Three-quarters of these are criminologists or other social scientists, while the remainder have qualifications in operational research. Most of the staff are located in the Unit's 'core' at the Home Office headquarters, but some are outposted to Prison Department and the Crime Prevention Unit of Police Department.

Background to the Unit's establishment

The chronology of events leading to the establishment of the Unit in 1957 has been described in detail by Lodge (1974) and also by Clarke and Cornish (1983). The contribution made by the social sciences to the war effort had given them some credibility in official circles and had lent weight to the views, expressed as early as 1936 by Margery Fry of the Howard League in a submission to the Home Office, that an organised programme of research was needed in order to deal effectively with the twin problems of juvenile delinquency and the treatment of offenders. These arguments were slow to gain general acceptance in the Home Office, despite the support it gave over the years to individual pieces of research. Milestones on the long route to the establishment of the Unit included: the last-minute inclusion within the Criminal Justice Act 1948 of a Private Member's clause which empowered the Home Secretary to undertake criminological research; the appointment in 1949 of a Home Office Statistical Adviser who subsequently became the Unit's first Head; and the award in 1951 of the Home Office's first small grants for research to the Universities of Oxford and Cambridge and to the London School of Economics. This latter grant was for a prediction study of the reconviction of borstal trainees (Mannheim & Wilkins, 1955) the success of which seems to have been instrumental in mobilizing support for research within the Home Office. By 1955, the Home Office appeared to have reached the following conclusions: that a coherent programme of social research was needed, especially one concerned with the effectiveness of penal treatment; that the resources to undertake the volume of necessary work did not exist within the universities; and that, if the research were to be undertaken to a timetable set by the Home Office and in a manner that would yield the most useable results, this would require the establishment of an in-house research unit. These views found favour with Mr R. A. Butler, newly appointed as Home Secretary in 1957, and in March of that year the Unit was founded. The initial complement was small, but growth was quite steady so that by 1968 the professional staff numbered 23 and five years later had reached more than twice that number. (The deteriorating economic situation had by the mid 1970s put paid to plans for further increases.)

Achievements

Given the fundamental conflict identified in the Introduction between the objectives of the scientific and political processes, any attempt to harness the former to the service of the latter is bound to result in an uneasy and perhaps fragile compromise. Judged by this standard the Unit must be regarded as remarkably successful, if not least because of its longevity. During the nearly 30 years of its existence, many government social research units have come and gone, while others have seen their functions reduced to the provision of low-level information for administrators or to the servicing of an extra-mural programme. Although smaller than it once was, the Unit still represents one of the largest concentrations of social researchers within government (even though the Home Office itself is not one of the larger government departments). But it is in terms of its published output that the Unit can truly be considered successful: within its own major series (since 1971 known as the *Home Office Research Studies* and prior to that time as *Studies in the Causes of Delinquency and the Treatment of Offenders*) more than 100 reports have appeared, while many times that number of lesser reports, journal articles and chapters in books have been published. In addition, the Unit produces a bi-annual *Research Bulletin* containing original articles and summaries of research and an annual *Programme of Research*, the 1984/85 edition of which contains more than

60 projects, half of which were being undertaken by the Unit itself. This wealth of output[1] dealing with a wide range of topics, together with the Unit's funding role, has given it a central place in British criminology.

Many of the Unit's reports concern detailed aspects of the functioning of the criminal justice system or studies of particular kinds of offences or groups of offenders. This work has usually been undertaken in response to the expressed needs of policy-makers for specific items of information and the results have therefore been of specialist interest,[2] but some of the Unit's output has attracted academic recognition both in Britain and abroad.[3] In our view, however, the Unit's major contribution to knowledge rests in its work on the prevention and control of crime. In an earlier publication (Clarke and Cornish, 1983) we attempted to chart the way in which this policy concern was interpreted by way of a series of linked research projects beginning – at the very inception of the Unit – with work on the treatment of offenders and shifting more recently to work on police effectiveness, deterrent sentencing and the 'situational' prevention of crime. Each stage of this research has been informed not only by the results of previous stages, but also by a changing and developing view of criminal motivation. The early work on treatment was embedded, perhaps inevitably, in the 'medico-psychological' model which had dominated criminology for half a century. This saw the determinants of crime as resting within the individual personality and, in particular, as being the outcome of emotional disturbance resulting from unsatisfactory family relationships (Healy and Bronner, 1936; Bowlby, 1946; Stott, 1950; Glover, 1960). The primary task of the penal system was interpreted as being the treatment and reformation of offenders and, for the first fifteen years of its existence, most of the Unit's resources were devoted to supporting this end.

The eventual outcome of this work (cf. Brody, 1976, for a review) and of similar research undertaken in the United States and elsewhere (cf. Martinson, 1974) is well known – the abandonment of both the rehabilitative ideal and the medico-psychological model which had fuelled it for so long. The Unit went on to develop an 'environmental-learning' theory to explain the short-lived effects of treatment and extended the 'situational' aspects of this theory in work it undertook later on the other forms of crime control mentioned above. This 'situational' viewpoint was most apparent in the Unit's work on crime prevention which, rather than being concerned with ways of modifying fundamental social causes of crime (an approach too uncomfortably close to that of treatment), was focused on ways of reducing the situational inducements and opportunities for crime (Mayhew, Clarke, Sturman and Hough, 1976). This work on 'situational crime prevention' has been recognised in textbook discussions of the causes of crime (cf. Downes and Rock, 1982; Barlow, 1984) and has also had a direct effect on Home Office policy: influenced by the many successful examples of situational preventive measures documented by the Unit, the remit for the Home Office Crime Prevention Unit (established in 1982), has been largely situational. The most recent developments in the Unit's crime control research – the British Crime Survey (Hough and Mayhew, 1983; 1985) and work on offender decision making (cf. Clarke and Cornish, 1985, for a review) – should also make a significant contribution both to criminal policy and to academic thinking.[4]

Ingredients of success

There can be little doubt that, without a substantial record of undertaking useful research, the Unit would not have emerged relatively unscathed from the last decade. During this period, the environment for government social research has become increasingly hostile: initial optimism about the ability of the social sciences to find a solution to crime and other social problems has long since disappeared; the public and politicians seem ever more distrustful of social scientists;[5] and pressure to reduce the size of the Civil Service has been unrelenting.

So what has been the formula for the Unit's successful research output? To answer that question one must return to the original remit for the Unit as given expression in the government White Paper, *Penal Practice in a Changing Society* (Home Office, 1959). As well as confirming the need for further research into effective penal treatment, this outlined a credo for government-sponsored research which, while frankly pragmatic, was rather broader than a purely operational approach. In brief, it was determined that the Unit would 'apply the basic principles of scientific method and attempt to produce results in quantitative terms'; that it would not cling to the methods of any particular discipline or school of thought but would 'seek to provide answers to specific questions by whatever means appear most appropriate'; and lastly that, 'in co-operating with outside research workers by providing facilities or grants, the Home Office will similarly be guided only by the apparent suitability for their purpose of the methods proposed to be used and the likelihood that the research will provide information in a form that can be used as a starting point for a further advance in knowledge' (*ibid.*, Appendix B, paragraph 21).

The White Paper's credo – pragmatic, interdisciplinary, positivist, correctional and reformist – while in keeping with the views of social science current at that period (Wootton, 1959) has also proved to be a very suitable foundation for government social research. The demand that research should be practically relevant – though not necessarily of immediate operational application – has provided Home Office administrators and Unit managers alike with a yardstick by which to judge the value of particular studies. The interdisciplinary composition of the Unit has made it difficult for individual research workers to retreat into narrow specialisms and also made them cognisant of the need for clear and simple communication – something especially necessary when the audience for research is hard-pressed administrators. Whatever its limitations (Trow, 1984), a quantitative bias has undoubtedly secured benefits beyond those of scientific method in that the conclusions of research have been seen to rest on a basis of 'hard' evidence: this has increased their perceived authority and utility in the eyes of administrators who, for their own purposes (cf. Weiss, 1980) traditionally require statistical indicators and other information expressed in numerical terms. Finally, the correctional and reformist ideals have served to give the Unit a particular identity, somewhat different from the rest of the Home Office, in the eyes of the liberal establishment – academic criminologists, pressure groups, informed journalists and Members of Parliament – which has been so influential in the development of British penal policy. On occasion this has resulted in support being given to the Unit from these quarters when its future existence has seemed to be under threat.

Equally important for the Unit's success as the initial credo, however, has been the understanding – endorsed by successive political administrations – that the results of research should be published. Without publication, external support for the Unit would have been minimal, but an equally important benefit has been the attention research has thereby received from administrators: reports that are to be published cannot be stuffed away in drawers or otherwise 'shelved'. They have to be read and digested and any policy implications have to be addressed; they must either be adopted or responded to in some other way – for example, they may need to be dismissed on grounds of cost or public acceptability. This close attention from administrators – hostile as it may sometimes have been – has conferred the additional benefit of strengthening the Unit's research proposals and improving both the presentation and logic of its published reports.

One other important aspect of publication has been that from the very beginnings of the Unit all reports have carried the names of their authors. This has provided an incentive to individual productivity, especially for those research workers who have seen their long-term future as being within the universities. That there has always been a sizeable cadre of such individuals has again worked to the Unit's advantage: while the

Unit has been large enough to provide a reasonably satisfactory career structure for some of its most able researchers it has been too small to provide secure careers for all of them. The fact that so many of these people have been able to obtain employment in universities has promoted the turnover of high quality staff and the regular infusion of 'new blood' that serves to maintain the vitality of any research organisation.

Criticisms

Successful as it may have been, the Unit has not been without its critics. These are divided between those administrators who see its work as insufficiently relevant to their needs and those academics who see it as insufficiently independent of government pressure. The harshest academic criticisms were voiced in the early 1970s and came from the ranks of the National Deviancy Conference (NDC), a group of younger sociologists mainly from the newer universities and polytechnics who were united by their dislike of establishment criminology. In fact, the main target for their invective was not the Unit but the Cambridge Institute of Criminology, then at the height of its influence, but which, because it received so much of its research money from the Home Office, was seen by the members of the NDC as an arm of government. The NDC criticisms of establishment criminology (e.g. Cohen, 1974; Wiles, 1976) concerned those very elements of the credo we have identified as being responsible for the Unit's success: the correctional and reformist ideals were seen as precluding a proper understanding of the deviant's motivation and perspective (deviant conduct may not only be entirely understandable and even normal in certain circumstances, but might also represent a political statement); pragmatism, so far from being a valuable disciplining force, was regarded as constraining and impoverishing intellectual effort; and the aspirations to scientific respectability were seen as a retreat into scientism and spurious quantification in the face of intellectual bankruptcy.

Not all these criticisms were simply motivated by the usual academic jealousies. However laudable, correctional and reformist ideals have proved sadly unrealistic. There is little doubt that a deeper understanding of the offender's perspective will enrich criminology and – while not intended by deviancy sociologists – may also result in improved crime control policies. And some of the quantitative exercises – especially those which ignored the dark figure of unreported crime – rested on very shaky foundations. On the other hand, much of the criticism was also unfair. It is difficult to see, for example, how the myth about the effectiveness of penal treatment could have been so convincingly dispelled without hard, quantitative evidence about the lack of long-term effects. Even if it was not to the liking of deviancy sociologists, a theory (the medico-psychological model) did underlie the research on treatment and the Unit, in particular, did develop a model ('environmental/ learning theory') to explain the failure of treatment. Indeed, we have argued elsewhere that the demand for practical relevance, far from leading to the neglect of theory, has meant that the Unit has made a unique contribution to the development of criminological theories which are relevant to practice and policy (Clarke and Cornish, 1983). In contrast, academic theories freed from the demands of relevance frequently prove to be useless in any practical way (cf. Wilson, 1975; Lazarsfeld and Reitz, 1975; Scott and Shore, 1979).

Possibly the most unfair criticisms, however, were those concerning alleged subservience to government interests. It should have required little imagination to see that the negative results of the treatment research would be unwelcome to the Home Office. And, more recently, the published results, for example, of work on police effectiveness (Clarke and Hough, 1980, 1984), on disparities in sentencing and prosecution (Walmsley, 1978; Tarling, 1979), on the extent of unrecorded crime (Hough and Mayhew, 1983), and on the use of police stop and search powers (Stevens and Willis, 1979) have appeared only following protracted arguments within the Home Office. The fact that this work has eventually been published says as much for the senior management of the Home Office as it does for the Unit itself. Whether the arguments would have been less protracted – we can recall one case where negotiations went on for over a year and involved nine or ten redrafts of the offending article – had reports routinely carried a 'disclaimer' by the Home Office is by no means certain. Some administrators would probably still have wanted reports to omit unfavourable interpretations of data or to express them in anodyne terms.

While the Unit may have resisted direct censorship of its results, it is difficult to know how far authors have exercised self-censorship in avoiding controversial interpretations and there is little doubt that on occasion the Unit has not undertaken research on particular subjects either because of their sensitivity or because the responsible administrator was known to be hostile to research. In fact, provided that the Unit continues to be sensitive to administrators' wishes about the timing of publication and the content of press releases, it would seem to have little to fear. In the first place, it would be politically difficult for Ministers to interfere with the long-standing tradition of publication: many more difficulties have been caused for the Home Office by accusations of censorship than by the actual contents of a Unit report. Also, the fact that the Unit's current projects are listed each year in the

Programme of Research means that it is difficult for a report simply to 'disappear' – something that is now even less likely as the result of a newly-instituted policy of sending out all major reports for academic review prior to publication. Finally, reports whose publication has been delayed have sometimes been leaked to the press – not always, it would seem, by Unit staff.

As for the criticism that the Unit's work has been insufficiently policy relevant, here again the position is not straightforward. If by relevant is meant leading directly to a change in policy or practice, this reflects a naive view of the policy process (Kallen et al., 1982). Policies are very rarely dictated only by 'the facts'; they are more usually the combined products of facts, values and perceptions, economic realities and political expediences. As Weiss (1980) suggests, a more accurate description of the processes involved can be summed up in the terms 'knowledge creep' in relation to the influence of research in policy, and 'decision-accretion' as a depiction of the way in which policy emerges. But, since facts are the major currency of social research, this inevitably limits its direct impact on the world; there are, nevertheless, some examples of policies that have been importantly influenced by research.[6]

Current role and position

Despite the above achievements, it is nevertheless true that too many pieces of Unit research have been difficult to relate to policy[7] or have arrived too late to influence the critical decisions. These failures stimulated attempts made over the years to improve the internal management of the Unit's programme as well as communications with Home Office administrative divisions. One important development was the adoption in 1973 of the Rothschild 'customer-contractor' principle of research management (Civil Service Department, 1971), which stipulated that no research should be undertaken by government or funded in a university unless a clear administrative 'customer' existed for the products of the research.[8] Some other steps were taken at about the same time: the Unit's senior management made a determined effort to reduce the time-scale of research projects so that they would typically run for no more than a couple of years, and a principal research officer was designated for secondment to the newly-formed Crime Policy Planning Unit to ensure that research had its proper place in the policy planning process.

The present structure of the Unit is the outcome of another such initiative – in this case, a major re-organisation undertaken in 1981, prompted largely by government policy to reduce the size of the Civil Service. The resulting reviews of Home Office scientific and research establishments led to the abolition of the post of Chief Scientist (one of only five Deputy Secretary posts in the Office) and the re-assignment of its former responsibilities. Following the review undertaken by its head, the Unit lost about one quarter of its social research posts these being replaced by ten from a disbanded operational research department. At the same time, the opportunity was taken to abolish the Crime Policy Planning Unit (which had not been part of the Chief Scientists' command) and to put two of its administrative posts within the re-named Research and Planning Unit.

This reorganisation achieved not only a net reduction in scientific and research posts (although the large Police Scientific and Development Branch escaped unscathed) but also served somewhat to reorient the Unit's efforts. From being a primarily criminological research unit, it became one more explictly concerned with operational and policy issues. This identification was assisted by the outposting of staff directly to administrative divisions and by the Unit's organisational positioning alongside Criminal Department which has responsibility, among other matters, for the co-ordination of Home Office policies.

The reorganisation of 1981 should be seen not so much as a turning-point for the Unit as just one further step taken by the Home Office to ensure the Unit's resources were directed to assisting with the policy concerns of the day. In fact, the Unit's remit remained largely as before: to undertake and publish a programme of social (and operational) research; to manage an extramural programme of Home Office funded work in universities and other research institutes; and to provide a continuous service of social science-based advice and support to policy-makers. Indeed, the main result was not to change the character of the Unit's work but rather to give administrators more direct control over it.[9]

Alternative ways of delivering social science research to government

In the section above we examined one solution to the problems of reconciling the professional goals of social scientists with those of governments in order to procure social research for policy formation. There we concluded that, given the fundamental conflict between these goals, institutional arrangements along the lines of an in-house quasi-autonomous unit can provide a viable solution – in terms of relevant and effective output; investment in, and development of, expertise and knowledge; stability and continuity of long-term research strategies; and the nurturing of links both with policy departments and with the academic community.

We emphasised, however, that such an arrangement always represents an uneasy compromise; despite the fund of goodwill and trust that may painstakingly be built up over the years amongst the parties involved, tensions wax and wane as existing arrangements are tested out, re-evaluated, challenged and modified on both sides (cf. Kogan and Henkel, 1983; Clarke and Cornish, 1983). It is because of these inherent, though manageable, problems of control and conflict that other models of research delivery exist which attempt to provide solutions to the three most difficult problems government departments have to face when considering the contracting of research: those of drawing up prioritised shopping-lists of policy-relevant research; of selecting researchers able and willing to produce the needed results; and of supervising the contractors during the duration of the project.

In this section we examine four alternatives in order to assess whether, in relation to all or any of these problems, the solutions they offer represent more attractive compromises – both to government and to social scientists – than that of the in-house unit.

Location within administrative divisions

The direct recruitment of social scientists to administrative positions within the civil service represents one general means by which government gains access to social science expertise, while at the same time controlling the ends to which such skills are devoted. But even were the recommendations of the Fulton Report to be more fully implemented,[10] the level of skill and expertise offered by graduate entrants is necessarily limited and dates quickly. As a more limited and specific solution, research workers may be brought in to develop a research capability within particular policy divisions of a ministry. (A variant of this model is provided by outposting of research staff from a departmental 'core' unit; as mentioned above, this is done to a limited extent in the Home Office.)

To the ministry, the advantages of such 'outposting' are seductive. In line with the Rothschild (customer–contractor) formula, the customer policy division develops a shopping-list of research requirements and the contractor (outposted member of the central research unit or directly-recruited researcher) then delivers the expertise and the research. Location of researchers within the division concerned guarantees their thorough familiarity with the latter's needs, and ensures that administrators can exercise a closer control over the work itself, the results, their interpretation and dissemination, and the use to which they are put. This is made possible by the administrative framework within which the work is done which ensures the crucial dependency of the researchers for both rewards and job-satisfaction on receiving satisfactory reports from the customer division concerned – a dependency which is underlined by the salary and status differentials which usually exist between administrators and research workers.

We believe, however, that many of these alleged advantages are more apparent than real and that they are, in any case, accompanied by enough disadvantages in the longer term to cancel out any short-term benefits. For the administrative division the acquisition of useful research depends primarily on two factors: its skills in identifying and specifying its research needs; and its ability to provide effective supervision of, and control over, the research process. But it at once appears that these factors are by no means independent of each other. The patchy implementation of the Fulton Report's (1968) proposals, together with the relatively short periods that administrative staff stay within the same policy-division, have a number of consequences for research planning and management. First, they make it unlikely that administrators will usually be able unaided to identify the research needs of the division: instead the task will tend to be shared with research liaison committees, the central research unit (if there is one) or outside consultants. Second, similar considerations would question the division's ability to commission research appropriate to identified issues or to provide effective oversight of research staff without considerable assistance. But the provision of such help, by the researchers themselves or (especially) by the central research unit at once reduces the division's control over its research programme, its implementation and over the staff involved – that is, those very features which made outposting so apparently attractive in the first place.

And what of the impact on research under such an arrangement? The likelihood that parochial short-term information-gathering exercises will take up the bulk of researchers' time cannot be discounted and the costs of paying skilled personnel to perform what are often essentially tasks for research assistants should not be underestimated. A disposition for research to be reactive rather than proactive, with little questioning of policy-assumptions and a dearth of genuine policy-analysis, might well be the outcome. Moreover, concentration upon the production of internal memos, briefings and reports as primary outputs will reduce the amount, value and wider impact of any research while at the same time protecting it from impartial and professional scrutiny.

Nor is such subservience to administrative needs the only price which the researcher pays for security and limited preferment: while promotion prospects even within specialised units have their effective ceiling well below those within the administrative grades, the position of the outposted or contracted research worker is even more uncertain. With little prospect, because of his or her 'excessive specialisation', of access to the higher administrative positions or – because of a lack of published work – of outside employment (cf. Cotgrove and Box, 1970), and the scene is set for an even greater subservience to administrative goals at the expense of providing precisely that kind of specialist advice and expertise which divisions have the right (although not always the perspicacity) to expect. At the least, promotion would be likely to involve movement back to the central unit or outposting to another division, thus imposing upon research a pattern of career management which may well be unsuitable to its professional needs.

In such circumstances it is all too easy for the line of least resistance to be adopted – either by supplying advice, masquerading as research data, which is no more than lay opinion, or by so relaxing methodological criteria that the scientific credibility of the work is compromised. Leaving aside the damaging effects to both policy-making and the reputation of the social sciences of such outcomes (Weiss, 1982), the effects on the research workers themselves are likely to be an increasing disillusionment accompanied by a marked long-term fall-off in the quality of work. Nor, against these disadvantages, should it be expected that familiarity will breed mutual understanding and tolerance between researchers and administrators: prolonged exposure to the value-systems of one group by the other may simply exacerbate differences in outlook, impair working relationships and further reduce the perceived value of a social science input into the policy-making process.

The position of the small core research unit under such extensive outposting arrangements would scarcely be better. Denied the powers, personnel or opportunity to carry out its own programme of research, its main functions would surely dwindle to those of providing information and advice when requested.

The small procurement secretariat

A logical extension of the ideas discussed above – of a largely outposted research capability – is the transformation and reduction of the core unit's role solely to one of research procurement in liaison with policy departments. This brokerage function, and the servicing of extra-mural programmes which it entails, could be combined with the sort of information-gathering, referencing and briefing tasks which already form a substantial part of the Home Office Research and Planning Unit's day-to-day work. Once again it is the apparent reductions in costs and increase of control which make this option so attractive. On the cost front, research staff would be employed only as required on particular one-off projects of interest to the department concerned, their

day-to-day supervision being largely delegated to the academic community, whose institutions could then defray many of the costs (including a
number of hidden ones).[11] This reduction in the ministry's direct
research overheads is, so the argument goes, accompanied by an increase
in control over the product. Thus, through a careful process of tendering,
procurement and negotiation, the customer department, assisted by its
secretariat, can specify exactly what is wanted, while contractual obligations buttressed by a system of deadlines, yearly reports and part-
payments to the contracting institution ensure that the goods as requested are delivered on time. Lastly, the worrisome degree of autonomy and
professional respect which might have to be accorded an in-house
research unit and its products is avoided by such arrangements. A body
staffed by experienced research managers and personnel is now replaced
by one consisting largely of information officers and researchers turned
administrators; and that powerful and politically-sensitive commodity –
the information generated from research – is now supplied by way of a
fragmented and weakened marketplace of individual research contractors who are competing for a diminishing national social research budget.

Against this eminently commercial approach to the commissioning of
research have to be put a number of disadvantages for the ministry itself.
The first concerns the credibility of the secretariat in its crucial role as
broker. Since the secretariat engages in no research of its own, either
directly or through outposted staff, its abilities to assist in developing
divisions' shopping lists, to commission viable research and adequately
to supervise and monitor its progress must be in some doubt. Indeed,
distrust on the part of administrators of this body's ability to evaluate
research proposals may only be equalled by their suspicion (though for
different reasons) of a body that could. Under these circumstances a
plethora of costly liaison and steering committees designed to bring
together policy-makers and those in the academic community who could
provide a meaningful expertise would be apt to develop (cf. Kogan and
Henkel's [1983] telling case-study of the attempts made by the Department of Health and Social Security to implement Rothschild in this way).

Moreover, although the practice of using academics not only as unpaid
research directors, but also as unpaid advisors during the processes of
establishing research needs, vetting research proposals and reviewing
project reports (the Home Office now pay for this latter work) might
seem at first sight a cost-effective solution to the problem, a number of
problems arise – especially during a period of recession – when experts
are used in this way. It is, for example, common commercial practice to
pay the market rate for expert advice, on the commonsense grounds that
you get only what you pay for, and that advisors are apt to take more

trouble over, and feel more responsibility for, advice which is purchased. For these reasons alone, free advice may not always be the soundest or most carefully-considered. Since also the busiest (and perhaps most successful) academics might be expected to have less time to spare – and even less inclination to provide it gratis – than their colleagues, there is also the danger that such a system would fail to provide an adequate screening of the better as well as the worse research proposals. More importantly, since no payment is being made to those who might themselves well look to the ministry concerned for research grants in the future, an element of implied patronage is inevitably built into the system as its most regular advisors increasingly define the knowledge-market from which future research is to be commissioned, and build up both credit and obligation with the ministry. Even the possibility, let alone the reality, of such patronage is enough to make such a practice both unprofessional and damaging to the academic community.[12]

So far as monitoring ongoing research is concerned, the likelihood that quality-control could be maintained in the face of the dilution of expertise and diffusion of responsibility represented by the above arrangements might seem remote. But it might be argued that the contracting-out of research effectively buys the necessary supervision – and at very favourable terms, since research projects will characteristically be undertaken within academic institutions and under the direction of a senior academic. Indeed, he or she could reasonably be expected to carry responsibility for the organisation, implementation, supervision and completion of such research as part of his or her contractual obligations to the educational institution concerned. Thus, it might be said, the academic would be under strong obligations not only to the funding agency but also to his own organisation to complete the project satisfactorily.

Unfortunately, the realities are often rather different. Against the view that a market of outside social researchers anxious and able to be 'relevant' exists to be commissioned, should be set Kogan and Henkel's (1983) disappointing conclusions about the quality of research proposals which found their way unsolicited to the Small Grants Committee of the Department of Health and Social Security. Academics do not necessarily have the variety of research skills, breadth of practical experience and detailed knowledge of the field of enquiry that the professional researcher may bring to a new project; and there is no guarantee that others in their institutions will be able to supply these lacks. Other constraints and priorities operating in academic life may further hamper the proper supervision and execution of large-scale research projects (cf. Cornish and Clarke, 1981). Chief among these are career demands which make commitment to long-term research projects in the social sciences (especially where these result in joint-authored reports) less attractive than short theoretical papers or those describing limited empirical exercises.

Again, the demands of teaching make more than intermittent involvement in, and supervision of, research a virtual impossibility except during vacations.[13] It is for this reason that the bulk of the research efforts may devolve upon comparatively junior personnel, who are either bought-in as research assistants for the duration of the project, or try to combine this work with that for their doctoral dissertations. (And the priorities and objectives of doctoral work are not necessarily those of contract research for policy-purposes.) In these circumstances, the procurement secretariat may find it has rather little effective control over those who have access to settings and data which may be politically sensitive, over how its research is carried out or, in the final resort, over whether and in what form the results are made public. Given the context, it should not be surprising that the customer's needs may not always take prime place.

Where purchase-of-service policies are pursued, the government department's imperfect acquaintance with the knowledge-market will, of course, make a limited degree of patronage inevitable. A quite proper aversion to risk, coupled with a desire to build on existing expertise has the effect of establishing *de facto* oligopolies as accumulated experience and satisfactory track-record increasingly favour established individuals and centres of research at the expense of new ones. Likewise, research awards will tend to be spread around the associated knowledge-networks.

But the weaknesses of the procurement secretariat and the slow, cumbersome, costly and ineffective advisory committee system which its own inadequacy as a broker inevitably spawns accentuates these problems while failing to exploit the advantages. Where, dazzled by a false vision of the economies to be made by contracting-out, administrators operate a purchase-of-service system, this may damage not only the effectiveness of the ministry it serves, but also the future of research in the areas with which it interacts. Without the informed overview of a field which an in-house research capability can provide, research is taken up and dropped piecemeal as fashion – dictated solely by political pressures from inside and outside the ministry – decrees, while the system of short-term contracting without satisfactory supervision, continuity of employment or proper career-structure which reflects these political processes can frequently lead to in an extremely unsatisfactory research environment (cf. Platt's, [1976]), detailed survey findings).

Lastly, it is naive to suppose that governments, as consumers of research, are 'customers' in the everyday commercial sense of the word (Kogan, Korman and Henkel, 1980). So long as government directly controls so large a part of the finance (and often access to data) which makes social science research possible (Smith, 1982), contractors are unlikely to be able to secure adequate recompense, and the scene is thereby set for a variety of distorting market influences. Given the opportunity to do so, the temptations for government to try to impose a particular view of research priorities beyond its own remit, and to avoid paying a fair price for the advice or research it actually commissions, are strong ones; and, since those making such decisions are unlikely to see or appreciate the detrimental longer term effects (or be brought to book for them), the short-run gains of such policies must render them well-nigh irresistible.

Apart, then, from exacerbating all the usual problems of contract research management, procurement systems like the model outlined above are unlikely – in the face of political pressures and demands – to be able strenuously to maintain the delicate and ambiguous role of client/ patron. And without this, they cannot fulfil their wider obligations to social research, upon which depends the continued health, viability and independence of research in the academic disciplines which provide the knowledge-base for policy.

Support of large-semi-autonomous units

If in-house research units pose potential problems of control and relevance for the policy-maker, and procurement secretariats may fail to deliver effective research, then one compromise solution is the establishment of semi-autonomous research units, independent of government but funded by it. Such units could be supported either directly via the universities, or indirectly via the research councils.[14]

There are a number of advantages to such arrangements from the point of view both of the government and of criminological research. For the government, in addition to the financial benefits of purchase-of-service are those which go with the development of centres of excellence – a concentration and development of expertise; greater continuity of staffing, research programmes and interest; government influence upon the direction and cost-effective development of long-term research programmes; growing capability for policy analysis; and provision of advice and proposals for future policy-relevant research. To these advantages can be added those of proper supervision, accountability and control. The fact that all such advantages are bought only as required and that government can extricate itself comparatively rapidly from its research commitments, is yet another powerful attraction.

For researchers many of the same advantages also apply. In such an environment, long-term job prospects – even for contract researchers – are more secure, while the specialist setting and the demands to supply policy-relevant contract research provide for the development of a wide and marketable variety of research skills (instead of the few characteristically provided by doctoral research) and the means to obtain a broad background of relevant scholarship. Moreover, the commercial pressures on contract-funded units to complete and write-up research to deadlines, and the tighter and more expert supervision which can be offered by its staff, reduces the likelihood of the 'failure to complete' syndrome which has in the past been such a waste of human and economic resources on British doctoral programmes and any associated research projects.

Against this catalogue of advantages it has to be recognised that most are realisable only given a high quality of research staff, a tightly-administered research programme, and careful supervision of the unit's progress by the government department. Moreover, although the creation of semi-autonomous units may seem cost-effective, of themselves they provide a solution only to the problem of supplying government with quality research; the problems of identifying research needs and of supervising external contractors remain. As was mentioned above, a procurement secretariat without the expertise to assist policy-divisions in the development of customer-requirements, or unable to assess the merits of unsolicited research proposals, is unlikely to be in any position to exert satisfactory control over the direction or quality of work of a specialist external research unit. For such tasks, outside advisors are no substitute for expertise within government; and satisfactory levels of expertise can only be maintained in-house by providing the job-experience and career-structure which foster and reward these skills – an argument, perhaps, for preserving at least a residual research capability within the government department concerned.

Problems may be anticipated, too, for the research institution which allows a large part of its activities to be underwritten by government monies. Even if the customer–contractor relationship is in fact no more than a commercial arrangement, others will be quick to identify hints of collusion, especially in the establishment of research objectives, and in the presentation of sensitive research findings (an example relating to the Cambridge Institute of Criminology was given above). The fact that – as in medical research – the funding of outside units uses up large chunks of the overall budget for research may well mean that, in supporting the work of one particular institution, overall research priorities in the field become distorted along particular lines. While this shaping of research direction may well appear justifiable to governments it may at times divert resources from issues of substantive, although longer-term policy-relevance in order to minister to short-run political pressures. In other words, semi-autonomous units may be subject to the same pressures (and criticisms) as in-house counterparts.

External research units can protect themselves from some of these pressures in a number of ways. First they can ensure that they continue to seek funding from a variety of sources, governmental, commercial and charitable. With a wide enough portfolio of research contracts, an institution can avoid an overdependence on any one customer. In addition to securing a measure of independence, this will enable the institution to pursue those research interests in which it feels best qualified to engage. Second – and this is particularly the case for units in the higher education sector – staff should be encouraged to carry out teaching duties within the institution to which they are linked: a system of joint appointments can considerably reduce the burden of staff overheads.

Most importantly, the unit might consider the benefits of offering specialist training courses in its fields of expertise. In the United States, for example, the establishment of a number of schools of criminal justice (particularly those at the University of Maryland, Rutgers University and SUNY at Albany) provided a base for both specialist academic training programmes and for policy-relevant research. In this country, apart (with reservations) from the Cambridge Institute of Criminology, nothing comparable exists, and yet the advantages such an arrangement offers are clear. By providing courses at degree, postgraduate and post-experience level to criminal justice personnel – the police, prison officers, probation officers, civil servants – such institutions can make an effective contribution to training in areas commonly agreed to be poorly served by existing arrangements. Clustering vocational courses in a centre of excellence could be expected to attract good students and provide good research workers with greater financial security and with experience in communicating ideas.

Although government resourcing and validation of such training programmes would inevitably place certain constraints upon the institution, these are apt to be exaggerated.[15] It would, of course, provide a better basis for continuity of research interests and staff employment, and a calmer environment in which to do research than one in which much of the time of senior researchers was taken up in touting for money or drawing up speculative research proposals – and that of junior staff in exploring alternative job opportunities as contracts neared termination. It would also provide an environment in which the fostering of a policy-oriented attitude to research came from within the institution as well as from its customers, as a result of the mutual communication between researchers and practitioners on the training courses, and as the numbers of practitioners acquiring the skills to undertake research in their own areas grew. There is, therefore, no reason to expect that such institutions would become unduly influenced by their funding sources. Over the years, the professional expertise gathered by the more effective of these would eventually provide them with a power-base from which they could play a part in analysing and shaping criminal justice policy.

Policy-analysis units

The discussion so far has examined a range of possible solutions to the three major tasks – drawing up prioritised shopping-lists of research, selecting suitable contractors, and ensuring effective super-vision – which governments have to tackle in order to secure policy-relevant social research. But it is upon the first of these tasks that the others crucially depend (Rawsthorne, 1978). Potential assistance abounds: from administrators in the relevant policy-areas; from in-house research unit staff, either within the central unit or outposted to divisions; from *ad hoc* or more permanent research liaison and advisory committees; and from outside consultants, including existing or past contractors. But the effectiveness with which these sources of help can be harnessed depends upon the quality of policy-analysis which the government can muster from within its own resources.

In order to examine this issue, it is worth looking more closely at some of the ways in which the Home Office has tackled this question in relation to its criminological research needs. As we saw earlier, solutions to this problem have varied over the lifetime of the Research Unit. Immediately before the establishment of the Unit, the government had been content to contract with the universities when it was felt (rarely enough) that policy-formation might be assisted by a particular piece of research (cf. for example, Carr-Saunders, Mannheim and Rhodes' report on *Young Offenders*, published in 1942). It was largely as the result of the success of a later venture (Mannheim and Wilkins, 1955) that the Home Office began to appreciate the likely advantages of having its own research capability. It is important to recognise, however, that when some three years later, in 1959, the government outlined its research strategy and requirements in its White Paper, *Penal Practice in a Changing Society*, (HMSO, 1959) it clearly envisioned these as being as much policy- as research-led. The Unit's increasing involvement in large, long-term research commitments and in generating its own research initiatives, however, inevitably meant that its role as a source of policy-analysis –

that is, among other things, of helping to identify departmental research needs – failed to develop to a comparable degree.

Meanwhile, a concern with the quality of policy-making and, as one consequence, with finding ways to improve communications between social scientists and policy-makers was itself becoming an important policy issue (Blume, 1982). During the 1970s, interest turned to the development of policy-analysis both as a formal discipline (Trow, 1984) and as a means of improving medium and long-term policy-formation. The resulting proliferation of 'think tanks' and 'planning units' represented experiments in ways of formalising this knowledge-broker role. At Cabinet level the Central Policy Review Staff (CPRS), under the leadership of Lord Rothschild, was established in 1970. In 1974, as an outcome of one of the Fulton Committee's (1968) recommendations, the Criminal Department of the Home Office set up its own Crime Policy Planning Unit (CPPU) (Moriarty 1977) – its jobs being to analyse longer-term policy requirements of the Department, develop and co-ordinate policy initiatives, encourage a more strategic approach to criminal and penal policies, and act as an information-broker between researchers and policy-makers. One of its functions was directly relevant to the issue of identifying research priorities: it was to provide Criminal Department with policy-relevant information, including reviews of the research literature on particular policy issues, and to make suggestions for further research – a policy-analytic role which might have seemed appropriate for the Research Unit itself, but which had not hitherto taken up a large part of the latter's work.

These moves clearly indicated important policy needs – a signal that did not go unnoticed by the Research Unit (from which, incidentally, a senior researcher had been outposted to the CPPU). If, as Rawsthorne (1978) commented, policy-makers needed to think more about research, and researchers more about policy, then, by emphasising the need for strategic thinking and long-range policy analysis, the CPPU experiment encouraged both Criminal Department and the Research Unit to develop their own expertise to meet these objectives. As a consequence, the Research Unit's own strategy throughout the 1970s was to become more responsive to policy-departments' requirements. In research terms, this led to a reduction in large-scale experimental and prediction research in favour of smaller and quicker projects, surveys (some contracted out) and demonstration projects. These changes were accompanied by the espousal of a much more explicitly policy-analytic role, resulting in the production of more literature reviews (in-house and commissioned), position papers, and information-provision; and, backed by an increasing amount of out-posting, more advice to divisions on research needs and implementation.

But the CPPU experiment was not to last. And the more responsive the Research Unit became, the more it must have seemed to offer a satisfactory alternative home for those of the CPPU's functions which were to be retained. The Research Unit, after all, already contained amongst its own staff (sociologists, psychologists, lawyers, statisticians and administrators) the very skills, backed by the relevant technical resources and expertise, which were crucial ingredients for successful policy-analysis, and for advising on policy-relevant research needs. In organisational terms, the Research Unit's move from the Rothschild-inspired Office of the Chief Scientist into Criminal Department – where, as the Research and Planning Unit, it took on some of the functions of the defunct CPPU – provided formal recognition of its new roles.

Since both the CPRS and the much less exalted CPPU came to untimely ends, it is perhaps worth speculating on the reasons: what, in general, contributed to the difficulties of (British) think-tank initiatives in achieving a long-term viability; and what, in particular, were perceived as the advantages of encouraging the Research Unit's policy-analytic role in preference to the CPPU's one. The answer to the first question lies perhaps in the vulnerability of the policy-analysis unit. Bodies like the Research Unit, with its large professional staff, solid base of technical expertise, long track-record of academically respectable and policy-relevant research – practically all of it on public record – and a recognised (if insecure) place in Departmental structure, can achieve a certain independence and credibility which provides some defence against the vicissitudes of the political environment which it inhabits.

The position of the typical policy-analysis unit, such as the CPRS or CPPU, however, could not be more different. Almost entirely dependent for survival upon the uncertain and temporary goodwill of ill-defined, changing and often incompatible sets of political masters, forging alliances and attracting powerful patrons when and where they can, their lives are precarious in the extreme. Whatever their theoretical obligations to policy-analytic ideals, their work is characteristically dictated primarily by the need to remain acceptable. As a result, the work tends to be short-term, opportunistic and eclectic (Plowden, 1981) – paradoxically, the very factors which limit the ability of many policy-analysis units to carve out a viable long-term role for themselves.[16] These problems are further enhanced by the constraints under which they often labour: their small size and limited in-house expertise and resources enjoin them to avoid more than the occasional longer-term, larger-scale strategic project which, while politically risky, might enhance their reputation. And this difficulty in achieving outside credibility (and hence, alternative sources of support) is exacerbated by their lack of control over the publication of their reports.

As to the organisational viability of such policy-analysis units at the departmental level – considered for the moment solely in terms of their role as research identifiers in the overall research delivery process – some more general doubts must be raised. Separated-off as they tend to be from both their customers (other administrators in policy-divisions) and would-be contractors (such as the Research Unit), they exemplify – as, in their own ways, do the procurement secretariat and semi-autonomous research unit – the dangers of allowing an analysis of the process of commissioning government research to dictate the way in which this is translated into organisational practices. For recognition that separate (and perhaps conflicting) powers, functions or interests exist within this process does not necessarily imply that their reification into correspondingly separate organisational arrangements will provide the best solution. An over-elaboration of bureaucratic structures in which none of the independent elements has, on its own, the expertise to carry out a general remit can exacerbate rather than reduce conflict; and it may well impede rather than facilitate the production of the policy-relevant research which is the object of the exercise.

The answer to the second question – of why it was the Research Unit, rather than CPPU, which survived – lies perhaps in the case-study which formed the first part of this chapter. Other factors – such as the greater public visibility of the Research Unit and the greater difficulty of redeploying a large body of specialist staff – doubtless also played a part. In addition, it is perhaps not unduly cynical to observe that, staffed by relatively non-mobile specialists (the bulk of whom are of comparatively lowly status in the departmental hierarchy) rather than by career administrators,[17] the Research Unit's policy-analytic role can be more easily regulated. This can be achieved either by restricting its activities to considerations of tactics rather than strategy, or by maintaining a tight control over presentational aspects of its work – in particular, the channels and forms by which the information it gathers is fed into the deliberations of policy-makers. Hence, unlike the CPPU, it runs no danger of usurping control of prestigious administrative functions, and of creating an elite within an elite.

Conclusions

We began this chapter by referring to the inevitable conflict between the values and objectives of the scientific and political processes. In the quest for policy-relevant research the issue, then, is not how to avoid this conflict, but how best to manage it. If there is a single conclusion to be drawn from the above discussion it is that the problems of delivering policy-relevant social research are not susceptible of an organisational or bureaucratic solution. Each of the models discussed – in-house research unit, divisional outposting, procurement secretariat, semi-autonomous research unit, and policy-analysis unit – has its particular set of limitations. Our own experience of the Home Office's Research and Planning Unit suggests that, of these alternatives, the in-house unit has perhaps the fewest drawbacks.

But not all such units have prospered – even those which appeared to share a similar research philosophy and pursued a robust publication policy. Nor is it likely that the Research and Planning Unit has been unusually fortunate in its staff, since for the major part of its life most of these have arrived via the centralised recruitment system run by the Civil Service Commission. It may be that the explanation lies rather in the Unit's ability to provide an environment in which professional expertise and reputations could flourish. To our minds this has had a number of important consequences, of which the most visible are the quality of publications and the development of long-term programmes of research. Other benefits have been the periodic injection of new blood brought about by a steady turnover of staff, able through their work at the Unit to secure academic and allied posts. But the major beneficiaries of this professionalism have been the customers: professionalism has reinforced the Unit's independence and this, in turn, has enabled it to provide policy-relevant advice and information, not only as required but also as necessary.

If this analysis is correct, then – paradoxical as it may seem – the key to successfully managing the conflict between research and policy may well be to make it a more, rather than less even struggle. This would imply granting the in-house research unit more organisational status and professional independence.[18] For if a research unit is to offer more than demand-led policy-analysis, it must be able when necessary to resist pressures to undertake 'quick and dirty' work (Weiss, 1982) in order to meet political deadlines. Useful as short-term work may sometimes be, social scientists cannot allow themselves to become restricted to the same brief timescale as the policy-maker. To do so would be to neglect and devalue their most valuable contribution – the critical examination of substantive policy issues, which can only be achieved through commitment to a longer-term perspective utilising methodologically sophisticated research techniques. When government social scientists are employed in this role, it will also have to be recognised that government itself is only one of the clients for their work. Their primary objective will be to contribute to the public debate which, in a democratic society, should be the source of rational policy (Trow, 1984).[19]

NOTES

1 Current publication levels have taken some time to achieve. In particular, there was a period during the 1960s when, in the view of many, too few publications emerged from the Unit. The problems resulted, to some extent, from the very lengthy projects being undertaken at that time. But beliefs among some senior managers about the limited value of publishing research intended for administrators' use also played a part. Many more smaller projects are now being undertaken – all of which result in publications – and researchers are now encouraged to write a variety of smaller reports and articles rather than to produce one single all-purpose volume; in addition, such rewards as promotion or attendance at overseas conferences have been made increasingly contingent on publications. As a result the ethos of the Unit, while not quite 'publish or perish', has become more competitive.

2 Some of these reports, particularly in the earlier years of the Unit's existence, suggest a degree of intellectual isolation. Again, numerous efforts have been made to deal with this problem: for many years there has been a regular series of Unit seminars with outside speakers and some full-scale workshops have been organised; attendance at relevant conferences has generally been encouraged; leaves of absence have been granted so that researchers can accept temporary research posts elsewhere; staff have been permitted to register their work for higher degrees; collaborative publications with university researchers have been encouraged; consultants are regularly employed either to supply general academic advice or specialist knowledge; and, most recently, a system of academic refereeing of all major Unit publications has been instituted.

3 For example, certain of the Unit's methodological contributions concerned with the prediction of offending (Simon, 1971), statistical methods of classification (Macnaughten-Smith, 1965), experimental designs for evaluation research (Clarke and Cornish, 1972) and with the description and evaluation of institutional regimes (Sinclair, 1971) find their way quite regularly onto the reading lists of university courses in criminology and other social sciences.

4 The British Crime Survey, first undertaken in 1982 and repeated in 1984, is designed to yield a range of information on such matters as the dark figure of unrecorded crime, fear of crime, the circumstances of victimization, and public perceptions of crime seriousness which will provide an essential background of information for criminal policy. If repeated regularly it should provide a more reliable measure than the *Criminal Statistics* of trends in crime (cf. Hough and Mayhew, 1985). Studies of offender decision making, so far represented in Britain mainly by research into burglary (Walsh, 1980; Winchester and Jackson, 1982; Maguire 1982; Bennett and Wright 1984), will provide an additional dimension of knowledge which should influence thinking about deterrence and prevention of crime.

5 One example is provided by the Conservative Government's threats in 1982/83 to the continued existence of the Social Science Research Council. The crisis was weathered, but not without a reduction in the Council's budget and a significant change of name (to Economic and Social Research Council).

6 One early example concerns the abolition of preventive detention following Unit research (Hammond and Chayen, 1961) which showed that this sentence was being used not for dangerous criminals, but for persistent petty offenders. Other examples, include: the extension of community service following a favourable evaluation of its experimental introduction (Pease, Billingham and Earnshaw, 1977); the routine use of a prediction instrument developed by the Unit in parole decision making (Nuttall, 1977); the 'situational' remit referred to above for the Home Office Crime Prevention Unit; and the notably less favourable attitude recently taken to police manpower as a result of research showing that expanding the police force is unlikely to have much effect on crime (Clarke and Hough, 1984). (If this latter work alone led to only a 1% reduction in police establishments, the resulting savings in just a couple of years should more than pay for the Unit's costs over its entire existence.) Other work, particularly on treatment ineffectiveness and on the nature of crime (as portrayed by the British Crime Survey), is likely in the long-term to have profound effects on the criminal justice system which are as yet difficult to fully anticipate.

7 This is not always because the research was ill-conceived; sometimes the policy options raised could not be pursued without first obtaining fresh information (cf. Clarke and Sinclair, 1974).

8 The customer–contractor principle as originally enunciated by Rothschild was limited to the relationship between government and scientific research and development; indeed, the social sciences were specifically excluded by Rothschild from his recommendations. It also tends to be overlooked that Rothschild recommended that the heads of government research departments should be allowed to spend 10% of their total resources on pure research.

9 Even this, however, should not be overstated. Prior to the location of the Unit under the Chief Scientist's command, it had for many years before been under the direction of the Deputy Secretary in charge of Criminal Department. More important in practical terms is the fact that a reduction in the Unit's staff accompanied by an increase in demands for its services inevitably affected its future capacity for undertaking large-scale or longer-term projects.

10 The main intention of the Fulton Report's (1968) recommendations was to ensure that decision-making within the civil service was better informed by specialist knowledge. This was to be achieved *inter alia* by improving the status and career-mobility of specialists and, in particular, by providing them with enhanced opportunities for entering line management. Most of the recommendations have yet to be implemented.

11 Charges for overheads may, of course, be written into grant applications. However, running as they characteristically do at about 30% (in contrast to 60% in the USA) these inducements scarcely represent much of a financial incentive for universities to house research teams. Furthermore, since the academic concerned will have to retain his teaching post in order to afford the luxury of supervising his research project, and since (especially in the current

economic climate) his employing institution will be able to offer him little relief from his teaching and administrative commitments, these may well go by the board to devolve informally upon his equally hard-pressed colleagues. The mutual damage to research and teaching represented by this state of affairs is a far cry from the picture of mutually reinforcing activities which is usually given.

12 One official response to these issues is summed up in a letter of October 1980 from the then Chief Scientist of the Department of Health and Social Security to one of the present authors, who had regretfully declined to continue acting as an unpaid referee to the Department's Small Grants Committee. His refusal was based on the concern, *inter alia*, that provision of free professional advice might unwittingly be financing the Department's rundown of its own already vestigial in-house social research capability. The following passages are taken from the Chief Scientist's letter:

> ... this Department has never paid for the external scientific refereeing of applications for research funds. Rightly or wrongly we continue to hope that scientists in Universities and elsewhere will continue to provide this support in future ... I can assure you had you chosen to do so you would in no way have 'contributed to a further contraction of job opportunities'.

13 In the United States many academics are paid their salaries on the basis of a nine-month academic year. They can then engage in consultancy or research for the remaining three months if they so choose and, where the research is in the form of a government contract, write their salary requirements for this period into their research budget. With the agreement of their institution, this money may also be used, where necessary, to 'buy-out' of some of their teaching duties during the academic year.

14 Within criminology, the closest parallels are those of the Cambridge Institute of Criminology and the Oxford Centre for Criminological Research, both of whose research programmes have been largely supported by Home Office grants. At no time, however, have the monies disbursed to these bodies approached the amount of funds allocated to supporting the Research Unit itself.

15 There are precedents: the Central Council for Education and Training in Social Work, for example, carries out periodic reviews of courses offering training for its professional social work qualification.

16 It is richly ironic (but hardly surprising) that the policies advocated by the CPRS – the simplicities of the Rothschild customer–contractor blueprint for policy-relevant research (cf. Kogan et al., 1980), and the replication of the CPRS's style of policy-analysis throughout government – enshrined many of these defects.

17 Or, as in the case of some members of CPRS, prestigious outside consultants. The combination of secretiveness, arrogance and insecurity characteristic of government leads to suspicion of outside experts, who might at any time either usurp important policy-functions or turn into powerful and disruptive watchdogs.

18 At present the Head of a government research unit is typically of Assistant Secretary status, and his or her staff of correspondingly lower status when compared with their administrative colleagues. As far as professionalism is concerned, more attention needs to be given to career-management and the provision of study-leaves and sabbaticals. It follows that, wherever possible,

members of a unit ought to be encouraged to become authorities in their fields.

19 A rider to this is that where knowledge conflicts with policy the social scientist's duty will be to make this clear. Escape routes from the research unit into outside employment may therefore have to be continually kept open, not only by individual researchers but also by the unit's management. This can only be achieved if the unit can, through its commitment to professionalism and integrity in its social science research, maintain its links with the academic community.

REFERENCES

Barlow, H. D. (1984), *Introduction to Criminology* (3rd. ed.), Boston, Little, Brown.

Bennett, Trevor and Richard Wright (1984), *Burglars on Burglary*, Farnborough, Hants, Gower.

Blume, Stuart S. (1982), 'A framework for analysis', in *The Future of Research*, ed. Geoffrey Oldham, Guildford, Surrey, Society for Research into Higher Education.

Bowlby, John (1946), *Forty-Four Juvenile Thieves*, London, Baillière, Tindall and Cox.

Brody, S. R. (1976), *The Effectiveness of Sentencing*, Home Office Research Series No. 35, London, HMSO.

Carr-Saunders, A. M., H. Mannheim and E. Rhodes (1942), *Young Offenders: An Enquiry into Juvenile Delinquency*, Cambridge, Cambridge University Press.

Civil Service Department (1971), *Framework for Government Research and Development*, Cmnd 4814, London, HMSO.

Clarke, Ronald V. and Derek B. Cornish (1972), *The Controlled Trial in Institutional Research: Paradigm or Pitfall for Penal Evaluators?*, Home Office Research Studies No. 15, London, HMSO.

Clarke, Ronald V. and Derek B. Cornish (eds.) (1983), *Crime Control in Britain: A Review of Policy Research*, Albany, New York, State University of New York Press.

Clarke, Ronald V. and Derek B. Cornish (1985), 'Modeling offenders' decisions: a framework for research and policy', in *Crime and Justice: An Annual Review of Research*, Vol. 6, eds. M. Tonry and N. Morris, Chicago, University of Chicago Press.

Clarke, Ronald V. and J. M. Hough (eds.) (1980), *The Effectiveness of Policing*, Farnborough, Hants, Gower.

Clarke, Ronald V. and J. M. Hough (1984), *Crime and Police Effectiveness*, Home Office Research Studies No. 79, London, HMSO.

Clarke, Ronald V. and Ian Sinclair (1974), 'Towards more effective treatment evaluation', in *Collected Studies in Criminological Research*, Vol. XII, Strasbourg, Council of Europe.

Cohen, Stanley (1974), 'Criminology and the sociology of deviance in Britain: a recent history and a current report', in *Deviance and Social Control*, eds. Paul Rock and Mary McIntosh, London, Tavistock.

Cornish, Derek B. and Ronald R. V. Clarke (1981), 'Government research: Cinderella of sociology', *Transactions of the Annual Conference of the British Sociological Association, 1980*, London, B.S.A.

Cotgrove, Stephen and Steven Box (1970), *Science, Industry and Society: Studies in the Sociology of Science*, London, Allen and Unwin.

Downes, David and Paul Rock (1982), *Understanding Deviance*, Oxford, Oxford University Press.

Fulton Report (1968), *Report of the Committee on the Civil Service: 1966–1968*, Cmnd 3638, London, HMSO.

Glover, E. (1960), *Selected Papers on Psycho-Analysis*, vol. 2, *The Roots of Crime*, London, Imago.

Hammond, W. H. and E. Chayen (1961), *Persistent Criminals*, Home Office Studies in the Causes of Delinquency and the Treatment of Offenders No. 5, London, HMSO.

Healy, W. and A. Bronner (1936), *New Light on Delinquency and Its Treatment*, New Haven, Conn, Yale University Press.

Home Office (1959), *Penal Practice in a Changing Society: Aspects of Future Development*, Cmnd 645, London, HMSO.

Hough, J. M. and Patricia Mayhew (1983), *The British Crime Survey: First Report*, Home Office Research Series No. 76, London, HMSO.

Hough, J. M. and Patricia Mayhew (1985), *Taking Account of Crime: Key Findings from the 1984 British Crime Survey*, Home Office Research Series No. 85, London, HMSO.

Kallen, D. B. P., G. B. Kosse, H. C. Wagenaar, J. J. J. Kloprogge and M. Vorbeck (eds.) (1982), *Social Science Research and Public Policy-Making: A Reappraisal*, Windsor, Berks, NFER–Nelson.

Kogan, Maurice and Mary Henkel (1983), *Government and Research: The Rothschild Experiment in a Government Department*, London, Heinemann

Kogan, Maurice, Nancy Korman and Mary Henkel (1980), *Government's Commissioning of Research: A Case Study*, Uxbridge, Middlesex, Department of Government, Brunel University.

Lazarsfeld, P. E. and J. G. Reitz (1975), *An Introduction to Applied Sociology*, New York, Elsevier.

Lodge, Thomas S. (1974), 'The founding of the Home Office Research Unit', in *Crime, Criminology and Public Policy: Essays in Honour of Sir Leon Radzinowicz*, ed. Roger Hood, London, Heinemann.

Macnaughton-Smith, P. (1965), *Some Statistical and Other Numerical Techniques for Classifying Individuals*, Home Office Studies in the Causes of Delinquency and the Treatment of Offenders No. 6, London, HMSO.

Maguire, M. (in collaboration with T. Bennett) (1982), *Burglary in a Dwelling*, London, Heinemann.

Mannheim, Hermann and Leslie T. Wilkins (1955), *Prediction Methods in Relation to Borstal Training*, Home Office Studies in the Causes of Delinquency and the Treatment of Offenders No. 1, London, HMSO

Martinson, R. (1974), 'What works? – Questions and answers about prison reform', *The Public Interest*, No. 35 (Spring), 22–54.

Mayhew, Patricia, Ronald V. Clarke, Andrew Sturman and J. M. Hough (1976),

Crime as Opportunity, Home Office Research Studies No. 34, London, HMSO.

Moriarty, M. J. (1977), 'The policy-making process: how it is seen from the Home Office', in *Penal Policy-Making in England: Papers Presented to the Cropwood Round-Table Conference, December 1976*, eds. Nigel Walker and Henri Giller, Cambridge, Institute of Criminology.

Nuttall, C. P. (with E. E. Barnard, A. J. Fowles, A. Frost, W. H. Hammond, P. Mayhew, K. Pease, R. Tarling and M. J. Weatheritt) (1977), *Parole in England and Wales*, Home Office Research Studies No. 38, London, HMSO.

Pease, Ken, S. Billingham and I. Earnshaw (1977), *Community Service Assessed in 1976*, Home Office Research Series No. 39, London, HMSO.

Platt, J. (1976), *Realities of Social Research*, London, Chatto (for Sussex University Press).

Plowden, William (1981), 'The British Central Policy Review Staff', in *Policy Analysis and Policy Innovation*, eds. Peter R. Baehr and Bjorn Wittrock, Beverly Hills, CA, Sage.

Rawsthorne, A. (1978), 'The objectives and content of policy-oriented research', *Research Bulletin No. 6*, London, Home Office Research Unit.

Scott, R. A. and R. R. Shore (1979), *Why Sociology Does Not Apply: A Study of the Use of Sociology in Public Policy*, New York, Elsevier.

Simon, F. (1971), *Prediction Methods in Criminology*, Home Office Research Studies No. 7, London, HMSO.

Sinclair, Ian (1971), *Hostels for Probationers*, Home Office Research Studies No. 6, London, HMSO.

Smith, Cyril S. (1982), 'The research function in the social sciences', in *The Future of Research*, ed. Geoffrey Oldham, Guildford, Surrey, Society for Research into Higher Education.

Stevens, P. and C. Willis (1979), *Race, Crime and Arrests*, Home Office Research Series No. 58, London, HMSO.

Stott, D. H. (1950), *Delinquency and Human Nature*, Dunfirmline, Fife, Carnegie United Kingdom Trust.

Tarling, R. (with M. Weatheritt) (1979), *Sentencing Practice in Magistrates' Courts*, Home Office Research Series No. 56, London, HMSO.

Trow, Martin (1984), 'Researchers, policy analysts and policy intellectuals', in *Educational Research and Policy*, eds. Thorsten Husen and Maurice Kogan, Oxford, Pergamon Press.

Walmsley, R. (1978), 'Indecency between males and the Sexual Offences Act of 1967', *Criminal Law Review* (July), 400–7.

Walsh, Dermot P. (1980), *Break-Ins: Burglary from Private Houses*, London, Constable.

Weiss, Carol H. (1980), 'Knowledge creep and decision accretion', *Knowledge: Creation, Diffusion, Utilization*, I (3), 381–404.

Weiss, Carol H. (1982), 'Policy research in the context of diffuse decision-making', *Social Science Research and Public Policy-Making: A Reappraisal*, eds. D. B. P. Kallen et al., Windsor, England, NFER–Nelson.

Wiles, Paul (1976), 'Introduction', in *The Sociology of Crime and Delinquency in Britain*, vol. 2, *The New Criminologies*, ed. Paul Wiles, London, Martin Robertson.

Wilson, James Q. (1975), *Thinking About Crime*, New York, Basic Books.

Winchester, S. and H. Jackson (1982), *Residential Burglary: The Limits of Prevention*, Home Office Research Studies No. 74, London, HMSO.

Wootton, Barbara (1959), *Social Science and Social Pathology*, London, Allen and Unwin.

CHAPTER 11

The work of the Commission for Economic and Social Change in Germany

LISL KLEIN

Introduction – background and methods

This is an account of an attempt in Germany to harness social research in a broad framework and on a large scale, to help policy-makers formulate a rational, humane strategy for managing technical change and its social implications. In the British observer it arouses two, by now familiar, reactions: on the one hand a feeling that things don't work quite like that and, on the other hand, the wish that such a broadly based and rational approach was not quite so alien to British policy-makers and institutions.

This account first arose in a different context. I have been concerned for some time with the utilisation of social science in organisations, especially industrial organisations. Funding to collect and analyse case studies of such attempts was obtained from the Anglo-German Foundation for the Study of Industrial Society, and this brought with it a requirement to find cases in both countries. However, some prior knowledge of the work of the Commission for Economic and Social Change (Kommission für wirtschaftlichen und sozialen Wandel) suggested that this was in fact more characteristic of a 'German approach', if there is such a thing, than the cases in organisations; and at the same time it was striking how similar the issues that arose for the Commission and its work were to those with which one is familiar at organisational level.

Background

Both historically and in terms of scientific traditions, the German context for social science utilisation is quite different from that of Britain or the United States. In both Britain and the United States, traditions of practical relevance in social science research and concern for its application began during the First World War, continued between the wars, and were substantially strengthened during the Second World War. In Germany, the years before and during the Second World War created a major discontinuity in social research.

When university departments were built up again after the war, and research traditions and different 'schools' evolved, their main focus of interest was theoretical and methodological. There was not the same history of involvement with the problems of practice, and where social scientists did empirical work it was to gather data for theory verification. However, research studies of this kind came gradually to be used as a basis for consulting, occasionally at a managerial level but mainly at a political level. Their function then was one of feedback.

The thrust towards more direct use and usefulness of the social sciences came later, and from a different source. It was Government, and particularly some of the programmes of the Social Democratic Government, which stressed the need to base social policy on research and to influence the world of practice with the methods and findings of the social sciences. So, for example, a clause was introduced into the Company Law of 1972 which requires that 'proven scientific findings about the workplace must be applied'. This sounds strange to British ears, where research involving people at work has been very context-specific and where the emphasis in application has been on cases and experiments rather than on the broad application of generalised 'knowledge'.

This legal requirement is clearly influenced by a natural science model which requires general laws, free from the fallibility and variability of human interpretation and intervention. In turn it has had considerable influence both on the sponsorship and on the nature of research carried out since it was passed. It is also one instance of institutionalised, government-based concern for the use of knowledge. Three others may be cited: substantial work on social indicators; a Government programme to 'Humanise Life at Work' which began in 1974 and which is jointly based on the Ministry of Research and Technology and the Ministry of Labour and Social Affairs; and the work of the Commission for Economic and Social Affairs, which will be the subject of this chapter.

Methods

In order to produce this account, a first draft was written on the basis of documents, some published and one unpublished.[1,2,3] Some passages from these documents have been translated or paraphrased *in toto*, and I am grateful for permission to do this.

On the basis of the first draft, interviews were held with:

(a) Some members of the Commission:
     Prof. Dr Karl Martin Bolte (Academic Member and Chairman)
     Dr Gerhard Leminsky (nominee of the Trade Union Federation)
     Dr Werner Dräger (nominee of the Employers' Federation).
(b) Some members of the Commission's scientific staff:
     Mr Helmut Kohn
     Mr Friedrich Latzelsberger
     Mr Hans-Jürgen Bieneck.

All of these commented on the first draft and have influenced the final one.

In addition, valuable written information and comments have been received from:

Dr Günter Friedrichs (Industriegewerkschaft Metall)
Mr Alfred Hassencamp (Secretariat)
Prof. Dr Herbert Hax (Academic Member)
Dr Herbert Schmidt (Ministry of Labour and Social Affairs).

The Commission and its origins

The Commission for Economic and Social Change was set up in 1971 by the then Chancellor, Herr Willy Brandt. Its mission was to produce a report on 'what economic, social and education policy options are available for furthering technical and social change and for fashioning it in the interests of the population, within the framework of a market economy'.

In the speech with which he launched the Commission, the Chancellor said:

> Our present and future are marked by permanent economic and social change. The development and use of new technologies, the rapid expansion of knowledge, the dynamics of our economy, are all components of continuous structural change which not only determines our broad economic and social development but whose consequences reach far into the lives of individuals. This presents both a challenge and an opportunity: the challenge to confront the situation and master it in the direction of social progress; and the opportunity to set about consciously shaping our common future ... Our citizens should not have to look with anxiety at technical, organisational and economic progress as a threat, but see in it a natural accompaniment and precondition of greater welfare.
> This requires far-sighted policies which mean to use scientific developments in a framework of social values and draw the relevant

conclusions from such developments early enough. For this reason the Federal Government has decided to set up a Commission for Economic and Social Change.

The Commission's existence thus owed much to the visionary and strategic approach of Willy Brandt; but there were, of course, other antecedents.

During the nineteen-sixties there had existed in the Federal Republic an institution called 'Concerted Action'. This consisted mainly of a meeting, several times a year, of representatives of the Employers' Federation and the Trade Unions with the Economics Minister, for an exchange of views about the economy.

The Metalworkers' Union (IG Metall) had, at several of its congresses in the mid-sixties, criticised the then Government for short-sightedness and inaction about future problems which were likely to arise from technical change and its consequences. In particular it drew attention to the United States National Commission on Technology, Automation and Economic Progress which had presented a report on the economic and social problems of technical change, which was widely debated in Germany.

In the Coalition Government of 1966 one of the critics, Prof. Karl Schiller, became Economics Minister. The trade unions then used the opportunity provided by the forum 'Concerted Action' to get a specialist working party on automation established. Its remit was in fact broader than the title implies, automation being only one topic among others. The 'Automation Group' concerned itself with the criteria and instruments for furthering technical change, with the analysis and solution of the undesired consequences of such change, and with the question of how the high demands on the mobility of both people and capital in an ever more complex world could be managed.

The Automation Group existed from 1968 to 1970. It consisted of four academics, four representatives each of the employers and the trade unions, and four senior civil servants, two from the Ministry of Economics and two from the Ministry of Labour and Social Affairs. The civil servants took it in turns to chair the sessions and, since this also meant that they strongly influenced the programme, some dissatisfaction with the arrangements began to develop.

The Automation Group initiated some forty-five research projects. (Cynics say that it was given to the trade unions as a kind of toy to play with, so that they should do research on the consequences of automation instead of worrying about the possible loss of jobs through automation.)

The presence of the Ministry of Labour and Social Affairs represented a significant shift towards the consideration of social aspects of the topic and away from an exclusive concern with economic matters. However, after two years' work, the members of the Working Party decided that they would prefer to be independent of the governmental bureaucracy altogether. They had also reached the conclusion that the base of research, which had been about technical development, had been too narrow: technology had to be seen as one social phenomenon among many if it was to be properly understood and if a real grasp and control of future economic and social developments was to be obtained. The approach to research would therefore have to be much broader and more systemic, and the Automation Group commissioned a societal 'system study' which should serve as the basis for a new programme.

Organisation and work of the Commission

The Government accepted the views expressed by the Automation Group. When the Commission for Economic and Social Change was created, it had a much broader remit. It was also substantially independent of government, which was no longer represented as a member. Apart from the obligation to produce a final report, from which it was hoped to derive guidance for legislation, there were no 'strings' tying the Commission to government departments or policies. The Commission could recommend as it wished, but it was asked not to make interim policy statements, i.e. to wait until its final report was ready. Funds were made available to finance a secretariat of eight scientific staff with the necessary technical and administrative back-up, and to commission research. The total costs eventually came to about DM 13 million, about DM 5.5 million of which was spent on research contracts.

The Commission consisted of seventeen members, eleven of whom had been members of the earlier Automation Group. Trade union and employers' organisations were invited to nominate five members each, and seven academics were invited on a personal basis. They consisted of two sociologists, two economists, one industrial economist, one expert in the economics of education, and one engineer. The emphasis on the economy as the basic frame of reference was strong. Some of the representatives of the employers and trade unions were economists by training, and even the two sociologists had come to sociology from economics. Although technical and, in particular, social issues were to play a very important part in the work of the Commission, it was difficult to get out of the habit of seeing social factors as dependent rather than independent variables. The balance of membership, in which the academics outnumbered – and could therefore outvote – members of either interest group, attracted considerable attention. It signified, at least at that stage, the emphasis put on research and knowledge for the development of policy as outweighing – by a nicely judged small amount – the component of politically worked out agreement.

The emphasis on systematic knowledge as a basis for policy was also exemplified by the 'system study' which was inherited from the Automation Group. This had been carried out together with a Study Group for System Research, some of whose members were at the University of Heidelberg. It set out forty-three themes or problem areas relevant to technical, social and economic change, and these were accepted as the basis for the Commission's work. They are shown in Fig. 1. One great advantage of the way the Commission's task had been formulated was its broad, global quality. However, this very breadth also brought problems of how to set about doing the work, and the 'system study' was an attempt to bring some structure to the task.

The members of the Commission met once a month, usually for a two-day session. The first thing they did was to go over the list of forty-three problem areas and attempt to arrive at some ordering in terms of priority. Fig.2. shows the result of this exercise, which was carried out by a system of voting.

It was at this stage that some members of the Commission began to recognise the consequence of its composition. It had no political sociologist or specialist in administration. They later drew on the services of a political sociologist, but they continued to feel the absence of expertise in the problems of public policy.

Once the list of priority topics was clarified, there developed two main streams of activity: one of these was that the Commission's scientific secretariat began to prepare a series of discussion and analysis papers about the various problems, and these were used as the basis of discussion during the Commission's monthly meetings. One outcome of this process was that the topics in the original system study came to be re-grouped into fourteen major problem areas. (This grouping is already shown in Fig.1.) It was these that became the main focus of the Commission's work and they essentially constituted the chapters of its final report.

Discussion of the secretariat's analysis papers revealed what were thought to be gaps in knowledge or information, and thus began the Commission's second main activity, namely the commissioning of research.

The research programme

Altogether, some 145 research projects were commissioned. (As one of the researchers involved, I can record my astonishment on discovering,

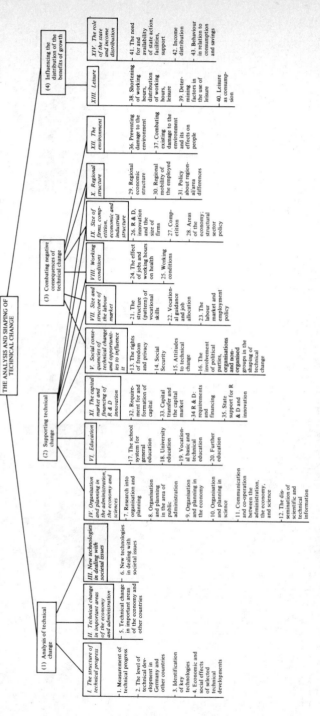

Fig 1 System study on technical, social and economic change

Number

Number		Votes
1	Measurement of technical progress	
2	The level of technical development in Germany and other countries	
3	Identification of key technologies	
4	Economic and social effects of selected technical developments	
5	Technical change in important areas of the economy and administration	
6	New technologies in dealing with societal issues	
7	Research into organisation and planning	
8	Organisation and planning in the area of public administration	
9	Organisation and planning in the economy	
10	Organisation and planning in science	
11	Communication and co-operation between the administration, the economy and science	
12	The dissemination of scientific and technical information	
13	The rights of freedom and privacy	
14	Social security	
15	Attitudes to technical change	
16	The involvement of political parties, Organisations, and non-organised groups in the shaping of technical change	
17	The school system for general education	
18	University education	
19	Vocational basic and technical education	
20	Further education	
21	The structure pattern	
22	The structure pattern of vocational skills	
23	The labour market and employment policy	
24	The effect of jobs and working hours on health	
25	Working conditions	
26	R & D innovation and the size of firms	
27	Competition	
28	Areas of the economy; structural sector policy	
29	Regional economic structure	
30	Regional mobility of the employed	
31	Policy about regional/area differences	
32	Requirement for and formation of capital	
33	Capital transfer and the capital market	
34	R & D: requirements and financing	
35	State support for R & D innovation	
36	Preventing damage to the environment	
37	Combating existing damage to the environment and its effects on people	
38	Shortening of working hours, distribution of working hours, leisure	
39	Determining factors in the use of leisure	
40	Leisure as consumption	
41	The need for and availability of state action, facilities, support	
42	Income distribution	
43	Behaviour in relation to consumption and savings	

■ 12 or more votes

▨ 9–11 votes

☐ 0–8 votes

Fig 2 Weighting of subject areas

when I was invited in 1973 to review theoretical developments and European experience in new forms of work organisation, and a contract was formulated, that this was designated as 'project no.57'. The vista which this seemed to open up, both in terms of scale and in terms of the programmatic nature of research efforts, was unprecedented in my experience.) Most of the projects eventually led to publication and, together with the 45 projects inherited from the Automation Group, they yielded 140 volumes of published research. These appeared as a series published by the Verlag Otto Schwartz and Co., Göttingen. Their authors and translated titles are given in the Appendix. A few reports were published independently by their authors. Some twenty projects collapsed or their reports were judged to be of poor quality. Two or more members of the Commission looked after each project.

Two features about the process of commissioning the research projects are worthy of note: one is that, unlike the more usual method of research funding, the Commission did not wait for applications from researchers but actively went out into the field to find researchers for topics that it wanted tackled. On some topics it knew or took advice about which researchers to invite to do the work; on most topics it advertised the work it wanted done, for open competition. The openness of this process made it possible for younger, lesser-known researchers to compete on equal terms with the more established figures in the world of research and for new or unconventional ideas to surface and be considered. On the other hand, it required the creation of a whole new and quite laborious apparatus of assessing the applications and administering the contracts. This experience itself formed the subject of one of the reports (Vol.140). In some instances the same project was commissioned from two different researchers, or a second opinion was sought, if a researcher was thought to be politically biassed but knowledgeable. There was considerable controversy about such items.

The second special feature of this research programme was that it tended, on the whole, towards state-of-the-art reports, i.e. the collection, summarising and interpretation of existing knowledge rather than new, fundamental research. The Commission's particular remit did not give scope, in terms of either time or money, for programmes of new or basic research, and on most topics it was considered that an analysis of the existing state of knowledge was in itself very necessary. They therefore concentrated on assessing and evaluating existing and earlier research, which had frequently been neglected. They discovered in the process that research whose boundaries coincided with those of existing institutionalised political fields was much more likely to have been taken up and used than research on problems going across such boundaries.

It is said in Germany that the publicity which was generated for the Commission's research topics by this public process of advertising and commissioning in itself acted as a stimulus to other research. A number of research institutions began to give attention to topics such as leisure, policy planning, and consumer and environmental issues because of the evidence of policy-level concern which was demonstrated by the Commission's publicly advertised projects. The same, publicly demonstrated, evidence of policy concern enabled some civil servants inside various Ministries to push for emphasis on this kind of topic. The state bureaucracy itself came under noticeable pressure.[4] At the same time, the Chairman felt that the way the Commission was constituted had biassed the selection of topics for research and that topics such as the Church, the family and changing values did not get sufficient attention.

Preparation of the report

The process of commissioning the research programme took quite a long time in relation to the Commission's anticipated life-span, i.e. about eighteen months. After that, the Commission returned in a more concentrated way to the task of formulating its own views for its final report, and with this began its real problems.

The academics and members of the secretariat prepared 'theme papers' on the basis of the research material as it came in, while the social partners (as employers and trade unions are generally called in Germany) prepared 'position papers' on the same topics. Within both the employers' and trade unions' organisations, but more within the latter, there were back-up staffs that accompanied the work, reading research reports and preparing analyses and opinions for their representatives on the Commission.

The first problem was who should draft the integrated text, combining both themes and positions. The social partners did not trust each others' representatives to do the drafting and were also unwilling to entrust it to the secretariat. Eventually the academics each took on some chapters, were allocated research assistants and obtained leave of one semester from their universities for the work.

The first drafts were discussed in a laborious and painful two-week meeting, during which began the politicisation of the Commission's work. The drafts turned out to be controversial – the academics had thought they were writing in a politically neutral way, but were accused of taking political positions, or of behaving like an interest group themselves, or challenged to reveal their political positions. In turn, the academics gained the impression that the employers were opposed to any proposals involving real change, while the trade unions were opposed to anything which implied criticism of current government policy (many ministers and secretaries of state came from the trade union movement).

Controversy about various recommendations led to increasingly frequent threats by one or other group to resign from the Commission. The academics themselves met together as a group to discuss what to do if this should happen, and decided to guarantee each other that they would in any case finish writing a report and issue it with an explanation of events, even if the Commission should collapse. The announcement of this decision to the rest of the Commission unleashed a considerable storm because it was felt that the academics did not take the reality of political problems seriously enough and were themselves acting as an interest group; but it had the effect that threats of withdrawal grew less. A second draft was prepared and this was taken back into trade union and employers' organisations for very detailed discussion.

The work during this phase was concentrated in working parties. The Commission divided itself into groups dealing with different topics, and for each topic a working party was formed. Employers and trade union members were now involving their back-home institutions in the work, and brought specialists along to the working parties. Plenary sessions of the Commission had a smaller role and were mainly concerned with co-ordination.

In this way there gradually emerged clarity about the boundaries of consensus and disagreement. A system of recording minority opinions was agreed on, whereby a group which could not agree with a majority recommendation could record its views, provided it contained at least three people. This was, however, only permitted where there was a real majority recommendation which could not be accepted; it was not a matter of just putting different opinions side-by-side. It was this system which made completion of the report possible, and members of the Commission now see the mixture of consensus and majority and minority opinions as a very positive feature of the report. In the process of using this system for a third and final draft, there developed many detailed improvements, many genuine compromises, but also a certain loss of substance.

The final report[5] contains 83 minority opinions (out of 1,367 content paragraphs). It was not, however, possible to produce an agreed official short version. This would not have adequately represented the mixture of main text and minority votes, and the social partners were also uneasy about producing a short version by voting on texts. The trade unions and employers have each produced their own short versions.

The inputs to the final report were therefore: the various papers which had been produced throughout, the research findings, and the views of the interest groups, particularly as they had been represented during the latter stages in the various working parties. To some extent the processes of research and recommendation had diverged. Some of the outcome of the research was not yet available at the time opinion was being formed and position papers considered for the final report; in some phases there was simply too much research material coming in to be absorbed and integrated; and, of course, in some instances research itself became part of political controversy. It is said that, when some hitherto impeccably 'scientific' sources were investigated, the results were 'devastating'.

A change in emphasis and climate

The work of the Commission took 5½ years. The report which emerged from all this work is in fact rather different from what the terms of reference and origins of the Commission might have led the reader to expect. Already during the setting of priorities or topics, the Commission had begun to come away from seeing change only as a consequence of technical change. In the event the report turns out to be strongly concerned with the furthering of technical change in the service of the economy and emphasises economic goals at least as much as social ones. A glance through the list of research publications, read in conjunction with and compared with a summary of the report itself, will also serve to show the divergence in trend.

There are a number of reasons for this change in emphasis and some difference of opinion about why and how it came about. One factor was the way in which, during the drafting of the report, both trade union and employers' bodies began to take a stronger hand in influencing the work of their representatives on the Commission. The role of the academics changed, and the balance shifted considerably from scientific to political, or rather interest-group, influences. Since the whole framework was one of reform, it is the employers' side which was most often on the defensive and which tabled most of the minority statements.

A second, and most important, factor in the changed emphasis was the fact that, while the Commission was carrying out its work, the economic climate changed and the oil crisis of 1973 hit the industrialised nations; a third was undoubtedly the fact that Chancellor Brandt resigned from office in 1974.

The Commission had begun its work during a time of full employment. The industrialised nations 'had just begun to permit themselves the luxury of talking about the quality of life' (Bieneck, unpublished, 1977). This discussion had been initiated in Germany at a conference of the

Metalworkers' Union. The creation of the Commission, as well as the list of projects, demonstrate optimism, both about the underlying economic situation and about the possibilities of innovation and reform. (The equivalent optimism in the UK can be seen in the setting up of the Social Science Research Council in 1965 and other explicit attempts at that time to integrate social science into economic life.)

Changes in the economic climate which followed the Arab oil embargo did not so much affect the research projects, which by that time were already under way, but had a profound effect on the thinking and work of the members of the Commission. They had to think up responses to the changing situation from within their own resources with little input from the research; ideas coming from the trade union side met with increasingly self-confident resistance on the part of the employers, and the trade union members themselves began to concentrate more narrowly than had been envisaged on questions of job security.

The original aims, of presenting an essentially long-term strategy, of showing the interdependence between subject-areas and in particular of treating economic considerations to some extent as means rather than ends all suffered to some extent, and the main result of this lies in the salience of the economic chapters of the report. The hand of professional economists is very strong in the drafting, so that even non-economic matters are couched in an economic framework.

Nevertheless, a good deal of the original perspective, particularly with regard to the long-term and interdependent requirement on policy-making, does remain in the Commission's report. And the joint work, extending over several years and including the presence of academics, led to a broadening of perspective among members of the Commission which in turn had some influence on their home institutions.

Unfortunately, there is no space here to give more than the chapter headings and sub-headings to give a flavour of the breadth of the report.

I. The development of proactive and future-oriented policies
II. Strategy for planned expansion
    From quantitive to qualitative growth
    Increasing private investment
    Increasing public expenditure
III. Shaping of economic growth via structural policies
    Sector policies
    Research and technology policy
    The organisation of space (i.e. regions)
    The environment

IV. Securing and consolidating economic growth
   Stabilisation
   Competition
   Consumer policy
 V. Full employment with the aid of labour market policy
VI. The mutual adjustment of education with the structure of occupations
   Skill requirements
   Educational and career guidance
   Improving the dual system
   Special aid for problem groups
VII. Income distribution and social security
   The distribution of income and wealth
   Social policy
   Health
VIII. Working conditions
 IX. Conditions for the successful shaping of economic and social change

Publication of the report

By the time the report was ready, there had also been a change in political climate. Chancellor Brandt had resigned, and his successor Chancellor Helmut Schmidt had a more pragmatic approach. Moreover, 1976 was an election year. Although the report was ready in June, the social partners thought it would be better to delay delivering it until after the election, which was due in October. However, after the election the government was being formed, and then preparing its work programme, and appeared to have no time to receive the report. The date was repeatedly postponed until the Commission declared that they would hand the report over on 10 January 1977, if only to the porter!

The report was formally received by two ministers, but there was some disappointment that the Chancellor did not receive it in person.

At a press conference it was clear that many journalists were expressing opinions about the report without having read it. They criticised the fact that the report contained minority views, whereas the Commission thought that the overall proportion of consensus was encouraging and the fact that its limits were defined very important and necessary. Some of the minority views are particularly well thought through and constructive, and contain analyses which are still referred to. Press reports picked out sensational aspects of the report, i.e. areas of disagreement, but this at least meant that there was substantial press coverage. There had been conversations with the press at some earlier stages, as individual research reports came out, but it appeared that journalists were only interested in views they could attribute to government. It was very difficult to get attention for a distanced position.

The length and complexity of the report made it difficult to absorb, and it was a disadvantage that it had not been possible to produce a short version. Individual points were quickly picked out for criticism, especially by particular interest groups affected; and great disappointment has been expressed at the frivolity and superficiality of many comments, not only in the media but among politicians who, it is said, commented on the report without bothering to read it.

Here is one Commission member's view of the situation:

> During its work the committee enjoyed a high degree of autonomy. For a period of five years – a long time for a politician, who thinks in terms of election periods of 4 years – the committee could organise research and prepare its report with practically nobody else caring about it; government had guaranteed the committee's financial and organisational independence. For the scientist these seem to be ideal working conditions. But when the committee came to an end with the report, it seemed that the contact with government had been lost. Unfortunately there had been major changes in government. There was still the same coalition of Social-Democrats and Liberals, but there was a new Federal Chancellor, there were new ministers in charge of economic, social and labour affairs. The committee members had the impression that the government behaved like somebody who gets something he has not ordered. The politicians who had initiated the committee's work were no longer in charge, and their successors were rather benevolent about it, but quite understandably they did not see what might be expected from the committee and what they should do with answers to questions they had not asked.[6]

Problems of implementation

Three important characteristics of the report are:

firstly, its delineation of the areas of consensus and disagreement, which have been mentioned;

secondly, its orientation towards long-term societal goals rather than the short-term ones dictated by the four-year cycle of elections. Two examples are ecology, and the economic interdependence between generations – the burden on the middle generation of having to support the young and the old;

thirdly, and in particular, its emphasis on the interdependence between problems and subject areas. Two examples are the links between the education system and the structure of occupations; and not just aiming for 'economic growth', but qualitative growth objectives aimed at evening out regional and sectoral imbalances; etc., etc.

However, such a systemic approach is difficult for individual ministries to work with. A strategic level of thinking takes place at high levels – in Germany this is the Chancellor's Office – but there strategy can only be specified in a very general sense and not in action-level detail. One of the trade union members of the Commission has discussed the fact that, while in the long term the Commission's report will undoubtedly make a significant contribution to greater integration of policy, the very fact that it came up against problems of the differing levels of responsibility of the Chancellor's Office and the ministries, as well as between federal and regional authority, shows how necessary it was.[7]

There is also, of course, a question of the power relations between different levels of the same institutions. It was pointed out that the trade unions are confronted with the problem of whether economic structure is more important than the next strike.

At the political level, 'the era of political reform was ending and the era of crisis management beginning'. The change in economic climate limited the freedom of action of those members of parliament who had been particularly interested in the work of the Commission.

The Chancellor's Office distributed sections of the report to the different ministries, and thus emerged the main problem of use and implementation: whereas the main thrust of the Commission's work was systemic, dealing with issues and crossing the boundaries of the conventional sub-division of disciplines and subject areas, there were no institutions for taking action in such a holistic way. The ministries represent subject areas (economics, labour, research and technology, etc.) and are in turn organised internally according to subdivisions of these subject areas. It was a basic dilemma that the policy thinking was not matched by institutional change.

It is also simply very difficult to relate strategic and comprehensive thinking to the pressures of everyday administration. Moreover, the more senior the people, the less time they can make available 'and in the end it boils down to people'. Thus the general tenor of the responses of the civil servants on whose desks the report landed is said to have been: 'It can't be done; we are doing it already; it costs too much'.

On the other hand, partial aspects did work their way through into administration. In the Ministry of Labour the report had considerable influence, for instance with respect to pensions policy. Again, the economics chapters put great stress on structural policy in relation to industrial sectors and this has influenced the way in which information and statistics have come to be built up. Institutes of Economics have oriented their statistical reporting more towards industrial sectors.

There has also developed a more integrated way of reporting labour market statistics, through the Federal Institute of Labour.

The greatest use is said to have been made by the Ministry of Research and Technology, which was young at the time and whose staff were glad to be able to refer to 'sources'. Indeed it is said that some concepts were picked up too uncritically. But one direct and important outcome was the institution of support for research and development staff costs of small and medium-sized firms. Another has been the setting up of advisory centres on innovation for technology transfer. The Minister for Research and Technology at the time, Mr. Matthöfer, expressed explicit agreement and acceptance of the recommendations regarding research and technology policy.

The least positive response is said to have come from the Economics Ministry, where the ideas of sectoral structure policy came up against strong political opposition. Even there, however, more recent pronouncements seem to show the influence of these ideas, without explicit reference to them.

On the whole, those ministries which had been involved with the Commission took the report most seriously.

Other consequences of the Commission's work

Many people say that, although direct consequences are difficult to trace, the work of the Commission has had considerable indirect effect. The series of research publications has met with undisputed approval. Its effect is of course impossible to assess, and individual items may be criticised. But many of the reports have become standard works and are widely taught and referred to, and overall the research programme represents an unprecedented bringing together of the current state of knowledge. It is said to have had important, though frequently indirect, effects. For example it is said that, although the attempt, in one project, to bring together the various disciplines represented in the 'science of work' into a more integrated framework did not succeed; nevertheless subsequent legislation on safety and health at work shows a much greater integration and problem-orientation than would have been the case without this attempt.

It is also said to be very important that the various organisations, interest groups, committees, etc., which concern themselves with these matters now have a common base of knowledge to draw on, and that this makes it much more likely that they can achieve results. The fact that the need for interdisciplinary and problem-centred work is increasingly accepted can also be seen in the efforts (not necessarily successful) made by those senior trade unionists, employers' representatives and academics who commission work under the government's programme to 'humanise life at work', begun in 1974. The programme itself can be seen as a consequence, not so much of the Commission's work, as of the same impulse as that which gave rise to it.

There is a proposal to found a new institute, 'work and technology', to work on these problems in an interdisciplinary way. There is no tradition in the Federal Republic of working in an integrated way on problems, and there is now recognition that it has to be got onto an institutional basis or the impulse will be lost again.

Also among the indirect benefits has been the experience gained in the process of commissioning research. An analysis of the costs and quality of the researches that had been commissioned led to substantial learning about the institutional circumstances that were most likely to produce good and useable research, and this has strongly influenced policy and the funding of research and research institutions. The Ministry of Research and technology benefitted greatly from this pre-work and made substantial later use of the research institutions (and of the instruments for commissioning research) which had been stimulated by the work of the Commission.

It must also be mentioned that the work of the Commission had a very strong influence on the officials who took part in it, and who after all went back into public service. Among other things they learned how 'consciousness-raising' takes time, and how people want to devise solutions for themselves and do not necessarily want to have this done for them.

It seems to be a characteristic of broad-based and systemic analyses, that they have far-reaching indirect benefits, but that it is much more difficult to point to direct consequences. The experience of the Commission for Economic and Social Change which has been described exemplifies the difficulty of evaluation, and therefore also the degree to which this depends on personal optimism or pessimism. Here are two views of the same experience:

> With such comprehensive terms of reference, success lies in making the political actors more aware of the problems. One does not know what all the consequences have been, the important thing is that a process has been set in train.

On the other hand,

> There were so many good ideas, and so little has happened, and the next generation turns to something else.

NOTES

1 Helmut Kohn and Friedrich Latzelsberger: 'Steuerungsprobleme in Wirtschaft und Gesellschaft; zum Gutachten der Kommission für wirtschaftlichen und sozialen Wandel.' In *Aus Politik und Zeitgeschichte*. Beilage zur Wochenzeitung das Parlament Vol. 18/77. 7 May 1977. (Mainly for a summary of the Commission's report.)

2 Karl Martin Bolte: 'Die Arbeit der Kommission für wirtschaftlichen und sozialen Wandel', *Hamburger Jahrbuch für Wirtschafts- und Gesellschaftspolitik*, 23, 1978. (Mainly for a history of the work.)

3 Hans-Jürgen Bieneck: 'Ein deutsches Experiment: die Kommission für wirtschaftlichen und sozialen Wandel.' Unpublished, 1977. (Mainly for a discussion of the processes involved.)

4 Hans-Jürgen Bieneck: Innovationsforschung zwischen Konsolidierung und Überforderung. In *Wirtschaft und Wissenschaft*, 1976, No.2.

5 Der Bundesminister für Arbeit und Sozialordnung: *Wirtschaftlicher und sozialer Wandel in der Bundesrepublik Deutschland. Gutachten der Kommission für wirtschaftlichen und sozialen Wandel.* Göttingen, 1977.

6 Herbert Hax: *An Enquiry on Economic and Social Development. European Coordination Centre for Research and Documentation on Social Sciences. Round Table Conference on Social Sciences and Policy Making*, Bucharest, 1978.

7 Günter Friedrichs: 'Persönliche Stellungnahme zur 'Kommission für wirtschaftlichen und sozialen Wandel', Paris, OECD, 1977.

Appendix: Publications of the Commission for Economic and Social Change*

(Translated titles)

Vol. 1
Thomae, H. and Lehr, U. with Dreher, G. and Opgenoorth, W. (1973)

Occupational performance among middle-aged and elderly adults. An analysis of the state of research.

Vol. 2
Witte, E. (1973)

Organising for decisions about innovation. The model of the promoter.

Vol. 3
Müller, J. H. (1973)

Regional structure policy in the Federal Republic. A critical evaluation.

Vol. 4
Külp, B. and Mueller, R. (1973)

Alternative uses of increasing leisure: economic and socio-political implications.

Vol. 5
Booz-Allen and Hamilton with a critique by Hartmann, H. (1973)

Meeting the challenges of German management.

Vol. 6
Winterhager, W. D. (1973)

Requirements of an occupational training system from the point of view of society, the individual, and the organisation.

Vol. 7
Brandenburg, A. G. (1974)

Success in learning of adults. Results of psychological, sociological and educational research.

---

* Published by the Verlag Otto Schwartz & Co, Annastrasse 7, 3400 Göttingen.

Vol. 8
Littman, K., with Krüger, B. and
von Obstfelder, V. and
Ulbrich, R.
(1974)

Damage to the environment –
socio-economic counter-concepts.

Vol. 9
Schneider, W., Heim, H. and
Wacker, P.A.
(1975)

Selection tests for specific tasks. Problems
of their development and application.

Vol. 10
Grefermann, K., Oppenländer,
K. H., Peffgen, E.,
Röthlingshöfer, K. and Scholz,
L.
(1974)

Technical development and the patent
system.

Vol. 11
Edding, F., Boehm, R.,
Dybowsky, G. and Rudolph, H.
(1974)

The structure and financing of vocational
training and further education.

Vol. 12
Barck, K., Mickler, O. and
Schumann, M., with Gerlach, F.,
Osterland, M., Schaufelberger,
H. J., Schröder, R. and Wulf,
H.A.
(1974)

Perspectives of technical change and the
interests of social groups. An empirical
study on the attitude to technical change
of top managers, scientists and engineers
from industrial research and development,
and commercial staff in industry.

Vol. 13
Werth, M.
(1974)

An analysis of the motivations that inhibit
mobility.

Vol. 14
Lenz-Romeiss, F.
(1974)

Leisure and everyday life. Problems of
increasing leisure.

Vol. 15
Kuntz, K. M.
(1974)

The motivation and direction of decisions
about education in different social classes..

Vol. 16
Brandenberg, A. G. Brödner,
P., Hetzler, H. and Schienstock,
G. with Arndt, I., Felde, M. R.
and Hamke, F.
(1975)

The decision to innovate. Reasons
determining the readiness to invest in new
technologies.

Vol. 17
Scherhorn, G.
(1975)

Consumer interests and consumer policy.

Vol. 18
Böhle, F. and Lutz, B.
(1974)

The effectiveness of agreements to protect
against the effects of rationalisation.

Vol. 19
Mackenson, R., Vanberg, M.
and Krämer K.
(1975)

The problems of regional mobility.
Findings and gaps of current research in
the Federal Republic.

Vol. 20
Klein, L.
(1975)

*The development of new forms of work
organisation.* International experiences
and current problems.

Vol. 21
Scholz, L.
(1974)

*Technology and innovation in industrial
production.* A theoretical contribution and
empirical analysis, using the example of
micro-electronics.

Vol. 22
Seifert, L. and Uebele, H.
(1974)

*Occupational training in large
organisations.*

Vol. 23
Gaugler, E., with Huber, K. and
Rummel, C.
(1974)

Manpower planning in industry. An
analysis of the literature.

Vol. 24
Ulrich, E. and Lahner, M.
(1974)

*The methods and information
requirements of technological forecasting.*

Vol. 25
Rath, M. with a preface by
Lohmann, U.
(1974)

Guaranteeing the right to work.

Vol. 26
Lutz, B. and Sengenberger, W.
(1974)

*The structure of the labour market and
public labour market policies.* A critical
analysis of objectives and tools.

Vol. 27
Schatz, H.
(1974)

*The system of policy planning in the
political system of the Federal Republic of
Germany.*

Vol. 28
Scharpf, F. W., with Mehwald,
L. and Schmitges, R.
(1974)

The political feasibility of internal reforms.

Vol. 29
Klein, K.
(1974)

*The opportunities and problems of
occupational integration of school leavers
who complete their schooling without the
final certificate.*

Vol. 30
Eichhorn, P.
(1974)

Social accounting in organisations.

Vol. 31
Bessoth, R.
(1975)
The effectiveness of suggestion schemes in industry. An analysis of research findings.

Vol. 32
Jarre, J.
(1975)
Environment damage and its impact on different social classes.

Vol. 33
Hödl, E.
(1975)
Economic growth and environmental policy.

Vol. 34
Mückl, W. J.
(1975)
Wealth policy concepts in the Federal Republic of Germany. Analysis of objectives, methods and effects.

Vol. 35
Linnhoff, U. and Sauer, B., with Szucs, L.
(1976)
The occupational training opportunities of women. An analysis of the literature of the Federal Republic of Germany, France, Sweden as well as of Czechoslovakia, the DDR and USSR.

Vol. 36
Rupp, E.
(1976)
Technology transfer as an instrument of state support for innovation. An international comparison of transfer mechanisms.

Vol. 37
Müller, U., with Stahldecker, P.
(1975)
Competition, the concentration of firms and innovation. An analysis of the literature on competition as a stimulus to discoveries.

Vol. 38
Jüttner-Kramny, L.
(1975)
The size of firms, their concentration and technological development. An analysis of the literature.

Vol. 39
Klemp, A. and Klemp, J.
(1976)
The distribution of working time and the use of leisure. A projection about the possibilities of redistributing working time and their effects on the leisure of the population.

Vol. 40
Zielinski, H.
(1975)
The discrepancy between the development of tasks of communities and their financing.

Vol. 41
Brück G. W. and Eichner, H., with Kuhkalani, M.
(1974)
Perspectives in social policy. A synopsis of the social policy ideas of the Federal Republic, the political parties, the Trades Union, and the Federations of Employers.

Vol. 42
Littmann, K. with Krüger, B.
(1975)

The state's component in the Gross National Product. Definitions and development

Vol. 43
Oberhauser, A.
(1975)

Policies for stability with an increasing state component of GNP.

Vol. 44
Flickinger, H. and Summerer, S.
(1975)

Legal and administrative conditions for successful environmental planning.

Vol. 45
Abels, H., Klemmer, P.,
Schäfer, H. and Teis, W.
(1975)

The business and labour market. An empirical study.

Vol. 46
Franmeyer, F. Schultz, S.,
Schumacher, D. and Seidel, B.
(1975)

The influence of the European Community on regional policy in the Federal Republic of Germany.

Vol. 47
Kreuz, D. W. and Schultz-Wild,
R. with Fischer H.
(1975)

Traffic and communications.

Vol. 48
Rosenberg, P.
(1975)

Possibilities for the reform of health care in the Federal Republic of Germany. A literature analysis.

Vol. 49
Schulte-Hillen, J., with Sprengel,
U. and Treinies, N.
(1975)

Aerospace policies in the Federal Republic of Germany.

Vol. 50
Krupp, H.
(1975)

Possibilities for the improvement of income and wealth statistics. The concept of distribution accounting for the Federal Republic of Germany

Vol. 51
Teichler, U. and Teichler-Urata,
Y.
(1975)

The labour market for academics in Japan.

Vol. 52
Jüttner, E.
(1975)

The labour market for academics in Sweden.

Vol. 53
Tessaring, M. and Werner, H.
(1976)

An international comparison of the employment problems of graduates.

Vol. 54
Armbruster, B. and Leisner, R. *Citizen participation in the Federal*
(1975) *Republic.* Leisure activities of different
groups of the population in selected fields
for participation (churches, political
parties, citizen initiatives and clubs).

Vol. 55
Pfromm, H. *Conflicts of solidarity within wage policies.*
(1975) Economic and social problems of
differentials within negotiated wages
structures.

Vol. 56
Höbermann, F. *The polarisation of work and leisure.*
(1975)

Vol. 57
Back, H., Böhle, P., Löser, J. *The regional planning of institutions of*
and Pieper, R., with Bünte, H., *vocational education.*
Henning, P. and Hirschfeld, C.
(1975)

Vol. 58
Frank, H. *New media and technologies for teaching*
(1975) *in schools and vocational education.*

Vol. 59
Görzig, B. *The differential effects of inflation in the*
(1975) *private and public sector.*

Vol. 60
Mückl, W. J. and Hauser, R. *The effects of inflation on the distribution*
(1975) *of income and wealth.* Two literature
studies.

Vol. 61
Roesler, K. and Stürmer, W., *The co-ordination of policy in the*
with Moser, H. *organisation of space.*
(1975)

Vol. 62
Frerich, J. and Pötzsch, R. *The tertiary sector and regional policy.*
(1975)

Vol. 63
Walser, P. *Macro-economic accounting. A revision*
(1975) *and extension of methods.*

Vol. 64
Fürstenberg, F. *The concept of an inter-disciplinary science*
(1975) *of work.*

Vol. 65
Schumacher, D. *Perspectives of an international policy for*
(1975) *research.* The example of the European
Community.

Vol. 66
Littmann, K., with Bornemann, I. and Paulenz, R. (1975) — *The possibilities of governmental control of innovations.*

Vol. 67
Lenz-Romeiss, F. (1975) — *Policies for leisure in the Federal Republic.*

Vol. 68
Wiemann, G., with Böse, K., Biermann, H., Düffert, J., Heilhoff, P., Knopp, A., Kappler, H. and Markert, C. (1975) — *Suggestions for the solution of the problems of unskilled workers.*

Vol. 69
Kühlewind, G. and Tessaring, M. (1975) — *Arguments for and against occupation-oriented education policy. A literature analysis.*

Vol. 70
Mergner, U., Osterland, M. and Pelte, K., with Görres, H. (1975) — *Working conditions in process of change*

Vol. 71
Heilmann, M. (1976) — *Redistribution of incomes occasioned by the state in the Federal Republic during the years 1960–1972.*

Vol. 72
Teriet, B. (1976) — *New ways of distributing working time.* Possibilities, conditions and consequences.

Vol. 73
Buhné, R. (1976) — *International interdependency of environmental problems.*

Vol. 74
Kapp, K. W., with Baumann, H. and Wachtl, P. (1976) — *State support for 'environment-friendly' technologies.*

Vol. 75
Bott, H. (1976) — *The part played by state/administrative prices in the cost of living index.* An empirical investigation for the period 1950 to 1973.

Vol. 76
Weser, A., with Annuk, I. (1976) — *Product descriptions – a means of consumer information*

Vol. 77
Egle, F., Ernst, A. and Schnur, P. (1976) — *Concealed unemployment.* Problems of measurement in the Federal Republic.

Vol. 78
Engelen-Kefer, U. and Klemmer, P. (1976)
The scope for regional action in labour market policy.

Vol. 79
Stamer, P. (1976)
Environmental policy in relation to quality-levels and structure. An analysis of instruments and an international comparison.

Vol. 80
Siebert, H. with Vogt, W. (1976)
Instruments of environmental policy. Information needs, conditions for success, analysis of effectiveness.

Vol. 81
Ewringmann, D. (1975)
The flexibility of public expenditure. An analysis of the limits of freedom in expenditure policy.

Vol. 82
Henke, K. (1975)
The distribution of goods and services at different levels of population. A literature analysis of problems of measurement and of political effectiveness.

Vol. 83
Schweikert, K. and Grieger, D. (1975)
The influence of certificates and formalised training for the employment system.

Vol. 84
Schmid, G. (1975)
Systems for influencing the labour market. A comparison of France, Great Britain, Sweden, the DDR and the USSR with the Federal Republic of Germany.

Vol. 85
Bräunling, and Harmsen, D. (1975)
Principles and measures for the support of research and technology policy. An analysis of their effectiveness.

Vol. 86
Pankoke, E. Nokielski, H. and Beine, T. (1975)
New forms of social self-regulation in the Federal Republic of Germany. A discussion of examples from education, social security and community self government.

Vol. 87
Kögler, A. (1976)
The development of marginal groups in the Federal Republic of Germany.

Vol. 88
Eichner, H. and Wagner, U. (1976)
Career advice and vocational guidance.

Vol. 89
Ellwein, T., Lippert, E. and
Zoll, R., with Bald D.
(1975)

*Political participation in the Federal
Republic of Germany.*

Vol. 90
Brinkmann, G.
(1976)

*The tasks and capacity of public
administration.*

Vol. 91
Lauffs, H. and Zühlke, W.
(1976)

Political planning in the Ruhr district.

Vol. 92
Lederer, K. and Mackensen, R.
(1975)

Levels of social need. The possibilities and
limitations of their scientific assessment.

Vol. 93
Baars, B. A., Baum, K. B. and
Fiedler, J.
(1976)

Policy and coordination. An investigation
of selected methods of co-ordination
within and between different subject areas
and between federal and regional levels.

Vol. 94
Heilmann, M.
(1976)

*The redistribution effects of the income-tax
reform of 1975.*

Vol. 95
Bombach, G. and Blattner, N.,
with contributions from Bauer,
C., Blattner, N. and Hoffarth,
A.
(1976)

Technical progress. A critique of concepts
for measurement and forecasting.

Vol. 96
Brandenburg, A. G.
(1975)

*Further education and labour market
policy.*

Vol. 97
Brösse, U.
(1975)

*Policy for regional planning systems as a
facet of integrated development policy.*

Vol. 98
von Schweitzer, R. and Pross,
H., with Boetticher
(1976)

*Households in process of economic and
social change.*

Vol. 99
Kock, H., Leifert, E., Schmid,
A. and Stirnberg, L.
(1976)

Stability policy. A review of current
discussion and new perspectives.

Vol. 100
Streissler, E., Beinsen, L.,
Schleicher, S. and Suppanz, H.
(1976)

*The stability of money values as a relative
goal.*

Vol. 101
Grünärml, F.
(1975)

Multi-national organisations and national economic policy.

Vol. 102
Kummere, K., Schwarz, N. and Weyl, H.
(1975)

The Federation's concepts for the ordering of regional structures.

Vol. 103
Braun, J. and Mathias, W.
(1975)

Leisure and the regional infrastructure. The problems of increased leisure for the regional infrastructure with particular relevance for areas of population concentration.

Vol. 104
Möller, J.
(1975)

Perspectives and problems of development relating to (geographical) space.

Vol. 105
Höpfner, K.
(1975)

Economic alternatives to the employment of foreign workers.

Vol. 106
Fehlau, K. and Neddens, M.
(1975)

The information for citizens in the development of political consciousness. A study towards the planning of the environment and infrastructure.

Vol. 107
Müller, J. and Hochreiter, R.
(1975)

Position and trends in the concentration (of industry) in the Federal Republic of Germany.

Vol. 108
Jochem, E., Hertz, H., Bossel, G. and Hoeflich, M.
(1976)

Motorisation and its effects.

Vol. 109
Rumpf, H., Rempp, H. and Wiesinger, M.
(1976)

Technological development.
Part 1: General lines of development.

Rumpf, H., Rempp, H. and Wiesinger, M.
(1976)

Part 2: Energy, transport and traffic, information, raw materials

Rumpf, H., Pahl, M., Rempp, H., Reinhardt, H. and Wiesinger, M.
(1976)

Part 3: Selected sectors (chemicals, machine tools, building technology, foodstuffs).

Vol. 110
Albrecht, J., Koch, C., Narr, W., Riehle, R. and Schmitz, K.
(1976)

The state and science policy. An analysis of research and technology policy of the Federal Republic.

Vol. 111
Decker, H., Langenbucher, W.   *Mass media in the post-industrial society.*
and Nahr, G.
(1976)

Vol. 112
Hackforth, J., with Heiner, I.,   *Mass media and their effects.*
Holtz, C., Möller, H., Noelke,
W., Pöhler, W., Rieskamp, I.,
Stein, D. and Voss, S.
(1976)

Vol. 113
Hamke, F.   *Private investment for the state's research*
(1976)   *policy.*

Vol. 114
Heckhausen, S.   *Deficits in the household-related*
(1976)   *infrastructure in the regions of the Federal*
    Republic of Germany.

Vol. 115
Denso, J., Ewringmann, D.,   *Efficiency and motivation in public*
Hansmeyer, K., Koch, R. and   *administration.* Incentives for the
König, H. and Siedentopf, H.   economic use of public funds.
(1976)

Vol. 116
Lüder, K. and Budäus, D.   *Efficiency oriented planning of budgets*
(1976)   *and administration of funds.* A study on
    the problem of incentives for the
    economic use of public funds.

Vol. 117
Hammer, H.   *The effects of political measures for*
(1976)   *influencing the employment of foreign*
    workers.

Vol. 118
Lauferr, H., Görgmaier, and   *Leisure policy at federal, regional and*
Laufer-Heydenreich, S.   *community levels.* An analysis and an
(1976)   attempt at a new orientation.

Vol. 119
Albers, W.   *Possibilities of a social policy which is*
(1976)   *more goal-oriented.*

Vol. 120
Reich, N., Toner, K. and   *Consumer and the law.*
Wegener, H.
(1976)

Vol. 121
Rüth, W. with Schmidt, G.   *The causes of premature inability to work.*
(1976)   (Invalidity).

Vol. 122
Grube, F., Richter, G. and
Thaysen, U.
(1976)

*Political planning in the political parties
inside and outside Parliament.*

Vol. 123
Damman, K., Faltin, G. and
Hopf, C.
(1976)

Further education for public service.

Vol. 124
Hübener, A. and Halberstadt,
R., with Feldhusen, G.
(1976)

Monitoring policy planning. Attempts and
problems in the Federal Republic of
Germany.

Vol. 125
Zapf. W.
(1976)

*Social accounting, possibilities and
problems.*

Vol. 126
Brinckmann, H., Burckhardt,
L., Heyse, E., Meyfahrt, M.,
Meyfahrt, R., Pfromm, K. and
Pfromm, R.
(1976)

*A policy for infrastructure needs
communication.*

Vol. 127
Blum, H., Heil, K. and
Hoffmann, L., with Gross, G.
(1976)

Urban development – claims and reality.

Vol. 128
Röper, B. with Berndt, L.,
Schmid, J. and Wassenberg, G.
(1976)

*The theory and practice of common
ownership.* An analysis, using the example
of common ownership enterprises.

Vol. 129
Weiss, J.
(1976)

*A projection of input/output tables for the
Federal Republic of Germany for the years
1980 and 1985.*

Vol. 130
Krelle, W. and Pauly, R.
(1976)

*Consumption and investment of the state
up to 1985.*

Vol. 131
Wieken, K.
(1976)

*An international comparison of the
organisation of consumer interests.*

Vol. 132
Mensch, G.
(1976)

Innovation in a mixed economy.
Alternative organisational forms for the
state's research and technology policy.

Vol. 133
Part 1: Blume, O. and Müller, G. (1976)
Part 2: Röper, B. with Heiduk, G., Heuwing, M., Kaempf, B., Marfeld, R. and Wassenberg, G. (1976)

Advertising for branded goods. Consequences for knowledge about the market and prices.

Vol. 134
Seidl, W. (1976)

Environmental damage to natural cycles.

Vol. 135
Kmieciak, P. (1976)

The structure and change of value systems.

Vol. 136
Reyher, L. (1976)

Gaps in labour market research.

Vol. 137
Röper, B. with Marfeld, R. (1976)

Is there such a thing as planned obsolescence?

Vol. 138
Görzig, B. (1976)

The age structure of investment capital. An ex post analysis and simulations of alternative investment strategies till 1985.

Vol. 139
Czerwonka, C., Schöppe, G. and Weckbach, S. (1976)

The active consumer: communication and co-operation.

Vol. 140
Kohn, H. (1976)

On the process of contracting out research in economics and the social sciences. The experience of the research programme of the Commission for Economic and Social Change with an appendix about the activities of the Commission.

II Methodologies for policy research

CHAPTER 12

Varieties of methodology: strengthening the contribution of social science

MARTIN BULMER

For social science research to have an effective influence, it must be well-grounded and soundly executed. Effective influence requires competent and rigorous research. Without good ideas and able scholars to execute them, this will not be achieved. A third quality is also necessary, the ability to command the appropriate methods with which to investigate society and the dynamics of change. Methodology indeed provides the underpinning of the social science effort, and nowhere is this truer than in policy research. Politicians, officials and advisers are unlikely to be impressed by studies that are strong on theory and weak on evidence. The warrant for the points made and conclusions reached is likely to be the first feature of research to be examined. This is usually interpreted to mean the merits of the design of the research, the selection of cases for study, the way data has been collected and analysed, and the relationship between this analysis and the conclusions arrived at. The methodology of policy research is therefore a particularly important aspect of the relationship between social science research and government. This section as a whole considers certain aspects of the subject, while this chapter provides a brief overview to set the chapters which follow in context.

A common distinction made in discussions of policy research is between basic, pure or fundamental research on the one hand, which is theory-based and discipline-oriented, and applied research on the other which is problem- and practice-oriented. By implication, most of the research which is done for government is applied research. Though the distinction contains an element of truth, it is not ultimately a very satisfactory one. A hard and fast line cannot easily be drawn between pure and applied research, and a more satisfactory conceptualisation may be a threefold one between basic, strategic and tactical research (Bulmer, 1978, pp. 8–9). Even in terms of research which government sponsors, not all research supported is applied research. The U.S. government, for example, through the research programmes of its armed forces and of the National Institutes of Health, supports some basic social science research. A more useful question to ask is where research is carried out.

The location of research is an aspect of its institutionalisation which was touched on in the previous section. Seven different types of location may be distinguished, which have some influence on the type of methodology used. The first is 'in-house' government research, of the type described by Walker and by Cornish and Clarke in the previous section. The second is research done under the auspices of government in para-governmental bodies, which in Britain are dubbed 'quangos', Quasi Non-Governmental Organisations. Examples in Britain would be organisations such as the Commission for Racial Equality, the Equal Opportunities Commission and the Sports Council. In a sense governmental commissions are a kind of temporary *ad hoc* para-governmental body, though they lack executive functions and their aim is to deliberate and make policy recommendations. They too undertake research. Thirdly, commercial market research firms use survey methods to carry out some government-funded policy-related research, as a small part of a much wider range of opinion polling and product testing carried out for commercial sponsors. Fourthly, there exist in the United States (though scarcely at all in Europe) social research enterprises (some for-profit and some not-for-profit) which undertake contract social science research for government. Firms such as Abt Associates Inc. of Cambridge, Massachusetts, Mathematica Inc. of Princeton, Westat in the Washington DC area and SRI at Stanford grew rapidly through the 1970s in response to government demands for an applied research product which could be tendered for and delivered within a shorter time-span than many academics could meet. Mathematica, for example, managed the New Jersey–Pennsylvania Negative Income Tax Experiment (Kershaw and Fair, 1976), which was designed and directed by academic economists from the Institute for Research on Poverty at the University of Wisconsin. Sometimes these consultant and research companies (those around Washington DC and Baltimore termed the 'Beltway bandits') do not themselves gather data but subcontract this stage to university or commercial survey organisations. Largely because of the much smaller scale of applied social science, such firms have not appeared in Europe. The nearest equivalent are concerns like Social and Community Planning Research in London, an independent survey research agency which conducts policy research for government and academic clients, described by Hedges in Chapter 14.

What is common to both North America and Europe are a fifth type, large government or foundation-funded independent research institutes, without direct academic affiliation, such as the Brookings Institution in Washington and the National Institute of Mental Health on its outskirts, the Policy Studies Institute in London, and the Max Planck (formerly Kaiser Wilhelm) Gesselschaft in West Germany. European practice varies. The German tradition of establishing research centres independent of universities has not been followed in Britain, where the Research Councils have preferred to establish units within universities. The Policy Studies Institute, like Brookings has relied largely upon support from foundations and the business community.

A sixth type is the large university-based research institute, with external funding, which may be devoted to research in a particular substantive area or to methodology, or a combination of the two. The classic American examples are discussed by McKennell in Chapter 13, the Institute of Social Research at the University of Michigan, the Bureau of Applied Social Research at Columbia University, and the National Opinion Research Center at the University of Chicago (although the latter is formally independent of the university). All three were and are devoted to the advancement of survey methodology among other things. In Britain, SCPR hosts a more modest research centre with similar aims (Hoinville, 1985). There exist in universities a considerable number of institutes and units, with full-time research staff without teaching appointments, devoted to substantive research in areas such as health, social services, race relations and industrial relations research, funded variously by the Department of Health and Social Security, the Medical Research Council and the Economic and Social Research Council.

Finally, some applied policy research is conducted in academic teaching departments by teaching staff, who may or may not obtain outside funding for research help or to bring themselves out of teaching, and who may have a letterhead for a research 'centre', but who are university teachers who do research part of the time. In the United States, joint appointments between academic departments and research institutes of the sixth type are not unknown, but in Britain these are less common. Indeed, there are intractable problems of grafting larger scale research enterprises onto academic teaching departments which mean that once research activity reaches a certain scale, a separate structure is needed to organise and manage it effectively (Rossi, 1964; Bulmer, 1983). However, a good deal of social science research by academics is conducted on a modest scale. Though some of it is basic research, a surprisingly high proportion is strategic or tactical research which has implications for applications to policy (Perry, 1976).

One implication of the variety of locations for policy research, particularly significant for methodology, is that university teaching departments occupy a comparatively small corner of the map. Some considerable part of the cumulative methodological expertise of applied social researchers is developed outside the orbit of academic teaching departments. In large American centres like ISR, Michigan and NORC, a felicitous blend of academic expertise and practical policy orientation has been achieved, and McKennell in Chapter 13 is concerned in part with how such a link might be fostered more successfully in Britain. Other developments, however, like large-scale social experiments, have been advanced outside the academic orbit, and this is true also of some evaluation research. The scale of GAO involvement which Rist documents in Chapter 16 is ample evidence of this. The influence of universities should not be underestimated. They are the major training ground for applied social researchers, and academic staff act as consultants and advisers in all of the five types of non-academic research setting. It is worth emphasising, however, the extent to which applied policy research is being carried on outside the academic orbit.

Another major implication of the diversity of settings lies in the greater resources available for research, and to researchers, in non-academic settings. Government, for example, has access to very large bodies of administrative data as well as to the results of censuses and large-scale continuous surveys (Hakim 1987). Large-scale survey research is costly, but professional survey organisations are geared up, and funded, for that scale of activity. This in turn means that their capacity for methodological experiment and innovation is enhanced, and may be considerably superior to that available to individual academics. Although academic researchers have made major contributions to survey research, social indicator work and evaluation research, the input from the non-academic research sector is very sizeable. This is reflected in the fact that three of the five chapters which follow are written by authors who work in non-academic research settings. One of them, Rist, is an ex-academic, but by the same token, the academics who wrote Chapter 13, McKennell, Bynner and Bulmer, all worked at one time or another for the Office of Population Censuses and Surveys in London.

The chapters which follow address important questions about the appropriate methodologies to use in applied social science research, but do not exhaust the kinds of applied research which may be distinguished in terms of their methodology. Certain omissions should be made clear lest the unwary reader is given an oversimplified picture. The cake may be cut several ways, but if four types of research are directly addressed here, two others are not and another field of research which is undoubtedly important is not discussed here.

The four fields covered are social survey research, social indicators, evaluation research and social experimentation. Two areas not covered are the aetiology of social problems and qualitative policy research. Research on policy formation and the process of research utilisation within government is also omitted from discussion. Some of these research methods are descriptive, some seek to diagnose causes, others to evaluate outcomes. They are not all strictly comparable, but they do represent distinct approaches which are crystallised sufficiently to threat separately. The social survey is the most common methodological digging tool of the applied social researcher, and its use is considered in the chapters by McKennell and Hedges. The procedures of conducting surveys are well explicated in standard texts, and a good deal has been written on the organisation of social survey research in Britain and the United States. These two chapters examine the three-way relationship between academics, professional survey researchers and government policy-makers, the experience of an independent survey agency in dealing with government, and the institutionalisation of survey research in universities. McKennell's chapter could have been placed in the preceding section, but since its subject-matter is a particular type of methodology, it appears here.

A different kind of mapping of the present state of society is represented by the social indicator movement. There is now a considerable literature on the subject (for example, Bauer, 1966; de Neufville, 1975; Carley, 1981; Land, 1983; MacRae, 1985) and British developments were treated in an earlier collection (Bulmer (ed.), 1978, pp. 201–67). Social indicators aim to provide policy-makers with succinct descriptive diagnoses of the state of society. Compared to standard economic indicators like GNP or the price index, the problems of doing so are formidable, and not lightly overcome. Denis Johnston's chapter represents an informed and critical reflection upon the experience of social indicator work within the American federal government during the 1970s. In a sense Johnston's chapter also belongs in the last section, since the work was another victim of the early Reagan cuts, but its primary interest lies in reflecting about the conditions under which effective indicator work can be done.

Both surveys and indicators provide snapshots of the condition of society. Surveys may, additionally, be used for analysis of the causes of particular conditions. An influential view which has gained ground in the last fifteen years is that social science's contribution to policy lies in the measurement of policy outcomes as much as in the initial formulation of policy. 'What government and the public most need to know in the aftermath of (the policy) process is whether there was anything to show for the effort, and if so what' (Moynihan, 1969, p. 194). Evaluation research has developed in response to this demand. Ray Rist's account of the evaluation research function within the U.S. General Account Office is a very interesting example of the extent to which social science is perceived as relevant within the U.S. system of government. At the behest of Congress, what is in effect a large research institute has been created to monitor the outcome of legislation. This example of evaluation research has been included because it is so close to the centre of U.S. government.

Social experimentation represents the 'hard' end of policy research, the most hard-nosed attempt to apply scientific method to the applied study of social processes. The United States has been unusual in being willing to mount large-scale costly social experiments to test the feasibility of certain social policy innovations (cf. Ferber and Hirsch, 1982). The best known of these are the negative income tax experiments, but others have been concerned with housing allowances, youth unemployment and health insurance. In one sense, such experiments are merely a rigorous form of evaluation, but because of their distinctive research design, they may effectively be treated as a separate type. Robert Boruch in Chapter 17 provides a comprehensive review of the types of randomised policy research experiments which have been carried out in different fields.

Two types of methodology are not considered here. Studies of the aetiology of social problems are part of the warp and woof of social science. Basic and strategic research blend into one another when the causes of phenomena are concerned, although policy-makers are much more interested in those causal influences which are susceptible to policy manipulation than in those which are not. Survey research and social experimentation may involve delving into the underlying and preciptitating causes of social conditions, but a good deal of survey research is primarily descriptive, while large-scale social experiments are primarily designed to test the effects of particular policy interventions (usually underpinned by a particular theory of social behaviour). When considering policies to tackle urban poverty, or juvenile delinquency, or racial conflict, policy-makers and their social science advisers may draw upon a considerable body of research in each area. Further investigation may well be called for, focusing on variables which policy can influence, but a good deal can be learned from examining the existing body of research and its presupposition. The Moynihan report of 1963 on the black American family generated much controversy (cf. Rainwater and Yancey, 1967) but it also demonstrated the importance of the theoretical framework and type of explanation used to account for the existence of particular problems. These issues about causal inference in policy research have recently been considered more fully elsewhere (Bulmer, 1986).

Qualitative policy research is not dealt with here in detail because that too is discussed elsewhere (Bulmer, 1986, ch. 9; Walker, 1985) and because it is as yet a rather small part of the policy research scene. Research of a small-scale, interpretive type is on the increase, for example, within the Home Office Research and Planning Unit discussed in Chapter 10. In the future it is likely gradually to assume a greater importance.

Research on the policy process and upon the process of social science utilisation is not a distinct type of methodology, but it has some relevance in discussing methodologies for policy research. More empirical research is needed of this type, both within particular societies and comparatively. A historical dimension in examining use and non-use of social science is indispensable. A particularly necessary feature of such research is to examine the policy-making process itself and the ways in which social science is perceived to be relevant by the participants (to the extent that it is) and how social science is actually used in the process (to the extent that it is). In the meantime, there is some value in accounts by social scientists of their own involvement in particular policy domains, such as D. P. Moynihan's analysis of what went wrong with the War on Poverty (1969) and David Donnison's account of his five years as Chairman of the Supplementary Benefits Commission (1982). Critical assessments of social scientists' involvement by observers are also of particular interest (cf. Aaron, 1978).

There is a certain asymmetry in the comparative element in the chapters which follow. This is deliberate, but should be highlighted so that the reader is aware of it. The two chapters on survey research are by British authors, and focus primarily on British experience, although McKennell makes extensive reference to the model provided by the large American academic survey research institute. There is no attempt here to describe the very wide range of government surveys conducted in each country, from the U.S. Current Population Survey and National Crime Survey or the UK Labour Force Survey or General Household Survey downwards in scale (see Bulmer, 1986, Ch. 5). The important role in government survey research of the U.S. Census Bureau (in some respects the counterpart of OPCS Social Survey Division, writ large) should not be overlooked. There is no attempt to characterise the market research industry in either country, which does some policy-relevant research. The growth of independent research firms referred to earlier is an American phenomenon which deserves detailed study. The focus upon ISR, Michigan and NORC, Chicago should not be read as implying that they are the only U.S. university-based survey organisations, rather that they were the pioneering institutions which still today remain pre-eminent. Despite its preoccupation with British concerns and relatively narrow focus, the next chapter does bring out the salient differences at the frontier between academics interested in surveys and policy research in the two countries.

The asymmetry is more obvious in the case of social indicators. The absence of a chapter on social indicator work in Britian should not be taken to mean that it is absent from the scene, rather that it has already been treated in several published sources (Bulmer, 1978, pp. 203–67; Thompson, 1978; Carley, 1981). The annual review *Social Trends* continues to be published, and the government statistical service survived in somewhat reduced form after a review by Mrs Thatcher's business efficiency expert Mr Derek Rayner (Rayner Report, 1981; Hoinville and Smith, 1982). Nevertheless, certain differences should be briefly noted. Although there are distinct parallels in the indicator work within the central statistical units in each country, leading to the production of *Social Indicators* and *Social Trends*, the American scene is once again the more expansive one. Within the Federal government and its associated agencies there is more readiness to undertake indicator work and publish its results. A striking example is the U.S. Commission of Civil Rights which in 1978 produced *Social Indicators of Equality for Minorities and Women*. No comparable British work is available, and indeed British social scientists are still arguing among themselves as to whether acceptable measures of race and ethnicity can and should be devised (cf. Bulmer, 1980; 1986b; Booth, 1985).

Another marked difference is in the extent to which academic experts have been involved in social indicator work. In the U.S., they have advised on the production of *Social Indicators*, contributed to two special journal issues providing commentary on that volume (*The Annals*, 1978; 1981) and participated actively in the (U.S.) SSRC's long-running programme on social indicators, which included until 1983 a Washington-based research coordination center (*Items*, 1983). Though some British academic work developing social indicators has been carried out, this has been largely independent of government. There has been little academic input into the work of the Central Statistical Office. The gap is more serious than for other types of methodology because in the construction of indicators, government holds most of the basic data and alone possesses the resources to synthesise these effectively into summary form. In economics, a much tighter relationship has existed in both countries between academics interested in improved measurement and developments within government to improve economic indicators. This is an important exception, but it has not had much impact upon social indicator work. Even Sir Richard Stone's attempt at Cambridge to construct a system of social and demographic statistics by linking them into a single set of accounts has been of greater interest to economists than it has either to other social scientists or to British government officials working on social indicators.

The absence of discussion of evaluation research and social experimentation in Britain is intended to highlight the salience of both in America and their low visibility or absence in Britain. The picture should not be painted too black and white. There is considerable interest in evaluation among a minority of social science researchers, and attempts to apply such approaches have been made on a small scale in fields such as criminology (cf. Clarke and Cornish, 1983; Farrington, 1983), and social services research (cf. Goldberg and Connelly, 1981). There have also been very modest and small-scale experimental tests of limited measures in fields such as penal policy and education, but not involving major expenditure. Nothing resembling the large-scale American social experiments have been conducted in Britain, nor even contemplated. Some greater use of experimentation has occurred in West Germany (cf. Hellstern and Wollman, 1984) but again not on a massive or expensive scale. In general, however, these two types of methodology for policy research are characterised by their high visibility in the United States and invisibility in Britain.

The reasons for this state of affairs can be read from the first two chapters and the contributions in Part I. Four specific factors may be highlighted. Leadership of social scientists in influential positions as head of department, senior officals or advisers, played a part. Consider, for example, Moynihan's evidence to a Senate subcommittee on executive reorganisation in 1966 which put eloquently and forcibly the case for a Congressional evaluation research capability, staffed by professional social scientists, to review judgements made by executive departments.

> The simple fact is that a new source of knowledge (evaluation research) is coming into being; while it is as yet an imperfect technique, it is likely to improve; and if it comes to be accepted as a standard element in public discourse it is likely to raise considerably the level of that discourse. This source of knowledge should not remain an executive monopoly. (1969, p. 200)

As a former Assistant Secretary for Labour for Policy Planning and Research, this testimony carried the weight of a Harvard Professor who had also served in the Federal Government. There were a variety of contributing factors leading to the GAO initiative, but such leadership was an important component.

Another important quality lies less in the American faith in scientific method *per se*, though this played some part, as in the explicit statement of social goals and the desire to monitor systematically progress toward such goals. Speaking at the height of 1960s optimism, Moynihan in the testimony cited above said:

> We have set ourselves goals that are, in some ways, unique in history; not only to abolish poverty and ignorance, but also to become the first genuinely multi-racial and, we hope, in the end non-racial democracy the world has seen. I believe that in moving toward these goals, and in seeking to change the present reality, an unflincing insistence on fact will be a major asset. (1969, p. 201).

Twenty years on, the achievement of such goals seems as elusive as ever, but the belief in the role of social science as a means of monitoring and evaluating progress shines through. There has been a receptivity to potential of applied social science which has carried it along even in the face of disappointments such as the lack of conclusiveness of the results of large-scale experiments (cf. Bulmer, 1986, Ch. 8). In Britain this receptivity and faith in science has either been lacking or where it existed, much more muted.

A related difference is the often-remarked entrepreneurial spirit which is more characteristic of the United States than of Britain. This is reflected, for example, in the history of the university system, which displays much greater diversity – private alongside public, denominational alongside secular institutions – and has since the late nineteenth century been highly competitive, leading institutions vying with each other for pre-eminence and innovating in a variety of ways to foster research and expand budgets (Shils, 1978). This restless and competitive spirit is reflected in the national characteristic of 'hustling' for business much more than in Britain, true of academic research as in other areas. There also appears, perhaps as a result, to be a considerably greater willingness to cross boundaries between the academic, federal government and commercial spheres than is apparent in Britain.

The maturity of the social sciences also has played some part. An important factor in the different development of survey research in the two countries has been the much longer history of academic social science research of an empirical kind, and the strength which this provided for the 'take-off' of more policy-oriented research during and after World War Two. In Britain the immaturity of the social sciences and that over-rapid expansion of the 1960s and early 1970s has had considerable costs. This is shown by one of the two large-scale demonstration action-research projects which are perhaps as close as Britain has come to mounting a large-scale social experiment. These, the Educational Priority Area (EPA) and Community Development Programme (CDP) projects (Bulmer, 1978, pp. 139–200), both involved pilot schemes in a small number of local areas, each of which had an action team to introduce change and a research team (with an academic base) to evaluate the before and after situation. The CDP research teams rapidly concluded that the brief they had been given, to evaluate improved co-ordination between workers and services at the local level as a means of alleviating individual social problems, was based on a false diagnosis of the real problems of these areas, which were located in the regional, national and international economies (Loney, 1983). They then proceeded to abandon the research brief they had been given and undertake a political analysis of the problems of industrial decline. Opinions differ about the value of this exercise, and of the whole experience of challenging the Home Office definition of the problem, but what is clear is that the research teams rapidly subordinated their academic research aims to broader political ones. Relatively little rigorous research was conducted as a result, though some useful studies were done and a good deal of polemical literature produced. Social science took second place to social advocacy. This case does not typify British social science, but it does show a strain toward politicisation which is either absent in the United States or treated in a much more sophisticated fashion.

The chapters which follow thus examine four different methodologies used in policy research and extend the comparison made in Part I of the place of social science in the British and American system of governments. This is not to lose sight of the difficulties with which the social sciences have had to contend within both societies during the 1980s, a subject treated in the final part. The battles they have fought in London and Washington have distinct parallels. But one should not neglect the fact that the American battle was fought from a much greater position of strength than the British, reflecting enduring differences between the place of the social sciences in the government of the two societies.

REFERENCES

Aaron, H. (1978), *Politics and the Professors*, Washington D.C., Brookings Institution.
Annals, The (1978), *America in the Seventies: Some Social Indicators*. Special issue, Vol. 435 (January), pp. 1–294.

Annals, The (1981), *Social Indicators: American Society in the Eighties*. Special Issue, Vol. 453 (January), pp. 1–253.

Bauer, R. (ed.) (1966), *Social Indicators*, Cambridge, Mass., M.I.T. Press.

Booth, H. (1985), 'Which "ethnic question"? The development of questions identifying ethnic origins in official statistics', *The Sociological Review* 33(2) (May), pp. 254–74.

Bulmer, M. (ed.) (1978), *Social Policy Research*, London, Macmillan.

Bulmer, M. (1980), 'On the feasibility of identifying "race" and "ethnicity" in censuses and surveys', *New Community* vol. 8 (1–2), pp. 3–15.

Bulmer, M. (1983), 'The social sciences', in *The Western University on Trial*, ed. J. W. Chapman, Berkeley, University of California Press, pp. 100–17.

Bulmer, M. (ed.) (1985), *Essays on the History of British Sociological Research*, Cambridge, Cambridge University Press.

Bulmer, M. (1986a), *Social Science and Social Policy*, London, Allen & Unwin.

Bulmer, M. (1986b), 'Race and ethnicity' in R. Burgess (ed.), *Key Variables in Sociological Investigation*, London, Routledge & Kegan Paul, pp. 54–75.

Carley, M. (1981), *Social Measurement and Social Indicators*, London, Allen & Unwin.

Clarke, R. V. G. and Cornish, D. B. (1983), 'Editorial introduction', in *Crime Control in Britain: a review of policy research*, ed. Clarke, R. and Cornish, D., Albany, N.Y., State University of New York Press, pp. 3–54.

De Neufville, J. I. (1975), *Social Indicators and Public Policy*, Amsterdam: Elsevier.

Donnison, D. V. (1982), *The Politics of Poverty*, Oxford, Martin Robertson.

Farrington, D. P. (1983), 'Randomised experiments on crime and justice', *Crime and Justice: an annual review of research* 4, pp. 257–308.

Ferber, R. and Hirsch, W. Z. (1982), *Social Experimentation and Economic Policy*, Cambridge, Cambridge University Press.

Goldberg, E. M. and Connelly, N. (eds.) (1981), *Evaluative Research in Social Care*, London, Heinemann.

Hakim, C. (1987), *Research Design: Strategies and choices in the design of social research*, London, Allen & Unwin.

Hellstern, G-M., and Wollman, H. (eds.) (1984), *Experimentelle Politik*, Opladen, Westdeutscher Verlag.

Hoinville, G. (1985), 'Methodological research on sample surveys: a review of developments in Britain', in *Essays on the History of British Sociological Research*, ed. M. Bulmer, Cambridge, Cambridge University Press, pp. 101–20.

Hoinville, G. and Smith, T. M. F. (1982), 'The Rayner review of government statistical services', *Journal of the Royal Statistical Society* A, 145(2), pp. 195–207.

ITEMS (1983), 'The Council's Program in Social Indicators', *ITEMS*, Special Issue, vol. 37(4) (December), pp. 73–103.

Kershaw, D. and Fair, J. (1976), *The New Jersey Income Maintenance Experiment*: volume 1, *Operations, Surveys and Administration*, New York, Academic Press.

Land, K. C. (1983), 'Social Indicators', in *Annual Review of Sociology* 9, ed. R. H. Turner and J. F. Short Jr, Palo Alto, Calif., Annual Reviews Inc., pp. 1–26.

Loney, M. (1983), *Community Against Government: the British Community*

Development Project 1968-1978 – a study in government incompetence, London, Heinemann.

MacRae, D. Jr (1985), *Policy Indicators: links between social science and public debate*, Chapel Hill, University of North Carolina Press.

Moynihan, D. P. (1969), *Maximum Feasible Misunderstanding: community action in the war on poverty*, New York, Basic Books.

Perry, N. (1976), 'Research settings in the social sciences: a reexamination', in *Demands for Social Knowledge: the role of research organisations*, ed. E. Crawford and N. Perry, London, Sage, pp. 137–90.

Rainwater, L. and Yancey, W. (eds.) (1967), *The Moynihan Report and the Politics of Controversy*, Cambridge, Mass., M.I.T. Press.

Rayner Report (1981), *Government Statistical Services*, Cmnd. 8236, London, HMSO.

Rossi, P. (1964), 'Scholars, researchers and policy-makers: the politics of large-scale research', *Daedalus* 93 (4) (Fall), pp. 1142–61.

Shils, E. (1978), 'The order of learning in the United States from 1865 to 1920: the ascendancy of the universities', *Minerva* 16 (Summer), pp. 159–95.

Thompson, E. J. (1978), '*Social Trends*: the development of an annual report for the United Kingdom', *International Social Science Journal* 30, pp. 653–9.

U.S. Commission on Civil Rights (1978), *Social Indicators of Equality for Minorities and Women*, Washington D.C., U.S. Commission on Civil Rights.

Walker, R. (ed.) (1985), *Applied Qualitative Research*, Aldershot, Hants., Gower.

CHAPTER 13

The links between policy, survey research and academic social science: America and Britain compared

AUBREY MCKENNELL, JOHN BYNNER AND MARTIN BULMER

The reasons why the development of survey research has been so different in Britain from the United States, and other countries that have followed the American lead, are complex. Britain has a large and thriving survey research industry but, almost alone among developed nations, has not established until recently any major university-based survey research centre. The consequence has been loss of the mutual benefits gained from the closer connections between social policy, survey research and social science which are to be found in the USA. Some of the reasons for this state of affairs and some of the consequences will be considered in this chapter.

Figure 1 represents the three-way relationship between social policy, social surveys, and academic social science. These triangles reflect the situation in the two countries. Both have a solid base reflecting the fact that policy makers fund a great flow of social surveys in Britain much as they do in other advanced nations. It is the further links with academic social science that are particularly weak in the UK. A flourishing survey research industry does exist but a central fact about the professional

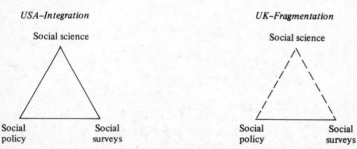

Fig 1 Integration and fragmentation

244

organisations that conduct this work is that they have grown up outside the university system. As a result the mainstream survey work in the UK largely bypasses the academic social science community.

This is in contrast with North America where there are 'transfusion effects' round the whole system because a good part of the flow goes through university-based institutions. The UK lacks such organisations, staffed by career academics who are also survey experts, and carry out a wide range of policy-oriented surveys while still retaining an allegiance to their discipline. (Moss, 1972; Sheatsley, 1982).

Although there is a long tradition of survey research stretching back to the surveys of poverty conducted by Booth and Rowntree in the last century, the foundations of the modern approach were not laid until the period during and immediately after the second world war. Wartime experience in Britain as well as America stimulated a demand for surveys of the home population. But in America quantitative social science was already well established in the universities. American social scientists contributed to the war effort in various ways including the running of surveys in the wartime agencies. When the agencies shut down after the war it was these returning social scientists who set up the original academic survey centres (Sheatsley, 1982). In Britain quantitative social science was still in its infancy even a decade after the war. Thus the Government Social Survey set up as a wartime agency and continuing in peacetime, developed largely independently of the kind of academic social science inputs that were shaping survey research in North America (Moss, 1972).

American survey research

The survey scene in the United States is vast if the activities of the Bureau of the Census and the several excellent opinion polling and market research organisations are included. Consideration of ISR and NORC alone does not do justice even to the variety of university-based survey organisations. There are now many such centres. We focus on the two original ones because we know them best, they have proved remarkably durable, are probably still the largest, and differ sufficiently to bring out what is most salient and general in the comparison with British survey research.

There may be reassurance to be gained from noting that American survey research did not develop initially within universities but was grafted on to them after it had grown up elsewhere. ISR and NORC are, even today, kept at financial arms length by their host universities. They are direct cost organisations with virtually no funds from sources other than their own projects. Both organisations have striven to maintain the difficult balance between basic research and applied research, with one foot in the academic world and one in the world of government departments. Both organisations have tried to do this through a policy of joint appointments, by which the survey researchers are affiliated with a teaching department in the university. (At ISR many of the senior survey staff have tenured university appointments, at NORC only the Director.) This arrangement has worked splendidly in the case of ISR, but less so for NORC. Partly for that reason, NORC's history is more relevant to a British observer. But we begin with ISR because it is perhaps the best known American survey organisation in Britain.

The Institute for Social Research, University of Michigan

ISR's success may have stemmed from a uniquely favourable combination of circumstances that are unlikely ever to be repeated. The Institute was born in 1946 when an eminent psychologist, Donald Marquis, and Theodore Newcomb a leading sociologist, both at the University of Michigan combined together to invite Rensis Likert to move on to the campus bringing with him several of the team who had been working under him in the Division of Program Surveys of the US Department of Agriculture in Washington, which functioned as an all-purpose survey facility for Federal agencies during the war (Cannell, 1984). The young social scientists gathered round Likert in Washington who came with him to ISR were a remarkably talented group, some already well-known and others destined to become so: Angus Campbell, Dorwin Cartwright, Charles Cannell, Leslie Kish, George Katona, Daniel Katz. They made up the core of the Institute and remained on its staff throughout their careers. Other scholars of international repute were attracted to the circle, Phillip Converse and Robert Kahn in the early days and others since. It is due to their combined talents that ISR has been able to establish such an unusual degree of autonomy in developing its research programs. There is an important sense in which the organisation has been able to deal with its funding environment in its own terms. Continuing the tradition, ISR today carries out some projects in response to 'Request for Proposals', but as many as seventy-five per cent are unsolicited, resulting from proposals submitted by staff on their own initiative to prospective sponsoring agencies. Research volume of about 15 million dollars annually is obtained mainly from the Federal Government, especially the Department of Health and Human Services and the National Science Foundation (Cannell, 1984).

In addition to the Survey Research Center ISR comprises Centers for

Group Dynamics, for Research on the Utilization of Scientific Know-ledge (CRUSK) and for Political Science, but the national sample survey remains the dominant mode of investigation. The basic production units of ISR are its research programs, consisting of a set of repeated projects, persisting and renewing over time, and dedicated to the investigation of some defined research domain. The oldest is the Economic Behavior program, initiated by George Katona, in which national surveys are conducted annually. The results are widely used by government agen-cies, business groups and economic analysts. Other major programs of research include the Organisational Behavior Program, Social Environ-ment and Health, Youth and Social Issues and Social Indicators.

Each program is the responsibility of one or more program direc-tors, whose career commitment is to its domain of theory and research. The depth of that commitment is indicated by the remarkable stability of the ISR program director group. Of the original founding members, eleven remained until their retirement; only three left before that. Of the next cohort, thirteen program directors have been on the staff for more than twenty years and only one has left. The Institute now includes some 35 Program Directors and a number of senior research scholars who perform similar functions. In 1980 ISR employed 90 Ph.D. level research scientists, several hundred research support per-sonnel and a field interviewing staff of 300. Few younger staff have tenured faculty appointments but many are pursuing academic careers. Though the projects they direct are mainly funded by policy-makers, the annual output of scholarly work based on ISR projects remains impressive.

In addition to such substantive programs, ISR has also a very full program in Survey Methods, which includes among other things the research into interviewing techniques by Charles Cannell, and into question wording by Howard Schuman. Sampling at ISR under Leslie Kish, now succeeded by Graham Kalton, is also world renowned. Multivariate analysis procedures have been pioneered by members of the staff such as Morgan, Sonquist and Andrews.

The Institute also plays a major part in the training of social science students in survey methods through the Detroit Area Study in conjunc-tion with the Department of Sociology at Michigan. This course which has now run for more than 30 years is unique in its combination of training in sample survey methods with the actual execution of a substantial survey research project. Students participate in all stages of the survey (Schuman, 1977). Other educational activities include the ICPR Summer School, held each year at ISR, and the contributions of a number of senior staff to University of Michigan courses.

The National Opinion Research Center (NORC) at the University of Chicago

NORC, which also began during World War Two, is nearer in its mode of operation to survey organisations found in Britain. The first academic director of NORC was Clyde Hart, a sociology professor also involved in wartime survey research. It was Hart who envisaged NORC as a major academic social research institution, located at the University of Chicago rather than at the University of Denver. Previously it had operated as a wartime agency there under Harry Field, but there had been hardly any academic participation (Sheatsley 1982).

In its long history NORC has carried out surveys of health care, housing, drug abuse, ageing, crime, mental health and a host of other areas of policy interest. Like ISR its funding comes mainly from the Federal government. Where NORC differs from ISR is in making its data collection facilities more generally available. NORC has been very successful in obtaining work as a subcontractor for large studies that require only the execution of a survey where the prime contractor bears the responsibility for the design, analysis and report stage. Demands for this kind of service grew rapidly and became the core of NORC's financial support. Total revenue reached thirteen million dollars in 1982.

Today, NORC describes itself as both a research institute and a survey research laboratory. The latter term is justified because even as a data collection facility it is more than just a service bureau. Alongside the data collection work, study directors have carried out a sustained grant-aided programme of investigations into interviewing, question wording and response effects for which NORC is well-known.

Substantive research done at NORC has included work in the fifties on occupational prestige, Bradburn's study of psychological well-being in the late sixties, and more recently James Coleman's 'High School and Beyond' project. The General Social Survey, funded by the National Science Foundation, was launched in 1972 and has been fielded annually to provide social indicators of change in the attitudes and behaviour of Americans in a number of important areas.

Many American academics who are also survey experts served their professional apprenticeship working at ISR, NORC or one other academic centre of survey research – the Columbia Bureau of Applied Research, one of the earliest. But this never had its own field force. It was very much the product of one great man, Paul Lazarsfeld. His many-sided contributions included the theory for elaborating causal inferences from survey data (Lazarsfeld, 1955), possibly the greatest single conceptual advance in the field since probability sampling. But the 'great man' theory of survey organisations provides a poor model for originating and maintaining similar developments elsewhere. Following Lazarsfeld's death in 1976 the Bureau has changd out of all recognition and virtually ceased to exist. These were the pioneering institutions. Their example has spread. Numerous American universities now have their own organisations engaged primarily in sample survey work.

British large-scale survey research

It is not possible to do justice here to the full complexity of the British survey research scene. Market research firms still do considerable work for the public sector, and social survey research has been institutionalised in a number of independent, non-partisan, not-for-profit research institutes, such as the influential Institute of Community Studies, one of the earliest, and the Policy Studies Institute (PSI, incorporating PEP). Though PSI has carried out notable survey-based policy research, and a nucleus of staff have agency survey experience, it does not itself do the fieldwork for surveys. These centres have not achieved the creative fusion of academic input, policy relatedness, and sustained methodological interest in survey research as tightly as does the best work coming out of ISR and NORC. The account below focusses on the more comparable Social and Community Planning Research (SCPR) and the Social Survey Division (SSD) of the Office of Population Censuses and Surveys (OPCS), Britain's two main non-profit organisations operating in the public sector. In respect of survey professionalism their work is the equivalent of anything carried out in academic centres overseas, though in other respects these two organisations differ significantly from the overseas centres and from each other.

OPCS Social Survey Division (SSD)

The Social Survey Division of OPCS is the government's own survey organisation. Much of its work resembles that of the American Bureau of the Census, monitoring the population in the sense of providing detailed facts in such areas as population, housing, employment, health, use of services, household income and expenditure etc. to supplement and update information obtained through administrative channels and via the national census. About 70 per cent of SSD expenditure on social surveys providing national coverage now goes into maintaining the continuous surveys (with fieldwork spread out evenly over the year) which include the General Household Survey (GHS), the Family Expenditure Survey (FES, which provides a basis for the Retail Price Index), the International Passenger Survey and the Continuous Labour Force Survey, and the main regular survey, the Annual Labour Force Survey, carried out throughout the EEC (SSD, 1985).

But the SSD also performs functions that are more like those of NORC than the US Bureau of the Census. From the start it was set up as a social research agency tackling a wide range of surveys, including surveys of attitudes as well as behaviour, designed to contribute to policy formulation and evaluation (Moss, 1972). Over the years an impressive number of major benchmark studies have been turned out by SSD, each typically based on a large, complex, high quality exercise in sampling, data collection and data processing and often breaking new ground in operational survey research techniques. In addition to its programme of regular data collection, the SSD has done a wide variety of ad hoc surveys for almost every government department, as well as major pieces of work for Royal Commissions and special enquiries. (For a recent review and bibliography of the work of the Division see Whitehead, 1985).

It is part of SSD's official function to provide consultancy advice on survey research to other government departments. Recruitment of graduates from a range of social science disciplines has ensured that social science interests have had a voice. Some work such as the research for the Plowden Committee (1967) has made major contributions to the social science research literature. Our own direct experience of SSD dates from the 1960s when two of us were involved in surveys which required methodological work on the psychometrics of attitude measurement (McKennell, 1966, 1967; Bynner, 1969; McKennell and Bynner; 1969). The official index used in legislation about aircraft noise annoyance was arrived at from the regression analysis of data from a survey round Heathrow airport (McKennell, 1969). A long programme of research into smoking behaviour and attitudes started in the 1960s with highly analytical surveys (McKennell and Thomas, 1967; Bynner, 1969) and was carried further recently with a survey (Alan Marsh, 1982) part of which was as tightly modelled round a theory of attitudes (Fishbein's) as anything emerging from academic centres overseas. The requirements of policy clients rarely call for such academically well-modelled surveys, though there are other surveys that entail theoretical or intensive academic-style subject-matter inputs. Current examples are the survey of Unemployment and Poverty, and the survey of Disability. The survey of Disability requires the scaling of different handicaps for severity and the research officer in charge (Jean Martin), herself with a background in psychological testing, is tackling the formidable measurement problems involved in consultation with academic specialists.

The major methodological areas on which the SSD has been innovative are those more closely connected with the sampling and data collection process. The emphasis has varied in different periods, but the dominant thrust of the organisation has been and still is towards the production of descriptive data rather than analytical surveys. This has pushed both survey reports and methodological interests towards the production of tables and the resolution of issues of sampling, question-naire design, coding and interviewing, to ensure their validity, cost effectiveness and operational quality. Jean Atkinson's *Handbook for Interviewers* has been acknowledged (e.g. Catherine Marsh, 1982, p. 34) as the best guide to interviewing that there is. Some of the most significant work on the value of random sampling in survey research such as the classic paper by Gray (1950) was carried out at SSD. More recently SSD has pioneered the use of the Postcode Address File maintained by the Post Office as a sampling frame.

There has not been in Britain the same flow of ideas between the academic and the policy research sectors which characterises the American scene. Louis Moss, the founder of the Government Social Survey (now SSD) and its Director until 1971, noted of the immediate post-war period: 'at that time we did not know that parallel develop-ments were taking place in the United States and there was nothing of the same sort in this country which seemed suited to the kinds of problems that were coming to us. Our advisers however did represent a very special group of British researchers who had in earlier years elaborated their own methods of social enquiry ... So we drew from British not American sources. The Survey was a home grown product' (Moss, 1972). To simplify somewhat, Louis Moss, supported by a highly professional staff including such people as Percy Gray, W. F. F. Kemsley, Lesley Wilkins, Amelia Harris, Tom Corlett, and H. D. Willcock set high standards of sampling and data collection in this country and established a role for themselves as providers of relevant data to policy makers, so that neither side felt much need for academic contributions on either the technical or the interpretative aspects of survey research. The same is broadly true of the postwar growth of the British market research industry which was later to provide the original staff for SCPR. So it came about that the main professional survey organisations in the U.K., having grown up outside the academic social science community, inher-ited a tradition of insulation from it.

Social and Community Planning Research

Following the great increases in social welfare expenditure in the 1960s, the demand for survey data on social conditions expanded rapidly. Work for the public sector became a major growth area for the market research industry during this time. Social and Community Planning Research (SCPR), Britain's only major independent non-profit survey organisation was born out of that development. It was formed as a charitable trust in 1969. The founders, Roger Jowell and Gerald Hoinville, came from the market research firm, Research Services Ltd. and were joined by others with a similar background. They brought with them a solid grounding in survey research and a willingness to carry out contract work and engage in competitive tendering (Hoinville, 1985; SCPR, 1980).

Originally the service offered by SCPR was very much that of the survey research agency with the emphasis on a quick turnround of surveys to meet client needs. Subsequently SCPR was able to expand its own work as a survey agency undertaking substantial studies on a very wide range of policy-related subjects for a variety of funding organisations including universities. Staff members, about half of whom are graduates, reached about 50 in 1980 and 70 in 1984. Income rose from around one million pounds in 1979 to double that figure in 1984.

Since 1979 SCPR has been located adjacent to City University in London. City University does not have large social science departments and SCPR is not integrated into the university setting in the manner of the American centres. But links have been formed. Three members of the SCPR staff (Gerald Hoinville – who has now left SCPR – Roger Jowell and Martin Collins) were appointed as visiting professors, and a Master's degree in survey research methods with an annual intake of 12 students a year has also been established. Success in attracting funding for methodological work led in 1980 to the setting up of SCPR's Survey Methods Centre, in association with The City University, as one of the newly constituted SSRC (now ESRC) Designated Research Centres, which runs until 1988. A seminar series was launched with the support of ESRC, and visits from leading academic social researchers from the US became a regular feature. Until recently SCPR did not have any continuing survey series but in 1984 the British Social Attitudes Survey (Jowell et al., 1984, 1985) was launched with funds from a variety of sources including private foundations and ESRC. It is planned as an annual national survey on the lines of NORC's General Social Survey to provide for the first time in Britain a regular monitoring of changes in values and beliefs among different sections of the public. Academics play a part in the design of the questionnaire part of which is standardised to allow cross-cultural comparison with similar surveys by academic institutes in several other countries.

In many respects SCPR is the closest there is in Britain to a university-based survey research institute along the lines of ISR and NORC. It not only provides a research service of the highest quality to public service clients but does a great deal to facilitate the development of survey practice. Where it differs from the US institutes is chiefly in its conception of what constitutes survey research. The emphasis has been principally on the collection of descriptive data of the highest quality rather than on the use of the survey as a tool of scientific investigation, though this emphasis has shifted recently. The current programme of the SCPR Methods Centre, for instance, is academic in the best sense. It focuses predominantly but not entirely on methodological aspects of the data collection process – sample design, non-response, interviewing, question wording effects, telephone surveys, coder reliability and so on – in which SCPR is now an acknowledged national and international leader. One consequence of the dominance of university survey centres abroad, however, has been that research and teaching focussed round the data collection process comprises only one sector of their academic-style output. Most importantly they have done much to bridge the gaps between social science theory, data collection designs and advanced data analytical techniques. It is the latter kind of academic-survey linkage that languishes in Britain. Here if the integration takes place at all it has to take place across the boundaries of the survey organisation.

The picture is a variable one. Most SCPR project directors have carried out surveys either with or for academics (for example, currently, the British Election Survey, Time Budgets, Social Attitudes, and Economic Stratification), and can report good as well as bad examples of interaction with academics. But academics as clients or collaborators are not likely to make up the great bulk of SCPR mainstream project work compared to surveys funded by policymakers. The latter are always likely to want descriptive information in Britain just as much as in the USA. The difference is that more (and more generously funded) surveys of an analytical kind involving social science inputs are commissioned in the United States.

Other initiatives

There have been two serious but ultimately abortive attempts to raise the standards of academic survey research in Britain – the Division of Research Techniques at LSE (later to become the Survey Research Centre) and the SSRC Survey Unit. The reasons why neither group survived are complex, but as Hoinville (1985) has emphasised a principal difference between them and the key American university centres was that neither had any survey capacity of its own. The SSRC Unit had a particularly short life, being established in 1970 and closed in 1976. 'In setting up the Survey Unit, the SSRC thus created the opportunity for an academic approach but removed it from a survey agency environment where it could also have benefitted from professional survey expertise and research opportunity' (Hoinville, 1985).

The old SSRC Survey Unit was an attempt at a two-way link that failed in Britain. But the comparison with the Zentrum für Umfragen, Methoden und Analysen (Zuma) in West Germany serves to underline the lesson that what can flourish in one national culture will languish in another. As a national non-profit 'Centre for Survey, Methods and Analysis', Zuma operates as a repository for survey skills to be made available to the West German academic community through various advisory research services. Since its inception at Mannheim in 1974 it has become increasingly influential as a survey institute both in its own country and more recently internationally. Zuma undertakes more methodological research of its own into data collection, measurement and analysis than the SSRC Survey Unit did, but otherwise there are basic similarities in purpose and structure between the two organisations. Zuma is financed by the Deutsche Forschungsgemeinschaft (roughly the equivalent of ESRC), it does not have its own interviewing force and the surveys with which it assists stem mainly from the academic rather than the policy research sector. The formula seems to have worked in Germany where it failed in the UK because German academics take survey research more seriously and receive more funds to do surveys, the unit is more generously funded and staffed and the problem of access to the data collection process has been at least partially solved by playing an intermediate role, entailing close working relationships with one or two carefully selected commercial organisations. A benefit of 'Zuma's role as an intermediary is that the all too frequent isolation of the researcher from the empirical aspects of his project can be avoided. Instead of being delivered a set of data from external sources the researcher can then accompany the project through the crucial empirical stages and gain first-hand information about the weaknesses and strengths of his instrument' (Zuma, 1983).

The 'academic–survey gap' in Britain

On the one side in Britain there are the university-based social scientists mostly lacking expertise in or even the opportunity to obtain any direct experience of large-scale policy-oriented research. There are significant exceptions, and the position may be changing, but for the most part they have been either antipathetic or at best indifferent to the survey method itself. On the policy side, remote and largely insulated from the academic world are the professional survey organisations in which the nation's large-scale data collection skills have been developed and remain entrenched. Until recently communication between the two sides has been minimal. The distance still separating them is what is referred to here as the 'academic–survey gap'.

The survey practitioners see survey research as a discipline in its own right, standing outside any of the social sciences, in a direct relationship to their principal clients, the policy makers. The latter tend to be dominated by a nineteenth-century empiricist model of the relationship between research and policy, summed up in the catch phrase 'the facts speak for themselves' (Bulmer, 1982). At any rate the survey practitioners share with the policy-makers a view of survey research as a superior kind of fact gathering. The surveys they are asked to do are invariably of the descriptive kind. The need for 'authoritative facts' leads to an emphasis on high quality data which finds expression in methodological research into the data collection process. But practitioners have no pressing reason to concern themselves overmuch with the methodology of the analytical survey since such surveys have seldom been required. Analytical interpretations rarely go beyond the consideration of bivariate tables. A watered-down view of the potential social science contribution to survey research prevails. Academics tend to be regarded as theorists with little of practical value to offer. Statistics, as the only academic discipline with much sustained interest in survey research, is valued mainly because of its contribution to sampling problems.

On the social science side the influence of scholars with principled objections to any use of surveys may be waning. Some scholars do not question the value of survey research as a tool for information gathering, but are apt to question its intellectual merits as an academic activity, and to take a condescending view of those engaged in it. A general lack of direct experience of the complex problems of data collection goes along with low awareness of the possibilities as well as the challenge of formulating and testing theoretical arguments in survey terms. It is ironic that academics and practitioners both share an unnecessarily limited image of the survey method as purely descriptive in scope and are each led by it to write down and disparage the potential contribution of the other. Perpetuation of this image serves to reinforce the academic–survey gap and is one of the more subtle losses consequent upon it.

The line between the descriptive and the analytical survey is not one that can be sharply drawn. But the model of the descriptive survey encourages a view of design, data collection and analysis as distinct functions to be pursued by different specialists rather than phases of the total survey process to be integrated by practitioners, such as that shown in Figure 2. On such a view *de facto* specialisation can even be regarded as a useful division of labour. Sir John Boreham, lately Director of the Central Statistical Office, refers to national statistics offices, including OPCS, as 'statistics factories' rather than research institutes. Boreham argues that 'data producers' responsibility for the quality of the statistics should not be blurred by other work; they should be allowed to specialize in the data collection methodology. Research and analysis should be carried out by different and separate group of data analysts ...' (Boreham, 1975 as related by Hakim, 1982a, pp. 15–16, 24). Influencing this view is the recent emergence of a trend towards the secondary analysis of government surveys by academics. Facilitated by developments in archiving, data banks and computer technology, and encouraged by government, a small industry is growing in the secondary analysis of official surveys, mainly the large-scale continuous surveys designed for multiple descriptive purposes, particularly the GHS. (Hakim, 1982; Gilbert, 1983; OPCS, 1984, Chapter 13). This has been hailed as a move towards the similar collaborative research model with a much longer history in the United States. A crucial difference is that in the United States there are academic analysts who are also experienced in the data collection process. In Britain, the development, although good in itself, could serve to reinforce the organisational divide that now separates the data collectors from the theorists and analysts. The potential for analysis, even of surveys designed for descriptive purposes, could suffer as a result. It would be possible to write at length of the way the 'facts' emerging from descriptive surveys are influenced by each link in the chain of processes depicted in Figure 2. To take fieldwork alone, it is impossible for anyone who has not directly observed it to imagine the complexity of what occurs when an interviewer confronts a respondent. Or again, round each question in a schedule there is a penumbra of alternative wordings that have been considered, in some cases piloted,

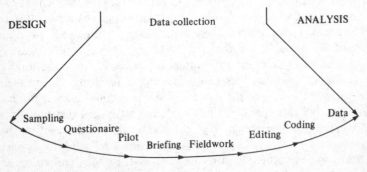

Fig 2 Design and analysis

before being rejected. Putting it briefly, academic analysts are less likely to take archive data as unproblematic, and their insights into multivariate properties and sources of error in the data will be richer where they have experience of the processes that have produced them.

Recent years have seen fewer major '*ad hoc*' surveys and more that are either repetitions of earlier ones or intended to be repeated. Data from the National Crime Survey (Hough and Mayhew, 1983) and the Workplace Industrial Relations Survey (Daniel and Millward, 1983) were archived even before the second round of data collection, and both these surveys have set new standards for collaboration with academics. It could be that continuing secondary analysis of both the regular descriptive surveys and the repeat surveys will lead in the long run to design inputs stemming increasingly from analytical considerations. As surveys do become more analytical, the concepts introduced at the design stage, and the way these concepts are operationalised at the data collection stage become progressively more dependent on analytical considerations. Where the data collectors are not the analysts they need to collaborate so that they come to share each others perspectives as far as possible. Forms of organisation that bring them together rather than keep them apart are what is required.

In the fully-fledged analytical survey the data is used to build and test explanatory models of social phenomena. At the design phase subject matter expertise is combined with theoretical perspectives from the academic social science disciplines. Measurement theory is required to handle the relationships between concepts and questionnaire items and multivariate analysis techniques to handle the relations between networks of variables. The American social science literature of the last decade or two provides eloquent testimony to the great advances that have been made in these areas. Several leading survey researchers, in addition to their substantive work, have themselves made original contributions to the technical literature on measurement and analysis. The academic survey institutes have personnel specialising in these advanced techniques. Nowadays they are referred to under the general title of 'sociological methodology', though on the measurement side this subsumes much that was formerly developed under the older label of 'psychometrics'. The British survey elite keep a wary eye on the sociological methodology literature but tend for the present to regard it as unnecessarily complex for their purposes. What distinguishes most British survey reports from many, equally policy orientated, issuing from the American centres is that as often as not the American investigator will have made some attempt to assimilate and apply the relevant portions of this literature.

Of the many comparisons that could be made there are two for which we have special experience of work on both sides of the Atlantic. A comparison for example of the British National Child Development Study (NCDS, Fogelman, 1976) with the Youth in Transition Study (YIT, Bachman et al., 1977, Bynner et al., 1981) based in ISR shows a totally different approach to analysis and to the selection of relevant variables and their measurement. NCDS is characterised by policy-makers' concern with monitoring for which data are sought through responses to single questions. In contrast YIT, though also policy orientated, comprises, a wealth of variables culled from the psychological and sociological literature to operationalise hypotheses about the origins and development of various teenage behaviours and attitudes. Theoretical models, for example concerning the development of adolescent self-esteem and its relation to achievement and delinquency, have been fitted to the data and rigorously tested. The second comparison is afforded by the 1970s surveys of perceived quality of life that were carried out in the two countries. The American investigators (Andrews et al., 1976, 1980; Campbell et al., 1976) made intensive efforts to resolve the conceptual and measurement problems that abound in this field. They examined the multivariate relations among the measures and also broke new ground in fitting theoretical models of the components of perceived life quality to the data (McKennell et al., 1980). The British investigation, conducted by the SSRC Survey Unit, albeit on a much smaller budget, was patterned on the American design, but relied mainly on descriptive reporting of the distributions on single rating scales together with some bivariate relations (Abrams, 1973; Hall, 1976).

Keith Hope (1978) has pointedly emphasised how few British social scientists, let alone survey practitioners, ever study the literature on sociological methodology. But some do. This kind of interest can be found among a few social scientists in British universities, some of whom have been responsible for the rare sporadic analytical surveys that do stand comparison with American work. Inevitably they look to reference groups abroad for standards of excellence, not infrequently working with American collaborators. Regrettably, outside statistical departments, they have until recently engaged in almost no dialogue with our home-grown professional survey researchers. Relatively small in number, thinly dispersed, this group of academics, while remaining an important source of potential influence, have so far made little impact on the British survey tradition.

The vacuum left by social scientists has been filled in Britain by statisticians. Though their contibution to survey method has been mainly on the sampling front, they are also probably the most frequent readers of the sociological literature on measurement and analysis. It is important to emphasise therefore that this literature has been developed in the United States by social scientists who combine substantive with technical quantitative interests, usually in survey research. For example, the classical method of attitude scaling that remains most widely used today is the one originated by Rensis Likert. Paul Lazarsfeld, as well as making important contributions to measurement theory, also made the initial breakthrough in the causal analysis of survey data from which recent developments have stemmed. These pioneers were not statisticians but academic social scientists, a psychologist and a sociologist, who were also survey practitioners. The tradition continues with people like James Davis (1971), John Sonquist and James Morgan (1973), Frank Andrews (1973), Duane Alwin (1974) and many more. Developments in social science methodology in the United States have been due in large part to academics with substantive interests (and their followers) pursuing them over decades, using successive surveys to refine their ideas, and being pressed to deeper analysis and more refined measurement to examine the more sophisticated issues that emerge.

The few outstanding analytical surveys conducted by academics in Britain (e.g. Butler and Stokes, 1974; Goldthorpe et al., 1980; Rutter et al., 1979; Brown and Harris, 1978; Himmelweit et al., 1981; Heath et al., 1985) have often depended on their collaboration with the professional survey agencies. There are hopeful signs that this kind of collaboration may be on the increase, though it is still rare. When academics do major surveys in Britain, they usually do only one or two in their lifetime. Even where there is more continuity, as with the regular election surveys conducted for a time until recently from the University of Essex, no infrastructure of data collection expertise remains behind in the university centre. The separation of the survey agencies from the process of university teaching effectively means that academics who wish to do surveys or teach survey methods have to learn the ropes for themselves. Few have had any professional training and still fewer any experience of the large-scale policy-orientated survey. Textbooks and courses on survey method are at best poor substitutes for direct 'time-line' experience of the design and conduct of large-scale surveys.

Meanwhile, for better or worse, surveys continue to be done by academics and social science graduates who are not properly trained (cf.Platt, 1976). To suggest that standards are universally low outside the professional agencies would be unfair to several researchers in the universities and in the non-academic sector who have reached an acceptable level of survey competence by their own efforts. But they are too few, too scattered and operate on too small a scale to make much difference to the national picture. The scale and continuity of operations necessary to achieve the highest standards of excellence in survey research is found only in the professional agencies.

To a large extent it is the policy-makers who call the tune on the kind of surveys that get done. That is why any bridging of the academic–survey gap has to be by way of the policy-maker. Policy-makers on both sides of the Atlantic fund large-scale descriptive surveys for the purpose of describing and monitoring social conditions. But in the United States they have been ready to fund more surveys in which social scientific perspectives are incorporated into analytical designs mounted on the data collection base. Fragmentation of the triangular set of relations between social scientists, survey practitioners and policy-makers, have prevented this happening to anything like the same extent in Britain. Possible cultural factors that have brought about this fragmentation are reviewed next.

Cultural reasons for the divergence

Why has the evolution of survey oranisations in the US and UK taken such different paths? Geography and wealth cannot in themselves explain it because there are examples of smaller countries such as Norway, Denmark and Israel where survey research institutes in the American mould can be found. And in Britain, outside the university system, the amount of social research being conducted in the public sector in the form of large-scale surveys, despite some reductions, has been and still is very considerable. The historical account given earlier of differences in the wartime and postwar development of survey research was less an explanation than a series of events that themselves require interpretation. To find the reasons therefore one needs to go further into the national culture which influences if not determines the funding environment in which the survey method operates, and consequently the uses to which it is put. Excursions into national culture have a tendency to become speculative, but some distinctive influential factors stand out. We look briefly at the way academic culture and civil service culture have affected the development of survey research in the two countries.

Arguably the phenomenon being looked at is just one of technical lag, but if so it has been compounded by shortfalls in the development when it did come in Britain of both psychology and sociology. ISR and NORC were initiated by leading figures in these core social science disciplines who shared, as their followers do today, a strong commitment to quantitative research methods. The dominant tradition in British academic sociology has been non-quantitative, orientated to anthropology, philosophy and history. Those who took charge of the rapid expansion of sociology in the 1960s in Britain were not generally sympathetic to survey research and sometimes even espoused arcane methodological positions that ruled out survey research along with much else that was empirical and quantitative. The psychology departments that were established in British universities in the 1950s, before sociology, although providing quantitative training, also failed, with rare exceptions, to provide academic support for survey research. A related factor has been the distancing of many of these academic departments from policy-related research. Surveys are by far the most expensive form of social research so that unless academics are prepared to link with the practical concerns of most funding bodies they are unlikely to be involved in much survey research. The report of the Social Research Association on *The State of Training in Social Research* noted that even among researchers in universities 'many of our informants found it unwise to recruit sociologists or social administrators because of their inadequate training, even though the majority of informants were themselves practising sociologists . . . This may point to the gulf that has come to exist [in those subjects] between university teachers and empirical researchers, despite the idea that both functions are part of the requirements of every academic post' (SRA, 1985, 41, 44).

If the university training of those who do survey research in the two countries is markedly different, the educational and cultural experiences of those in ruling circles who bear final responsibility for commissioning large-scale suveys is even more disparate. Until recently, the route to senior administrative positions in the Civil Service was a classical or historical education at Oxford or Cambridge. While economics has been favoured, these ancient universities have been slow to give credence to modern quantitative and empirical developments in other social science disciplines and have shown some ambivalence about accepting such disciplines at all. Even now the University of Cambridge has not fully accepted Social and Political Sciences as a faculty and has re-established the Chair of Sociology for one tenure only. Recently the Secretary of State decreed that the 'Science' should be removed from the Social Science Research Council, hence the change of name to Economic and Social Research Council. In recent years the Civil Service Staff College has been seen as a way of equipping new recruits with the necessary modern knowledge and skills, including social science, but inevitably the dominant and most valued discipline is seen to be economics.

Recruitment policies have of course broadened considerably in recent years and large numbers of social science graduates have entered government departments, particularly their own research units. Many of those who filled the expanding jobs in the non-academic sector of social research during the 1960s 'take off' were either non-social-science graduates or else came from the newly created social science schools with all the deficiencies in training referred to earlier. Those social scientists who took up posts in the local government or the voluntary sectors were often out on their own, regarded as experts in their calling, and put to applied research tasks including surveys which were not infrequently carried out appallingly. (For one example see Brown and Bowl, 1973.) Those who entered research departments in central government were more fortunate. They could learn on the job. But the dominant ethos in the departments they entered was not one that favoured theoretical social science insights in policy formulation. (Some of the problems of social scientists within government are further explored by Cyril Smith in Chapter 5 and by Robert Walker in Chapter 9.) Nor was there anything in their university training that made them aware of the great potential for testing such insights by means of analytical social surveys. If they required survey data they could plug into magnificent data collection machines in the shape of the government's own survey organisation, the better market research firms and later SCPR. Since the people running these survey organisations and so many of the policy researchers using their services owed so little of their professionalism to their academic training it is no surprise that in this country survey culture has come to be regarded as distinct from the culture of academic social science.

In the USA almost the reverse is the case. Because of the broad based nature of US university education continuing into graduate studies, many government officials will have had quite extensive exposure to social science methods and theories and will have higher expectations that social science inputs will be among the information available to them as they administer services and develop policy. In the submissions under the RFP (request for proposals) system by which government agencies secure research tenders in the United States, there is frequently the expectation and even the requirement that social science knowledge will be effectively integrated into the design. To a considerable extent the university-based survey institutes have themselves been instrumental in nurturing an informed constituency that has shaped their own funding environment and the way information needs are perceived by policy-makers. Alumni of ISR and NORC have not only fanned out to set up survey centres on other campuses, but they and their students have also gone into teaching and into policy research carrying with them a survey culture that is both academic and applied. These transfusion effects have taken place within a system where there was already a longstanding tradition of acceptance and high status accorded to quantitative social science in the major universities. The psychology and sociology professors who founded the original survey centres were even then heirs to that tradition. Not only has more attention been given to the teaching of basic statistics to American social science students but generations of such students particularly at graduate levels have received a thorough grounding in measurement, theory testing and analytical procedures applicable to survey research. Developments in sociological methodology have been particularly vigorous over the last two decades with Britain falling increasingly behind.

The future of survey research in Britain

The American experience may be of less value for suggesting forms of organisation and funding that could be transported across the Atlantic, than for the reflected light it sheds on the gaps between survey research, social science and social policy in Britain. The contrast between the picture of integration in the US and fragmentation in the UK has been drawn in deliberately stark terms in this chapter. The triangular set of relationships has been managed better in other developed countries and could, we believe, be managed better in Britain, but not necessarily in the same way.

The distancing of the academic researcher from the data collection process remains one of the main weaknesses in linkage between social science and the other two corners of the triangle in Figure 1. There are instances of inputs from academics in the design phases of major surveys, but involvement then typically leapfrogs to the data analysis stage and is more commonly and increasingly found there. What happens between the completed questionnaire and the data tape is often delegated entirely to the survey organisation. This is the most crucial part of the academic–survey gap. The Zuma type of intermediary role having failed once in Britain is unlikely to be resurrected again. The ISR formula where academics become directors of their own in-house data collection staff is not one that has been widely replicated in the United States and is not likely to be in Britain, if only on grounds of cost and lack of funding. The NORC solution in which survey practitioners work on a range of projects only some of which involve close interaction with faculty members seems more transportable. This pattern might well have developed more strongly in Britain if SCPR for example had happened to link with the London School of Economics where social science departments are strong rather than City University where they are minimal.

Currently the amount of interaction between survey practitioners and academics is meagre, but there are precedents for successful collaboration which might be expanded if suitable means can be found. It is difficult to see how academics could be given extensive on-the-job training, as occurs in the United States, but at least insights into the data collection process could be fostered and the worst effects of complete insulation countered. The agencies themselves are too hard pressed and locked into the system driven by funders to serve as training organisations for academics. But most do extend to the funders the well-established privileges of observing the different stages of the survey as it passes through the agency. An academic sponsored by the funder could have similar privileges.

That is a main idea behind a new ESRC initiative, the Survey Link Scheme, begun in 1984, which sets out to promote and legitimise special kinds of association between individual academics and particular large-scale policy-orientated surveys. A relevant academic is identified who is able to make inputs of a theoretical, subject matter or methodological kind at either the design and/or analysis ends of a survey carried out by a professional survey agency for a policy division or department. Under the aegis of the sponsoring department the academic is then able to observe the intermediate stages of data collection. Such observations can be of great value even though they stop a long way short of deep involvement in the data production process. In a way that books and courses on survey method can never do, observations down the time-line of a survey can reveal what is involved in efficient project management and how successive stages have been chained together to produce the eventual data tape. Encouragingly, research managers in about a dozen government departments, including all the major survey customers, have agreed to participate in the scheme. It has been generally accepted that contributions from carefully chosen academics can be useful and will be enhanced if they can be given opportunities to observe the data collection process in the survey agency. Over the last few years there have been a number of publications and inquiries and some official pressures for improving the education and training of social researchers with an emphasis on quantitative research methods. New postgraduate courses with that emphasis have been set up – for example at Surrey University, University College Cardiff, Manchester University, the Open University and City University (the SCPR MA course) – which still continue despite cuts in expenditure. There is still a long way to go.

American experience is also a potent factor making for greater awareness. There is a tendency for academic standards to be set internationally and for knowledge to advance along a cosmopolitan front, however unevenly. The three of us for example are British teachers of social research methods who have each spent periods as academic visitors to the United States, at ISR or the University of Chicago. (The contrasts we have been able to draw have been sharpened by the fact that we also happen to have worked in parts of what is now OPCS at earlier stages of our careers.) American influence can be seen in some texts on survey research. The revised edition of Moser's (1971) influential textbook included chapters by the new co-author, Graham Kalton (now at ISR), summarising the essential ideas behind attitude measurement and causal analysis. Texts by Martin Bulmer (1977, 1982) on research methods in social science and social policy stress the potential analytical contribution of survey investigations in strategic research. A recent book by Catherine Marsh (1982), addressed to British sociologists in particular, counters some of their metatheoretical objections to surveys and urges them to appreciate that the survey tradition of fact-finding is not their only intellectual heritage. The central theme of Marsh's book is the potential of survey research as a scientific strategy with an analytical purpose as exemplified in American work.

Among the hopeful pointers in the contemporary research scene has been the founding of the Social Research Association (SRA) in 1979. The SRA brings policy researchers, survey researchers and academics together and such a body is capable of taking a synoptic view of the situation. Its recent report on *The State of Training in Social Research* (SRA, 1985) draws attention to the inadequacies in quantitative training and makes proposals for improvement which ought to carry weight. The ESRC has sponsored a series of seminars on survey method which has run for several years now in both Edinburgh and London, drawing on a similar broad if very slightly different constituency. Seminar topics range widely and have included coverage of measurement and analysis procedures and feature leading American survey researchers from time to time. ESRC support also plays an important role through continuing support for the SCPR Methods Centre, the Link scheme, and surveys generated by ESRC committees. As noted earlier, another hopeful trend is the growth of secondary analysis by academics of official surveys.

The extent of future progress is problematic. The obstacles are not so much shortage of resources as institutional fragmentation and inertia. The three of us have great respect for those who have already made most effective use of survey research for policy purposes in the British context, and we share a concern that the potential of the survey method for integrating social science with policy research should be realised in Britain to the extent that has been achieved in the United States. Whether the trends just reviewed are the beginning of a pendulum swing in that direction is a matter of opinion.

NOTES

The authors would like to acknowledge the helpful comments on an earlier draft of this chapter by Roger Jowell, Roger Thomas, Bob Barnes and Graham Kalton.

REFERENCES

Abrams, M. (1973), 'Subjective social indicators', *Social Trends* 4 (London, HMSO), pp. 35–50.

Alwin, D. F. (1974), 'Approaches to the interpretation of relationships in the multi-trait multi-method matrix', in *Sociological Methodology*, 1973–4, ed. H. Costner, San Francisco, Jossey-Bass, pp. 79–127.

Andrews, F. M. (1973), *Multiple Classification Analysis*, Ann Arbor, Mich., ISR.

Andrews, F. M. and McKennell, A. C. (1980), 'Measures of self-reported well-being: their affective cognitive and other components', *Social Indicators Research* 8, pp. 127–55.

Andrews, F. M. and Withey, S. B. (1976), *Social Indicators of Well-Being*, New York, Plenum.

Atkinson, J. (1964), *A Handbook for Interviewers*, London, HMSO.

Bachman, J. G. and O'Malley, P. M. (1977), 'Self-esteem in young men', *Journal of Personality and Social Psychology* 35, pp. 365–80.

Boreham, A. J. (1975), 'How far should and could those who produce statistics engage in research and analysis?' (Invited Paper No. 14; Fortieth Conference of the International Statistical Institute; Warsaw).

Brown, G. W. and Harris, T. (1978), *The Social Origins of Depression*, London, Tavistock.

Brown, M. J. and Bowl, R. (1976), *Study of Local Authority Chronic Sick and Disabled Surveys*, Birmingham, Birmingham University Social Services Unit, mimeo.

Bulmer, M. (ed.) (1977), *Sociological Research Methods*, London, Macmillan.

Bulmer, M. (1982), *The Uses of Social Research*, London, Allen & Unwin.

Butler, D. and Stokes, D. (1974), *Political Change in Britain: The Evolution of Electoral Choice*, London, Macmillan.

Bynner, M. J. (1969), *The Young Smoker*, London, HMSO.

Bynner, J. M., Bachman, F. G. and O'Malley, P. M. (1981), 'Self-esteem, and delinquency revisited', *Journal of Youth and Adolescence* 10, pp. 407–41.

Bynner, J. M. and Parker, S. R. (1969), 'Correlational analysis of data obtained from a survey of shop stewards', *Human Relations* 23, pp. 345–59.

Campbell, A., Converse, P. E. and Rodgers, W. L. (1976), *The Quality of American Life*, New York, Russell Sage.

Cannell, C. F. and Kahn, R. L. (1984), *Some Factors in the Origin and Development of the Institute for Social Research University of Michigan*, Ann Arbor, ISR Working Paper 8034.

Daniel, W. W. and Millward, N. (1983), *Workplace Industrial Relations in Britain: The DE/PSI/SSRC Survey*, London, Heinemann.

Davis, J. A. (1971), *Elementary Survey Analysis*, Englewood Cliffs, New Jersey, Prentice Hall.

Fogelman, K. (1976), *Britain's Sixteen Year Olds*, London, National Children's Bureau.

Gilbert, N., Dale, A. and Arber, S. (1983), 'The General Household Survey as a source for secondary analysis', *Sociology* 17, pp. 255–9.

Goldthorpe, J. H. *et al.* (1980), *Social Mobility and Class Structure in Modern Britain*, Oxford, Clarendon Press.

Gray, P. G. and Corlett, T. (1950), 'Sampling for the Government Social Survey', *Journal of the Royal Statistical Society*: Series A 113, pp. 150–206.

Hakim, C. (1982a), 'Secondary analysis and the relationship between official and academic social research', *Sociology* 16, pp. 12–28.

Hakim, C. (1982b), *Secondary Analysis in Social Research*, London, Allen & Unwin.

Hall, J. (1976), 'Subjective measures of quality of life in Britain: 1971–75', *Social Trends* 7, London, 1976, pp. 47–60.

Heath, A., Jowell, R. and Curtis, J. (1985), *How Britain Votes*, Oxford, Pergamon.

Heyworth Report (1965), *Report of the Committee on Social Studies*, Cmnd. 2660, London, HMSO.

Himmelweit, H., Humphreys, P. and Jaeger, M. (1981), *How Voters Decide*, London, Academic Press.

Hoinville, G. (1985), 'Methodological research on sample surveys: a review of developments in Britain', in *Essays on the History of British Sociological Research*, ed. M. Bulmer, Cambridge, Cambridge University Press, pp. 101–20.

Hope, K. (1978), 'Indicators of the state of society', in *Social Policy Research* ed. M. Bulmer, London, Macmillan, pp. 244–67.

Hough, M. & Mayhew, P. (1983), *The British Crime Survey: first report*, Home Office Research Study No. 76, London, HMSO.

Jowell, R. and Witherspoon, S. (eds.) (1985), *British Social Attitudes*, Aldershot, Gower.

Lazarsfeld, P. (1955), 'Interpretation of statistical relations as a research operation', in *The Language of Social Research* ed. P. Lazarsfeld and M. Rosenberg, New York, Free Press, pp. 115–25.

Marsh, A. (1982), *Smoking Attitudes and Behaviour*, London, HMSO.

Marsh, C. (1982), *The Survey Method*, London, Allen & Unwin.

McKennell, A. C. (1966), *The Contribution of Psychologists to Government Social Survey Work*, London, Social Survey Division of OPCS, General Series Paper G46.

McKennell, A. C. (1967), *Use of coefficient alpha in constructing attitude and similar scales*, London, Social Survey Division of OPCS, Methodology paper 139.

McKennell, A. C. (1969), 'Methodological problems in a survey of aircraft noise annoyance', *The Statistician* 19, pp. 1–29.

McKennell, A. C., Atkinson, T. and Andrews, F. M. (1980), 'Structural constancies in surveys of perceived well-being', in *The Quality of Life*, eds. A. Szalai and F. M. Andrews, New York, Russell Sage, pp. 111–28.

McKennell, A. C. & Bynner, J. M. (1969), 'Self-images and smoking behaviour among schoolboys', *British Journal of Educational Psychology* 39, pp. 27–39.

McKennell, A. C. and Thomas, R. (1967), *Adults' and Adolescents' Smoking Habits and Attitudes*, London, HMSO.

Moser, C. A. and Kalton, G. (1971), *Survey Methods in Social Investigation*, London, Heinemann.

Moss, L. (1972), 'Survey Research in and on Administration' (Meeting of the Joint University Council for Social and Public Administration, London, mimeo).

OPCS (1984), *General Household Survey 1982*, London, HMSO.

Platt, J. (1976), *Realities of Social Research*, (London, Chatto & Windus/Sussex University Press.

Plowden Report (1967), *Children and Their Primary Schools*, London, HMSO.

Rutter, M., Mortimer, P. and Ouston, J. (1979), *Fifteen Thousand Hours*, Shepton Mallet, Somerset, Open Books.

Schuman, H. (1977), 'The Detroit Area Study after twenty-five years', *The American Sociologist* 12, pp. 130–7.

SCPR (1980), *A Report on the 1980's*, London, SCPR.

Sheatsley, P. B. (1982), *NORC: The First Forty Years*, Chicago, NORC Annual Repot 1981–2.

Sonquist, J. and Morgan, J. N. (1973), *Searching for Structure*, Ann Arbor, Mich., ISR Publications.

SRA (1985), *The State of Training in Social Research*, London, Social Research Association.

SSD (1985), *Social Survey Division Annual Report 1984–5*, London, OPCS.

Whitehead, F. (1985), 'The Government Social Survey', in M. Bulmer (ed), *Essays on the History of British Sociological Research*, Cambridge, Cambridge University Press, pp. 83–100.

Zuma (1983), 'Zentrum fur Umfragen Methoden and Analysen', Information sheet issued by Zuma, Mannheim, West Germany.

CHAPTER 14

Survey research for government

BARRY HEDGES

Introduction

British governments became familiar with sample surveys largely through the work of the Government Social Survey, now OPCS's Social Survey Division (SSD), whose importance lies not only in the surveys that it has conducted itself, but in the standards it has set and in the influence it has had on work done by others. Its firm adherence to probability sampling, for instance, has made this the norm for government surveys in Britain in spite of the widespread use and advocacy by commercial survey organisations of cheaper but less soundly based methods. But SSD does not have a monopoly of government surveys. Government Departments are unlikely to wish to confine themselves to one supplier, and in any case the volume of government surveys is too large and too diverse to be serviced by a single agency. As a result, a substantial proportion of government surveys are contracted out directly to external survey organisations.

The rapid growth of government surveys, in the sixties in particular, led to an expansion both of SSD and of the social research workloads of the leading market research agencies. In 1969, Social and Community Planning Research (SCPR) was set up as a charitable trust to undertake sample surveys exclusively in the public sector, for which it has developed a survey capacity comparable in scale with those of the larger market research agencies. It has, perhaps surprisingly, remained the only organisation of its kind.

The range of surveys that SCPR has undertaken for government has been very wide. They vary in scale, in specificity or breadth of objectives, in complexity, in urgency, in mode of commissioning, in the extent to which the specification is closed or open and in the degree of control

269

exercised by the sponsoring department. There is thus no basic pattern that can be described and commented on in an ordered way. Instead, a number of particular issues are selected for discussion.

Surveys and policy

Expenditure cuts and the preoccupations of the present government have increasingly required that government surveys should deliver results of immediate policy relevance. Where public money is to be used to fund more basic research, it is the Research Councils who are supposed to provide it – though within even these bodies there is a growing tendency to emphasise the practical value of research at the expense of its role in developing social theory.

'Policy relevant research' is a slippery concept. In practice, it is an umbrella for any kind of research providing information that policy-makers think will help or might interest them, however indirectly.

The way in which such information does in fact contribute to policy is difficult to assess, particularly for the outsider who is not party to most of the policy discussions that take place after the delivery of a survey report. Research results do not necessarily point conclusively, or even strongly, towards some particular policy action: rather, they provide the essential framework for evaluating issues and alternatives.

The main emphasis of policy research surveys tends to be on monitoring and evaluation, and they are less often called on to assist in the formulation of a new policy in the way that a manufacturer might use them in the development and marketing of a new product. Nevertheless, they play a vital role in policy formation, since an analysis of the success or failure of current policies is essential for designing modifications to them, or for evolving new ones.

Survey data form only part of the evidence available to the policy-maker, who is also in receipt of information and opinions from a wide variety of other sources. Policy decisions are the product of debate at many levels, at each of which the various forms of available evidence are sifted and interpreted. The decision-maker may directly absorb the survey results, or may rely on digests. The diffuseness of the process, and the nature of the information, both militate against clear-cut links between the survey and the decision. But the survey evidence will underpin and inform the whole debate. It will also make a further contribution to the government's steadily increasing knowledge of the various markets for which it is catering, and thus has a long-term as well as an immediate benefit.

Policy relevance does not imply that the research should have a narrow focus. Many policies do not aim at specific effects that can be measured by equally specific research. Even when they do, evaluative research must take account not only of what the policies themselves are doing but also of all the other forces at work. Policy research thus tends to be broad-based in content even where it originates in concern about some particular aspect of policy.

There has always been a certain amount of scepticism about the value of broad-based descriptive surveys that are carried out routinely rather than in response to policy concerns, and it might be expected that they would have suffered in the changing climate. In fact, the major continuous surveys, such as the Labour Force, General Household and Family Expenditure surveys, have maintained their place, though in some cases with some reductions in scale. Meanwhile, there have been notable additions to the stock of major national surveys that are, or are likely to be, repeated at irregular intervals. Two of the new surveys – the Department of Employment's Workplace Industrial Relations Survey and the Home Office's National Crime Survey – have already been repeated after a short interval in response to policy concern about these issues.

Problems in policy surveys

The emphasis thus far on the descriptive role of surveys needs some qualification. It may seem to imply a somewhat colourless collection of facts, but in the area of (for example) crime, numerous questions are posed that are, in effect, hypotheses that descriptive surveys can test. Is the amount of crime increasing? Are its victims to be found disproportionately in certain age, ethnic or other groups? Are some people repeatedly victims of crime, or is its incidence evenly spread? Is the volume of unreported crime greater than that of reported crime?

In attempting to find answers, the researcher may have to solve some difficult problems. Some of these are primarily technical, such as finding a valid questioning technique for establishing whether people have been victims of crime. They may or may not be soluble: there is no guarantee that such a technique can be developed.

But other research problems are more fundamental in character, and reflect unresolved issues in the policy area they are intended to address, or in the conceptual framework of the policy-makers. Solving the research problem logically demands the prior resolution of these issues. In practice, the attempt to design suitable research is one of the best ways of trying to resolve them. The process of translating policy concepts into a more concrete form in a questionnaire is likely to raise questions about these concepts and even about their validity. Examples are provided by some of the concepts employed in cost-benefit analysis: estimating the value of time, or of a human life, or of the monetary value that the public places on the removal of specific amounts of environmental disturbance. Their existence in models formulated at a high level of abstraction does not guarantee that they are measurable, or even that they correspond to any external reality. In the case of environmental disturbance, for example, there is reason to believe that evaluations are made by the public in ways that are unlikely, even in principle, to lead to the derivation of any consistent set of monetary values. It may be convenient for the policy-maker to reduce all elements in a decision to the common yardstick of money, but empirical research is more likely to question than to legitimise this procedure. Is the appropriate measure that of willingness to pay for the removal of a disturbance? If so, should replies be constrained by the resources of the respondent? Is it equitable that the removal of disturbances that affect the rich should have a prior claim on the public purse over those that affect the poor? Research designed to make such measurements comes face to face with some intractable problems of political philosophy. The discipline of thinking the issues through can be of great value, but the conventional policy approach is often too rigid to allow re-assessment of the concepts it utilises.

These examples are admittedly extreme, but policy research furnishes many such illustrations of fundamental, rather than merely technical, problems of measurement.

The scepticism of earlier years about the value of surveys appears to have given way to a sometimes too unquestioning faith in their ability to provide answers to any question, no matter how difficult. In such an atmosphere, and when researchers themselves promote it, there is a risk that the need to act, or to be seen to act, on rational, scientific principles may encourage the acceptance of pseudo-answers when real ones cannot be obtained.

Research on complex issues usually requires a preliminary feasibility study that will show whether the project is viable at all, on what scale it could usefully be carried out, and by what means. The need for feasibility studies, however, is all too often frustrated by timetable pressures. It is not easy for government departments to allocate funds to the development of methods in the absence of a pressing policy need for data. Once that need arises, the desirability of methodological work may well be accepted, but by then the opportunity may have been lost because of the urgency of obtaining substantive research results. It can thus happen that a survey on an unsatisfactory methodological base is later repeated without fundamental improvement because it has not proved possible in the interim to find a budget for the necessary development work.

Qualitative research

A particularly fruitful approach to many policy research problems, especially if the emphasis is on explanation rather than description, is provided by qualitative research, which has become part of the standard repertoire of research techniques in many survey organisations, though it makes little use of their central disciplines of sampling, questionnaire design, structured interviewing and large-scale data processing. Its value as a complementary technique has been recognised in commercial research for over two decades, but it has been much slower to become accepted by government, and even now it has not found an established place in all government departments. Although SCPR has undertaken qualitative studies since it was founded, it was not until 1984 that the Institute established a specialist unit to handle the growing volume of this type of work.

Qualitative research is usually conducted on a small scale, and its chief tools are the 'depth' (or 'unstructured') interview and the group discussion. Both are relatively free in form, being controlled by a loose topic guide rather than a set questionnaire. Statistical analysis is not customary, and indeed would not be warranted by the numbers involved. The interviews or discussions are tape-recorded, and analysed after repeated listening or by reading transcripts (or both). Various analysis systems, often complex, are used. The report is a commentary and interpretation by the researcher, usually illustrated with verbatim comments.

It is easy to see why this type of research should have been slow to become accepted by government departments in which quantitative disciplines hold an important place. In a statistical survey, the findings are presented both in tabular form (representing 'the evidence') and in a commentary (describing the evidence and perhaps interpreting it). The tabular format gives a comforting, if sometimes illusory, feeling of solidity and reliability, and the parallel presentation of both the conclusions and the evidence on which they are based appears to offer a safeguard against, or at least a check on, incorrect interpretation by the researcher. In qualitative research, the text is largely interpretative and the verbatim quotations flavour rather than justify the conclusions.

The great strength of qualitative research lies in the insights it provides into the way people perceive, and feel about, the issues being studied. Statistical surveys are well-suited to measuring behaviour, but less good at discovering why people behave as they do. The causes of people's actions often need to be sought simultaneously on many different levels, requiring a deeper study of each individual case than a structured questionnaire permits. This is particularly true where the behaviour pattern concerned is something that respondents have not consciously thought about or tried to explain to themselves.

The depth of understanding that qualitative research provides is invaluable both in developing ideas about fields that are comparatively unexplored and in subjecting established ideas to critical scrutiny.

Structured surveys tend to impose the conceptual framework of the researcher and client on the problem unless that of the population to be surveyed has first been sufficiently explored. Qualitative research is an ideal medium for this exploration, and research designs that involve a qualitative stage followed by a survey are frequently encountered. But the explanatory power of qualitative work can be deployed at other stages, for example by following up in depth some of the findings of a quantitative survey.

But qualitative work is often free-standing. Not all research problems need be, or even are capable of being, followed up in a structured survey after being investigated by qualitative methods.

It would be wrong to suppose that qualitative research is exclusively concerned with attitudes, beliefs, perceptions or other mental processes. These are often investigated in qualitative work, but are firmly linked to circumstances and to the behaviour it is hoped they will explain. Sometimes the subject matter is entirely 'hard', with no attitudinal or similar component at all, but the unstructured techniques of qualitative research may be needed because the facts are difficult to establish without extensive probing adapted to the circumstances of the particular case.

In spite of the fact that it is necessarily based on small samples that cannot be declared representative in a statistical sense, the insights that qualitative research provides make it a very valuable tool for which there is a bigger role in policy research than it has yet achieved.

Experiments

In the natural sciences, it is often possible to find explanations for phenomena by undertaking controlled experiments. It is much to be regretted that this powerful tool has such a limited role in policy research. There are examples, but they are not common. It is rarely practicable to select individual members of the population randomly to be the recipients of some form of policy action, because that is not the way most policies work, and even when it is practicable, political or ethical considerations may preclude it. The fact that co-operation must be voluntary – a principle rigidly adhered to in government surveys other than the Censuses – tends to interfere with the realisation of a rigorous design, since different experimental treatments can have different acceptance rates, and the groups to be compared may not be truly comparable.

Attempts are sometimes made to simulate policy effects by putting a sample of people into a situation resembling one that would result from the adoption of a particular policy. In one SCPR study, designed to predict the effect of a 50 per cent bus fares reduction, a sample of people in one city were given a special pass permitting them to travel at half-fare. But there is reason to doubt whether the resemblance between the simulation and real life is really close enough: there are various reasons why people's behaviour in the simulation might differ from what they would do in reality.

There is sometimes an opportunity for what may be termed quasi-experiments. An example is again provided by fares policy. One city maintained a low fares policy during a decade when fares elsewhere were rising steeply, and thus provided a 'test' area. A second city was chosen as a 'control' in a study of the effect of fares on the level of job search activity. The essential element of controlled randomisation is missing, and there are interpretative problems in determining how much of the observed difference in travel patterns is due to differential fares and how much to other things. Nevertheless, the exploitation of quasi-experimental situations that occur for reasons quite other than a wish to experiment is potentially of great value.

A more common role for research is in evaluating the experimental application of certain policies in selected districts or areas, analogous to the consumer goods manufacturer's 'test market'. It would be naive to suggest that research considerations should predominate in the choice of such areas for policy 'test-marketing', but some kind of randomisation, if only within a shortlist of areas, could perhaps be introduced more often than it is. It is all too easy for the choice to be made on some criterion that makes the test areas untypical and interpretation correspondingly difficult.

In the United States the 'test-market' concept is far more fully developed than is the case in Britain. It is difficult to imagine regional experiments in this country on matters such as tax structures, though they have been undertaken across the Atlantic. The difficulties are undoubtedly large. But the effects of major policy changes are both far-reaching and uncertain, and it is surely worth paying a substantial price to be able to evaluate their success before becoming irrevocably committed to them.

Modes of commissioning survey research

Government departments themselves initiate most of the work they fund. Although they have occasionally responded to grant applications from academics and independent institutes, this has become rarer as financial constraints have increased.

Commonly, an element of competition is involved, with either an open or a closed tender. Open tenders, in which social researchers are invited to respond to a public advertisement, are not common. The arms'-length procedure they inevitably involve – since the customer cannot have detailed discussions with what may turn out to be a large number of tenderers – is wholly inimical to the effective placing or conduct of survey research contracts. A modified version of this, operated for example by the Department of the Environment in its planning research programme, is really a closed tender since the initial advertisement asks merely for an expression of interest and relevant experience: a limited number of those replying are then invited to submit tenders.

The closed tender has been a familiar, though not invariable, feature of government surveys for many years. Its use has been reviewed and discussed both by the Rayner Review of the Government Statistical Service[1] and by the Merchant report on government's commissioning of surveys[2]. An extended critique of tendering will be found in a paper by Jowell[3].

Some surveys can be specified in great detail by the commissioning department. They are the best suited to tendering, since quotations can be requested on an (apparently) uniform basis. They include some of the largest government surveys, where the sheer scale of the work constitutes an additional reason to seek competitive tenders. But no survey brief can specify the end product in the same sort of way as an architect's specification for a building. The 'quality' of the work is hard to assess, since the final output – tape, tables or even report – does not directly reveal very much about how expertly and thoroughly all the underlying processes such as interviewing, coding and data checking have been carried out. Observing the work while it is in progress is a partial solution to the problem, but such monitoring is inconclusive if the work inspected is a demonstration piece rather than a random sample. A better way of assessing the calibre of the work is for the Department's researcher to play an active participatory role throughout, working alongside the survey organisation's researchers. This is demanding in staff time, but brings many benefits.

Automatic acceptance of lowest tenders is, properly, not regarded by government departments as an admissible strategy. Nevertheless, cost is often the paramount factor. It may be difficult for the Department's research staff to assess other factors, and, even more, to quantify these in a way that would clearly demonstrate to Finance Officers and policy-makers the justifiability of choosing a more expensive bid.

The difficulties of tendering increase as the project moves away from the fully-specified to the more open type of brief. In a competition for ideas, the costings of the organisation offering the best ideas will be hard to evaluate against those of others who will be offering different schemes. The usual solution to this problem is to ask for quotations for a project, specified in detail, but to invite both comments on the design and suggestions, and costings, for alternative specifications (or even alternative projects).

It may not be easy for contractors to respond to such an invitation. They may well feel that other designs would be preferable to those tabled. On the other hand, they may sense a substantial commitment on the Department's part to the specification as given, and may wonder whether the considerable cost of working up alternatives will be worthwhile when they have little chance of being acceptable.

Moreover, the required creative input to research design is a valuable resource, and the competitive process requires that much of it should be contributed without charge. One strategy, advocated by Merchant, is to have two stages rather than one. The first is a design phase (not subject to competition) to establish an appropriate methodology, and the second is the resulting survey, for which tenders are invited. This seems eminently logical at first sight. However, when the problem is difficult enough to warrant two-stage treatment, design and execution are usually too intimately linked to be satisfactorily divorced in this way. Possession of the creative ability needed to evolve a successful design should be a major asset in carrying out the work as a whole. When preliminary feasibility studies are needed, either to unravel conceptual problems or to develop techniques, contracts for them should ideally be placed with the explicit intention, subject to a satisfactory outcome, of negotiating the main contract with the same organisation.

One of the drawbacks of putting a survey specification out to tender is that it does not offer scope for an uninhibited exchange of ideas in advance between outside organisations and the commissioning Department. Among the most successful surveys are those whose designs have been jointly worked up by the Department and the survey organisation, with both parties making an essential and distinctive contribution. Tendering pre-empts decisions that should be left open until the work is well under way, since survey design is an organic process rather than a blueprint.

The negotiated contract, or 'single tender', is appropriate (and is not infrequently used) where one organisation possesses appreciably more relevant experience or expertise for a particular task than others do, as in the case of a follow-up to an earlier study in which a lot of time has been spent in acquiring familiarity with complicated issues and in developing solutions to difficult technical problems. Where the earlier study has been done efficiently and well, there is a strong case for deliberately capitalising on the investment by negotiating the next project with the same contractor. To change to another contractor on the basis of a marginally lower tender, as sometimes happens, is to run a large risk for a small return, or indeed for no return at all after the costs of the tendering process and of 'induction training' for the new organisation are taken into account.

Ironically, however, repeat surveys are by definition relatively easy to specify in detail, and thus seem to lend themselves well to tendering. If this path is chosen, the incumbent organisation's familiarity with the work can in some respects be as much a hindrance as a help, since it may know from experience that the project will impose greater demands than other tenderers may suspect, and its costings will have to reflect this.

Timetabling

Pressure on timetables over the last few years seems to have increased just as much as pressure on costs. Increased insistence on policy relevance has certainly been a contributory factor, and has been given added impetus in some Departments by direct ministerial involvement in decisions about survey research. But in view of the diffuseness of the notion of policy relevance, discussed earlier, this does not seem a sufficient explanation.

Short timetables and tendering do not sit well together. Given that time is needed to develop and agree the initial brief, as well as for the preparation of submissions and their evaluation, the tendering process can easily take up a substantial proportion of the available time for the project. The survey itself may then have to be done in a hurry. While it is possible that the need for speed may sharpen the mind and result in a more efficient operation, it is more likely that the work will suffer from undue haste. Procedures that are not the most efficient for achieving the survey's objectives may need to be adopted in order to get the work done by the specified date. Alternatively, that date has to be put back. In either case, the price paid for the loss of time occasioned by the tendering process can be heavy.

Budgeting

Survey costs usually have to be determined at a time when a good deal of the content is still to be decided. In particular, the core document, the questionnaire, has usually not been designed. Explicit assumptions can be made about interview length, and perhaps about the number of cards that will be punched. But what starts as an estimate, to be varied in the light of circumstances, must inevitably, under tendering conditions, become a fixed price for the work. It is, of course, universally accepted that if major changes are made to the specification as the work proceeds, the price will need to be renegotiated. But there is no mechanism for coping with the incremental effect of numerous minor increases in the demands of a project. An agreement to undertake a complex survey for a fixed price could, if the customer were unreasonable, prove to be an open-ended commitment.

The most efficient way of dealing with such problems, but one which governmental procedures rarely permit, is the contingency allowance, a discretionary budget that is to be spent if, and only if, the Department's officers are satisfied that it is necessary. The reason that contingencies are rarely built in appears to be a belief that money earmarked for potential spending will in fact be spent. It stems, perhaps, from the inflexible annual budgeting system that exerts pressure to spend budgeted amounts in full in order to fend off cuts in the following year: there is no prize, but only a penalty, for underspending. More flexible arrangements for external survey budgets would reflect the realities of the work.

Relationships and roles

Experienced researchers within government departments may require simply a fieldwork and data processing service, subcontracting only those parts of the work for which they cannot directly deploy resources. More often, they subcontract the entire project, while retaining a necessary supervisory role. Clients who are not themselves research specialists are likely to adopt the second of these two models.

From the point of view of the outside researcher, the two models are clearly distinguished by the fact that the second involves a substantive report, while the first ends with a data tape and brief technical report. In the actual design stages of the work the distinction between them may prove less clear-cut, since both are likely to involve a substantial collaborative effort with overlapping roles. Even in the first model, the task of designing much of the operational detail of the survey is likely to fall at least partly on the outside researcher, who controls the resources for undertaking the work, while in the second model the Department researcher's supervisory role and expertise may make it difficult for him or her to avoid participating in detailed discussions about the questionnaire and other matters. Nevertheless, there is likely to be a difference in emphasis. Where the client is not a specialist researcher the roles may become more sharply differentiated as a result of the smaller overlap in areas of expertise, and the outside organisation's influence on the conduct of the project may accordingly increase.

Its specialised knowledge of sampling and other technical aspects of surveys, its experience of analogous problems in other fields, and its different perspective should enable the outside organisation to make a useful contribution. This is particularly true while the project is in gestation, but in practice the constraints imposed by the principle of competition make it difficult for the Department to seek ideas at an early stage, and it is usually not till after briefs have been issued that the outside organisation can begin to comment. It is easier for it to offer constructive criticism if it is familiar with the Department's attitudes and practices, and if a relationship of mutual respect has already developed. Such relationships can develop only if departments are prepared to build them up with a limited number of suppliers, rather than feeling obliged to spread their work over a larger number in order to be seen to be evenhanded.

There are various outputs from the survey process. It is much rarer in government surveys than in academic surveys for the client to want copies of completed questionnaires (with all identification deleted), no doubt because staff resources are insufficient for analysing them. More often, but by no means always, there is a requirement for a data tape, again with identification deleted. Not all departments have computing departments used to handling data of this type, and the computing of some large data sets (such as the National Travel Surveys) has in the past been subcontracted to bureaux. Provision of a data tape (with a supporting technical report) often marks the end of the outside organisation's involvement. Where it is producing a substantive report, it is much less likely to be asked to provide a data tape, but copies of the full set of the computer tables drawn on in drafting the report are sometimes requested.

The outsider's share in discussions of the results is usually limited.

Even when he or she has written a full interpretative report, it is typically addressed to, and discussed only with, the link person (researcher, economist, statistician or psychologist), whose job it is to disseminate the findings within the Department. It is not usual for the outsider to take part in discussions of the findings with policy officials, let alone ministers. There are some good reasons for this. One is that to play a really useful role, the outsider would need more contextual information than it is usually possible to acquire, though close relationships help. Continuing involvement also represents a cost. And direct communication between senior officials and an outside organisation would tend to duplicate, and might on occasion threaten, the role of the inside researcher. In any case, it is a perhaps natural wish of civil servants to arrive at their own conclusions in their own way, unhampered by the presence of outsiders who are inevitably unfamiliar with personalities, practices and policies within the Department. The outside researcher may thus remain unaware of the kind of impact the project may have had, or of the ways in which it may have affected policymakers' thinking.

The amount of time spent by staff within the Department on a survey can be considerable. It has not hitherto been the custom within government to identify or cost such time, and perhaps the outside researcher should be grateful that this is so, since the true costs of conducting surveys would then be seen to be a good deal larger than they seem now. But it would provide a better perspective on the process as a whole. If the aim were to reduce the *total* cost of the operation, a greater premium would be placed on using organisations familiar with the department and its work. Marginal differences in external costs could easily be offset by internal savings.

In particular, the costs of tendering would be shown to be quite disproportionate, in many instances, to any savings made. These costs comprise not only those directly associated with writing the brief and evaluating replies, but those arising from the whole process of securing internal agreement on something sufficiently clear-cut to constitute a specification that can be put out to tender. Agreement must of course be reached, but the formal nature of the end product probably adds formality to, and protracts, the process itself. Once the contract is placed, there is likely to be a fresh cycle of internal consultation as the design continues to evolve. A telescoping of these two phases would almost certainly result in substantial net savings.

Confidentiality

Growing concern in the last few years about data protection, fuelled by the increase in computer applications, has led to widespread appreciation of the need for confidentiality to be guaranteed to those who respond to government surveys. There are practical as well as ethical reasons for this. Loss of public confidence in the professional secrecy of survey research organisations in relation to individual responses would impair the usefulness of surveys as an information-gathering tool.

Various ways of protecting the confidentiality of survey responses have been developed. The most important of these has been the move away from questionnaires bearing names and addresses to serially numbered forms linked to separately held address lists. SCPR's standard practice, for instance, is for interviewers to send back questionnaires and identification slips in separate envelopes, thus guarding against an identifiable questionnaire going astray in the post. The 1984 Data Protection Act exempts research from some of its requirements, but provides a context within which practices must be carefully reviewed.

Some government surveys require that a data tape is supplied to the commissioning Department. This poses no problem in household surveys, since the absence of names and addresses, and the spreading of small numbers of interviews over large areas, does not offer any real possibility of identification of individuals.

In some situations, however, difficulties can arise. The surveying of employers provides a notable example, since it is at least theoretically possible that some employers could be recognised from characteristics such as workforce size, industry and area. To safeguard against this, a tape provided to the Department for analysis must remove, or limit, data that might lead to identification. The broad-banding of size and industrial group and similar characteristics, together with the deletion of area codes, normally meets this objective. However, if the sample was selected by the Department in the first place (for example from a list of employers participating in a certain scheme), the chances of identification are greatly increased, and still more severe editing of the data tape may be needed, if indeed it can be provided at all. But broad-banding and editing of this sort can render the data much less amenable to secondary analysis.

It is clearly necessary for such problems to be thoroughly discussed, and solutions agreed, at the outset.

The fact that departments do not wish, and will not try, to identify individual cases does not absolve the research organisation from meeting its obligation to respondents to ensure that third parties will not be given access to identified, or identifiable, responses.

Publication

Most government surveys result in full published reports, although contracts stipulate that if the Secretary of State judges publication not to be in the public interest, permission may be delayed or withheld altogether. This clause seems to be increasingly invoked by some departments, particularly when sensitive policy areas are being investigated. This reflects a more managerial view of its function on the government's part. It sees itself as in business to take decisions in the light of the best information available to it. These decisions, it may argue, are difficult ones that involve conflicts of interest, often revolve round technical concepts, and may be hindered rather than assisted by the injection of survey results into public debate. But there are dangers in restricting publication of research results (unless the quality and integrity of the work itself is of insufficient standard). There is a narrow line between not publishing work on grounds of public interest, and not publishing it in the government's political interest. A government publishing selectively, or unduly delaying publication, might thus appear to be manipulating research. In any case, it seems reasonable that the public should have access to research it has contributed to and, ultimately, paid for; and desirable that discussion of policies and their outcomes should be as well-informed as possible.

Conclusions

Survey research can sometimes approximate to a production-line process, with well-determined and readily assessable outputs. More often, its character may be described as organic. To a certain extent, it develops its own specification as the work on it proceeds. Any attempt to specify every detail of the design in advance is unlikely to be successful, and may even be counter-productive. In order to obtain better data for evaluating submissions, survey briefs sometimes ask for details that it is not merely unnecessary but wrong to determine until work is well under way and an informed choice can be made on the basis of evidence that is not available at the outset.

Government's commissioning of surveys has evolved over a long period, borrowing techniques from other supplier-customer situations. Competitive tendering has an essential role, particularly for large and well-defined surveys, but is unsuited to the character of many others. For these, more use could be made of the single tender or negotiated price. Government's experience of survey costs is extensive and should enable it to assess single tender prices. Savings in internal time spent on tendering would – if costed out – often counter-balance any price advantage gained.

Outside organisations have a valuable contribution to make to survey design, not simply to execution. It is thus often desirable to involve them at an early stage, before the outline and budget become fixed, though evenhandedness makes this difficult to achieve where there is to be a competitive tender. The value of the outsider's contribution is likely to increase with familiarity with the Department's work. Continuity and close relationships are likely to be valuable assets.

Feasibility studies or other exploratory work may be required by the complexity of the problems addressed, but are often precluded by the speed with which many projects have to be undertaken. To combat this, some of the more fundamental problems could be tackled outside the context of a specific policy survey. The use of qualitative techniques for such purposes could usefully be expanded.

While the contribution of surveys to policy is indirect, in that they do not often point directly to particular policy actions, they provide a wide range of relevant information that cannot be obtained by other means, and cumulatively increase government's understanding both of the circumstances and processes to which policy is applied and of the results that it achieves.

NOTES

1 Rayner, Sir D. (1980) *Review of Government Statistical Services*, Cabinet Office report.
2 Merchant, J. R. (1981) *The commissioning of ad hoc social surveys*, Civil Service College mimeograph report.
3 Jowell, R. M. (1985) 'The Researchers' Perspective' in *Can you buy it off the shelf? Alternative methods of commissioning research*, ed. Lewis, J. and Jacoby, A., London, Social Research Association.

CHAPTER 15

The federal effort in developing social indicators and social reporting in the United States during the 1970s

DENIS F. JOHNSTON

Viewed in retrospect, the 1970 decade was a period of unusual promise for both social indicators development and social reporting by the federal government of the US. To begin with, the requisite data base had been greatly improved during the preceding decade – an improvement that continued unabated throughout the 1970s as well. Some of these gains were prompted by the information demands of the 'war on poverty' declared by President Johnson in the mid-1960s, but the underlying impetus was the growing awareness among policy-makers that the complex social problems that emerged from the turmoil of the late 1960s could neither be understood nor dealt with solely in terms of conventional economic indicators. In addition to major improvements in the decennial censuses and the Current Population Survey (the nation's main multi-purpose monthly survey of households), a number of major new surveys were inaugurated during this period, covering such diverse topics of social interest as time use, the quality of employment, the condition of the nation's youth and its retirees, participation in adult learning, improved measures of learning (as opposed to 'years of school completed'), and longitudinal surveys of the labour market experiences of youth and of older men and women. By the mid-1970s, the social data base had been further enriched by the establishment of such major data collection efforts as the 'General Social Survey' of the National Opinion Research Center, University of Chicago (begun in 1972); the national 'Health and Nutrition Examination Survey' (begun in 1971); the national 'Criminal Victimization Survey' (begun in 1972); and the 'Annual Housing Survey' (begun in 1973). According to a recent compendium of such data sets, one-third of them (numbering one hundred in all) were initiated in the 1960s, and thirty-six more in the 1970s (Social Science Research Council, U.S., 1982).

The academic community also exerted considerable influence on the thinking of federal officials in this area, both by the examples offered by several compendia of innovative studies and by extensive service on a vast number of advisory committees. By 1975, for example, over twelve hundred committees, with about twenty-two thousand members, were active in advising some forty-five federal agencies (Nelkin, 1979, p. 109). At least four major works in this field also made their appearance in the late 1960s (Bauer, 1966; Gross, 1966; The American Academy of Political and Social Science, 1967; and Sheldon and Moore, 1968). Viewed collectively, these works demonstrated the insights that could be obtained by examining the condition of American society from a holistic perspective; they also called attention to important data gaps and deficiencies still to be remedied (Biderman, 1966).

Further impetus toward a concerted federal effort in this general area was provided by the establishment, in 1970, of a Social Indicators Development Programme within the Organization for Economic Co-operation and Development (Organization for Economic Co-operation and Development, 1982, p. 7). Throughout the 1970s, the ongoing developmental efforts of the OECD's Working Party on Social Indicators were highly influential in providing both general guidelines and specific counsel in regard to the social indicator specification and social reporting activities of many OECD Member Countries, including the United States (Johnston, 1975, 1978).

As early as 1967, an attempt was made to establish a capability for comprehensive social reporting within the Executive Office of the President. Legislation proposed by then Senator Walter F. Mondale, under the title 'Full Opportunity and Social Accounting Act', would have mandated establishment of a 'Council of Social Advisors' within the Executive Office and would also have required the President to submit to the Congress an annual report on the 'social state of the nation'. Despite its subsequent modification and re-introduction, this Bill was never enacted into law. Congressional reluctance to support the mandatory issuance of annual social reports at the presidential level was consistent with the majority views of the academic establishment. In reviewing the recommendations of no less than three commissions formed in the late 1960s to consider the role of social sciences in relation to the federal government, Riecken (then President of the US Social Science Research Council) pointed out that none of them fully endorsed the idea of a Council of Social Advisors. Most of their recommendations were addressed to needed improvements in the quality of statistical data and greater support for a broad range of social science research (Riecken, 1971, pp. 111f).

But if social reporting was not considered to be a viable option for the Executive Office of the President, it was readily accepted as an appropriate activity within the then US Department of Health, Education, and Welfare. In response to a directive issued by President Johnson, a Panel on Social Indicators was formed in 1966. This panel, comprising forty-one social scientists and chaired jointly by Daniel Bell and William Gorham, was expected to provide general guidelines (and individual contributions) for what was envisioned as a comprehensive assessment of the condition of American society. To that end, a small staff established within the Department (headed by Mancur Olson and Alice Rivlin) began to assemble and analyse an enormous variety of statistical data to be included in a series of reports addressed to the different aspects of the 'quality of life' in the United States (Bell and Olson, 1969, pp. 72–105). However, the change in administrations brought about by the election of President Nixon in November 1968 also necessitated a quick termination of this ambitious effort. Instead, Wilbur Cohen, then Secretary of the Department, ordered the hasty preparation of a single 123-page summary report that was issued on the last day of the Johnson Administration (U.S. Department of Health, Education, and Welfare, 1969).

Toward a Social Report, despite its superficial treatment of its subject-matter and its many serious omissions, remains an outstanding example of a social report addressed to the general public and designed to facilitate informed public assessments of general social conditions. Each of its seven brief chapters was addressed to an issue of broad popular concern, such as 'Are we becoming healthier?' or (with reference to equality of opportunity), 'How much opportunity is there?' In calling attention to the kinds of statistical information that could illuminate public consideration of these issues, this report demonstrated the usefulness of such data; by trying to explain the significance of these data, it also encouraged their critical examination by its readers.

Despite the unwillingness of the Nixon Administration to continue the large-scale social reporting effort originally envisioned, it did express a strong interest in the use of social statistics in developing domestic policy initiatives. An outstanding example of this Administration's support for small-scale efforts in this area was the establishment, in July 1969, of the 'National Goals Research Staff' within the Domestic Policy Staff of the White House. This staff was given one year to review and report on 'emerging debates concerning alternative paths for continued societal development' (Executive Office of the President, 1970, pp. 22f). *Toward Balanced Growth: Quantity with Quality* differed substantially from *Toward a Social Report*, both in its treatment of statistical data and its orientation. Instead of organizing its presentation around subject-areas of general concern (such as health, education, employment, and the like), this report explored alternative paths toward the achievement of generally unquestioned instrumental values – especially the value of continued economic growth. The report carefully avoided any interpretations or arguments reflecting a particular viewpoint toward the causes or solutions of social problems; nor did it offer any assessment of the condition of American society. The statistical data it presented related largely to long-range demographic and economic projections, together with similar extrapolations of observed trends in selected factors thought to be significantly related to economic growth, such as expenditures on research and development or enrollments in higher education. Nevertheless, this report shared with its predecessor the major objective of promoting better informed public consideration of important issues affecting the continued economic prosperity of American society. In addition, it added an important dimension to such considerations by stressing the need for alternative projections of the future environment in which today's decisions would exert their effects.

A second initiative taken by the Nixon administration during the summer of 1969 was longer lasting. At that time, the Domestic Policy Staff decided to initiate preparation of a new series of comprehensive statistical chartbooks that would depict (mostly in graphic form) current conditions and emerging developments in the major sectors of American society. In the early planning of this report series, key roles were played by Senator Daniel Patrick Moynihan (then Counselor to President Nixon), Sir Claus Moser (then Director of the UK's Central Statistical Office), and Julius Shiskin (then Director of the Office of Statistical Policy, Bureau of the Budget, Executive Office of the President). Sir Claus's account of the preparation of the first of the UK's annual *Social Trends* reports and his plans for this report series were important factors in prompting a similar effort in the United States (Tunstall, 1974 and private discussions).

The new social reporting effort was far less ambitious than the one launched in 1966 by the Panel on Social Indicators. A single professional position was established in the Office of Statistical Policy for this purpose. However, its strategic location within the Bureau of the Budget facilitated considerable cooperation on the part of key subject-matter specialists throughout the federal statistical establishment. But the shift in emphasis from a narrative discussion of major conditions or key issues affecting the quality of life to a graphic presentation of selected statistical series with a minimum of interpretation critically altered the nature of the social reports that eventually emerged. The chartbook format that was adopted was designed to present an array of 'key' statistics, in time-series form where possible, offered both in tabular and graphic form, and organised around major 'areas of concern', such as health, education, employment, housing, and the like. The descriptive text that accompanied these data was largely restricted to summarising the highlights of the data. This approach would have been inescapable in any case, given the minimal level of support for the project. But the underlying reason for the adoption of the chartbook format was that it better reflected the dominant view that the presentation of statistical information by any agency of government should be as 'neutral' as possible and should therefore eschew any interpretation that might be construed as advocating a particular viewpoint or program of action.

The first of the comprehensive social indicator chartbooks was finally issued in February 1974, after four years of preparation. It was followed by two more reports in the series, issued in December 1977 and January 1981 (U.S. Office of Management and Budget, 1974 and 1977; U.S. Bureau of the Census, 1981). The first of these reports, *Social Indicators 1973*, was highly innovative in at least two respects. First, its elaborate use of color graphics (165 charts in all) made the report far more attractive than the usual statistical publications issued by government agencies. Second, its subject-matter was carefully organized around specified 'concern-areas' within each of the broad subject-areas. For example, 'life expectancy' was identified as a key area of concern within the general area of public health. Eight such subject-areas were covered in the first report: Health, Public Safety, Education, Employment, Income, Housing, Leisure and Recreation, and Population. The two subsequent chartbooks – *Social Indicators 1976* and *Social Indicators III* – adhered to the same format, but they included considerably more statistical data and expanded their coverage by eventually including additional chapters on Transportation, Social Security and Welfare, and Social Participation. As a result, each of these reports included over 300 charts, and was over 600 pages in length. These last two chartbooks also featured two innovations included in each chapter: a section on public perceptions and one on international comparisons. The latter feature was intended to take advantage of the assemblage of internationally comparable social indicators that was anticipated in response to the recommendations of the OECD's Working Party on Social Indicators, and was designed to call attention to the similar social conditions and problems to be found in all modern industrialized societies.

One further notable feature of the last two social indicator chartbooks was an arrangement with the American Academy of Political and Social Science to devote a special issue of their long-established bi-monthly journal, *The Annals*, to each chartbook. Each of these issues was edited by Conrad Taeuber and was composed of a number of essays, contributed by recognised authorities both in academia and in government, and addressed to the subjects covered by the separate chapters of the chartbooks or to important cross-cutting issues, such as the status of minorities (American Academy of Political and Social Science, 1978 and 1981).

When viewed together, the chartbook and *The Annals* issue devoted to it provided their readers with both an assemblage of descriptive statistical data and an independent (and often highly critical) interpretive essay addressed to the subject-matter covered by the statistics in question. These were the essential components of a social report, as originally envisioned. Unfortunately, their separate publication prevented many readers from examining these reports in relation to one another.

The three comprehensive chartbooks produced during the 1970s were by no means the only federal efforts in this general area. Important series of reports were also initiated, focusing on science, education, and health, respectively. *Science Indicators* is a biennial series, begun in 1972; *The Condition of Education* is an annual seies, begun in 1975; and *Health, United States* is also an annual series, issued since 1976. *Science Indicators* is designed to supplement the annual report of the National Science Board to the President of the United States by providing a quantitative assessment of the status of science and technology in the country (National Science Board, 1983). Responsibility for the preparation of these reports rests with a small professional staff within the National Science Foundation. An outstanding feature of this report series has been its candid and objective appraisal of conditions affecting the current status and prospective development of science and technology in the U.S. This achievement can be attributed largely to two factors: first, the establishment of the National Science Board as an autonomous body of distinguished scientists appears to have ensured continued support for more independent and critical appraisals than might otherwise have been possible. Second, the series has been responsive to the criticisms and expressed needs of the scientific community at large and has benefited especially from the detailed criticisms of the earlier issues (McGinniss, 1979; Elkana et al, 1978).

The Condition of Education has been patterned closely after the format of the comprehensive social indicator reports, except for its heavier emphasis on what might be termed educational 'inputs' (enrollments, teacher qualifications, budget and facilities, etc.) (U.S. Department of Education, 1983). Like those reports, *The Condition of Education* provides statistical tables of important data series, usually accompanied (on the facing page) by illustrative charts, together with a brief text that is limited largely to pointing out the highlights of the data. From a 'social indicators' perspective, however, the outstanding feature of these reports has been their inclusion of measures of educational performance – both average performance scores on standardised tests of different competencies, and measures of outcomes of higher education, such as earned degrees conferred.

The series of *Health, United States* reports is designed to provide their readers a comprehensive overview of the health status of the American people (U.S. Department of Health and Human Services, 1983). Like the two other series, *Health, United States* has gradually developed an excellent format for this purpose. It now consists of two parts: a group of articles addressed to selected topics of current interest, and a standardised set of detailed statistical tables that provide coverage (and annual updates) of the same topics in the health area from year to year. Beginning in 1980 and repeated triennially thereafter, the report also includes a supplement entitled 'Prevention Profile', that summarises current developments with respect to a variety of health conditions that are especially susceptible to behavioral modifications, such as control of high blood pressure, family planning, immunisation, control of toxic agents and radiation, prevention of injuries, improved nutrition, and control of smoking, alcohol consumption, and drug use.

One additional social indicator report to be issued during the 1970s merits particular attention for its effectiveness in providing supportive arguments in favor of affirmative action programs for particular minority groups. The report was entitled *Social Indicators of Equality for Minorities and Women* (U.S. Commission on Civil Rights, 1978). It was designed to serve one purpose above all: to heighten public awareness of the prevalence in U.S. society of serious and long-standing inequality, particularly among racial/ethnic groups and between men and women. The extent of this inequality was measured by means of a number of quantitative indicators representing conditions in four broad subject-areas: education, unemployment and occupational distribution of the employed, income and poverty, and housing. For each of these measures, the extent of 'inequality' was gauged by comparing the observed value for selected minority populations (by gender) to that of 'majority white males'. These comparisons were carried out for a total of fifteen population groups: 'majority white females', plus the males and females of seven racial or ethnic groups: American Indians/Alaskan natives, Blacks, Mexican Americans, Japanese Americans, Chinese Americans, Filipino Americans, and Puerto Ricans. The requisite statistical data were drawn from observations at three points in time; the 1960 and 1970 censuses, and a special sample survey conducted in 1976. In each of the comparisons, the procedure for making the comparison was the same: the observed value for 'majority white males' was set equal to 1.00 and the corresponding values for the other population groups were then expressed on the same scale. Because the data related to three time periods, it was also possible to show evidence of convergence or divergence among the several groups with respect to particular measures. For example, setting the median earnings of college-educated 'majority white males' in the calendar year immediately preceding the three reference dates equal to 1.00, the corresponding index value for college-educated Black males was 0.66 in 1959 (as reported in the 1960 census), had risen to 0.73 in 1969, and to 0.81 in 1975. In short, the data revealed that college-educated Black males earned, on average, only about two-thirds as much as their white male counterparts in 1959, but that they were earning about four-fifths as much by 1975.

Despite the fact that it was never repeated, this report was highly effective in achieving its intended objectives. The simple comparative technique employed throughout the report was readily grasped, even by statistically unsophisticated readers, and the findings were dramatically evident in graphic form. The narrative part of the report emphasised a single message: the persistence of glaring (and inequitable) inequality in American society. That focus precluded attention to some of the controversial aspects of the study, such as the absence of appropriate standardisation for its measures, its failure to consider the relative status of different ethnic groups within the broad 'majority white' category, and the inattention to the considerable evidence that many of the observed gaps between 'majority white males' and the other groups had narrowed sharply between 1960 and 1976. But for all its limitations, this report remains an outstanding example of the power of simple comparative measures to illuminate the relative status of different population groups, thereby calling attention to the disparity between reality and one of the society's avowed values: equality. As such, it fulfilled one of the useful functions of a social report – that of providing 'ammunition' for a particular social agenda (Bulmer, 1981).

In retrospect, it is evident that the three federally-issued, comprehensive social indicator chartbooks did not succeed in satisfying the informational demands of any readily identifiable group of readers. In contrast, the reports just discussed, addressed to single subject-areas, have enjoyed a sustained readership among clearly identified interest groups. Nevertheless, it is the comprehensive social indicator reports that most nearly exemplify the *idea* of a social report. We therefore return, in the remainder of this essay, to a review of the problems encountered (and lessons learned) in the course of their preparation.

Problems and lessons

Most of the problems encountered (and lessons to be drawn) in preparing the three social indicator reports can be grouped into four broad categories: conceptual problems, measurement problems, presentational problems, and valuational problems, as follows:

Conceptual problems

The first conceptual problem to be dealt with in preparing any comprehensive social report is the organisation of its subject-matter. In the United States at least, the sharpest issue in this respect has been that of a subject-matter organisation versus an organisation around population groups of particular interest. The preference in the U.S. reports and in all of the major national social indicator reports issued to date, at least by OECD Member Countries, has been for the conventional subject-matter organisation, with separate chapters focused on such topics as health, education, housing, employment, etc. But the critics of this mode of data presentation strongly object to the artificial compartmentalisation of conditions affecting human well-being that results from this episodic treatment. Even where, as if often the case, appropriate disaggregations are provided, readers with an interest in the overall situation of a particular population group can only find scattered bits of pertinent evidence among the several chapters of the report.

Despite these problems, this mode of organization can still be recommended, first because it is familiar to most readers. In addition, it affords the best assurance of a comprehensive coverage of at least the major aspects of human well-being. A subject-matter organisation is also congruent with the organisational subdivisions of the statistical institutions of most national governments. But most important, it is also consistent with the frame of reference established by the OECD's Working Party on Social Indicators, as well as those of other international research groups concerned with social indicators development (Zapf, 1975; OECD, 1982, p. 13).

A second conceptual problem is the appropriate role of analysis and interpretation. Does a good chart save a thousand words, or, as one critic put it, does a good chart *require* a thousand words? It is undeniable that many of our common social indicators offer unambiguous evidence of improvement or deterioration – e.g., a fall in the rate of infant mortality, or a rise in the rate of unemployment. But even in these cases, the need for a *ceteris paribus* clause and the ever-present possibility that apparent trends are due to statistical artifacts must be borne in mind. In other cases, the significance of an observed change in a given indicator is not obvious. For example, increased public access to health care (clearly a favorable development) may be reflected in an increased incidence of activity restrictions (time lost from work or from school), thereby indicating deteriorating health conditions in the given population (Wilson, 1981). But there is a deeper issue here as well: if the purpose of a comprehensive social report is to enable the reader to develop an independent assessment of the condition of the society, it is essential to provide that reader with some guidelines, or illustrative examples, of how that judgmental process might be carried out. This can only be achieved if the data presented are accompanied by some interpretation that goes beyond mere descriptions of salient features of the data.

The lesson here is straightforward: a chartbook cannot be a social report; the information presented in chartbook form can be both factual and comprehensive, but at best, it provides knowledge, not understanding.

A third conceptual problem relates to the need for criteria whereby particular statistics or derived measures may be selected as appropriate 'indicators' of given phenomena. In addition to the useful criteria for acceptable statistics (reliability, validity), two criteria were set forth in the introduction to *Social Indicators 1973*: that the data should 'measure individual and family (rather than institutional or governmental) well-being' and that they should 'measure end-products of, rather than inputs into social systems' (U.S Office of Management and Budget, 1974, p. xiii). It turns out that neither criterion is feasible. It is at least arguable that any statistic describing prevalent socio-economic or environmental conditions is relevant, directly or indirectly, to individual well-being or that of the primary groups in which they live and work. But the problem with a focus on 'output' measures is more severe, since it entails prior delineation of an appropriate 'input–output' framework. Such concepts enjoy considerable prestige, given their successful application by economists in studying business enterprises and the interrelations of industrial sectors in the national economy. But the extension of this concept to non-economic areas requires adoption of arbitrary and questionable assumptions. Most of the conditions affecting human well-being, such as health status, educational levels, levels of income, and the like, are not the result of any clearly identifiable set of 'inputs'. Furthermore, these conditions, in turn, function as 'inputs' to a host of other desirable social outcomes, such as greater productivity, greater freedom of choice, etc.

In this case, the lesson is again simple: the imposition of an 'input–output' matrix on complex social characteristics artificially constrains the reader's appreciation of their interaction. By the same token, an exclusive focus on 'output' measures (assuming they could be identified) reduces the reader's ability to appreciate their significance, since such appreciation requires their examination in relation to relevant inputs.

A fourth conceptual problem is the kinds and levels of disaggregation needed to permit important comparisons, weighed against the equally imperative need to limit the size of the report. One perceptive reviewer of the first chartbook objected to the routine employment of data relating to different characteristics of the population according to age grouping, gender, and race or ethnicity. She argued that the explanatory significance of these background factors in regard to observed variations in the phenomena being disaggregated is itself far from uniform. Her further concern was that an uncritical presentation of such disaggregations tends to encourage the notion that these factors are equally relevant (Ramsøy, 1974, pp. 46f). Another reviewer of the same report noted the paucity of disaggregations according to social class – a background characteristic that is widely understood to have considerable explanatory power (Zapf, 1974, p. 33).

One lesson that can be drawn from this debate is that a social report cannot fulfil the more demanding requirements of scientific analysis. Even if these (and other similar) disaggregations fail to provide adequate explanations of observed differences, they remain useful in calling attention to the normative implications of such differences.

Measurement problems

The demand for composite indicators is a persistent problem in the development of social reports because it is a difficult problem in measurement. The appeal of composite indices in social reporting is obvious, since such measures would greatly facilitate the readers' assessment of the condition of society. Here also, the example offered by the economists' 'gross national product' and similar constructs is misleading. In non-economic areas, the absence of a common metric (such as monetary exchange values) means than any attempt to combine a number of measures relating, for example, to the health status of a given population, entails arbitrary selection and arbitrary weighting of the components.

One of the deeper insights that emerges from any attempt to develop a 'system' of social indicators is that the concept of human well-being and our notions of 'quality of life' are inherently multi-dimensional, and that our assessments of these complex conditions cannot be carried out solely in terms of the norms of economic rationality (Diesing, 1950 and 1962, pp. 244ff).

A second measurement problem derives from the inescapable variation in the quality of statistical data. One of the unfortunate characteristics of such data, whether presented in tabular or graphic form, is that they convey the impression of great (and uniform) precision. Increased emphasis has been given to informing data users about the quality of statistical data in general terms by describing the approximate magnitude of sampling error (in the case of sample data) and by summarising the principal sources of non-sampling error or validity. This was done in the last two U.S. social indicator reports as well. But even if the requisite information was available, it would be difficult to provide data users with adequate warnings as to the structure of error associated with the many different statistics contained in comprehensive statistical compendia. One dilemma here is that such knowledge is only available for statistics of the highest overall quality; in fact, knowledge of the structure of error associated with particular data sets is itself a useful indicator of high quality. Hence the statistically unsophisticated readers may be prompted to question the reliability of better quality statistical data (about whose 'errors' much can be said) while remaining uncritical about relatively poorer data sets, whose error structure remains unknown.

A somewhat similar measurement problem arises in connection with the presentation of 'subjective' data – i.e., statistics describing public opinions, perceptions, or reactions toward particular events or conditions affecting their lives. The inclusion of such data alongside so-called 'objective' measures of social conditions is now widely recognised as one of the principal distinguishing features of a social indicators report. The essential argument here is that no assessment of the well-being or 'quality of life' of a given population group can be based solely upon an account of the objective conditions and characteristics that surround it; such an assessment must also take into account that group's perception of its condition. For that reason, the last two US social indicator reports included a section on 'public perceptions' in each chapter. However, the quality of perceptual data has been problematic. Many studies have revealed serious deficiencies in such data, including their extreme sensitivity to minor variations in question wording or question context, and inconsistencies in response patterns that often defy rational explanation (Turner, 1984, pp. 159–214; Marsh, 1984, pp. 565–91). Despite these limitations, there is considerable evidence that public opinion data bring to light significant differences between situations described in 'objective' terms and the same situations as defined or perceived by their principal actors (Schneider, 1975). In addition, perceptual data are often useful in gauging emerging public attitudes toward major policy issues (Rose, 1984).

Each chapter of the last two U.S. social indicator reports also included a section on 'international comparisons'. Such comparisons also pose serious measurement problems, particularly when they extend across societies having widely different cultural traditions or levels of economic development. For purposes of social reporting, the problem is not only one of measurement. Thanks largely to the long-term efforts of the UN Statistical Office and the affiliated statistical agencies of the other international organisations in the U.N. family, important advances in the international comparability of statistical information have been made. These gains have been achieved by means of the gradual adoption of standardised concepts, measurement procedures, and classifications in the collection of information in such major areas as economic activity, industrial production, demographic characteristics, and statistics relating to health conditions and levels of education. However, a further problem arises in trying to evaluate the *significance* of conditions in different cultural contexts. For example, in judging the significance of the divorce rate in different societies, it does not suffice to determine that the underlying concepts, definitions, and data collection procedures are identical or reasonably comparable. The deeper question relates to the significance of the phenomenon of divorce in the different cultures. Such concerns are hardly the province of statistical measurement techniques, but they are an important reminder that the problem of international comparability (or, for that matter, inter-group comparisons within a given society) cannot be resolved entirely by technical means.

Presentational problems

The most common presentational problems have already been mentioned in discussing the problem of appropriate levels of disaggregation. But the general practice in national social indicator reports has been to emphasise socioeconomic or demographic disaggregations (i.e., by age, gender, income class, race or ethnicity) at the cost of very limited geographic disaggregations. In consequence, these reports provide considerable information on the relative condition of different population groups within a given society, but they offer very little information on living conditions in different localities or in selected communities. Unfortunately, observed differences among the demographically-defined subgroups of a population may mask equally important differences among the residents of different communities within the given country. Ideally, national averages should never be presented without some accompanying indication of inter-regional variability; it follows that sample surveys designed to yield nothing more than national averages are of limited value for purposes of social reporting.

The emphasis on charts that characterised the U.S. social indicator reports offers some useful lessons in the graphic presentation of statistical information. To begin with, good charts cannot present the detailed information contained in statistical tables of the same size. Their design requires careful selection of the more important data elements or relationships. As noted previously, most of the charts in the U.S. reports were expected to convey factual information without the need for extensive commentary. However, the reports of the more serious users of these chartbooks (notably college teachers) indicate that even the simplest graphs were commonly misinterpreted, and that the ensuing discussion was often frustrated by the limited narrative that accompanied the statistical charts and tables. Once again, it is clear that a chartbook cannot meet the requirements of a social report (Peterson, 1979, pp. 532f; Carley, 1981, pp. 124f).

Valuational problems

The continuing debate as to the relation between social science and social values has been reflected in contrasting views as to the nature of social indicators. The view that social indicators are inherently normative is consistent with the idea that a judicious assembly of social indicators provides the essential ingredients for a social report (Bauer, 1966, p. 1; U.S. Department of Health, Education, and Welfare, 1969, p. 97). But a contrasting view defined social indicators in value-neutral terms as components of social science models designed to enhance understanding of social change (Land, 1970; Ferriss, 1975, p. 81). Much of the dissatisfaction of the academic community with the national social indicator reports that were issued by the U.S. government in the 1970s reflects this conflict between the aims of social reporting and those of social science research. To be sure, that conflict does not involve the basic data from which social indicators are constructed. The norms of scientific objectivity and verifiability clearly apply to the development of these constructs. But the selection of relevant measures and the definition of problems that are contained in any social report must reflect the values and goals of the society (Sederberg, 1984, pp. 42f; MacRae, 1985, pp. 345f). Perhaps it is necessary to recognise the functional differences between social science and social reporting while recognising the ultimate dependence of the latter upon the former (Bulmer, 1982, pp. 1673f; Doty, 1982, pp. 43f). In his careful analysis of the troubled relationship between social scientists and governmental policy makers, MacRae suggests a need to create and maintain a number of 'technical communities' that could better translate the findings of the research community into valuational terms that reflect the needs and outlooks of policymakers (MacRae, 1985, pp. 358f).

Valuational problems also arise in relation to more specific kinds of social indicators, such as measures designed to gauge progress toward particular goals or standards. As has been shown, the adoption of the condition of a particular population group (e.g., 'majority white males') as a standard against which to compare the corresponding status of other population groups reflects a prior value to the norm of equality among these groups. By the same token, the use of social indicators in illustrative projections reflects the prior judgment that prospective changes in that indicator's values are normatively significant. In fact, where appropriate time-series of social indicator values are available, their projection into the future on the basis of alternative sets of assumptions can be useful in the planning process by helping policy makers to evaluate the long-term implications of observed trends, together with the likely effects of alternative intervention strategies (Johnston, 1978).

The federal effort to produce comprehensive social indicator reports was terminated shortly after the publication of *Social Indicators III* early in 1981. Many reasons can be cited for this failure, such as the inherent weakness of descriptive statistics in explaining social phenomena, the inability of the reports to attract a significant audience, or the absence of adequate support for the enterprise from its inception. But a deeper reason was perhaps the discomfort of both governmental policy makers and members of the social science community with the need to entrust the preparation of such reports to anonymous civil servants, whatever their professional qualifications. For all their limitations, social indicators are conceptual constructs that guide and channel our perceptions of social reality. In doing so, they are capable, at least in principle, of challenging the insights and understandings that arise from different perspectives, particularly those of conventional economics. If the administration of the early 1970s was not prepared to underwrite a significant effort at social indicator development and social reporting, the administration that took control at the end of the decade was clearly opposed to any such undertaking.

The basic idea of a national social report is that it should convey to the public both a picture of social reality as it is perceived by the government and an account of governmental actions or policies designed to achieve specified goals or objectives. If that idea has merit, only the government can produce a national social report. Until the government decides to do so, the American public will be deprived of a unique and important form of societal intelligence.

REFERENCES

American Academy of Political and Social Science (1967), *The Annals*, 'Social Goals and Indicators for American Society', volume I (May) and II (September), edited by Bertram M. Gross.

(1978), *The Annals*. 'America in the Seventies: Some Social Indicators' (January), edited by Conrad Taeuber.

(1981), *The Annals*, 'America Enters the Eighties: Some Social Indicators' (January), edited by Conrad Taeuber.

Bauer, Raymond A. (ed.) (1966), *Social Indicators*, Cambridge, Mass., The MIT Press.

Bell, Daniel & Mancur Olson, Jr (1969), 'Toward a Social Report', *The Public Interest*, Number 15 (Spring).

Biderman, Albert D. (1966), 'Social Indicators and Goals', in Bauer, Raymond A. (ed.), *Social Indicators*, pp. 68–153.

Bulmer, Martin (1981), 'Applied Social Research', *Knowledge*, 3:2 (December), pp. 187–209.

Bulmer, Martin (1982), *The Uses of Social Research*, London, George Allen & Unwin, Ltd.

Carley, Michael (1981), *Social Measurement and Social Indicators*, London, George Allen & Unwin, Ltd.

Diesing, Paul (1950), 'The Nature and Limitations of Economic Rationality', *Ethics*, Volume 61, Number 1 (October), pp. 12–26.

Diesing, Paul (1962), *Reason in Society*, Urbana, Il., University of Illinois Press.

Doty, Pamela (1982), 'Values in Policy Research', in William N. Dunn, (ed.), *Values, Ethics, and the Practice of Policy Analysis*, Lexington, Mass., Lexington Books, pp. 33–45.

Elkana, Yehuda et al., (eds.) (1978), *Toward a Metric of Science: The Advent of Science Indicators*, New York, John Wiley & Sons, Inc.

Executive Office of the President, National Goals Research Staff (1970), *Towards Balanced Growth: Quantity with Quality*, Washington, D.C., U.S. Government Printing Office.

Ferriss, Abbott L. (1975), 'National Approaches to Developing Social Indicators', *Social Indicators Research*, 2:1 (June).

Gross, Bertram M. (ed.) (1966), *A Great Society?*, New York, Basic Books, Inc.

Johnston, Denis F. (1975), 'National Social Indicator Reports: Some Comparisons and Prospects', *World Future Society Bulletin*, IX: 4 (July/August), pp. 8–15.

(1978), 'Social Indicators and Social Forecasting', in Jib Fowles (ed.), *Handbook of Futures Research*, Westport, Conn., Greenwood Press, pp. 423–48.

Land, Kenneth C. (1970), 'On the Definition of Social Indicators', a paper presented at the annual meeting of the Population Association of America.

MacRae, Duncan Jr. (1985), *Policy Indicators*, Chapel Hill, NC, University of North Carolina Press.

Marsh, Catherine (1984), 'Do Polls Affect What People Think?', in Charles F. Turner and Elizabeth Martin (eds.), *Surveying Subjective Phenomena*, vol. II, New York, Russell Sage Foundation, pp. 565–91.

McGinniss, Robert (1979), 'Science Indicators 1976: A Critique', *Social Indicators Research*, 6:2 (April), pp. 163–80.

National Science Board (1983), *Science Indicators 1982*, Washington, D.C., U.S. Government Printing Office.

Nelkin, Dorothy (1979), 'Scientific Knowledge, Public Policy, and Democracy', *Knowledge*, 1:1 (September), pp. 106–22.

Organization for Economic Co-operation and Development (OECD) (1982), *The OECD List of Social Indicators*, Paris, OECD.

Peterson, James L. (1979), 'The United States *Social Indicators* reports in critical perspective', *International Social Science Journal*, vol. xxxi, no. 3, pp. 529–35.

Ramsøy, Natalie Rogoff (1974), 'Social Indicators in the United States and Europe: Comments on Five Country Reports', in Roxann A. Van Dusen (ed.), *Social Indicators, 1973: A Review Symposium*, Washington, D.C., Social Science Research Council, pp. 41–62.

Riecken, Henry W. (1971), 'The Federal Government and Social Science Policy', *The Annals* (of the American Academy of Political and Social Science) (March), pp. 100–13.

Rose, Richard (1984), 'Meta-policies for mega-government', *The Public Interest*, No. 75 (Spring), pp. 99–110.

Schneider, Mark (1975), 'The Quality of Life in Large American Cities: Objective and Subjective Social Indicators', *Social Indicators Research*, 1:4 (March), pp. 495–509.

Sederberg, Peter C. (1984), *The Politics of Meaning*, Tucson, Ariz., University of Arizona Press.

Sheldon, Eleanor Bernert and Wilbert E. Moore (eds.) (1968), *Indicators of Social Change*, New York, Russell Sage Foundation.

Social Science Research Council (U.S.) (1982), *National Social Data Series: A Compendium of Brief Descriptions*, Washington, D.C., Social Science Research Council.

Tunstall, Daniel B. (1974), 'Social Indicators and Social Reporting', a paper presented at the Joint American Marketing Association/British Marketing Research Society Conference on 'Changing Values and Social Trends: How Do Organizations React?'

Turner, Charles F. (1984), 'Why Do Surveys Disagree? Some Preliminary Hypotheses and Some Disagreeable Examples', in Charles F. Turner and Elizabeth Martin (eds.), *Surveying Subjective Phenomena*, vol. ii, New York, Russell Sage Foundation, pp. 159–214.

U.S. Bureau of the Census (1981), *Social Indicators III*, Washington, D.C., U.S. Government Printing Office.

U.S. Commission on Civil Rights (1978), *Social Indicators of Equality for Minorities and Women*, Washington, D.C., U.S. Commission on Civil Rights.

U.S. Department of Education (1983), *The Condition of Education*, Washington, D.C., U.S. Government Printing Office.

U.S. Department of Health, Education, and Welfare (1969), *Toward a Social Report*, Washington, D.C., U.S. Government Printing Office.

U.S. Department of Health and Human Services, (1983), *Health, United States*, Washington, D.C., U.S. Government Printing Office.

U.S. Office of Management and Budget (1974), *Social Indicators, 1973*, Washington, D.C., U.S. Government Printing Office.

(1977), *Social Indicators, 1976*, Washington, D. C., U.S. Government Printing Office.

302   Denis F. Johnston

Wilson, Ronald W. (1981), 'Do Health Indicators Indicate Health?', *American Journal of Public Health*, 71:5, pp. 461f.
Zapf, Wolfgang (1974), '*Social Indicators, 1973*: Comparison With Social Reports of Other Nations', in Roxann A. Van Dusen (ed.), *Social Indicators, 1973: A Review Symposium*, Washington, D.C.: Social Science Research Council, pp. 20–40.
Zapf, Wolfgang (1975), 'Systems of social indicators: current approaches and problems', *International Social Science Journal*, vol. xxvii, No. 3, pp. 479–98.

CHAPTER 16

Social science analysis and congressional uses: the case of the United States General Accounting Office*

RAY C. RIST

Introduction

Social science perspectives and the methodological craft generated by such understandings have come only recently to the United States General Accounting Office. But as can be anticipated from the very title of the agency, it was within the domain of auditing that the GAO had its origins, its rationale, and its mandate from the U.S. Congress. Indeed, since its inception in 1921, the GAO has played the dominant role in providing to the Congress verification of financial statements and management operations in the Federal government. It has also exerted considerable influence in shaping and framing the techniques and rules of evidence for the auditing profession. Standards developed by the GAO are now used to guide public sector auditing throughout the United States and have framed many of the practices of the private sector as well.

But in response to the changing information needs of the Congress, e.g., the actual effects of government programs and policies, the GAO has had to continually adapt and modify itself.[1] This is evident by changes made in existing methods of doing its work, in the qualifications and backgrounds of new staff recruited into the agency, and in the kinds of questions GAO is now undertaking to address for its Congressional users. Each of these three changes, interdependent as they are, has had a clear impact upon the agency. But the sum total has been to transform the GAO in the past ten years from a single focus,

* The views expressed in this paper are those of the author and no endorsement by the United States General Accounting Office is intended or should be inferred.

single method agency into a pluralistic center of analysis for the Congress – a center involving a wide range of disciplines, methodologies, and designs for its work.

Summarizing the mix of work in the GAO as of 1980, Mosher (1984: 145–6) has written:

> Financial auditing, which with legal work had been the bread and butter of its first quarter century, comprised only 7 percent of its total workload in 1980. Management studies in the interest of economy and efficiency narrowly defined, as developed after World War II, dropped to about 29 percent. Evaluations of ongoing programs, together with cost-benefit analyses of alternative approaches to problems for the future, comprised just about one-half, and the balance, about 14 percent, was made up of special studies of one kind or another – of methodology, techniques, surveys of needs for internal planning, and so forth.
>
> . . . today GAO's studies cover almost the entire spectrum of government work and many problems that are only partially governmental: the effectiveness of the food stamp program, problems of nursing homes, productivity in shoe manufacture, the war against organized crime, the fiscal future of New York City, the usefulness of rural post offices, the sale of airplanes to Saudi Arabia, the cost-effectiveness of the B-1 bomber, methods of introducing metric systems, and handgun control. It produces an average of about four reports each working day. Its reports and other memoranda go to the Congress – as a whole or to committees or individual members – to the executive agencies concerned, to the OMB, and to the media.

It is to a description and assessment of the social science contributions within the mosaic of GAO activities that the remainder of this paper is devoted. The emphasis is not that of detailing specific methodological nuances among social science groups within the agency nor is it one of attempting to categorize by disciplines all those who would identify themselves broadly as social scientists. Stated somewhat differently, the institutional labels used in the academic community to sort and classify are not especially germane to an understanding of the roles and contributions of social scientists within the GAO. The only exception, and it is a partial one at that, is for the economists who are hired into the agency with a position classification entitled 'economist'. Most all other social scientists coming into the agency are hired under either the broad position classification termed 'social science analyst' or that of 'evaluator'.

The GAO context

A brief description of the GAO is warranted. The agency is staffed with approximately 5100 persons and has a yearly budget of above $300 million. The agency has a unique status in that it is simultaneously both a Congressional support agency and a center for independent investigations and evaluations of all aspects of the Federal government. Approximately half of its work comes from Congressional requests and approximately one half from self-initiated work. It disseminates its findings and recommendations through formal reports to the Congress and to individual government departments and bureaus, through briefings to Congressional members and their staffs, through testimony to many Congressional committees, and through issuing countless legal decisions. Any material produced by the GAO that is not classified for reasons of national security is available free to the general public.

Succinctly, the mandate given to the GAO is one of working to ensure the activities of the federal government are conducted in an efficient and effective manner. The concerns range from studying financial systems, to the organizational efficiency of offices both large and small, to assessing the effectiveness of government supported or government administered policies, programs, and agencies.

The GAO is internally organized into fifteen regional offices and seven headquarters divisions. (The staff are approximately equally divided between regions and headquarters.) A key strength of the GAO is the existence of the regional offices where there are literally several thousand staff who are involved in primary data collection and analysis. The work of the regional offices is done on site – be that a military installation, a nuclear power facility, a national forest, a failing bank, a youth employment and training program, or a water pollution treatment plant. Working in conjunction with the headquarters divisions where the central planning and prioritizing of work for the agency is undertaken, the regional offices provide a world-wide capability to gather and analyze data relevant to the needs of Congressional users.

The headquarters divisions are structured in two ways. Four of the divisions are called 'programming divisions' and are organized to reflect the organization of the Executive Branch of the government, e.g., the National Security and International Affairs Division is responsible for the activities of the Departments of Defense and of State. Three other divisions are termed 'technical divisions' and each carries a set of responsibilities that cross-cut all government systems. One of the three is responsible for accounting and financial systems, the second for information and computer systems, and the third for assessing program effectiveness by conducting evaluations.

It is the last of these three technical divisions, the Program Evaluation and Methodology Division, that has the largest number of social scientists in the GAO. Perhaps a full 70 per cent (60 persons) of its professional staff are social scientists. Recruiting is done in universities, public and private research agencies, and in other branches of the government to bring in persons with advanced degrees and who have strong backgrounds and experience in designing and conducting program evaluations.

Persons with social science backgrounds are also found in other parts of the GAO. Each of the four programming divisions have both an 'Economic Analysis Group' and a 'Design, Methodology and Technical Assistance Group' that provide assistance to their respective divisions. Here social scientists would be involved in job design, in developing the measurement approaches, and in the analysis of data. Finally, there are small numbers of social scientists in other parts of the agency as well, though not located in settings that deliberately seek to sustain a critical mass of persons with social science backgrounds. There are approximately 200 social scientists in the GAO.

The social science contributions

The focus for this paper is on the variety of contributions that social science work within the GAO is providing to help meet the information needs of the Congress through supplying sound, carefully crafted, and objective information in a timely and appropriate fashion. It is an underlying premise here that social science analysis is applicable to a broad range of policy and program questions, but it is social science analysis of a particular type. The distinction is between 'question driven' and 'theory driven' analysis. In the GAO, the concern is entirely with the former. Any theoretical development from the work of social science analysis within the agency is a beneficial byproduct – but not one sought or rewarded.

Consequently, while several hundred social scientists are at work in the GAO, the number of theoretical articles or theoretically framed research articles based on Office work and published in the academic journals is quite small. But having said that, the number of substantial reports, briefings, and analyses transmitted to the Congress is quite large. Social science work within the GAO is being conducted, disseminated, and used. It is, quite simply, that the rationale, reference groups, and reward structures are not oriented towards or based on those found in the universities or in private research organizations.

The social science community or, more precisely, the social science communities in the United States are now so large that there can literally be hundreds of social scientists working in one arena, here the Congressional policy-making arena, and be quite distinct from those in other arenas. The research literature produced by these communities need not coincide or ever appear in the same publications. Likewise, the promotion opportunities are on entirely different and not even parallel tracks, and the influence exerted by leaders in one area may not even be known, let alone respected, by persons in other areas. The end result is that an understanding of the role of social science within the GAO has to be approached within the context of the agency mission, the questions posed by the policymakers in the Congress, and the particular phases of the decision-making process where analysis and information can be used.

The framework for this paper will rely on a three part assessment of the kinds of questions posed by policymakers and how it is that each kind of question informs a different aspect of the responsibilities of the U.S. Congress. Specifically, the focus will be on the posing by policymakers of descriptive, normative, and cause and effect questions (cf. U.S. G.A.O., 1984: 1–2, 18). It is in the context of these different kinds of questions that the dialogue is built between the producer and user of social science information. Further, the framing of the analysis for this paper in this way allows an examination of how the use of information gathered from one of these three types of questions can inform decision-making for both policies and program.[2]

A necessary caveat here is that examining the options for Congressional use in this way will not capture all the social science work in the agency nor all the variety of requests from the Congress. But such an approach does allow for analysis of various intersections of social science data and the policy-making process.

In sum, the social science work within the GAO is catholic in its orientation and applications. It is methodologically diverse, cuts across the programmatic and policy areas of the federal government, involves the work of several hundred analysts, and is used to answer different informational needs of Congressional users. Finally it is strongly applied in its orientation, with a clear emphasis upon the responsiveness of the work to the questions posed.

Information area 1: descriptive questions

When a Congressional user poses a descriptive question, the intent is to seek information, as the name implies, about specific conditions or events – the characteristics of individuals receiving benefits from a particular government program, the performance trends for a particular piece of military hardware, the range of training activities provided to unemployed veterans, the construction costs of various nuclear power plants, and so on. Though the development of descriptive material and information is, at first glance, of less complexity than for normative or cause and effect questions, the needs for this kind of information are multiple. Simply stated, being able to provide information on 'What's going on' is not unimportant to policymakers. (Judgements about whether the events, activities, or procedures described are what they ought to be or what impacts they are having lead to normative and cause and effect questions, respectively. These will be discussed in the next two sections.)

Descriptive questions are relevant to a number of Congressional information needs. First, descriptive data are especially important in clarifying the nature of a perceived 'problem'. A good deal of Congressional effort is focused on responding to 'problems' within the country. However, coming to understand just what exactly is the problem, what population is impacted by the condition, what strategies are now in place for responding, what has been the shape of the problem over time, and so on are all questions for which descriptive data are relevant. As but one example, consider the present situation of teenage pregnancy. While there is broad-based agreement currently in the United States that teenage pregnancy is a problem, gathering descriptive information on the characteristics of target populations, trends, existing programs, etc. are all relevant prior to any effort at shaping an appropriate federal response.

What has contributed to this interest in describing and tracking existing problems in recent years is that the Reagan Administration has cut back in many different areas on data collection efforts (cf. Chelimsky, 1985). Health, education and labor statistics are but three areas where there have been notable cuts in support for collecting longitudinal data. The end result of these cut-backs is that the Executive Branch is less able to state what are the current conditions of the problems that they are responsible to address. The Congress, consequently, has had to turn to the GAO and its other Congressional support agencies for increased assistance in gathering and analysing data that describe the problems at hand.[3]

A second use of descriptive data comes from the need for information on how new initiatives sanctioned by the Congress are being implemented. A concern with program and policy implementation is essentially a concern with the process of execution. A number of authors have recently focused on the implementation phase of the policy process as the least understood, and perhaps most critical. The documentation of this lack of attention to the various aspects of implementation is now quite widespread (cf. Rist, 1981: 29). Indeed, Hargrove (1975) already a decade ago described the implementation process as the 'missing link' between policy formation and program operation.

Wollmann (1984: 120–1) describes the limitations in perspective and focus prior to the late 1970s within the social science and policy communities that inhibited any sustained attention to the matter of implementation. He writes:

> The emergent and then dominant approach of evaluation research concentrated on monitoring and causally interpreting the effects and outcomes of policies and programs, while still neglecting the process dimensions of policy and program implementation. This was certainly because of its preference for quasi-experimental designs and quantitative methods that were to meet the methodological requirements of 'few variables, many cases'. Thus, there were difficulties to handle the multiplicity and changeability of variables in the implementation process.

Pressman and Wildavsky (1979: xxi) focused on the link between policies and programs as the appropriate analytic framework for the study of implementation:

> Policies imply theories. Whether stated explicitly or not, policies point to a chain of causation between initial conditions and future consequences. If X, then Y. Policies become programs when, by authoritative action, the initial conditions are created. X now exists. Programs make the theories operational by forging the first link in the causal chain connecting actions to objectives. Given X, we act to obtain Y. Implementation, then, is the ability to forge subsequent links in the causal chain so as to obtain the desired results.

This concern with how the program has developed a set of appropriate strategies to link 'actions to objectives' is of continuing interest to the Congress. Oversight committees in both the Senate and the House of Representatives have as one of their responsibilities the on-going monitoring of existing programs. These oversight committees serve to provide to the Congress a continuing flow of information on the activities, practices, and resource allocations of programs administered by the Executive Branch (cf. Art, 1985). One critical reason for the existence of these oversight committees is that experience has taught that seldom are programs implemented as intended. Without a continuing and systematic attention to the process of implementation, neither sponsors nor detractors from existing programs are able to say just what precisely the program is doing, let alone how well it is doing what it is suppose to do.

One evaluative approach being developed within the Program Evaluation and Methodology Division of the GAO that focuses specifically on implementation analysis is termed the Program Operations and Delivery of Services Examination (PODSE). This examination is designed to provide timely and descriptive information about existing programs. As described in an April, 1983 Methods Paper on the PODSE:

> ... the approach may be used to address congressional interest in one or more of the following topics:
> — the way public programs operate in general, including their objectives, organization, activities, and procedures for addressing problems such as fraud and abuse:
> — how service sites operate for programs that deliver services to individuals, including what services are delivered, how they are delivered, and who provides the services:
> — the views of people associated with public programs – program staff at the Federal, State, and local levels, clients, and others – regarding program operations and service delivery;
> — information about whether actual operational activities, program services, and participation characteristics match legislative requirements;[4] and
> — the identification of any issues requiring congressional consideration.

The PODSE approach has had two field tests to date. The first was used to examine the Runaway and Homeless Youth Program in the Department of Health and Human Services (HHS). The entire field test, from congressional request in October 1981 to the delivery of testimony in May 1982, took 7 months (1983: i).

In the time since that first test, an additional test has been run to further refine the approach. The second test involved an assessment of the practices used in three states on how and where residential placements are made for youth when circumstances dictate that the youth can no longer remain in their home environment. The strength of the PODSE approach is that it is flexible and allows its users to structure data collection and analysis plans to address the specific evaluation questions with which they are concerned. The limitations found in both tests are the same – non-generalizability when judgemental samples are drawn and the data describe conditions at only one point in time.

Information area 2: normative questions

The answers to normative questions always involve a comparison – a comparison between an observed outcome and a stipulated or expected outcome. Normative questions focus on matters of program compliance, conformity, and consistency. These areas are also of considerable interest to the Congress. Whether the question has to do with measuring actual airline repair practices against those established by the Federal

Aeronautical Administration, actual safety procedures in place at a nuclear power plant compared to requirements established by the Nuclear Regulatory Administration, or the number of poor persons receiving food supplements in comparisons to the targets set in the legislation authorizing the program, the Congress frequently comes to the GAO asking for such assessments.

Normative questions add an element not found in descriptive studies – that of a benchmark or criteria against which an observed situation is to be judged. Normative questions need a descriptive base, but they also need a statement of expected level of performance or achievement. The strength of a normative study (when all goes well) lies in the ability to determine whether the performance is as it should be. The weakness lies in the development and acceptance of criteria that can be used as the benchmark against which to compare existing conditions to desired conditions.

This latter point deserves additional elaboration. While it may appear that criteria are self evident for measuring the performance of a program, the actual specifications are frequently much more difficult to achieve than one might think. For example, developing and assessing the standards of care in a nursing home, developing and assessing organizational effectiveness in a complex organization, or tracking dollars through the maze of the Department of Defense procurement practices to see if the funds have been spent correctly are all difficult and time-consuming tasks. In each of these three examples, e.g., the reaching of consensus on standards of health care for Medicare patients in a nursing home, there is the very real possibility that no consensus is even possible. Thus when the findings from a normative study are released, those who are in disagreement frequently direct their attack on the criteria against which the performance is to be judged. And given the judgment call that eventually has to be made on whether any particular criterion is or is not appropriate to the question, there is an inherent vulnerability that cannot be dismissed.

One rationale for Congressional interest in normative questions is that they can be either prospective or retrospective, they can be used to pose questions involving forecasting as well as program evaluation. Framing normative questions prospectively directs attention to whether a program is or is not likely to achieve a stipulated cost savings, rate of participation by a target group, or, for example, reach a goal of constructing a given number of units of low-income housing. While the use of forecasts carries the inherent risk of incorrect projections, they are continually tantalizing to policy-makers because they open a window on the future, however hazy the view might be.

The other way of posing normative questions is to frame them retrospectively – to ask about what has or is presently occurring. Questions of this type find their answers useful in oversight hearings held by different Congressional committees, as well as in the various budget committees where actual performance, when measured against expected performance, becomes a salient consideration in the funding of existing programs. Retrospective analysis, the classical forté of program evaluation, allows for definitive statements on actual program or policy outcomes – the goal was or was not met. There is a constant interest in the Congress for answers to questions of this type ranging from progress in meeting a timetable for the clean-up of hazardous waste sites to bringing a new fighter plane onto operational status.

For the social scientist, answering normative questions is not normally thought of as part of the general methodological repertoire. Focusing on a comparison of observed conditions to expected conditions has been less in the domain of the social sciences and more in auditing, organizational management, and operational research where studies of organizational economy and efficiency predominate. The movement of social scientists into this area has coincided with more attention to the measurement of the performance criteria. Further, social science emphasis upon construct validity has played an important role in being able to say just what exactly is being compared or contrasted. Operationalizing concepts like 'adequate nursing home care', 'successful completion of operational tests' for a missile, and restoring polluted rivers to a condition where they are 'swimable and fishable' can create the measurement challenges of interest to many social scientists. Working in the GAO has created a number of opportunities to explore the social science contributions to the answering of normative questions. Considerable expansion of social science efforts in addressing questions of this type can easily be anticipated over the next five to ten years.

Information area 3: cause-and-effect questions

To answer a cause-and-effect question is to answer whether the observed conditions one finds can be attributed to the program policy designed to impact that condition. In its most classical form, the social science approach to cause-and-effect questions has been through the use of experimental or quasi-experimental designs. By comparing one group of individuals, one neighborhood, one natural forest campsite, or one job training program to a comparable group or setting when there is as much similarity as can be achieved, save for the important (or perhaps not so important as the outcomes may attest) difference that a program, policy, or treatment is present in one and not the other, one can test for the impact of the intervention. To say an intervention had an impact necessitates testing for alternative explanations and only when they have been examined and justifiably discarded, can one posit that the observed outcome is the result of the program or policy.

The answers to cause-and-effect questions are especially helpful to the Congress in holding accountable those individuals and organizations responsible for the administration and performance of government initiatives. If a cause-and-effect relation can be established between the program or policy and the existing condition or event, then the decision-maker is confronted with the bottom-line: has the measured performance of this policy or program been such that it warrants further support. Here is where accountability and performance becomes linked.

The challenge for the social scientist working on studies of this type is a most difficult one. Cause-and-effect questions are the hardest to answer confidently. There are frequently problems of measurement, sampling, dealing with situations or events where there are likely to be multiple causes and multiple effects, and where the condition or event to be studied is undergoing such continuous change that to focus on outcomes is to try and hold still that which cannot be done. Nevertheless, cause-and-effect studies are undertaken within the GAO. Examples from the Program Evaluation and Methodology Division would include measuring whether existing retirement policies in the U.S. Marine Corps are encouraging early retirement among the higher quality officers, and what impacts constructed water pollution treatment facilities have had on the quality of various rivers and streams.

Though cause-and-effect studies are surely the most difficult to conduct (in comparison to descriptive or normative studies), the consequences can be greater and longer lasting. Good analysis of the impacts of a program or policy not only address the basic question of utility, but can loop back to influence either existing implementation strategies or the next round of policy and program formulation. That is, judgement and guidance necessary to decision-making can be derived in part from information on the impacts, consequences, and outcomes of current or previous efforts. Cause-and-effect studies can provide the linkage between knowing about current responses to a problem or threat and making judgements on what to do (or not to do) next.

It should be apparent from this discussion why there would be congressional interest in having the GAO conduct cause-and-effect studies. There are uses for such analysis in the oversight committees, in the authorizing committees where legislation is considered to authorize new programs as well as reauthorize or eliminate existing programs, and in the appropriations committees where data on current impacts can influence decisions on levels of financial support. Thus in all three basic types of congressional committees, focusing on the impacts of existing policies and programs provides opportunities for congressional use of the information.

But, lest it be assumed that the GAO rushes into conducting as many cause-and-effect studies as is organizationally and methologically possible, a disclaimer is needed. A realistic estimate would be that approximately five to ten percent of the studies GAO has underway at any one time are answering cause-and-effect questions. This is so for a variety of reasons. First, they tend to be long term, and not many congressional committees want to wait eighteen months or two years for data from such a study. Second, studies of this type tend to be methodologically complex and technically most difficult to execute. Thus, the risks in undertaking such a study are greater. Third, the necessary data simply are not always available. There are many more good impact questions to be posed than there are good data to answer them. And fourth, they tend to absorb the greatest amount of staff resources, i.e., conducting one cause-and-effect study may equal the staff allocation necessary for two studies that pose descriptive or normative questions. The end result is that making the judgement to undertake a cause-and-effect study has to be done in the context of recognizing costs as well as benefits. While there are many aspects to such a study that are highly attractive, there are constraints that will not go away. Consequently, across the range of studies that the GAO would have underway at any one time – and there were approximately 900 studies underway in May 1986 – only a small portion of them can or should take on the challenge of determining cause-and-effect relations within a policy or program.

Congressional questions, social science answers

While this is not the place to start a second chapter, there are a few brief comments necessary to complete the discussion. First, this paper has not sought to deal with the matter of utilization. While much has been written on the subject, and indeed, there are a variety of models which portend to explain the relation of social science research to the decision-making process (cf. Anderson, 1984; Weiss and Bucuvalas, 1980), suffice it to say here that the uses of GAO work by the Congress happen in multiple and sometimes totally unpredictable ways. Any effort to portray the linkage as linear has to be resisted. This paper is not predicated on the point that social science work is always used, but only that it is frequently and continually asked for. The uses do seem to be there, but, candidly, the view from the vantage of the producers is sometimes blurred. There are only those few occasions where the complexity of the decision-making process diminishes, and some direct linkage – however tenuous – can be made between a particular piece of analysis and a particular decision.

Second, what this paper has also not addressed, but seems to be an interesting topic to explore is the relation between the development of social science research capability in the Executive Branch and in the congressional support agencies. I think it fair to say that the Executive Branch began sponsoring broad scale social science research and bringing its findings into the decision-making process some five to ten years earlier than did the Congress. But what needs further study is the way in which a new form of information in one sector of the government drove needs for a parallel and countervailing source of that information in another. It was as if social science work became a destabilizing force in the balance of power between the executive and congressional branches of government.

Placing this strain in the midst of the expansion of the government's role in domestic social programs in the 1960s meant that without its own source of such information, the Congress was left with what social science research and findings the Executive Branch chose to share. The establishment of the Office of Technology Assessment in 1972, the Congressional Budget Office in 1974, and the Institute for Program Evaluation (to become the Program Evaluation and Methodology Division) within the GAO in 1980 are but three examples of responses within the Congressional domain of efforts to strengthen scientific and analytic capabilities. (Parenthetically, something of the same scenario is now working itself out between the federal government and the various state governments. As the federal government devolves responsibility for more and more programs to the state level, the states are having to develop their own analytic capabilities. Depending upon federal data sources to manage and guide state-level policies and programs is a circumstance increasing numbers of state officials do not enjoy.)

Finally, and while it may seem somewhat presumptuous to say, the future is encouraging for social science work being used in Congressional deliberations. The nature of the problems and threats being addressed by the federal government are growing more and more complex. No one mode of analysis, no one strategy for forecasting or modeling will suffice, no one definition of the situation is any longer unquestioningly accepted. The Congress has become a marketplace for ideas, debates, perspectives, ideologies, and facts. Further, the staffs working on the various committees and for the individual members now frequently have advanced graduate training and can use sophisticated analyses as a routine part of their work. It is not far from the mark to say that many of the Congressional offices are now staffed with their own small 'think tanks'. Technocrats are in the ascendancy in many of the more than 250 Congressional committees and subcommittees.

There is, very definitely, a demand for good analysis – a demand outpacing supply. GAO has responded to these shifts in a number of ways. One has involved increasing its capability to conduct social science work. How that has been happening and what questions social scientists subsequently have been addressing has been the theme of this chapter.

NOTES

1 A number of commentators on the GAO have cited the Prouty Amendment to the Economic Opportunity Act of 1967 which required the GAO to assess the effectiveness of the 'Great Society' poverty programs as the turning point in Congressional expectations and demands for new types of information and analysis (cf. Mosher, 1984; Wisler, 1986). By 1969, GAO had produced almost fifty reports on the poverty programs.
2 The opportunity to address both policies and programs is important because of the interactive relationship between policies and programs: formulating policies has to be done within the context of what programmatic options are available to bring that policy into reality; likewise, experience and expertise in developing programs and generating operational infrastructures impact upon the range of considerations for policy formulation. Policies represent objectives, agendas, perspectives, and decisions on direction; programs represent structural and organizational means by which policies are translated into activities, efforts and resource allocations.
3 This concern has been evident in congressional inquiries on both domestic social issues and a number of foreign policy and national security matters. For example, if longitudial data indicate that the problem or the threat has changed, what implications does that have for existing programs and policies. Likewise, and perhaps no less important, what implications are there for existing policies and programs if conditions have not changed, but there was an anticipation that there would be change. Congressional concern frequently expresses itself, consequently, by means of requests for information that tracks conditions over time, be these levels of poverty, available health care to the elderly, number of minority students gaining access to college loan programs, or combat readiness of U.S. troops in Europe.
4 It is here that the PODSE methodology shades over into a concern with normative questions as well. The emphasis on comparing actual conditions to stipulated requirements is what generates the normative question.

REFERENCES

Anderson, D. (1984), 'The Use of Social Science Knowledge in Formulation of Policy Advice', Canberra, Australia, National Clearinghouse for Youth Studies, Australian National University.

Art, R. (1985), 'Congress and the Defense Budget: Enhancing Policy Oversight', *Political Science Quarterly*, vol. 100, No. 2, pp. 227–49.

Chelimsky, E. (1985), 'Budget Cuts, Data, and Evaluation', *Society*, vol. 22, No. 3, pp. 65–73.

Hargrove, E. (1975), *The Missing Link: The Study of Implementation of Social Policy*. Washington, D.C.: The Urban Institute.

Mosher, F. C. (1984), *A Tale of Two Agencies: A Comparative Analysis of the GAO and the OMB*, Baton Rouge, LA, Louisiana State University Press.

Pressman, J. and A. Wildavsky (1979), *Implementation*. (2nd ed.) Berkeley, University of California Press.

Rist, R. C. (1981), *Earning and Learning: Youth Employment Policies and Programs*, Beverly Hills, CA., Sage Publications.

United States General Accounting Office, Program Evaluation and Methodology Division (1983), *Program Operations and Delivery of Services Examination, Methodology Transfer Paper No. 2*, Washington, D.C.

United States General Accounting Office, Program Evaluation and Methodology Division (1984), *Designing Evaluations, Methodology Transfer Paper No. 4*, Washington, D.C.

Weiss, C. H. and M. J. Bucuvalas (1980), *Social Science Research and Decision-making*, New York, Columbia University Press.

Wisler, C. (1986), 'Topics in Evaluation', *GAO Review*, Vol. 20, No. 2.

Wollmann, H. (1984), 'Emergence and Development of Policy Research in the U.S.A.', in G. Thurn, et al., *Development and Present State of Public Policy Research: Country Studies in Comparative Perspective*, Berlin, West Germany, Wissenschaftszentrum, pp. 101–30.

CHAPTER 17

Comparative aspects of randomized experiments for planning and evaluation

ROBERT F. BORUCH

You remember what Quetelet wrote '... Put down what you expect from such and such legislation, after ... see where it has given what you expected. But you change your laws and your administration of them so fast, and without an inquiry after results past or present, that it is all experiment, see-saw, doctrinaire, a shuttlecock between two battledores.'

Florence Nightingale Letter to Sir Francis Galton 7 February 1891

0. Introduction

Miss Nightingale's remarks are no longer as accurate as they once were, of course. Governments do, at times, try to discover the results of their action. Her letter is relevant to contemporary problems, however, in that the discovery process often involves haphazard methods or post facto inquiry that fail to yield relatively unambiguous evidence.

This paper covers a special approach to producing less equivocal evidence about the effect of government action: randomized field experiments. The idea of randomized tests is not new. Its origins lay in Sir Ronald Fisher's (1935) work early in this century. What is new is the increasing use of the technology, in the U.S. and elsewhere, to produce evidence, and the development of administrative, scientific, and political skills to apply the technology in field settings.

In particular, this is an analytic account of the use of the technology of randomized tests and the policy uses of data that the technology produces. The stress is on comparative issues, including historical development, in a variety of discipline areas. The areas include medicine, education, criminal justice and law enforcement, tax compliance, manpower training, welfare, and mental health.

The analysis, though primitive, suggests some ways to better understand why, when, and how randomized field tests are sensible. The general conclusion is that common problems of field experiments are old and not confined by discipline boundaries. Indeed the similarities in perspective and problems are striking.

1. Definition and examples

Randomized experiment here means the random assignment of individuals (or institutions or other units) to one or two or more program regimens in order to permit a fair comparison of the relative effects of the regimens, and (b) a quantitative statement about one's certainty in the comparison. Fair comparison means unbiased estimates of effects, estimates that are not tangled by competing explanations about what caused the effect (Riecken, et al., 1974). The procedure is denominated as a randomized clinical trial (RCT) in medical research (e.g., Moses and Brown, 1984) and as randomized field experiment in the social, behavioral and economic literature (references below).

The examples given next illustrate some recent field experiments designed to inform policy and the applied social sciences. See Boruch, McSweeny and Soderstrom (1978) for an early bibliography.

1.1 Employment and training

Tests of new training and employment programs have been supported by the U.S. Department of Labor and the Rockefeller and Ford Foundations, among others. In the best of these field experiments, eligible individuals were randomly assigned to a special training and income support regimen or to a control condition in which only conventional services were offered (e.g., Manpower Development and Research Corporation, 1980). The object of such a randomized experiment has been determining whether the special programs would increase wages and employment relative to ordinary services. The random assignment avoided the chronic problem of earlier econometric analyses. For instance, individuals usually select themselves into novel and existing programs. Individuals selecting new programs can be expected to differ in unknown and unknowable ways from those who select conventional services. The self selection effect is inseparable from the effect of the program in most analyses unless one makes heroic assumptions *or* one randomizes.

1.2 Tax compliance
Recent U.S. Internal Revenue Service interests lie in understanding which of several administrative strategies would increase
payment of delinquent taxes. Delinquent taxpayers were randomly
assigned to the alternative IRS strategies, then tracked to determine
which strategies yielded the best returns on investment. The random
assignment procedure obviates a variety of inferential problems engendered by simply introducing a management change and monitoring its
effect. For instance, geographic variation in press coverage of convicted
delinquents is substantial. But the effect of such press coverage on
reduction of delinquency is usually impossible or difficult to estimate
precisely despite the IRS's belief that 'press coverage works' (Perng,
1985). Controlled tests in which small geographic areas are randomly
designated to prosecute cases that are especially newsworthy are at times
feasible to gauge the effect of coverage. Procedures other than press
coverage, such as the tone and content of warning letters, are important,
too, and warrant experimentation.

1.3 Police procedures
In the Minneapolis Domestic Violence experiment, the object
was to understand how police should handle calls on domestic violence
cases (Sherman and Berk, 1984). Within certain limits set by police,
cases (calls to a home) were randomly assigned to three different
methods of handling: arrest, mandatory mediation, or immediate temporary separation. The main object was to determine which of these
regimens produced the lowest level of subsequent domestic violence in
households.
The integrity of the determination was sustained by the randomization. That is, families in each regimen were equivalent on account of
the random assignment. Competing explanations common in earlier
nonrandomized studies could be ruled out. Such competing explanations
included differential police preferences for one or another way to handle
the violence complaint. The experiment helped to inform a fifteen-year
debate on handling such cases and is likely to be repeated in other cities
to assure the generalizability of the findings (Sherman and Hamilton,
1984).

1.4 Treatment of mental depression
The National Institute of Mental Health has undertaken multi-
site trials to understand the effectiveness of different forms of psycho-
therapy for various patient populations. The trials involve random
assignment of patients from a pool of relevant consenting patients to one

of three promising approaches to treating therapy: a specialized brief form of cognitive behavior therapy, pharmacotherapy with clinical management, and placebo with clinical management. The purpose of randomization in this arena is no different from the purpose in randomized clinical trials of new surgical techniques or drugs. The main object is estimating relative effectiveness of treatments in a way that assures that estimates are not *systematically* contaminated by unknowable extraneous influences such as physician or patient preferences and beliefs (Collins and Elkin, 1985). The groups being compared are equivalent in the long run by virtue of randomization; the measurement is 'blind' in the jargon of the medical researcher.

1.5 Experiments and discipline area

Randomized experiments have been conducted in a variety of other discipline areas. To get some sense of the differences in frequency across area, consider Table 1. The table includes experiments reported between 1927 and 1978. Criminal and civil justice experiments are high in frequency. They include police experiments as well as experiments to improve court procedures described later. Field tests of education and training regimens are even more common. Most of the education experiments, however, involve small samples, e.g., 30–50 students with some being assigned to a new teaching approach, the remainder being assigned to a conventional one.

The social welfare experiments are much less frequent by comparison but are large in size. The MDRC experiment cited earlier involved over 1,500 participants, for instance. Similarly some of the experiments in information collection are dedicated to testing various ways to reduce respondent burden or to increase respondent candor in surveys. These can involve several thousand participants.

Table 1 *Categories of randomized experiments*

1. Criminal and civil justice	76
2. Mental health	36
3. Training and education	96
4. Mass communications	6
5. Information collection, transmission, and retrieval	47
6. Research utilization	11
7. Commerce, industry, and public utilities	17
8. Social welfare: casework, housing, insurance and other support programs	18
9. Fertility control	12

2. Understanding the effects of programs and projects

2.1 Episodic interest in evidence

Understanding whether societal programs work and how well they work is not a new problem. But formal government attention to quality of evidence bearing on that understanding has been episodic, as Nightingale suggests.

In the fourteenth century, for instance, the North African polymath, Ibn Khaldun, urged his readers to seek the causes of institutional and social change vigorously, to be skeptical of simple before-after analyses of government policy, and to assay conscientiously the quality of numerical evidence on change and of government action. The Mogul emperor Akbar supported development of the Institutes, a compendium that helped to describe economic and other aspects of the Indian empire. These anticipated John Graunt's (1662) magnificent *Bills of Mortality*, a statistical effort to describe the state and course of British institutions and to present some data for use in policy.

In the United States, as elsewhere, exploiting high-quality information about social problems was episodic, rather than sustained, until the 1960s. For instance, it was not until the nineteenth century that the country systematically confronted major flaws in the decennial censuses, taking longer to rectify them, despite the periodic recognition of problems in Europe, and elsewhere as early as the fourteenth century (Davis, 1972).

Rectification was stimulated by crisis. In the 1840 census, for example, black residents of entire villages were enumerated as insane by interviewers with more political zeal than integrity (Regan, 1973). The remedial action, appointments of census directors and regular staff partly on the basis of merit rather than on politics alone, helped. But another 80 years passed before the Census Bureau initiated a program of routine side studies on the quality of census data.

The occasional efforts of citizen's groups to collect reliable data bearing on social programs is also detectable in nineteenth-century Europe. Lecuyer and Oberschall (1968), for instance, attribute the appearance of local statistical societies in England during the 1830s to the general interest in social reform. The societies apparently organized social research of a quantitative sort to investigate health, prostitution, working conditions of the poor, and education. Similar groups appeared in post-revolutionary France and in Germany during the middle 1800s. For the United States, Kaestel and Visnovsky (1980) suggest that it is 'no accident that the appearance of the first systematic school statistics coincides with the educational reforms of the late 1830s and 1840s. The data were a crucial tool for reformers in their public relations efforts' (p. 10). The spirit of the enterprise reappeared in England in 1927 with the mass observation movement, propelled by the belief that *anyone* can make systematic inquiries about social phenomena (Barnes, 1979, pp. 51–2).

2.2 Randomized experiments: invention and early use

Sir Ronald Fisher produced the unique logical contribution to appraising evidence that is of special interest here: the randomized experiment. The most common early applications of the method were in Sir Ronald's arena – agriculture. He argued that parcels of a field ought to be randomly assigned to one or another of different fertilizer to understand the relative effects of nutrients. The point was to estimate effects despite complex variation in soil composition, drainage, and other factors. The introduction of randomized tests to agriculture was not accomplished without debate. Logic, rather than clear evidence on the usefulness of the method or mathematical theory, seems to have been used to gain acceptance for the idea. The method is generally accepted in agricultural research as the preferred one for making comparisons. Still, demonstrations of the design's utility appear occasionally, perhaps to keep at bay the aggressively naive experimenter (e.g., Harshberger, 1974).

There were early attempts to introduce the technology of randomized experiments to other arenas. They include experiments on sanitation instruction in Syria during 1931–3, on the benefits of raw versus pasteurized milk at Lanarkshire (Student, 1931), and tests of alternative methods for encouraging people to vote in the U.S. Presidential election of 1924 (Gosnell, 1927).

The earliest randomized field tests of medical regimens were undertaken in the early 1930s. But large scale well-designed randomized field tests in medicine did not become common until the 1960s. The Salk trials, designed to compare alternative ways to reduce polio incidence, were a milestone (Meier, 1972). The proportion of such trials reported in medical journals has increased from 9 per cent in 1963 to 46 per cent in 1978. Of the remainder, most appear to use no controls at all (Chalmers & Schroeder, 1979.) A fair number of poorly designed evaluations continue to be carried out (Cochran, 1976).

The execution of randomized field tests of projects in the physical sciences has not been especially routine. Judging from Braham (1979), efforts to mount scientific tests of weather modification methods can be traced to 1946, for example. This is despite a long history of elaborate rituals alleged to produce rain and naive attempts to estimate the effects

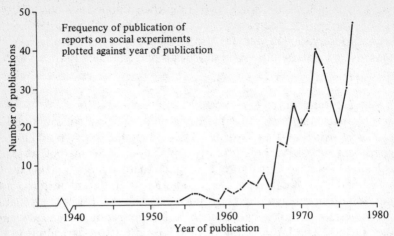

Fig 1 Frequency of publication of reports on social experiments plotted against year of publication

of the rituals. Braham suggests further that the first fifteen years of these tests led to no useful information about cloud seeding, but they did yield research tools useful in the tests. Actual randomized trials were not mounted until the 1960s.

2.3 Contemporary interest in randomized experiments: social programs

In the United States, government interests in using randomized field experiments to plan and evaluate social programs began in the late 1950s. To understand the dramatic rise in randomized experimentation from 1944 to 1977, see Figure 1. It is based on a bibliography on *virtually* all social experiments mounted during the period, and listed in Boruch, McSweeny, and Soderstrom (1978). Surgical experiments are excluded.

The main scientific justification for interest of the 1960s was less biased, less ambiguous estimates of the effect of programs, notably evidence on the success of welfare and education programs for the poor. This concern was reflected in products of U.S. organizations dedicated to science policy, e.g., the President's Commission on Federal Statistics, the President's Science Advisory Committee, the Brookings Institution, and the Social Science Research Council.

In the early 1970s, for instance, the Social Science Research Council was asked to take stock of the experiments and develop suggestions for policy. The SSRC work led to a state of the art monograph (Riecken et al., 1974). It was the best single treatment of managerial, political, institutional, ethical, legal and scientific problems engendered by doing good experiments. It outlined problems in each area and partial solutions that were relevant to most of the social and behavioral sciences.

Randomized tests are still a *minority* among methods used in contemporary efforts to evaluate programs and projects. This is true in agriculture, despite the work of Fisher and others. Bengston's (1985) review of agriculture research, for example, suggests that *ex post facto* research methods are dominant. The material examined by Farrington (1983) suggests that randomized tests constitute, at most, 20 percent of the evaluations of crime and justice programs. Randomized tests are in a minority in educational project evaluations (Boruch, et al., 1981), tax compliance, health services research and other areas.

This minority status does not imply they are unimportant. Indeed, their importance far outweighs what one might expect from their frequency.

2.4 The role of evidence in expansionist and reductionist policies

In the United States, the 1960s and 1970s were expansionist in the sense that government provided increasing services to the disadvantaged. The Great Society ideas were often innovative. Where there was opportunity to innovate, there was also opportunity to experiment formally, to assess the consequences of the innovation. And in fact, the major economic experiments were undertaken during this period.

This interest in assessment is a fine *scientific* rationale for experiments. It may also serve the scholar-bureaucrat well. The rationale does *not* appear to be sufficient to initiate controlled experiments early in an expansionist period, however. Rather, the demand for evidence from the competing *nonexpansionist* camp appears to have led to demands for better evidence at least in the United States. For the cautious legislator, evidence from field experiments may have also played a role in deciding whether and how to support or oppose legislation.

The Reagan Administration, unlike the previous administrations, has been reductionist in orientation. This, in Reagan's first term, led to drastic cutbacks in programs *regardless* of evidence on their worth.

During the second term of office, however, the administration has exhibited considerably more interest in learning more about evidence for effectiveness of new variations on *existing* social programs and new approaches to cost reductions, law enforcement and compliance-related programs. Some of the pressure to present evidence comes from the opposition party. Randomized experiments are a natural vehicle for obtaining evidence in both areas.

For example, the Internal Revenue Service Conference on Tax

Compliance Research (January, 1985) put strong emphasis on the use of experiments to better understand whether and why new tax compliance programs work to encourage people to pay their taxes. This extends earlier efforts by Schwartz and Orleans (1967) to experiment formally on alternative moral appeals to encourage thorough reporting of taxable income. Similarly, law enforcement is a high priority for conservative governments. Under the Reagan administration, the stress is reflected in efforts to mount city-wide tests on effective police handling of domestic violence (e.g. Sherman and Berk, 1984).

3. Framework: pre-theory

Consider a simple framework to guide thinking about the use of *any* information, including the technology of randomized experiments. A rudimentary but sensible framework involves addressing four questions:

(a) Does the prospective user of information, such as the technology of randomized experiments, *know* about the information (i.e., the technology)?
(b) Does the prospective user *understand* the information?
(c) Is the user *capable* of using the information?
(d) Is the user *willing* to use the information?

This is a pre-theoretical approach. It lends itself, however, to a small 'theory of information utilization'. Each question implies measurement, for instance. Further, a probabilistic model is implicit in the sequential process suggested by the questions.

4. The technology of randomized experiments and its uses

4.1 Knowing

In 1960 there existed no major textbooks dedicated to randomized field experiments in economics, law or criminal justice, mental health, or education. By 1985, the Federal Judicial Center (1983) produced a major monograph on court experiments. The economic community received Ferber and Hirsch (1982), an excellent work on field experiments designed to understand the effects of negative income tax on welfare reliance and work behavior, of housing supports for the poor, and of peak load pricing in energy consumption. For research in mental health, Fairweather and Tornatsky (1977) produced a fine volume on how, when and why randomized tests of rehabilitation programs can be run. These and related monographs usually cite Campbell and Stanley's

(1963) work on ways to get evidence. It was distinctive in informing the reader about randomized experiments, especially in education. It was much more distinctive in strengthening understanding of the merits and shortcomings of alternatives to randomized texts.

Apart from textbooks, there have also been major changes in who appears to know about experiments. Whereas in 1965, few members of the U.S. General Accounting Office were informed about the topic, in 1985 an entire division is dedicated to relevant techniques, i.e., the Program Evaluation and Methodology Division directed by Eleanor Chelimsky (see Chapter 16). Similarly, the Evaluation Division of the Food and Nutrition Service of the U.S. Department of Agriculture has well-informed staff who write about the methods *and* tell legislators what they can do to increase the quality of evidence at their disposal. Much the same can be said of the National Institute of Justice, the U.S. Department of Education, the National Center for Health Services Research. This is based on the contracts issued by such organizations and on the published papers of their staff members (e.g. Chelimsky, 1985).

There are certainly variations in knowing within such organizations and within the disciplines that they may draw on. But it would be difficult to maintain that only a few scholars 'know', given the incidence of journal articles in education, psychology, sociology, law, social services and elsewhere on the topic.

Knowing about the technology at the political level is another matter of course. It is clear that politicians must be educated and reminded about what constitutes fair tests of projects, at least in the United States, for their training and backgrounds often do not include serious attention to numerical evidence. And moreover, political appointees are short lived – a term of office of 1.4 years is average. The responsibility for educating these migrant laborers falls to the scholar-bureaucrat.

4.2 Understanding

Understanding randomization is essential in scientific forums that lead to choice about how to design an experiment. The understanding did not come easily to Fisher himself. Nor did he always find it easy to communicate to colleagues.

He explained it in homely ways, in response to critics who maintained that one ought to select and assign purposively, i.e., to assure similarity of the groups to be compared. 'Systematic arrangements (the purposive selection) are devised to deal with only certain sort of devilish scheme', he said. 'But the devil may choose any arrangement, even that for which the systematic design is least appropriate . . .' (Box, 1978, p. 145). To avoid the devilish scheme, Fisher argued that one ought to rely on chance as well as on what is known.

The theory of chance is an important ingredient for the argument. It was developed for experiments between 1918 and 1923 and debated until at least the 1930s in agriculture in the face of an older generation of agricultural experimenters (Box, 1978).

The debate about whether randomized experiments are ideal continues in the applied research at the local policy level. But there are a variety of scholarly review papers in various disciplines that display *no* essential disagreement about the scientific merit of randomized tests. This includes Farrington (1983) on criminal justice, Freeman and Rossi (1981) on health services research, Hollister (1985) and others on manpower experimenters.

Differences that *do* appear in scholarly debate about randomized tests often concern two issues:

(a) Do other methods produce as accurate an estimate of project effect as a randomized experiment? That is, what do we know from *empirical comparisons*?

(b) Are randomized experiments feasible? More to the point, have they been conducted?

The issues are also considered in policy forums insofar as academic scholars contribute to these, and to the extent that forum participants are scholar-bureaucrats or are well informed political representatives.

Empirical comparisons, the idea of comparing outcomes of a randomized experiment to results achieved in nonrandomized trials, is not new. To clarify Fisher's arguments with Gosset in the 1930s, Fisher himself appears to have tried such a comparison in experiments on wheat (Box, 1978, p. 269) and in reanalyzing Charles Darwin's data on stock fertilization. In the first case, it is clear that results of the experiment differ from those of the quasi-experiment. In the second, they do not.

Similar comparisons have been undertaken by medical researchers. Randomized trials on the Salk vaccine, for example, gave estimates of the vaccine's effect that differed from estimates based on nonrandomized quasi-experiments (Meier, 1972). The battle over when randomized tests are appropriate in medicine is not done, in the U.S. at least (Fried, 1974). What remains to be done in this arena includes increasing capacity and willingness to do experiments, if we may judge from the Institute of Medicine's new report on post-marketing surveillance for drugs and other technologies.

A major recent set of comparisons have been undertaken in manpower training and employment. The tradition of evaluating programs in this area has been based on econometric models. That is, in the absence of a randomized trial, one posits an explicit statistical model on which to base estimates of program effect. That conventional models are often *wrong* seems clear from work by Fraker and Maynard (1985). In particular, a broad array of such models produced results that differed widely from randomized tests of programs on similar populations for youth. They did *not* differ appreciably for samples of welfare-supported women with children. The important lesson here, as in the Salk trials and in other cases (Boruch, 1976), is that one cannot be sure beforehand that a nonrandomized design will produce the same results as a randomized set-up.

Other persuasive evidence stems from investigating groups of program evaluations. Gordon and Morse (1975), for example, found remarkably different estimates of social program effects when the evaluation design was taken into account. Glass and Smith (see Light and Pillemer, 1984) found differences in tests of the effect of class size on students' learning, when the quality of experimental design was taken into account. In a fascinating series of papers, Chalmers and his colleagues find analogous differences (see Chalmers, et al., 1982, and references therein). Little recent evidence of a similar sort, however, appears to have been generated in nutrition research, criminal justice, or law enforcement.

The randomization procedure avoids the need for elaborate statistical models whose assumptions, though explicit, are often untestable. The battle between modellers and randomizers began in 1935 between Fisher and Neyman (Box, 1977, p. 265). It continues insofar as modellers are willing to trust their model and cannot invent (or imagine) experiments that help to test that trust. It continues insofar as the experimentalists distrust the models, plump for experiments, and do not have the resources to conduct the experiments that help to test the models.

An ostensible difference among all discipline areas is the stress on nonrandomized approaches to estimating project or program effects. In psychology and education, the relevant methodological work falls under the rubric of 'quasi-experimentation'. The work on this topic, by Campbell and Stanley (1963) has been translated into at least four languages and is seminal.

The word quasi-experimentation is not common in literature on medical trials or economics. Mantel (1976) uses it, but he makes no reference to earlier work; nor is there any reference to it in any issue of *Clinical Trials* at hand. Some of the analytic techniques in biometrics and econometrics clearly fall into this arena. The linkages are among methods unrecognized on account of disciplinary parochialism, jargon, or both.

4.3 Capacity to experiment

Randomized experiments are more feasible than one might expect. About 300 are cataloged in Boruch, McSweeny, and Soderstrom (1978). The review papers cited earlier give evidence on field experiments mounted since then. We know also that pilot testing of field tests is warranted where there is no precedent (Boruch, 1982). The more interesting issues concern the conditions under which they are most feasible. This leads naturally to discussion of one's capacity to experiment and willingness to use experiments.

'Capacity' here means access to competent staff, resources such as money and time, the control that is needed and can be exercised to experiment, and the tolerability or tractability of constraints on the randomization process.

Staff. No good experiments are mounted without an able cadre that has *some* assurance of sustained support. In the U.S., the resources expended on program evaluation generally have led to private, for-profit and not-for-profit organizations developing the requisite skills. These organizations engage in a competitive bidding process to provide the human resources necessary to plan and execute the field experiment.

Some are specialized. The Manpower Development Research Corporation (Gueron and Nathan, 1985) and Mathematica Policy Research (Hollister, Kemper, and Maynard, 1984), for example, dedicate their attention to experimental tests of human resource programs. The Police Foundation in Washington, D.C. has undertaken tests of police patrol strategies and alternative ways of handling domestic violence (Sherman and Berk, 1984). Organizations that cast a wider net in their applied social research, such as Abt Associates, have done fine experimental tests of alternative ways to reduce costs of daycare programs for pre-school children and to find effective methods of nutrition education (St. Pierre, et al., 1982). Rand's health insurance experiments are well known (Newhouse, et al., 1979). The Stanford Research Institute has had considerable experience in the negative income tax arena (Ferber and Hirsch, 1978; 1982). These are supplemented often (and displaced at times) by university based groups, e.g., Hahn and Friedman (1981) at Brandeis University

No similar private organizations have achieved national eminence in conduct of experiments on theraputic programs in mental health or in evaluating education programs, or law-related programs.

Control and constraints. An important lesson of Ross Conner's (1977) study of twelve field experiments is that controlling the randomization process counts heavily in a successful social experiment. Control is no less important in medical randomized trials of course. Nordle and Brantmark (1977), for example, took pains to discuss whether plans for randomization in drug effectiveness experiments can be too easily subverted by clinicians involved in the trials.

The lack of control over randomization accounts at least partly for failures of TV experiments in El Salvador, and the Roos et al. (1977) trials in health services. It accounts partly for the problems encountered by Bickman (1985) in studying nutrition programs for the elderly.

The mechanism for exercising control varies considerably. In the Internal Revenue Service tax compliance experiments described by Perng (1985) centralized control over randomization is a natural part of the administrative process. Hard-won experience with more loosely coupled social systems lead to the use of centralized random assignment (by telephone) in the MDRC work/welfare tests that Gueron (1985) describes. That is, welfare program staff provided some client information to MDRC and assignment to alternative regimens was made from random numbered tables constructed to generate blocks and groups. Telephone-based blind assignment was also used by Collins and Elkin (1985) in tests of treatment of mental depression and by Goldman (1977) in experiments on how to reduce time in court using pre-trial hearings.

The Police Foundation's approach has been less direct in that policemen were responsible for assigning based on a 'randomization pad'. But here, surveillance was possible to assure adherence to rule (Sherman and Berk, 1984).

Exercising control also implies limits on control: the physicians' relinquishing part of their influence over the treatment of a patient in experimental tests of surgical techniques, for instance, and this presents a major ethical problem (Fried, 1974). Similar tension over diminished or shared professional power, is evident in judicial experiments (Goldman, 1977), police experiments (Sherman and Berk, 1984), educational experiments, and others. Exclusionary rules are crucial discretion for the courts (for example, the pre-trial hearings experiments), to program staff (for example, the Minneapolis Domestic Violence Experiments) or to assure compliance with statute (Breger, 1983) or regulation (for example, the Work/Welfare Initiatives project).

The lesson of these is that exclusions must be prescribed. If exclusionary rules or custom cannot be anticipated, then pilot randomization tests are warranted. The pilot test tactic has been used well in research

332   Robert F. Boruch

by Corsi (1983) in preparing for administrative law experiments, among others.

Negotiation and control. A social experiment is, as Riecken and others (1974) observe, a political act. It demands recognition of political-institutional realities, including the need to negotiate with a variety of stakeholders.

For example, the early discussions leading to Corsi's (1983) experiment concerned whether due process in welfare appeals cases was indeed met through telephone hearings instead of the more conventional in-person hearings, whether administrative agencies had authority to use the innovative telephone approach, whether random assignment was really necessary to compare telephone to in-person hearings. The negotiations involved a half dozen government agencies, assorted public administrators and lawyers; discussions gradually clarified concerns of these stakeholders.

Sherman and Berk focused on the law enforcement decision chain in the Minneapolis experiment. The sponsoring agency's concerns about ethical issues were handled partly through discussion of the sparse evidence concerning police effectiveness of handling of domestic violence. Interest groups' objections had to be met with evidence and argument too. Mayoral support in two administrations had to be developed. Meetings and retreats with beat cops and their supervisors appear to have been frequent and effective in handling concerns and objections.

The Work/Welfare Demonstrations (Gueron, 1986) also demanded considerable negotiation and planning, partly because eight state governments were involved. And as in many such ventures, the negotiation can be productive in both assuring that the experimental design is executed and in capitalizing on local expertise to nail down details, introduce good ideas, and assure realism.

Resources: time and money. No useful information on how much experiments cost has been consolidated. No journal articles or books reporting results report such information. This prevents benefit-cost analysis of individual experiments and comparing relative costs and benefits across discipline areas (e.g., Mosteller and Weinstein, 1985). All this is despite the Social Science Research Council's efforts, among others, to encourage such reports (Boruch, 1976) and complaints of economists, such as Nobel Laureate Theodore Schultze (1982) that economists, do no benefit-cost analyses of their own work. There are few exceptions, notably the Abt Associates' Analysis of Day Care experiments. The experiment itself concerned whether relaxing federal regulations on credentials of day care staff would have negative effects on children. The results were used to alter regulations. The use resulted in the experiment's paying for itself in less than five years.

4.4 Willingness to experiment

If the prospective user of information is unwilling to use *good* evidence, the experimental design is irrelevant. Unwillingness may stem from experience. For instance, Fisher's superiors were experienced and well regarded colleagues, but they failed to adopt Fisher's methods early in their own work (Box, 1977, p. 153). The lack of persuasive theory also appears to have affected theoreticians' willingness to advance the idea. Moreover, the availability of a plausible, often-used alternative, i.e., systematic designs, doubtless affected willingness. In 1936, for example, Gosset advocated a specialized systematic design before the Royal Statistical Society after 13 years of correspondence with Fisher (Box, 1978, p. 268).

Being able to explain *why* a randomized experiment is desirable, in principle and practice, and to debate the matter in public forums is essential. For if the arguments cannot be made explicit, we have no business trying to run a randomized trial. Incentives, apart from reason, that facilitate or meet motives are warranted then and so this kind of planning is also considered below.

Reasons. The scientific justification for randomized assignment, of course, lies in generating a less equivocal, unbiased estimate of the relative effects of a regimen or program, one that is coupled to a formal statement about one's certainty in results.

These reasons for controlled tests are persuasive to the scientist. They will *at times* be persuasive to individuals sensitive to scientific evidence, such as some judges in court experiments, but not all of them. They will, at times, be useful to welfare program decision-makers who must be able to justify their choices of welfare rules in public forum, if we understand correctly Gueron's (1986) assessment. And they will be appropriate in environments that are not as open to public scrutiny and are technically oriented, to judge from Perng's (1986) description of tax experiments and Collins and Elkin's (1986) essay on tests of treatment of depression. Public debate can itself influence a decision about whether a randomized test is warranted. So, for example, a rationale for the Sherman–Berk experiment was helping to resolve a twenty year debate over how police can most effectively handle domestic violence cases.

The main point is that the rationale of better evidence is commonly used in arguing for experiments across all the substantive areas. That it alone is often not sufficient to generate support for an experiment is also clear. Other incentives are often employed.

Incentives. Especially when the experiment is demanding, the incentives that are based on money must be put first simply because they are obvious and they appear to work at times. That is, if people are paid to participate in a randomized experiment, they will experiment to the extent they are able. If they are not paid, matters are less promising.

For government, the fiscal vehicle for incentives is usually the Request for Proposal (REP), i.e., a formal invitation from government to businesses or universities to conduct field research. When an RFP prescribes randomization in medical tests, for instance, hospitals are willing to collaborate and often able to mount an experiment. We may judge this from the cooperative clinical trials undertaken since the Salk vaccine experiments. The Treatment of Depression trials mounted by the National Institute of Mental Health described by Collins and Elkins (1986), are among the first to use this mechanism in the evaluation of treatments for mental illness.

The Work/Welfare Initiatives described by Gueron and Nathan (1985) took a different approach to incentives. Ford Foundation funds could be leveraged by a state to make additional funds available for mounting tests of new work-fare and employer subsidy programs. In the Rockefeller Foundation's Program for Minority Female Single Parents, community-based organizations are supported to mount a program and supported further for their participation in randomized tests of the program.

Bickman (1986) took special pains in his state-wide education experiments to assure that 'control' schools received support for their participation – funds and technical assistance. Similarly payments have been used with individuals assigned to control groups in other field experiments where the burden of participation (and fact of receiving no special treatment) invites noncooperation.

Reduction in negative incentives is also germane. For example, the experimenter may try to reduce a drain on local resources engendered by an experiment by providing additional staff to the agencies involved.

Monetary incentives have *not* been uniformly successful. Institutions have agreed to randomize, for example, and then have not, finding that they were unable to implement the design. Threats to withdraw funding or failure to deliver are, in principle, usable. But we are unaware of good illustrations of research sponsored by governments or private foundations that have been terminated on this account.

5. Discipline-specific issues

The commonality among the disciplines, with regard to experiments, is more obvious than discrepancy. Still, there are major differences in degree and kind of concern that are tied to the discipline area. This affects the appropriateness and feasibility of randomized tests in the various settings.

Suppose such issues are classified into four broad categories as Riecken and Boruch (1978) have done: ethical and legal; managerial; political and institutional; and scientific. What can be said about distinctive concerns?

5.1 Ethical and legal issues

The ethical issues are gravest in the medical sector, but only to the extent that an experimental treatment in medicine seriously affects mortality and morbidity. The concern has led to deliberate termination of trials on anti-diabetic drugs for instance (Fried, 1974). We are unaware of any social experiments terminated for a similar reason.

Social experiments can pose economic and psychological risks rather than biological ones. These are usually (not always) *less* serious than the biological ones by any standard. Moreover, the character of the risk differs: degraded individual privacy and confidentiality of data is a more frequent concern than other kinds of harm (Boruch and Cecil, 1974). The presence of *any* risk, however small, has led to federal regulations that require the social experiment be reviewed by an Institutional Review Board empowered to prevent or terminate the research. The development of such IRB's for the social sector stems partly from models in the medical arena. The subtle differences between ethical issues in each area has led to distinctive treatments of each, e.g., Fried (1974) in medicine, the Federal Judicial Center (1983) in law, and Breger (1983) in welfare experiments.

5.2 Managerial issues

Organizational constraints emerge differently in each area. In educational research, for instance, it is often difficult or impossible to randomly assign individual children to classrooms. But randomization of classrooms or schools or regions is possible and has been done, e.g., Bickman (1985). In medical research, in evaluations of manpower training programs, and in many psychological studies, randomized assignment of individuals is often sensible and feasible. In court and justice settings, randomizing by time period or groups seems most feasible simply because the flow of clients is constrained in time (Goldman, 1977).

Organizational issues also concern sample size. The average effects of medical or social programs are usually small; large samples are often needed to detect these effects. How feasible it is to generate large samples depends on context, notably organizational setting and the time available to accumulate the appropriate sample.

In particular, clients are not always as easy to identify as one might expect. The difficulty varies with disciplinary context. Youth employment program experiments often only engage 60–70 percent of their target participants. Local police research has faired better probably on account of the control that can be exercised. Court experiments have recently faired still better partly because earlier squabbles over insufficient sample size produce more time to do the experiments properly. The negative income tax experiments seem to have done well on this account also because of early conscientious attention to the need for statistical power in the experiment.

5.3 Political and institutional issues

Political constraints on any field research vary with discipline. Medical and health services research in the United States seem less susceptible to naive political influence because the medical professional community is so politically influential, and American fear of illness or death and regard for physicians are so sturdy. In economic work, the large-scale experiment is more arguably a political act. Indeed, the origins of recent economic experiments lie in law. Consequently, the choice of experimental sites and decisions to experiment within a state may attract the attention of legislators interested in assuring that funds are spent in their areas. Similarly, sizeable education experiments usually require the cooperation of multiple schools and state departments of education.

The smaller experiments can be susceptible to local political influences, of course. But things are much less clear at the city level. One may escape the influence of local as well as federal and state politics, if the experiment is innocuous. What is innocuous, however, depends on local custom. In the Minneapolis Domestic Violence experiment, for example, women's groups argued for the experiment in the interest of reducing abuse of wives and children. If the experiment focused on abuse of husbands, it is doubtful that much interest in doing any experiment would have emerged.

5.4 Scientific issues

In the scientific category, a great many differences appear across discipline. The differences can be organized on the basis of the simple elements of any experiment: a treatment variable and random perturbations that together yield the third element, a response.

In medicine at any rate, there is often no debate about what response ought to be measured. Mortality or health status, measured in a variety of ways is conventional. There is occasional debate over the quality of the 'ways' to measure for a particular malady. Similarly, it is often easy to reach agreement about what measures are essential in economic experiments: hourly wages, hours worked and so on, are usually among the variables that are important.

The matter of what to measure has become a bit more complicated even in medical and economic work, however. Duration and periodicity of measurement are often debatable. Reliability of measurement, of wages say, may be relatively low (as in cases where trainees are asked to recall their income levels). See for instance Hollister (1985) on employment and training and Newhouse, Marquis, Morris, and others (1979) on the health insurance experiments.

It seems fair to say that choice of a response variable and measurement is more difficult in psychological work. The difficulty may be engendered by disagreement over what constitutes a decent measure of severity of schizophrenia (using all candidate measures usually becomes the compromise solution). It may be exacerbated by the difficulty of measuring reliably. Attitude tests are often responded to poorly in field research, for instance, e.g., Hollister, (1985) on attitudes affected by training programs.

Education falls somewhere in between the extremes. Standardized achievement tests and other assessment devices are available and are used in controlled experiments. When debates occur, they usually involve disagreements about the relevance of the achievement test to the educational program being examined. Similarly, there is usually agreement that recidivism should be a response variable in criminal justice experiments. Disagreements may turn around those who believe severity of crime rather than incidence ought to be measured.

There are differences of practical and theoretical import if one examines the treatment variable, of course. Fixing a medical treatment, such as a dose level, is often easy in practice and desirable, within limits, in principle. The ostensible treatment in negative income tax experiments – money – seems simple. It is as simple as 'dose' until one considers the variety in people's understanding of conditions for receipt of a welfare payment or the variation in the way the support funds are disbursed through a welfare office. Similarly, the treatment called 'arrest' in the Minneapolis Domestic Violence experiments is ostensibly simple. But there is still variety in policemen's ways of executing the arrest. This affects the precision and interpretability of the experimental results.

More complex, or at least more difficult to observe and understand, are the interventions in education and psychology. Part of the difficulty lies in the resources needed to observe implementation of a treatment over a considerable time. Part lies in the complexity of the treatment itself. The treatment as 'cognitive therapy' may appear simple. It may even be clear in principle to its advocates. But the label disguises complex processes that cannot always be understood well even when they can be observed. But the problem seems more common if not more severe in the social and psychological arena than in medicine and economics.

Differences in the difficulty of implementing a regimen seem more a matter of degree than kind. In drug research for example, patients fail to take their pills or turn out for their special treatment; surgeons vary in the extent to which they operate in accord with standards quite apart from variation in the patients' needs. Meterological experiments have been jeopardized on account of unexpected failure to seed clouds (Braham, 1979). Teachers asked to employ an innovative approach may alter the approval so as to make it recognizably and comfortably different from the one planned. Patients (or therapists) may doze in therapy. Training program participants may be absent. And so on. The point here is that every discipline area has the problem of assuring implementation and that implementation varies.

Consider the final scientific element of experiment: the random variation that contributes to any observation. One might expect this variation to be greater in the social sector than in the medical sector simply because the reliability of measurement in the latter is greater than in the former. It *is* greater if one confines attention to simple variables such as mortality. It is not if one considers that reliability in measuring blood pressure, standardized achievement, and 'health status' are of the same order of magnitude.

The random variation that seems more pertinent is attributable to variation in human behavior – variance in reaction to a drug in contrast to, say, variance in reaction to an education or law enforcement regimen. Further, it is likely that there is more regional variation in response to an economic or educational program than to drug regimen. There seems to have been no serious intellectual attention to measuring such variety on a common scale. It is not at all clear that a common scale can be conceived. Still, the topic seems worth exploring.

REFERENCES

Armitage, P., 'Trials and errors: The emergence of clinical statistics', *Journal of the Royal Statistical Society* (Series A), 1983, 146(4) 321–34.

Barnes, J. A., *Who should know what? Social science, privacy, and ethics.* New York, Cambridge University Press, 1979.

Bengston, D. N., 'Economic Evaluation of Agricultural Research', *Evaluation Review*, 1985, 9(3), 1985.

Bentler, P. M., and Woodward, J. A., 'Nonexperimental evaluation research: Contributions of causal modeling. In L. E. Datta and R. Perloff (eds.), *Improving Evaluations*. Beverly Hills, CA: Sage, 1979, pp. 71–102.

Bickman, L., 'Randomized field experiments in education: Implementation lessons', *New Directions for Program Evaluation*, 1986, in press.

Boreham, J., 'Present position and potential developments: Some personal views (on) official statistics', *Journal of the Royal Statistical Society*, (Series A), 1984, 147(2), 174–85.

Boruch, R. F., 'On common contentions about randomized experiment', in G. V. Glass (ed.), *Evaluation Studies Review Annual*: 3, Beverly Hills, CA, Sage, 1976, pp. 158–94.

Boruch, R. F., 'Problems in research utilization: Use of social experiments, results, and auxilary data in experiments', *Annals of the New York Academy of Sciences*, 1973m 218, 56–77.

Boruch, R. F. and Cecil, J. (eds.), *Solutions to ethical and legal problems in social research*, New York, Academic Press, 1983.

Boruch, R. F., McSweeny, A. J., and Soderstrom, J., 'Bibliography: Randomized field experiments for program planning, development and evaluation', *Evaluation Quarterly*, 1974, 4, 655–96.

Boruch, R. F., Cordray, D. S., and Pion, G., 'How well are local evaluations carried out?', in L. E. Datta (ed.), *Local, state, and federal evaluation*, Beverly Hills, CA, Sage 1982.

Boruch, R. F., 'Recommendations from the Holtzman Report: Experimental tests of education programs', *American Statistician*, 1982, 36, 1–7, (A–102).

Box, J. F., *R. A. Fisher: The Life of a Scientist*, New York and Chichester, John Wiley and Sons, 1978.

Braham, R. E., 'Field Experimentation in Weather Modification', *Journal of the American Statistical Association*, 1979, 74 (365), 57–104.

Breger, M., 'Randomized social experiments and the law', in R. F. Boruch and J. S. Cecil, *Solutions to legal and ethical problems in applied social research*, New York, Academic Press, 1983, pp. 97–144.

Campbell, D. T., and Boruch, R. F., 'Making the case for randomized assignment treatments by considering the alternatives: Six ways in which quasi-experimental evaluations in compensatory education tend to underestimate effects', in C. A. Bennett and A. A. Lumsdaine (eds.), *Central issues in social program evaluation*, New York, Academic Press, 1975, pp. 195–297.

Campbell, D. T. and Stanley J. C., (1963), 'Experimental and quasi-experimental designs for research on teaching', in N. L. Gageler, *Handbook of Research on Teaching*, Chicago, Rand McNally.

Chalmers, T. C. and others, 'A method for assessing the quality of a randomized control trial', *Controlled Clinical Trials*, 1981, 2(1), 31–50.

Chelimsky, E. (ed.), *Program evaluation: Patterns and directions*. Washington, D.C., American Society for Public Administration, 1985.

Cochran, W. G., 'Early development of techniques in comparative experimentation', in D. B. Owen (ed.), *On the History of Statistics and Probability*, New York and Basel, Marcel Dekker, 1976, pp. 1–26.

Collins, J. F., and Elkin, I., 'Randomization in the NIMH treatment of

340   Robert F. Boruch

depression collaborative research program', *New Directions for Program Evaluation*, 1986, in press.

Conner, R. F., 'Selecting a control group: Analysis of the randomization process in twelve social reform programs', *Evaluation Quarterly*, 1977, 1(2), 195–243.

Corsi, J., 'Randomization and Consent in the New Mexico Teleconferencing Experiment: Legal and Ethical Considerations', in R. F. Boruch and J. S. Cecil (eds.), *Solutions to Ethical and Legal Problems in Social Research*, New York, Academic, 1983, pp. 159–170.

Cox, D. R., 'Present position and potential developments: Some personal views (on) design of experiments and regression', *Journal of the Royal Statistical Society* (Series A), 1984, 147(2), 306–15.

Davis, R. M., 'Social research in America before the Civil War', *Journal of the History of Behavioral Sciences*, 1972, 8, 69–85.

Fairweather, G. W., and Tornatsky, L. G., *Experimental Methods for Social Policy Research*, New York, Pergamon, 1977.

Farrington, D. P., 'Randomized experiments on crime and justice', *Crime and Justice: An Annual Review of Research*, 1983, 4, 257–308.

Federal Judicial Center, *Social Experimentation and the Law*, Washington, D.C., FJC. 1983.

Ferber, R. and Hirsch, W. Z., 'Social experimentation and economic policy: A survey', *Journal of Economic Literature*, 1978, 16, 1379–14.

Ferber, R., and Hirsch, W. Z., *Social experimentation and economic policy*, Cambridge, Cambridge University Press, 1982.

Fienberg, S. E., Singer, B., and Tanur, J. M., 'Large-scale social experimentation in the United States', Chapter 12 of A. C. Atkinson and S. E. Fienberg (eds.), *A celebration of statistics: The ISI centenary volume*, New York, Springer-Verlag, 1985, pp. 287–325.

Fisher, R. A., *The design of experiments*, Edinburgh, Oliver and Boyd, 1935.

Fraker, T., and Maynard, R., *The Use of Comparison Group Designs in Evaluations of Employment-Related Programs*, Princeton, Mathematica Policy Research, 1985.

Freeman, H. E., and Rossi, P. H., 'Social Experiments', *Milbank Memorial Fund Quarterly: Health and Society*, 1981, 59(3), 340–74.

Fried, C., *Medical Experimentation: Personal Integrity and Social Research*, New York, American Elsevier, 1974.

Gilbert, J. P., Light, R. J., and Mosteller, F., 'Assessing social innovations: An empirical base for policy', in Fairly and F. Mosteller (eds.), *Statistics and Public Policy*, Reading, Mass., Addison-Wesley, 1977, pp. 185–242.

Goldman, J., 'A Randomization procedure for trickle-process evaluations', *Evaluation Quarterly*, 1977, 1(3), 493–98.

Goldman, J., *Ineffective Justice: Evaluating the Pretrial Conference*, Beverly Hills, CA, Sage, 1980.

Goldstein, H., 'Present position and potential developments: Some personal views (on) statistics and the social sciences', *Journal of the Royal Statistical Society* (Series A), 1984, 147(2), 260–67.

Gordon, G., and Morse, E. V., 'Evaluation research', *Annual Review of Sociology*, 1975, 1, 339–61.

Gosnell, H. F., *Getting out the vote*, Chicago, University of Chicago Press, 1927.

Gueron, J. M., 'The demonstration of work/welfare initiatives', *New Directions in Program Evaluation*, 1986, in press.

Gueron, J., and Nathan, R., 'The MDRC work/welfare project: Objectives, status, significance', *Policy Studies Review*, 1985, 4(3).

Hahn, G. J., 'Experimental design in the complex world', *Technometrics*, 1984, 26(1), 19–31.

Hahn, A., and Friedman, B. (with C. Rivera and R. Evans), 'The effectiveness of two job search assistance programs for disadvantaged youth: Final Report', Waltham, MA, Heller Graduate School, Center for Employment and Income Studies (CEIS), Brandeis University, 1981 (DOL Grant 99–8–1979–33–410YP).

Hargrove, E. C., 'The bureaucratic politics of evaluation: A case study of the Department of Labor', in H. E. Freeman and M. A. Solomon (eds.), *Evaluation Studies Review Annual*, 6, Beverly Hills, CA, Sage, 1981.

Harshbarger, B., 'An example of how a designed experiment saved research workers from false recommendations', *American Statistician*, 1974, 28 (4), 128–9.

Hausman, J. A., and Wise, D. A., (eds.), *Social experimentation*, Chicago, University of Chicago Press, 1985.

Hendricks, M. 'Service delivery assessment: Qualitative evaluations at the cabinet level', in N. L. Smith (ed.), *New Directions in Program Evaluation*, 1981, *12*, 5–24.

Hollister, R., *Report of the Committee on Youth Employment Programs*, Washington, D. C., National Academy of Sciences, 1985.

Hollister, R. G., Kemper, P., and Maynard, R., *The national supported work program*, Madison, Wisconsin, University of Wisconsin Press, 1984.

Kaestle, C. F., and Vinovsky, M. A., *Education and social change in nineteenth-century Massachusetts*, New York, Cambridge University Press, 1980.

Kruskal, W., 'The significance of Fisher', *Journal of the American Statistical Association*, 1980, 75(372), 1019–30.

Lecuyer, B., and Oberschall, A. R., 'The early history of social research', in D. L. Sills (ed.), *International encyclopedia of the social sciences*, New York, Macmillan and Free Press, 1968, pp. 1013–31.

Light, R. J., and Pillemer, D. B., *Summing up: The Science of Reviewing Research*, Cambridge, Mass., Harvard University Press, 1984.

Manpower Development and Research Corporation, *Summary and findings of the National Supported Work Demonstration*, Cambridge, Mass., Ballinger Publishing, 1980.

Mantel, N., 'A personal perspective on statistical techniques for quasi-experiments', in D. B. Owen (ed.), *On the history of statistics and probability*, New York, Marcel Dekker, 1976, 103–30.

Meier, P., 'The biggest public health experiment ever: The 1954 field trial of the Salk Poliomyelitis vaccine', in J. M. Tanur, F. Mosteller, W. H. Kruskal, R. F. Link, R. S. Pieters, and G. Rising (eds.), *Statistics: A guide to the unknown*, San Francisco, Holden-Day, 1972.

Moses, L. E., and Brown, B. W., 'Experiences with evaluating the safety and efficiency of medical technologies', *Annual Review of Public Health*, 1984, 5, 267–92.

Mosteller, F., Gilbert, J. P., and McPeek, B., 'Reporting standards and research strategies for controlled trials: Agenda for the editor', *Controlled Clinical Trials*, 1980, 1, 37–58.

Mosteller, F., and Weinstein, M. C., 'Toward Evaluating the Cost Effectiveness of Medical and Social Experiments', in J. A. Hausman and

D. A. Wise (eds.), *Social Experimentation*, Chicago, University of Chicago Press, 1985.

Newhouse, J. P., Marquis, K. H., Morris, C. N. and others, 'Measurement issues in the second generation of social experiments: The Health Insurance Study', *Journal of Econometrics*, 1979, 11, 117–30.

Perng, S. S., 'Accounts receivable treatments study', *New Directions for Program Evaluation*, 1986, in press.

Regan, R., 'Statistical reforms accelerated by sixth census errors', *Journal of the American Statistical Association*, 1973, 68(343), 540–6.

Riecken, H. W., et al., *Social Experimentation: A Method for Planning and Evaluating Social Programs*, New York, Academic, 1974.

Riecken, H. W., and Boruch, R. F., 'Social experimentation', *Annual Review of Sociology*, 1978, 4, 511–32. (A–39).

Risman, B. J., 'The Kansas City preventive patrol experiment: A continuing debate', *Evaluation Review*, 1980, 4, 802–8.

Robins, P. K., Spiegelman, R. G., Weiner, S., and Bell, J. G., *A Guaranteed Annual Income: Evidence from a Social Experiment*, New York, Academic, 1980.

Robins, P. K., and West, R. W., *Labor Supply Response to the Seattle and Denver Income Maintenance Experiments*, Menlo Park, CA, SRI International, 1981.

Roos, L. L., Roos, N., and McKinley, B., 'Implementing randomization', *Policy Analysis*, 1977, 3(4), 547–59.

Rossi, P. H., Berk, R. A., and Lenihan, K. J., *Money, Work and Crime: Experimental evidence*, New York, Academic, 1980.

Schultze, T. W., 'Distortions of Economic Research', in W. H. Kruskal (ed.), *The Social Sciences: Their Nature and Uses*, Chicago, University of Chicago Press, 1982, pp. 121–34.

Schwartz, R. D., and Orleans, S., 'On legal sanctions', *University of Chicago Law Review*, 1967, 34(274), 282–300.

Sherman, L. W., and Berk, R. A., 'The Specific Deterrent Effects of Arrest for Domestic Assault', *American Sociological Review*, 1984, 49, 261–72.

Sherman, L. W., and Hamilton, E., *The Impact of the Minneapolis Domestic Violence Experiment*, Washington, D.C., The Police Foundation, 1984.

Stafford, F., 'Forestalling the demise of empirical economics: The role of microdata in labor economics research', in O. Ashenfelter and R. Layard (eds.), *Handbook of Labor Economics*, New York: North Holland, 1984.

St Pierre, R. G., Cook, T. D., and Straw, R. B., 'An evaluation of the nutrition education and training program: Findings from Nebraska', *Evaluation and Program Planning*, 1982, 4, 335–44.

Student, 'The Lanakshire Milk Experiment', *Biometrika*, 1931, 23, 398–406.

Wortman, P. M., and Yeaton, W. H., 'Synthesis of results in controlled trials of coronary artery bypass graft surgery', in R. L. Light (ed.), *Evaluation Studies Review Annual*, 1982, 8.

Yeaton, W. H., and Wortman, P. M., 'The evaluation of coronary bypass graft surgery using data synthesis techniques', *International Journal of Technology Assessment in Health Care*, 1985, 1(1), 125–46.

III The Political Context

CHAPTER 18

The social sciences in an age of uncertainty

MARTIN BULMER

Applied social science is not carried on in a vacuum, but within a political context. For reasons outlined in the opening chapter there was a rapid growth in government funding of social science during the 1960s. The 1960s and most of the 1970s were good years for the social sciences in both the United States and Britain, and a period in which the scope of social science research for government expanded greatly. This was not fortuitous, for there was a common perception, on the part of those in government, that the social sciences could illuminate the policy choices they faced, and on the part of social scientists that they had something to offer. The bonds were strengthened by the strong links forged by particular groups, as Cyril Smith suggests in Chapter 5, but also more generally by the movement of social scientists into government posts of various kinds.

If the election of John Kennedy in 1960 and of Harold Wilson in 1964 marked (though they did not cause) the expansion of the social sciences, the election of Margaret Thatcher in 1979 and of Ronald Reagan in 1981 have been widely seen as marking a change of climate in the relations between government and social science. The attempts of education secretary, Sir Keith Joseph, to abolish the SSRC and of David Stockman as budget director to emasculate the social science budget of NSF, were a direct attack upon the standing, credentials and funding of the social sciences which were greeted with great alarm by the social science community. In the next chapter, Paul Flather tells the story of the attempt to close down SSRC while in Chapter 20 Roberta Miller recounts the role of COSSA in co-ordinating opposition to the Stockman cuts. The aim of the present chapter is briefly to set these events in context.

Writing about recent events is a hazardous undertaking, and writing about such events in which one has been oneself involved is even more hazardous. The aim here is neither to pontificate about the controversies of the early 1980s nor to engage in crystal-ball gazing about the uncertain future. Two contributors to this section were sought who would be expected to have a degree of detachment, Flather as a journalist observer closely involved in reporting on the social science scene, Miller as a historian of the social sciences turned science administrator. Both provide a dispassionate account of struggles between leading politicians and the social science community in the two countries in the first half of the 1980s.

To focus exclusively upon these struggles, however, to treat the embattled social sciences as Davids threatened by Goliaths occupying cabinet office bent on their destruction, is to overdramatise the reality. Certainly the advent of right-wing governments has altered the terms of the debate, and the changed economic circumstances facing western industrial nations make the expansionist optimism of the 1960s seem dated indeed. This does not mean, however, that the Thatcher or Reagan administrations, even if they succeeded in their objectives of cutting sharply the social science budget (which they had not at the time of writing in 1985), would have been able to put the clock back to 1960 or 1945 or whenever. Despite the advent of unsympathetic ministers, applied social science in 1985 was very different from what it was around 1960.

In the British universities, the social sciences were now established in substance where hitherto they only existed in outline. In the United States, social science departments had expanded well beyond their modest size around 1960. In both countries, there had been extremely substantial growth in non-academic settings, some of it within government, some of it 'out-house'. The scale of the latter – in independent institutes, research contracting firms, 'think-tanks' and partisan intellectual groups – was far in excess of what was carried on 25 years before. Moreover, among pressure groups and the media there was a much greater receptivity to the output of the social sciences, though still problems in interpreting complex issues for a lay audience. Moreover, the social sciences had developed a receptive audience to some degree among the informed lay public. Two constituencies in particular were important in the immediate crisis posed by Stockman and Joseph: the natural scientists, and (in Britain at least) senior government administrators who took a broader view than their political masters. Times were leaner, but from the standpoint of the mid-1980s, the substantial achievements over two decades of both academic social science and applied social science looked set to last. This is not to imply a Whiggish view of things getting steadily better. There have been major reverses and significant cuts. But these had not killed the animal.

It is also the case that the political animosity to social science among members of the Thatcher and Reagan circles has been to some extent misinterpreted. There is less antipathy to social science as such so much as viewing economic and social phenomena within a different frame. This is very clear in economics, where the broad theoretical underpinning for these governments' economic policies is found in monetarist rather than Keynesian economics. Cyril Smith in Chapter 5 brings out clearly how the British economic consensus broke down. The same applies to social analysis and social policy, though the outlines are less clear. Smith in Chapter 5 discusses the influence of the Titmuss group and its decline. Though the outlines are hazy, one can discern the appearance of an articulated alternative philosophy with some intellectual pretensions. The star of Paul Flather's chapter, Sir Keith Joseph, is co-author of a work which opens: 'The object of this book is to challenge one of the central prejudices of modern British politics, the belief that it is a proper function of the State to influence the distribution of wealth for its own sake' (Joseph and Sumption, 1979, p. 1). Sir Keith's approach to the social sciences stems from his belief in the efficacy of free-market forces and his conviction that the social sciences tend to be 'statist' – i.e. to incorporate assumptions about the efficacy or beneficence of provision through the state which are not necessarily warranted. This applies particularly to the redistribution of income and wealth, an issue of central concern to the Titmuss group. More recently William Letwin, mentioned in the next chapter, has edited a collection mainly by right-wing academics attacking the logical bases of egalitarian ideas (Letwin, 1983).

In the United States, the leading apostle of the free market is Milton Friedman (cf. Friedman and Friedman, 1980) but there are a number of different approaches to monetarism. Also significant are social scientists with a broadly free market or laissez-faire approach to social issues, who are highly critical of nearly all forms of government intervention. They challenge strongly the liberal conventional wisdom, and base their argument upon a belief in the efficacy of market processes (cf. Sowell, 1980). George Gilder, for example, treats income, wealth and poverty from the point of view of supply-side economics (1981), in a work described by David Stockman as 'Promethean in its intellectual power and insight. It shatters once and for all the Keynesian and welfare state illusions that burden the failed conventional wisdom of our era.' Other writers such as Thomas Sowell have provided comparable analyses of fields such as race relations in the United States (1981, 1983). More broadly, a group of neo-conservative academic social scientists whose members, such as Nathan Glazer (cf. Glazer, 1976) provide intellectual support for the changed climate in the early 1980s (Steinfels, 1980). Some of this group are former liberal reformers who have become disillusioned with the effects of reform policies, and either doubt their efficacy or consider they have led to undesirable consequences. (For a similar British view, see Anderson, 1980.) For followers of Thatcher and Reagan, the question is not: social science or no social science? but: what kind of social science? This point has been insufficiently appreciated in the social science community.

In the civil service, too, the Thatcher and Reagan governments have made their influence felt. One of the first Thatcher decisions was to wind up the Royal Commission on the Distribution of Income and Wealth. Cuts in government statistical services followed, as part of a general reduction of civil service manpower. The 1981 Census schedule was the shortest for twenty years. Colin Campbell in Chapter 8 alludes to the decline of analysis among officials as the Reagan administration settled in. Yet as Smith suggests in Chapter 5, there remains more sympathy for social science in the permanent British civil service than among ministers, and officials may, as Flather suggests in the next chapter, have done something to tone down the more extreme views of ministers.

Funding, moreover, comes from plural sources. The main focus has been upon the channels by which government funds are directed to basic social science, through SSRC/ESRC in Britain and the social science part of NSF. This is the most salient and direct form of government support but it is not the only one. Though their budgets for social science have been cut back, British government departments have continued to fund a considerable amount of applied social research. DHSS, for example, continues to maintain a strong presence in the health and social welfare areas. The same is true of departments in Washington. Demand for social science research is still evident from quasi-governmental organisations and agencies, indeed they may make demands in areas where the social science community is ill-prepared to respond. In Britain, for example, the growing research programme of the Manpower Services Commission is focused upon training, an area in which basic social sciences lack special interest. Private sources of funding remain of great importance, particularly in the United States where the scale of foundation activity is much greater. Even in Britain, with the more modest resources which Patricia Thomas describes in Chapter 4, foundations can be a significant factor. The recently-mounted annual SCPR British Social Attitudes Survey, which began in 1984, for example, has been made possible by private foundation support.

The diffuse, pluralist and negotiated character of decision-making in industrial societies means that it is not simply a matter of Prime Ministers, Presidents or cabinet members setting down a line to follow (cf. Lindblom, 1980; Bulmer, 1986, Ch. 1). In Chapter 2 the fragmented and high negotiable character of politics and administration in Washington was sketched. The same is true in a different way in Britain. For while the Thatcher government has pursued vigorously a general policy of reducing government expenditure, individual ministers have taken different views, several of them less extreme than Sir Keith Joseph. Successive secretaries of state for social services for example have retained the DHSS research capability, partly no doubt under the influence of generalist administrators and professionals within the department. In the Department of Environment on the other hand, Michael Heseltine while secretary of state closed the departmentally-supported Centre for Environmental Studies. Its last director, Peter Willmott, observed in 1980 that it was a good thing that the government did not have a coherent policy on social research, for it would be likely to be unfavourable. There was a general hostility to the social sciences and social research, with tinges of philistinism, but the situation varied from department to department (Willmott, 1980, p. 2).

Viewed in a longer-term perspective, the retrenchment, soul-searching and mobilisation for political argument of the case for social science may indeed have been salutary. There was certainly considerable overoptimism in the 1960s about the potential social role of social science. 'Part of the blame for the reaction – the disenchantment – lies with ourselves . . . (I)n the late 1950s and early 1960s . . . we were, at that time, carried away by an almost euphoric sense that social science really could change the world in quite a short period to time' (Willmott, 1980, p. 3). The same was most emphatically true of the American War on Poverty of the 1960s, as D. P. Moynihan pointed out in an acerbic analysis at the end of the decade (1969).

The social sciences also continue to grapple with the difficult problems of objectivity and value commitment. Even economics, the most 'scientific' of the social sciences, is not free of the problem. The partisan allegiance of social scientists is most apparent when they work within politically committed groups and 'think-tanks', whether the British Fabian Society, Tawney Society, Bow Group or Institute of Economic Affairs, or larger American bodies like the Heritage Foundation or the American Enterprise Institute. Playing a dual role, as partisan and objective social scientist, is perfectly feasible, but is a difficult line to draw in practice (cf. Peston, 1980). These problems of objectivity and value-commitment make it more difficult to establish the credentials of the social sciences, but it is a problem best tackled not in the abstract, but by examining particular specific analyses of social issues. Smith's analysis of the Oxford Industrial Relations School is an excellent case in point.

Indeed, one way forward for the policy-oriented social sciences is to adopt a more adversarial mode, not in a partisan sense, but in seeking to confront alternative analyses of the same phenomena more sharply than has been done hitherto. In some fields, like British industrial relations policy under Oxford hegemony, it is all too easy for a cosy consensus to emerge. It can develop in other fields. Keith Hope, for example, has observed that there is a persistent tendency in British educational research to treat findings supportive of centre or left political positions more favourably than those congruent with a right-wing position (1978, pp. 259–62). He also suggests the need for more formal academic mechanisms for the systematic comparison and critique of research findings.

> What is required is the consciousness that the aims, design, execution, analytic acumen and lucidity of presentation of one's work will be subjected to rigorous scrutiny by competent and suspicious critics who may speak from a different social experience and a different political persuasion . . . [There is a need for] journals, circulating widely among a sizeable college-educated public and feeding material into the mass media, in which leading sociologists as a matter of routine evaluate the academic competence and social implications of each other's work . . . A formal assessment process [should be incorporated] in any research which is set up to answer questions that have general administrative and political implications . . . to interpret the results of the research to the policy-maker. (Hope, 1978, pp. 262–3)

This, he argues, is available in the United States much more than in Britain, a possible reason why it proved easier, as Miller explains in Chapter 20, to secure the support of natural scientists for the defence of social science against budget cuts. If the challenge of adversity encourages the social sciences to re-examine themselves and the basis on which they can be socially useful, it will have been no bad thing.

Hope's argument may also be linked to a view of social science research methodology put forward by Robert Weiss. He suggests that in certain respects the analytical social scientist reaching his conclusions resembles a lawyer arguing a brief more than a natural scientist dispassionately testing a scientific theory. General theories in social science are weak or so highly general as not to be usable in empirical research. Instead, the social scientist investigates his or her problem as assiduously as possible, marshals the evidence, and presents a convincing case. The line of argument is extremely important. 'The investigator may imagine himself addressing a somewhat sceptical audience to whom he must make his case step by step, including all relevant data, treating them fairly, and moving toward his general conclusion in a logical and steady progression' (Weiss, 1968, p. 305). The social scientist differs from the lawyer in including all relevant evidence, for *and* against his case. He is not arguing a purely one-sided case.

Without espousing a Toynbeean theory of challenge and response, Miller's analysis certainly suggests that the critical challenge of the early 1980s forced the social sciences to re-examine their relationship to government. Though overall funding levels were lower at the end of the period, the social sciences emerged stronger from the experience. Whether the same is true in Britain has yet to be tested. The political system and culture are very different, just as ALSISS is different from COSSA. The challenge of adversity prompted critical re-examination of cherished beliefs and practices, as well as changes in the research grant assessment and postgraduate training awards within ESRC not uniformly welcomed by the academic community. Continued growth came to a halt, but despite the painfulness of the process, most of the gains made during the 1960s and 1970s were successfully defended. In the last quarter of the twentieth century, in Britain as in America, the relation between government and social science has altered out of all recognition compared to a half or quarter century previously.

REFERENCES

Anderson, D. (ed.) (1980), *The Ignorance of Social Intervention*, London, Croom Helm.
Bulmer, M. (1986), *Social Science and Social Policy*, London, Allen & Unwin.
Friedman, M. and Friedman, R. (1980), *Free to Choose*, New York, Harcourt Brace Jovanovich.
Gilder, G. (1981), *Wealth and Poverty*, New York, Basic Books.
Glazer, N. (1976), *Affirmative Discrimination: ethnic inequality and public policy*, New York, Basic Books.
Hope, K. (1978), 'Indicators of the state of society', in *Social Policy Research*, ed. M. Bulmer, London, Macmillan, pp. 244–67.
Joseph, K. and Sumption, J. (1979), *Equality*, London, John Murray.
Letwin, W. (ed.) (1983), *Against Equality: readings on economic and social policy*, London, Macmillan.
Lindblom, C. (1980), *The Policy-Making Process*, Englewood Cliffs, N.J., Prentice-Hall.
Moynihan, D. P. (1969), *Maximum Feasible Misunderstanding: community action in the war on poverty*, New York, Free Press.
Peston, M. (1980), 'A professional on a political tightrope', *Times Higher Education Supplement* 11 July, pp. 10–11.

Sowell, T. (1980), *Knowledge and Decisions*, New York, Basic Books.
Sowell, T. (1981), *Ethnic America*, New York, Basic Books.
Sowell, T. (1983), *The Economics and Politics of Race*, New York, William Morrow.
Steinfels, P. (1980), *The Neoconservatives*, New York, Touchstone.
Weiss, R. S. (1968), *Statistics in Social Research*, New York, Wiley.
Willmott, P. (1980), 'A view from an independent research institute', in *Social Research and Public Policy: three perspectives* ed. M. Cross, London, Social Research Association, pp. 1–13.

CHAPTER 19

'Pulling through' – conspiracies, counterplots, and how the SSRC escaped the axe in 1982

PAUL FLATHER

On 22 December 1981, Sir Keith Joseph, the Secretary of State for Education was asked what appeared a routine question in the House of Commons about the work of the Social Science Research Council, which spent about £20m of public money a year on British social science research and training. The question was a plant. Sir Keith replied that he had in fact just set up an urgent independent review of the 'scale and nature of the Council's work'.[1]

So began a drama that was to last 10 months, the effects of which are still felt by the British social science community today. Of course it never hit the headlines, turning as it did on such issues as research funding levels, the independence of research from politicians, the prestige of social research, and allegations of left-wing bias. Yet for the social science community it was probably every bit as dramatic as the Falklands War, which was occupying the headlines at the same time. The episode also provided a window into the complex machinations that go on between Westminster and Whitehall. Finally, for many social scientists, forced to look beyond the campus and library, it turned out to be an important lesson in the relations between academe and the harsh world of politics.

The background to the review is significant. It had been clear that the social sciences in general and the SSRC in particular were in the firing line ever since the Conservatives came to power in 1979. The new Thatcher Government had entered Downing Street armed with the ideology of nineteenth-century liberals, very pro-market and very anti-state. A key figure in the new government was Sir Keith Joseph, often regarded as Mrs Thatcher's principal monetarist guru,[2] a man who had long harboured a dislike of the SSRC as a haven for 'subversive radicals'. He had apparently once openly complained, without evidence as it turned out, to Sir Andrew Shonfield, chairman of the Council from 1968 to 1971, that the SSRC's committee lists were filled by left-wingers. Joseph's dislike also seemed to derive from an All Souls snobbery (he is a fellow of this elite Oxford college) which holds as suspect any discipline that does not have its roots in antiquity, such as history or the classics, or is not empirically testable, like the natural sciences. The social sciences are regarded as upstarts, still to prove their worth.

Joseph also saw the Council as a fuelling post for young researchers hell-bent on proving the continuing importance of 'statist' policies like Keynesian demand management and the Welfare State. This rankled even more after Joseph had a Damascus Road conversion to Chicago-school monetarism in 1974. He even set up his own rival right-wing research unit, the Centre for Policy Studies, which became a focal point for the emerging school of monetarism and supply-side economics that was to underpin Mrs Thatcher's thinking after 1979.

With the Conservatives in power it was immediately clear that the Council was vulnerable. Conservative critics could point to the fact that three of the main four macro-economic forecasting groups, the National Institute of Economic and Social Research, the Cambridge University Growth Project Group and the Cambridge Economic Policy Group, which together accounted for a significant slice of Council money, were all neo-Keynesian. Also Michael Posner, the council's chairman at the time, was himself a neo-Keynesian, a member of the Clare Group of economists. They could also draw succour from a growing disillusionment with social science that had marked the later 1970s, particularly with economics itself, for so long treated as the most prestigious of the 'new' disciplines, but which, it seemed, could offer little to halt the decline of Britain.

A new kind of anti-intellectualism and petty sniping at social science became common in the popular press and in right-wing weeklies. In 1980 Posner was savaged by the Government's Public Accounts Committees, then in fact headed by a Labour MP, Mr Joel Barnett, over some of the esoteric research supported by Council, including for example a study of kinship in Polish villages. It was rightly pointed out that no one else – including Poles and Russians – was going to support such work, even though the sum in itself was relatively small.

The attack on social science and the Council began quickly after 1979 with a £1.5m cut in the £20m budget. But it was when Joseph was moved to the Department of Education and Science in a ministerial reshuffle in September 1981, that those in the know inside the Council began to brace themselves for the worst. The Whitehall grapevine soon confirmed something big was afoot. As the weeks went by details remained scant, but senior council staff worked out position papers, and some even began thinking about new posts. Then came the Commons announcement. At least it seemed the Council, in the traditions of natural justice, was being given a chance to explain and defend itself in the dock.

The omens, however, were graver. Joseph had asked Lord Rothschild, once a senior adviser to former Conservative Prime Minister Edward Heath, to carry out the inquiry. Lord Rothschild was head of the Central Policy Review Staff, or PM's 'Think Tank', from 1971 to 1974 and had headed a wide ranging inquiry into Whitehall research which had come up with the idea of the 'customer–contractor' principle.[3] He favoured a system whereby 'the consumer says what he wants, the contractor does it (if he can); and the customer pays'. This, suggested Lord Rothschild, a Cambridge biologist, would break down the formal buffer role played by the council between government departments and the research community largely based in universities, though his 1971 report had been based on an analysis of scientific research and specifically excluded social research. In 1971 the SSRC had been deemed to be still in its infancy and outside the scope of the review.

The new Rothschild inquiry also coincided with an announcement of yet another discriminatory £1.1m (4 per cent) cut in the Council's budget for 1982–3, a cut originally intended by Joseph to be £2m. The minister had decided, against the wishes of his scientific advisers on the umbrella Advisory Board for the Research Councils, in itself an unusual move, to make the extra cut in the SSRC budget and to divide the cash between the other four scientific research councils. It was a clear signal of what kind of work he thought most important. This meant the budget had been cut by almost 25 per cent in real terms since 1979, the number of postgraduate student awards had fallen to half the 2,000-a-year peak of the mid 1970s, and Whitehall contracts had fallen, worryingly, by a third over the same period.

As soon as he heard of the cut, Posner asked for an urgent meeting with the Minister to discuss the benefits social science was bringing to 'improve the efficiency of the national economy and the quality of life', to paraphrase one of the explicit aims for setting up the Council in the first place. He had his meeting. But it was then, just before Christmas, and the day before the official announcement in the House of Commons, that Joseph told him of the planned full-scale review of all Council work.

The terms of reference of the inquiry were: 'which areas, if any, of the SSRC's work should be done at the expense of the ultimate customer rather than the Exchequer; which areas rightly supported by the Exchequer could be done at least as well and as economically by other bodies, who would receive payment from the public purse either on a once-and-for-all or recurrent basis?' The bodies concerned should be identified, and which areas if any at present supported by the Exchequer through other bodies could better be covered by the SSRC. This clearly revealed that Joseph's hope was to find alternative ways of funding social research. The Council was now 17 years old and indeed, it could be argued, ripe for review. Joseph made it all seem like a sound act of government taken by an interested minister. But then suddenly the hidden political agenda was revealed when confidential Cabinet letters exchanged between Joseph and Sir Geoffrey Howe, then Chancellor of the Exchequer, were leaked to the press. That they emerged at all at a time of Government stringency over press leaks was itself testimony to the concern insiders felt about the issues.

The letters made plain Joseph's intention to try to abolish the Council. On December 10th he wrote that he had been pondering on the SSRC.[4] He explains how Lord Rothschild came to be invited, in effect, to complete his 1971 study by analysing in the same terms the work of the SSRC. It had been passed over because 'it was in its infancy', having been founded in 1965. He also confirmed that it was his junior education minister, William Waldegrave, once a member of the Rothschild Think-Tank, who reminded him of this point. 'I feel confident', he continues, 'about the quality and the conclusion which would emerge and the presentational advantages of proceeding with a *tried and trusted operator* are apparent . . . ' (my italics). He then outlined the proposed terms of reference for the inquiry, including the following clause which did not appear in the official announcement: ' . . . and whether if these changes in responsibility [over funding] were made, there would be continuing justification for the Council's existence'. Further on, he continues: 'The report must hold water, in both its practical and its philosophical parts, if it is to provide us with an effective *basis for action*, possibly action opposed by articulate and influential sectors of academic and political opinion' (my italics).

That letter went to Mrs Thatcher and 17 Cabinet colleagues. On December 16th Sir Geoffrey Howe replied, welcoming the review. 'You know from my correspondence with Mark Carlisle [Sir Keith's predecessor at the DES] the doubts my Treasury colleagues and I have about the value of some of those activities [of the SSRC] . . . I was indeed interested to hear of your intention to give greater priority to the natural sciences within the research councils' field. *This has my strong support*' (again, my italics).

It is remarkably unusual to have such revealing statements of the real intentions of ministers embarking on a policy shift, and not surprisingly it galvanised social scientists into responding. Indeed the fact that Rothschild received some 500 unsolicited submissions by his March deadline suggests that academics in the field had become only too aware of what was at stake. A typically angry public response came from Margaret Stacey, then president of the British Sociological Association, professor of sociology at Warwick University, who said the letters confirmed that social science had 'enemies in high places' and that the review was not just an attack on public spending but had 'philistine origins'.[5] Posner, however, remained very bullish, at least in public, confident that the work of the SSRC would be vindicated, and that the net result might be a strengthened council with a more assured future. In a letter to *The Times*[6] he defended his council's efforts to support work 'chosen for its excellence' which would be encouraged 'without fear or favour or political interference'. He also defended the council's macro-economic research portfolio, 'both those bits which ministers may seem to like and those they dislike' – a direct reference to the Keynesian versus monetarism debate.

Joseph for his part, refused to comment on 'private official correspondence'. But he affirmed that the review was to be independent, and that no action would be taken before a full public discussion after the review. As one SSRC staffman graphically put it at the time: 'It's as if the council is like the lady tied to the railway track with the train steaming down, and the two villains have suddenly been caught red-handed twirling their moustaches.'

Certainly a number of relatively new academic pressure groups prepared to enter the fray. They were among many new subject-based bodies born in the wake of major university cutbacks announced by the University Grants Committee in 1981. A survey[7] confirmed that some 27 universities faced significant cuts in social science following the 1981 announcement. Thus the Social Science Action Group, an *ad hoc* pressure group set up by a dozen leading academics in June 1981 planned an urgent meeting. The British Sociological Association, one of the more active academic societies, already monitoring cuts, now started shadowing the proposed review. A new umbrella society, the Association of Learned Societies in the Social Sciences, about to be inaugurated, put the review at the top of its agenda. The Social Research Association, founded in 1978 and representing 600 researchers in academic, government and independent units, promised its own review.

One major problem, however, lay in the relations between Michael Posner, the SSRC chairman, and such groups.[8] He was seen by many as too much an inside man, more attached to the corridors of power in Whitehall than the interests of academe. Many also found his style too abrasive and rumbustuous for their liking. Many had been angered by reforms he had pushed through the committee structure of the Council, replacing the original 15 disciplinary committees by 7 policy-oriented committees.[9] Opinion was divided on the reforms, but there were those who feared it would be a first step towards greater political control over the direction of publicly funded research. They objected also to the heavy-handed manner in which it was implemented, and also to the sacking of A. H. Halsey, professor of social and administrative studies at Oxford, the sternest critic of the reforms on the Council, after one term of office.[10]

Yet all in all it was clear that most leading academics saw an independent inquiry as their best hope of saving the Council from continuous sniping, given the obvious antagonism from Tory circles. Many were quite critical of council practices, the bureaucracy, the delays in processing applications, but were also convinced about the absolute need for an autonomous public funding agency. This was the view of a wide range of academics from Professor Wynne Godley, the Keynesian Cambridge economist, and Professor Halsey, both vehemently anti-Conservative, to others such as Professor Ralf Dahrendorf, then director of the London School of Economics, and Sir Herman Bondi, then chairman of the Natural Environment Research Council, more establishment figures. All were prepared to sit out the review, confident of the impartiality of Lord Rothschild.

It was against this background of suspicion and hope that Lord Rothschild got down to work in February under instructions to complete his inquiry within three months, a task he achieved with a remarkable display of consistent hard work. In his time the Third Baron Victor Nathaniel Rothschild had been a brilliant sportsman, a research biologist at Cambridge, a colonel of wartime military intelligence, research co-ordinator at Shell, and head of the Government Think-Tank, a job he got because of his well known inquisitive, sceptical and unorthodox approach to tackling issues. He espouses a kind of creative tension and is notoriously hard to impress. One colleague confessed: 'When I go to see him I can only speak the truth.' It was these qualities that were now focused on the SSRC.

The Council had been founded in 1965 following the Heyworth Committee report[11] to fill the buffer role between the political paymasters and the social investigators, to ensure the latter remained protected from political pressure. The Council's Royal Charter laid down that it must encourage and support social service research, fund postgraduate training, and provide for advice and disseminate knowledge on the social services.

An earlier government Committee set up by the wartime coalition in

1946[12] had foreseen the need for increasing social research but had warned strongly against the 'premature crystallisation of spurious orthodoxies' like sociology. But during the 1940s and 1950s more money had become available through the University Grants Committee and in the 1960s higher education in Britain itself expanded.[13] The number of students and trained social scientists increased, peaking in the mid 1970s, then levelling off in the late 1970s. In all then the Council enjoyed an S-shaped funding curve.[14] The question now facing Rothschild was: should the already flattened top of that curve now be bent further downwards?

Lord Rothschild announced a deadline for submissions and began, as he put it, to learn the ropes of social science. He proceeded in his usual thorough fashion – the scientist at work. He wanted the facts about the SSRC's spending, definitions of what social science was, and alternative options for funding social research. He asked SSRC staff for endless detail about their operation, pursuing them relentlessly until they delivered. Many useful statistics thus emerged, some for the first time. Above all he consulted a select group of experts plus a number of trusted colleagues. Without doubt this group had a decisive impact on Lord Rothschild's thinking on the subject. Many were drawn from his Cambridge circle, such as Professor Bernard Williams, a noted moral philosopher and Provost of King's College; Professor Jean Floud, an educationalist, then principal of Newnham College; and Sir Peter Swinnerton-Dyer, a mathematician, master of St Catharine's College, a former vice-chancellor, a powerful establishment figure, later to become chairman of the University Grants Committee. Others included his daughter, Emma Rothschild, economics professor at the Massachusetts Institute of Technology (MIT) in Boston; Lord Flowers, then rector of Imperial College, London, later to become vice-chancellor of London University, a close friend; Gary Runciman, a brilliant sociologist and Fellow of Trinity College, Cambridge; Dr Roger Scruton, a right-wing philosopher, once at Peterhouse, Cambridge, now a professor at Birkbeck College, London; Professor Dahrendorf; and Mr Leonard Hoffman, a barrister. He consulted one politician, Shirley Williams, and she only because of her past office as Secretary of State for Education and Science in the last Labour Government. Once he had his brief he did not even speak to Joseph again.

At the same time Lord Rothschild was being bombarded with submissions, the vast majority in favour of the Council's continued existence. The official list runs to 320, though many more were received after the deadline.[15] But even after the first few had arrived the messages from the academic community were reasonably clear: 'The Council alone can

fund long-term work' said the Social Research Association; an independent body is fundamental for a 'well-educated and self-aware society'
said the Bristol University social scientists; the Council has to 'look after
the interests of our grandchildren' said Professor Halsey; there are
'obvious and grave limitations' in relying on the 'customer–contractor
principle' said the Association of University Teachers, representing
34,000 members. Professor Robin Matthews, Council chairman from
1972 to 1975, now master of Clare College, Cambridge, also weighed in
with an article in the *Policy Studies* journal,[16] emphasising the importance of the SSRC's buffer role, in ensuring that social science research
was free of direct political interference.

Extracts from 28 submissions which for different reasons caught Lord
Rothschild's eye and covered some of the main arguments, were also
reprinted in the report itself.[17] Included were statements from the main
interested parties such as the University Grants Committee, the British
Academy, the Confederation of British Industry, the Trades Union
Congress, the Nuffield Foundation and the Royal Society, as well as
leading individuals. As the report notes[18] the overwhelming message was
in favour of the Council, though critical statements, notably from the
Conservative peer, Lord Beloff, are also included.[19] Overall no more
powerful case for saving the Council could be made than by simply citing
the evidence of those who should know best. Including it in the body of
the report ensured that it had to be read, a shrewd way of making the
point.

Lord Rothschild gave only one interview during his study[20] when he
hinted broadly that he thought social research was essential and the
Council would be reprieved. When the report appeared on 19 May the
message was even more blunt than expected. 'To dismember or liquidate
the Council', Lord Rothschild said, 'would be an act of intellectual
vandalism with damaging consequences for the whole country from
which it would take a long time to recover.'[21] Such a weighty endorsement was a severe rebuff for Sir Keith Joseph. The conspiracy had
backfired. The counter-plot had succeeded. It seemed all could now
relax.

Social scientists naturally welcomed the report warmly – qualifying
their delight only because of recommendation 21 to investigate charges
of bias levelled against one of the Council's specialist research units. It
just seemed a small political crumb for the minister, and soon enough
reports filtered through that Joseph was indeed mightily displeased.
Whichever way he read the report, the message was the same: 'Hands
off!'

In his general conclusions[22] Lord Rothschild recommended the

Council should be retained, its budget should be maintained irrespective of other cuts, otherwise important social research would not be done; and that it should be freed for at least three years from further inquisitions. He also made plain that neither the UGC nor the British Academy wanted to take over control of social science postgraduate training even if they were given the money. So if the Council was liquidated it would have had to be 're-invented' in some new form just for that. Lord Rothschild gave three reasons why public funding of social science research should continue through the Council. First, important new disciplines such as social anthropology, social psychology and human geography were critically dependent on public funding through the Council. Second, society needed a way of checking what he called 'entrenched common-sense', ensuring that social problems really were being tackled in right ways. Third, abolishing the SSRC would leave some important research simply not done, or would impose an impossible burden on 'consumers' who could not sustain research. Thus, as he puts it in the report, 'who would pay for work into compensation for illness and injury? The relevant Government departments, the victims, or the British people as a whole?'[23]

The report itself is elegant, pithy, sharp, full of interesting nuggets. Of course many have found it flawed, but that is hardly surprising considering the timescale within which it was completed. It well repays reading by any social scientist. Perhaps the most important paragraph, though not the most famous, is the one telling politicians to leave the SSRC alone. It is worth quoting in full:

> The need for independence from Government departments is particularly important because so much social science research is the stuff of political debate. All such research might prove subversive because it attempts to submit such policies to empirical trial with the risk the judgment might be adverse. It would be too much to expect ministers to show enthusiasm for research designed to show that their policies were misconceived. But it seems obvious that in many cases the public interest be served by such research being undertaken.[24]

The collective sigh of relief after the report was audible. The *Times Higher Education Supplement* headlined a report 'Saved by the Referee',[25] while Michael Posner spoke gratifyingly of the Council's 'Daniel'. Professor Halsey thanked Lord Rothschild for refusing to do 'a nasty hatchet job'; and John Eldridge, professor of sociology at Glasgow University, chairman of the ALSISS, said the report had given the council an important 'breathing space'. Professor Dahrendorf said simply: 'This is the right answer.'

The report though was not all soft-centred. Council practices came in for sharp criticism. There was the famous paragraph urging the council to spend £6.50 on four copies of Sir Ernest Gowers' *Plain Words* to improve its poor record of communication.[26] The Council is seen as too bureaucratic,[27] and in need of better referees.[28] The report also contained critical comments about sociology and sociology departments[29] and an independent inquiry was recommended into the council's industrial relations research unit at Warwick University, after it was accused by Lord Beloff of bias towards trades unions, as opposed to management, a charge akin to calling a politician corrupt or a clergyman immoral.

Lord Beloff it should be noted, is an intensely political man, a confidante of Joseph, founder of the Independent University of Buckingham, active in the Conservative Party Central Office. He was also eager at the time to launch his own Labour Affairs industrial relations centre.[30] His was the most critical statement about the SSRC as a whole. He had serious doubts if it should continue, and wondered if its creation had not been 'a mistake'. Lord Rothschild said he felt compelled to recommend Lord Beloff's accusations on the Warwick unit be fully investigated – what became the first ever public inquiry in Britain into alleged academic bias. Lord Beloff was after all a fellow of the British Academy and former Gladstone professor of government at Oxford University. Others felt the criticisms should have just been dismissed, the unit being seen as one of the Council's jewels. After meeting Beloff and other critics Lord Rothschild enumerated a number of points needing reply. The SSRC as instructed set up the inquiry, appointing Sir Kenneth Berrill, a former UGC chairman, to lead a team of three wise men to pass judgment. But it was to be a full year before the name of the Warwick unit was cleared and the charges declared insubstantial.

After the report appeared and Rothschild had departed the scene, a two-month period of public discussion began. On July 16th, Posner wrote to his minister explaining the steps Council was taking to implement the majority of recommendations addressed to it. Meanwhile, the social scientists began packing for the summer holidays confident that a major victory was now assured. They rallied behind the Warwick unit, though again most believed a public inquiry would see the unit vindicated and left in a stronger position than before. Only the sociologists kept their powder dry, preparing replies to the report's specific criticisms of their discipline.

Indeed for many this was seen as the only real blemish in the report,[31] put down to the Baron's empiricist background in Cambridge where sociology had long been held in low regard.[32] Insiders who really knew the extent of Joseph's hostility to the council, however, kept warning about counting the chickens too soon.

Joseph did receive a number of submissions almost all echoing Rothschild's conclusions, though the important evidence, as already noted, was in the report itself. That summer the matter was also raised in both Houses of Parliament. William Shelton, a junior education minister, told the Commons no decision had been reached and that Joseph had been 'open-minded' in holding the inquiry (to shouts of 'empty-headed') while a lengthy debate in the Lords opened, inevitably, by Lord Beloff, backed by Lord Vaizey, and the free-marketeer, Lord Harris of High Cross, should have tipped off the defence that the game was indeed far from over. 'The 'noble peer' was as trenchant as ever in his criticisms of the council and the 'scientific' nature of its work.[33]

In September after the summer lull it suddenly became apparent that DES officials had been instructed to have another look at the SSRC. Joseph also dispatched his new young political adviser, Oliver Letwin, a young right-wing Cambridge philosopher, the son of William Letwin, professor of government at the LSE and Shirley Robin Letwin, the author, friends of Sir Keith, to re-examine the Council and presumably come up with the 'right answer'. The issue was far from dead in spite of Rothschild's tight stitching. Gloom once again descended on the council's Temple Avenue headquarters as staff were forced to ferret away, answering the young Letwin's questions. Senior staff feared the worst, and Posner dropped public hints to that effect, hoping once again to galvanise academics behind the Council. Here, perhaps, strained links between Posner and the leading academic activists did not help. At least a timely and a useful defence of the SSRC by David Watt did appear in *The Times*.[34]

But could Sir Keith really get away with it? The answer, in the end, was no, though as much because he could find no body to agree to take on its basic tasks as because he had lost the arguments. Right to the end he was still hoping to hive off the SSRC's control over postgraduate training, and apply the customer–contractor principle at least to management research. There followed a series of meetings between Posner and Joseph. By late September it was clear the Council would be saved – but at a cost. After much re-drafting and various amendments Joseph wrote officially to the Council on 14 October outlining his decision on the SSRC, and Posner replied the same day.[35] When the details were officially revealed four days later there was some dismay in the social science community – but overall the feeling remained one of relief. It transpired that Posner had been forced to 'buy off' Joseph with a series of promised reforms – a gentleman's agreement – that he was duty bound to stick with, whatever the ensuing reaction.

Joseph had accepted the main Rothschild recommendation that the

SSRC was to be retained but he imposed another discriminatory cut in the SSRC budget of £6m (about 8 per cent) over three years. Here he was going against Rothschild, the Advisory Board for the Research Councils, and the express feelings of the social science academic community. He tried to buy off other academics by cleverly earmarking the 'saved' money to help pay for 'new blood' appointments of young lecturers aged under 35 in the universities, widely acknowledged as a pressing need.

Joseph also asked for the word 'science' to be dropped from the title of the Council on the grounds that it misled people by suggesting social research was testable and verifiable like scientific research. Finally he asked for changes in the way postgraduate student awards were distributed so that more were available in 'open competition' to the best students regardless of their choice of institution, and less to institutions to disburse to chosen students, the 'quota system'. Sir Keith also agreed to visit the Council in early November to explain his decision.[36]

Posner's reply is a masterpiece of restrained writing. It welcomed the main decision, drawing 'quiet satisfaction' from the fact that a line had at last been drawn after 12 months of uncertainty at the Council. He certainly expressed regret over the budget cut, but his strongest word was 'dismay'. Later he revealed that almost to the last minute he had felt the Council might be closed, and he 'banished to a Siberian saltmine'!

At a press briefing in the DES Joseph was closely questioned about his decision. He confirmed that the SSRC would survive and also that it would continue to operate under the wing of the ABRC – an important statement in view of the fact that for 12 months its budget had for all intents and purposes been handled, directly and roughly, by the minister himself. Justifying the cut, he said that he believed that the natural science councils spent money more effectively, and reminded critics that the SSRC only accounted for up to 20 per cent of all social research spending in the UK. On the record, he denied that he favoured more 'policy-orientated research' or that he disliked left-wing research. He also dodged questions on whether he had really wanted to abolish the council, saying that he had just wanted to 'stimulate a debate' over public funding of social science research. Yet it was known that his first reaction on receiving the Rothschild report was to pen a memorandum to the Prime Minister that was utterly dismissive of the findings. It had to be toned down by the civil servants.

In provoking a debate, Joseph had certainly succeeded. But what was surprising was how quickly it all died down again. Once it had become known the Council itself was to survive, the community, it seemed, was ready to return to academic routines, a scent of victory hanging in their nostrils. Somehow the opportunity to have a serious, lively, open discussion about some of the issues raised by Joseph and Rothschild was missed. Somehow social scientists fell between a mood of near euphoria and a wish not to say anything that might further rock the boat. To Posner and the Council insiders it was another illustration of how little the outside community really understood what was happening.

However, there were some ready to confront the minister. 'Nothing has been achieved by Sir Keith Joseph's review of the SSRC – except to prove what was anyway obvious to most observers, that a Secretary of State can fight a war of attrition but not a war of extermination against the SSRC', thundered the *Times Higher Education Supplement* in a leader.[37] Lord Rothschild also allowed himself one final word, congratulating the 'originality and intellectual penetration of the Secretary of State's proposal to substitute the old English word *Wissenschaft* for Science in the name of the SSRC'.

There was however quite a lot of small print left to sort out. First, had a line really been drawn around the SSRC? An answer came at a conference organised by ALSISS in London the following January, when the junior minister, Mr Shelton, was dispatched to pledge 'no further inquiries' into the troubled Council for at least three years.[38] Second, should the Council really bow and agree to change its name? Many admitted they could see the intellectual point Joseph was getting at. But they argued against it on principle, because it meant giving up some automomy to ministers, and, besides it was a trivial change that served no purpose except perhaps the political one of seeming to denigrate the seriousness of social research. This was certainly the view of Ernest Gellner, a Council member, now professor of social anthropology at Cambridge, and the majority of learned societies which openly opposed any change, not least because none of the alternatives were much liked. This was certainly one issue on which everyone seemed to have an opinion. The best alternative, Social and Economic Research Council, was unavailable because the recently named Science and Engineering Research Council had already taken SERC as an acronym.

In January the Council duly decided to make no change. Yet by May it had decided to become the Economic and Social Research Council. In the end members were convinced by three facts: that it meant no material changes in the Council's Royal Charter; that it was part and parcel of the gentlemens' agreement between Joseph and Posner; and by hints that Posner would make it a resigning issue. Michael Posner used to try and put the move into context by reminding people that Henry IV of France had once said: 'Paris was worth a Mass.' He changed his religion, the Council just changed its name, he joked. But somehow it symbolised the philistinism of the political New Right to social science.

Third, a new system of student awards was phased in with more than 50 per cent of the 800 annual awards to be distributed by 'open competition', up from about 35 per cent. Fourth, the bias inquiry ground on slowly, causing anguish to all parties. No one really knew how to proceed, nor indeed if it was worth proceeding.[39] The Unit's staff, left in the dock, were naturally annoyed at being made 'scapegoats' for the Rothschild report. A great deal was at stake, and not just the future of staff and the unit, previously endorsed by two confidential SSRC internal reviews in 1974 and 1980, many saw the inquiry as a test case for the continued independence of publicly funded research in politically sensitive areas. The charges – that the unit had chosen to research topics specifically suited to trade union interests and been too closely linked to the labour movement – themselves reeked of politics. In the event, however, the prosecution case just fizzled out for lack of evidence, and the final judgement when it appeared found the case 'unsubstantiated.[40] A nasty precedent had nonetheless been set.

But the most important problem though was coping with the budget cuts. Posner tried to bring home the seriousness of the new cut which in effect meant the SSRC budget had been reduced by a total 32 per cent in real terms in six years. The Council was forced to shed 30 posts provoking strong union opposition. Further cuts in research funding and studentships had to be planned, the four specialist research units and various designated research centres in universities round the country had to face extra cuts.[41] The aftermath of all these decisions was still filtering through the system several years later. Indeed the image of SSRC cuts was so great, it produced a big decline in funding applications.

Yet when the so called Rothschild truce of three years was up in 1985, further cuts were being considered. The Council had to make a special presentation to the ABRC illustrating and justifying the range of its current work. Many feared that the natural scientists, themselves short of money, had their eye on the £20 million SSRC budget, even though as one senior academic put it, 'it would be like storming the castle for a tiny breakfast'. But behind the scenes reports suggested that Joseph was once again on the war-path.[42]

Whatever the future holds, that the SSRC survived in 1982 can be put down to a number of key elements. The most significant is undoubtedly the 'counterplot' – a clever *Yes, Minister* manoeuvre to bring in Lord Rothschild on an absolutely *bona fide* pretext to produce an independent review before any axe could be swung. Those who arranged this, Waldegrave, Posner, perhaps Dahrendorf, senior DES officials, knew what they were doing. They guessed, rightly, that the strength of the arguments would prevail. Those in the know, who had read the 1971

Rothschild report carefully, knew all along that he had never supposed
the customer–contractor principle could be applied to the social sciences
anyway. That was perhaps the nub of Rothschild's conclusions, along
with the answer to Joseph's second question – that there was no other
body that could take on the SSRC's functions. It would have to stay.

A linked element was the strong favourable message from the establishment circle within which Lord Rothschild moved. It is important to
note that a great number of scientists shared (and still share) Joseph's
prejudices against the social sciences. Yet equally many were prepared to
abide by the evidence cited in the report. Once that had appeared with its
unequivocal message, Joseph's room for manoeuvre was always going to
be limited whatever Lord Beloff and other advisers urged. But just how
much help came from the powerful science barons? Certainly Sir Alec
Merrison, the ABRC chairman, personally drafted the board's important evidence to the Rothschild review, 'applauding' in general the way
in which the SSRC had managed research.[43] Posner and others are
convinced that the natural scientists played a key role in helping to
persuade Joseph to accept the continued existence of the Council. Few,
of course, were willing to put themselves in the firing line. But the
widespread feeling that the scientists were on the touchline enjoying the
spectacle appears unfounded.

The resonance of support among the wider social science community
was also certainly important. But it is doubtful if the opposition generated by ALSISS, the SRA, the BSA, the Social Action Committee, and
other bodies, really affected Joseph's view. His leaked Cabinet correspondence with Sir Geoffrey Howe revealed that he had in any case
expected hostile reactions. What counted far more were the views of the
academic establishment including Sir Alec Merrison, Sir Owen Chad-
wick, president of the British Academy, Meyer Fortes, former professor
of social anthropology at Cambridge, Lord Todd, president of the Royal
Society, and his All Souls colleagues, Peter Mathias, professor of
economic history at Oxford, and Amartya Sen, professor of economics at
Oxford, whose views supporting the SSRC are both printed in the
Rothschild report. Abolition after all this would have severely dented Sir
Keith Joseph's reputation as an 'intellectual politician' and be seen
simply as a move of ideological prejudice.

The secretive manoeuvering of Michael Posner and other Council
officers still rankles with many social scientists, most notably with the
vociferous community of sociologists. But the evidence does suggest that
the range of contacts built up over a lifetime by Posner in Whitehall and
the so-called academic golden triangle of Oxford, London and Cambridge, was crucial. He gambled hard. He kept up good relations with

Lord Rothschild and William Waldegrave and others in the academic research community throughout the inquiry period, while his officers in the Council, notably Dr Cyril Smith, the secretary, and Mrs Catherine Cunningham, the deputy secretary, used whatever influence they had among civil service contacts in the DES. The quiet but strong support of the senior economists, particularly, but also the psychologists and geographers must also be noted.

And yet the wider, more public campaign was also significant. If it had not occurred it would have limited the room for manoeuvre of the insiders, narrowed the scope for compromise and that final gentleman's agreement between Joseph and Posner, which was to some extent also a face-saver for the minister. To ensure the execution really was cancelled there had to be the means for Joseph to also emerge with 'something' from the exercise. How ironic it was then to see a bitter, angry exchange between Posner, the supreme insider, and Margaret Stacey of Warwick University, one of the most active outsiders, at the ALSISS conference in London in January 1983 over the tactics used in defence. Perhaps they knew they had had an unholy alliance to see the execution cancelled.

Yet Stacey could claim justifiably that Council officers and the academics sitting on SSRC committees had indeed become too remote from the wider community, leading to divisions, for example, over the reformed committee structure, which could not help the social sciences in the long run. Equally, though, Posner could claim that the social science community is very good at issuing public statements but contributes little to serious debate about what is possible under a resolute Thatcher Government and faced with declining resources. Certainly the Council, now under new leadership with Sir Douglas Hague,[44] long-time friend and adviser to the Prime Minister and Sir Keith Joseph, an economist from the Manchester Business School, as Chairman, and Mrs Suzanne Reeve, a former Department of Health and Social Security civil servant, as secretary, will be disappointed that more permanent features of the public debate that ensued in 1982 have not lasted. The structures, notably ALSISS, and the more recently set-up group of humanities and social science academics in the universities, are still active. But the energy, perhaps not surprisingly, has ebbed.

Three turning points can therefore be identified in defusing the Joseph conspiracy, which is what the story appears to have been about and saving the SSRC in 1982. First, the moves to 'persuade' Joseph to bring in Lord Rothschild to do the review, the counterplot. Second, the leaking of Joseph's private correspondence in January 1982, which galvanised the social science community to take the affair very seriously indeed. Third, the unambiguous wording and conclusions of the final report, coupled with the publication of evidence from key establishment figures in the report itself, overwhelmingly in support of retaining the Council. Just how important all these British Academy, Oxbridge, and Royal Society contacts are can be gauged from the fact that one important reason, given privately, why Rothschild had felt obliged to recommend a full inquiry into the Warwick industrial relations unit was that the charges had 'after all come from an FBA', that is a Fellow of the British Academy!

All this contrasts strongly with how social science research escaped similar Governmental attacks in France and the United States. This is not the place to examine just why social science was in trouble in so many countries at the same time in the late 1970s, suffice to say that in France the social science budget of the *Centre Nationale de Recherche Scientifique* fell in real terms by 25.8 per cent from 1976 to 1981. In the U.S., the incoming Reagan Administration attempted to slash the social science budget of the National Science Foundation by 75 per cent because it was 'relatively less important to the economy', a story discussed in the next chapter.

In France the trend was dramatically reversed when President Mitterand's Socialist Party came to power in 1981. The reverse was thus a spin-off of the general election and the detailed arguments for and against social science never had to be debated. In the U.S. the social science community took up the fight themselves, appointing full-time campaign staff, setting up a campaign office, and lobbying Congress remorselessly and effectively. The campaign is described by Roberta Miller in the next chapter. It appears there were three important reasons why the Americans were successful in forcing the Reagan Administration to reverse its policy of heavy cuts. First, the case for social science was well made. A great deal of time and trouble was spent explaining why social science was important. It was shown that Government departments themselves spent more than $780 million on social research in 1980, with the NSF accounting for just $50m. It was shown that such huge cuts would only serve to take the 'science' out of social research, ending surveys, closing data banks, curtailing econometric analyses and so on, hardly justified. Such a strong case was never publicly made in Britain beyond Rothschild.

Second, the natural scientists were pulled in to support the campaign, adding greatly to its force. The inclusion of the social science section within the multi-disciplinary NSF structure made this easier. But more effort to get senior natural scientists to come out publicly for their social science colleagues paid handsome dividends. In Britain this happened to some extent, but only among the higher echelons of the research establishment, and it remained largely behind-the-scenes support. Perhaps the scientists were simply too scared of Joseph and preferred ultimately to keep some distance from the SSRC in case the ship really was sunk. Finally, they ran a professional and unremitting campaign, and in the words of one senior campaigner: 'They did not whine.' This greatly improved the status of social scientists with the academic community at large. In Britain there was always a feeling that what Joseph was doing was 'unfair', which detracted from efforts to meet the minister's arguments head on. It should of course be added that the sheer size of the Reagan cuts added greatly to the sympathy factor for social scientists in the U.S.

At a public conference in October 1985 to mark the 20th anniversary of the founding of the SSRC/ESRC, Michael Posner, in a stirring paper, wondered aloud if in the end he really had not 'squeaked' loud enough in 1982. Some would agree that indeed he did not. More would probably say he played the game the only way he knew how – inside the liberal-Keynesian establishment, where so much of British politics is still run, even today. But such opinions, in at least one important respect, miss the point. The 1982 counterplot was a significant victory. It is never easy to beat a Government, especially a determined one, and such victories always have to be bought at a price.

This was a victory but on soft foundations. The real case for social science research is probably still to be made in Britain. It has probably not been taken beyond the arguments put by Lord Rothschild in Chapter 4 of his report. Until the politicians are convinced, it is likely that the Council will continue to lurch from one crisis to the next. At the time of writing in 1985, the Council has just made a special presentation to the ABRC showing the range of its work. It bodes ill coming just weeks after the end of the so-called three-year Rothschild 'truce', the Joseph–Posner gentleman's agreement. The Council had meanwhile also been forced by the threat of a further £1m budget cut to penalise 10 institutions for poor Ph.D submission rates and to threaten severer and wider sanctions. The pressure from outside on the Council, in theory an independent buffer between the politicians and the academics, is once again only too apparent. It seems the battles of the SSRC are far from over. In the United States, however, with the case well made, social scientists seem more able to leave political fighting and get back to research.

NOTES

1 'Review of Social Science Research Council', Department of Education and Science press notice, 22 December 1982, from the DES, London.
2 See for example, William Keegan's *Mrs Thatcher's Economic Experiment* (Harmondsworth: Penguin, 1984).
3 Lord Rothschild, *The Organisation and Management of Government Research and Development*, Cmnd 4814, 1971 (London: HMSO), a consultative Green Paper, led to a white paper, *A Framework for Government Research and Development*, Cmnd 5046, 1972, (HMSO, London).
4 A fuller analysis of the letters appears in Stuart Weir, *New Society*, 7 December 1982, p. 11.
5 See report in *Times Higher Education Supplement* (*THES*), 15 January 1982, pp. 1, 3.
6 Letters column in *The Times*, 14 January 1982.
7 *THES* University Social Sciences survey, 7 May 1982, p. 7.
8 See P. Flather, 'Conspiracies and Counterplots', *THES*, 22 January 1982, p. 8.
9 Outlined in *A Change in Structure for Changing Circumstances*, document from the SSRC, September 1981.
10 For fuller discussion see P. Flather, 'The Quiet Revolution', *THES*, 2 October 1981, p. 8.
11 *Report of the Committee on Social Studies*, chairman Lord Heyworth, Cmnd 2660 (London: HMSO, 1965).
12 Clapham Committee Report on *Provision for Social and Economic Research*, Cmd 6868 (London: HMSO, 1946).
13 The tone for this was set by the Robbins Committee Report on *Higher Education*, Cmnd 2154 (London: HMSO, 1963).
14 For details see, for example Edmond Lisle, Howard Machin and Sy Yasin, *Traversing the Crisis: the Social Sciences in Britain and France*, London, ESRC, 1984, p. 21.
15 The list is printed at the back of *An Enquiry into the Social Science Research Council* by Lord Rothschild, Cmnd 8554, May 1982 (London, HMSO), pp. 99–106.
16 See Robin Matthews, 'Rothschild on the SSRC: some reflections' in *Policy Studies*, Vol. 3 (1), July 1982, pp. 1–11.
17 *An Enquiry into the Social Science Research Council*, pp. 42–85.
18 *Op. cit.*, p. 42.
19 *Op. cit.*, p. 44.
20 See P. Flather, 'Rothschild qualifies principle', *THES*, 16 April 1982, p. 1.
21 Lord Rothschild is echoing the evidence of Professor Barry Supple in *An Enquiry into the Social Science Research Council* by Lord Rothschild, Cmnd 8554, HMSO, 1980, pp. 74–8.
22 *Op. cit.*, p. 4.
23 *Op. cit.*, p. 11.
24 *Op. cit.*, paragraph 3.12, p. 12.
25 See P. Flather, 'Saved by the Referee', *THES*, 28 May 1982, p. 7.
26 *An Enquiry into the Social Science Research Council*, p. 88.
27 *Op. cit.*, p. 86.
28 *Op. cit.*, p. 88.

29 *Op. cit.*, pp. 85, 86, 89.
30 See his own evidence in the Rothschild Report, p. 44.
31 See for example A. H. Halsey, 'Why Rothschild spared the Axe', in *New Society*, 27 May 1982, p. 336.
32 See P. Flather, 'A new champion in the lists', *THES*, 7 June 1985, p. 13; see also M. Bulmer (ed.), *Essays on the History of British Sociological Research*, Cambridge, Cambridge University Press, 1985, pp. 23–7 which details this.
33 *Hansard Parliamentary Debates*, Vol. 432, nos. 114 and 115, Cols. 288–321, 20 June 1982.
34 D. Watt, 'The Quango that should be Saved', *The Times*, 16 July 1982, p. 7.
35 Both letters are reproduced in full in *SSRC Newsletter* 47, December 1982. They were sent on 14 October 1982.
36 See P. Flather, 'Sir Keith plans a visit to the SSRC', *THES*, 22 October 1982, p. 1.
37 Editorial, 'Sentencing the SSRC', *THES*, 22 October 1982, p. 32.
38 See P. Flather, 'Government will leave SSRC alone', *THES*, 21 January 1983, p. 2.
39 P. Flather, 'Shuffling initials at the SSRC', *THES*, 13 May 1983, p. 2.
40 For a full analysis, see P. Flather, 'Briefing on Academic Bias', *THES*, 15 October 1982, p. 10.
41 See P. Flather, 'Council faces harsh decisions over cuts', *THES*, 21 January 1983, p. 2.
42 For a fuller review, see P. Flather, 'The Vultures Hover over Social Sciences', *New Society*, 11 October 1985, pp. 51–2.
43 See *An Enquiry into the Social Science Research Council*, pp. 44–6.

CHAPTER 20

Social science under seige: the political response, 1981–1984

ROBERTA BALSTAD MILLER*

Although social scientists in the United States have long studied the political process and many have attempted to influence public policy, they have traditionally been reluctant to take political action in defense of their own research budgets. Yet in 1981, when the newly elected Reagan administration proposed severe cuts in federal budgets for social science research, social scientists not only vocally defended their research, but they also established a new lobbying organisation to oppose the administration's social science budget cuts. The story of that organisation, the Consortium of Social Science Associations (COSSA), and its activities during the first presidential term of the Reagan administration is the subject of this essay.*

Background

Attacks on the social sciences were not without precedent. In the years preceding Mr Reagan's election, there had been congressional criticism of social science research in general and of the National Science Foundation (NSF) and its social science research grants in particular. Senator William Proxmire, a Democrat from Wisconsin, regularly awarded a 'Golden Fleece' to recipients of federal grants and contracts whose work he deemed unworthy or trivial and a waste of government

---

* The views expressed here are those of the author and not those of the U.S. National Science Foundation (NSF). The author was previously the founding Executive Director of the Consortium of Social Science Associations (COSSA). She wishes to emphasise that this account of COSSA's development and early activities is told from the perspective of one who was deeply involved in the activities described. Narrowing the focus of this account of social scientists' response to the budget cuts to COSSA's political activities is not intended to disparage nor to underestimate the importance of the many other fruitful efforts of social scientists to promote their common cause during this period.

money. Although the Golden Fleece awards went most frequently to defense contractors, those awarded for biological or social research received more publicity. The public, it appeared, was eager to read about congressional exposés of misspent government funds, particularly when those funds went to study such topics as the sex lives of insects, the nature of love, or, more specifically, the role of religion in the economic activities of Sherpa guides in Asia. That the research projects honored with a Golden Fleece could be successfully defended on intellectual and policy grounds made little difference, for the publicity surrounding the 'award' did not extend to a serious discussion of the research itself. As a result, periodic issuance of the Golden Fleece created in many people a disregard or even disdain for social science research.

In the House of Representatives, this disdain was exploited by Representative John M. Ashbrook, a Republican from Ohio. Mr Ashbrook annually pilloried social science research projects supported by the National Science Foundation (NSF) for being irrelevant, arcane, and, again, a waste of the taxpayers' money. For several years, Mr Ashbrook maintained his attacks on social science research each time the NSF budget was brought to the floor of the House, citing specific social science grants as examples of what was objectionable in the social sciences and introducing amendments to reduce the budget support for social science research at NSF.

Just as regularly as Mr Ashbrook rose to attack, the NSF and its social science research grants were defended by other Members of Congress, particularly Representative George E. Brown, a Democrat from California who was then Chairman of the House Subcommittee on Science, Research, and Technology, and other members of his Subcommittee. This periodic exchange took an unexpected turn in 1979 when Mr Ashbrook's ritualistic amendment to cut funds for social science research from the NSF budget was unexpectedly passed by a majority of the House. Since social science research was hardly a political issue at that time, it is likely that the proposed budget reduction itself – rather than the attack on the social sciences – was most attractive to Members of Congress who voted for Mr Ashbrook's amendment.[2]

Because budget appropriations are in the end a compromise between the House and the Senate, the Ashbrook amendment did not survive in the final NSF appropriation that year. However the vote demonstrated the willingness of Members of the House to reduce or eliminate social science research budgets. Although the research community as a whole paid little attention to the appropriations process, the vote alarmed some social scientists and the House Subcommittee on Science, Research, and Technology. The following spring, the Subcommittee held hearings on the NSF budget and six social scientists came to Washington to testify.[3]

Equally significant as the passage of the Ashbrook Amendment in 1979 was the reaction of a young Congressman from Michigan to budget pressures in 1980 who, with other conservatives in the House, prepared a model counter-budget that considerably reduced federal expenditures projected by the Carter administration. This budget totally eliminated support for the 'soft social sciences' from the National Science Foundation budget. Although the Representative, Mr David Stockman, did not see his recommendations adopted in 1980, he was in a better position to put them into effect as the newly appointed Director of the Office of Management and Budget (OMB) in the Reagan administration in 1981.

In short, the social sciences were vulnerable to both public criticism and possible budget reductions in Congress long before the Reagan administration so effectively made them vulnerable in the Executive Branch of the government as well. It is worth noting that both the attacks and defenses of social science research in Congress were carried on in the absence of active participation in the debate by the social science community.

The Reagan budget proposals

Although the Reagan presidential campaign had made little effort to attract the support of social scientists, there was nothing to suggest that in office the administration would be opposed to social science research. However, the first signs of the new administration's position came shortly after the election. As early as the first week in January, several weeks before the inauguration of the President, newly nominated OMB officials were familiar with details of the NSF social science research budget, a familiarity that, given the breadth and complexity of the federal budget and the relative insignificance of the social science budget at NSF, was ominous. Then in early February preliminary Reagan budget revisions for the coming fiscal year (FY 1982) were leaked to the press suggesting that there would be major reductions in NSF's support for social science research.

On 18 February 1981, a formal announcement was made that the Reagan administration, now in office, was revising the budget that former President Carter had prepared for FY 1982 before he left office. Among the proposed revisions were deep cutbacks in social science research budgets. At the National Science Foundation, for example, the principal source of support for basic research in the social sciences, the budget for the Division of Social and Economic Science was to be reduced by 75 per cent, that of the Foundation's programs in psychology and linguistics (in another NSF division) by 67 per cent, and anthropology by 39 per cent. These cuts were not confined to NSF. Throughout the federal government, social science research agencies and programs were identified for major budget reductions, although none were scheduled for cuts as deep as those at NSF.

There has never been an adequate explanation as to why the Reagan administration decided to impose such severe cuts on social science research budgets. The formal reason given in OMB budget documents was that social science research was 'of relatively lesser importance to the economy than the support of the natural sciences'.[4] Beyond this explanation, which was routinely given for budget cuts in other areas as well, the administration did not provide any justification for the social science budget cuts. Nor was there any explanation of the size of the cuts or why, if perceived economic contributions were so critical, the cuts were partial rather than total. In reality, the social science budget cuts were probably due to several other, unrelated factors.

First, many members of the Reagan administration identified social science research with the social policies of former President Lyndon B. Johnson, who built a number of the programs of his Great Society on the findings of social scientists. Certainly some individuals in the Reagan administration privately acknowledged that they had no intention of supporting research that would lead to an expansion – rather than a contraction – of federal programs. A second, related factor that may have accounted for the budget cuts is that many conservatives had long identified social scientists with liberal attitudes and life styles that were out of place in the new administration. As far back as the 1930s and 1940s, social science had been confused with social work and socialism. More recently, with the widespread university opposition to the Vietnam War, academic social scientists were perceived by many to be farther to the left than their colleagues in other disciplines. Finally, congressional debates on the value of social science research over the previous several years had demonstrated that there was political capital to be gained from attacks on social science research – at little political cost.

These are all suppositions. The 1981 budget cuts were undoubtedly the result of a combination of these and perhaps other impulses that surfaced in the weeks after the elections.[5] What was most important for social scientists at that time was less the motivations behind the budget cuts than the political reality of a newly elected administration moving quickly to curtail social science research funding.

Not only social scientists, but the scientific research community as a whole was taken aback by the extent and magnitude of the social science budget cuts. Initial statements by Philip Handler, then president of the National Academy of Sciences, and William D. Carey, Executive Officer of the American Association for the Advancement of Science (AAAS), made it clear that they felt the social science budget cuts were unwarranted. Within weeks, the organisations the two represented had taken further steps in support of the social sciences. The AAAS, through its weekly magazine *Science*, published a number of strong editorials supporting social science research. The series was followed by an editorial attack on the administration's budget policy for social science research by Mr Carey:

> ... The same act of public faith that legitimizes theoretical and applied research in the physical and life sciences has been withheld from the social and economic sciences because the benefits are less amenable to measurement. It is a Catch-22 situation, and it is not likely to improve unless the stronger scientific disciplines come to the relief of their embattled colleagues. Isolating the social and economic sciences means inflicting damage on the integrity of all scholarship.[6]

The National Academy of Sciences also supported the social sciences in the face of the budget cuts. Meeting in April 1981, members of the Academy passed a resolution that condemned the administration's budget cuts, particularly those at the National Science Foundation, and suggested that the Director of the Foundation, John B. Slaughter, reallocate funds from other NSF research budgets to provide additional funds for the social and behavioral sciences.

The stance taken by the Academy and the AAAS and the support later expressed by the National Science Board (NSB) were important because they helped to enlist the scientific community in support of the social sciences, thus providing social scientists with needed allies. In some ways, this was not surprising, for social scientists in the United States identified themselves with the broader scientific community rather than with the humanities. However the role they played in that community was modest, tempered by the belief – held mainly by physical scientists but also shared by some social scientists – that the social sciences were not quite legitimate as science. Whether because of inherent difficulties in the analysis of social behavior or because of some other cause, the social sciences were unabashedly observational and generally non-experimental – both of which reduced their claim to being 'science' in the eyes of physical scientists. Moreover, although social scientists had made significant improvements over the previous decade in the measurement of social behavior, there remained serious measurement problems in social science research that concerned natural scientists and social scientists alike. Despite these misgivings, the Reagan budget cuts, by reducing social science research budgets for apparently capricious reasons, led to a show of solidarity among scientists that was both unexpected and vitally important to the social science community.

The response of social scientists

It remained, nonetheless, for social scientists themselves to lead the opposition to the administration's budget proposals. Initially, social scientists were uncertain how to respond to the announcements of major social science budget cuts at NSF and other federal agencies. The research community had little experience in political activities on behalf of social science research budgets. The few earlier efforts that had been made in this area were isolated and quickly forgotten. At the same time, the Reagan budget cuts were deep and the costs of inaction were widely perceived to be great. For the first time, social scientists in large numbers wrote letters to Members of Congress and to government officials, protesting the proposed budget cuts. They testified before a number of congressional committees.[7] They spoke with reporters and wrote editorials attacking the administration's budget plans. Academic social scientists held frequent conversations about the budget cuts with social scientists and research administrators in the Reagan administration, hoping to reduce the opposition to social science research in the White House. In addition, social scientists in federal research agencies worked hard to persuade agency officials and advisory bodies of the value of their research.

But these efforts, though important and necessary, were not enough. For when the proposed budget cuts were sent to the Congress, they took on a political reality that could only be altered in a political context. By March 1981, there was a mounting sense that to be most effective, the social science community must undertake concerted political action.

At this point, some two months after the formal announcement of the President's new budget, the Consortium of Social Science Associations (COSSA) decided to establish a temporary office to lobby on behalf of social science research budgets. COSSA had existed since the early 1970s on an informal basis, bringing the executive officers of the social science disciplinary associations together from time to time to discuss issues of mutual concern. For example, in 1979 and 1980, the COSSA executive officers had met with representatives of the Social Science Research Council (SSRC) to discuss ways of dealing with the Ashbrook amendment to the NSF budget.

Now faced with the Reagan budget custs, COSSA went further. The disciplinary associations put together funds for a limited full time effort, and two people were hired to organise and co-ordinate a series of political activities in opposition to the cuts. COSSA only had resources for a three month effort. This was as long a period as the associations could commit funds to support what they were even then beginning to call a lobbying activity. The temporary office was housed at the American Psychological Association, one of the founding organisations.

Initial decisions made by COSSA shaped the new organisation's activities during its first three months. First, all the major social science disciplinary associations were to be represented in the effort and COSSA was from the beginning intended to be a voice for the social and behavioral sciences as a whole rather than a voice for specific disciplines. This was a departure from current practice. Although the scholarly associations, like researchers in the various disciplines, rarely acted in concert, the proposed budget cuts for social science research had ignored the differences between the disciplines and grouped them together as 'social sciences'. Thus COSSA was mobilised into political activity to respond on their joint behalf. The associations involved in the establishment of COSSA were the American Anthropological Association, American Economic Association, American Historical Association, American Political Science Association, American Psychological Association, American Sociological Association, American Statistical Association, Association of American Geographers, Association of American Law Schools, and Linguistic Society of America.

A second decision was to use social scientists rather than political operatives in the defense of the social sciences. This involved hiring social scientists as staff for the COSSA effort and as spokesmen for the social sciences. At the beginning of the Reagan administration, there were a great many individuals in Washington with extensive political and lobbying experience who had lost their jobs after the election because of the change from a Democratic to a Republican administration and from a Democratic to a Republican controlled Senate. Despite the availability and political experience of these professionals, the COSSA executive officers decided to employ a staff with social science backgrounds who could speak knowledgeably about research and could learn the politics of the situation on the job, rather than to employ politically experienced individuals who would need extensive education to discuss research in the various social science disciplines. This staff, in turn, relied heavily on joint efforts with social scientists in the universities.

The decision to rely on social scientists also extended to the development of political strategies. COSSA's activities in the organisation's first months were carefully planned in weekly meetings of a small committee consisting of COSSA staff and the executive officers of the American

Political Science Association, the American Psychological Association, the American Sociological Association, and the Association of American Geographers.

A third decision was to concentrate COSSA's attention on the budget of the National Science Foundation (NSF). The NSF was symbolically important to the social sciences. The fact that social science research was funded by NSF provided institutional acknowledgement of the scientific nature of social science research. The Reagan budget cuts not only threatened to cut off these important research funds, but also implicitly called into question whether the social sciences belonged with the physical and biological sciences at the Foundation.

There were, in addition, practical reasons for COSSA's focus on NSF. Of all the social science budget cuts, those at NSF were deepest and thus most serious. Second, the Foundation funded basic research in each of the disciplines represented in COSSA. A concentration on NSF budgets would therefore strengthen the support for the COSSA effort in the member associations. Because COSSA represented a venture into risky and unconventional waters for the scholarly associations, the executive officers could be assured that members of each of their disciplines, as well as the social sciences in the aggregate, would benefit from the efforts of the new organisation.

Finally, social science research support in other federal agencies was embedded in programs directly related to the mission of the agency – health, labor, education, and so on. Only at the National Science Foundation was the mission of the agency pure science. For this reason, political discussion of the NSF research budget could focus on the quality of social science research rather than on the effectiveness of research in dealing with issues and problems in, for example, health care, social security, or educational policy.

In the effort to restore social and behavioral science budgets in the National Science Foundation, as in other political activities in which COSSA was involved, three elements came into play. First, it was necessary to establish and communicate the position of the scientific community to those involved in budget decisions. As the following account will show, this was accomplished through congressional testimony, formal communications from the heads of disciplinary and scholarly organisations, and statements of support from the larger scientific institutions such as the AAAS, the National Academy of Sciences, and the National Science Board.

Second, it was critical to show support for social science research budgets in the grass roots political constituencies of Members of Congress, that is, social scientists needed to to demand help from their political representatives. COSSA was deeply involved in this activity but did not work alone. Other social science organisations, frequently co-ordinating their activities with COSSA, contacted Members of Congress and urged their members and boards to do the same. Moreover, many social scientists wrote spontaneously to their political representatives on the issue of social science budget cuts.

For these two elements to be successful, it was finally essential to influence the political process directly through the individuals who were involved in decision-making at all levels of the budget process. At a minimum, this included the staff of congressional committees and federal officials at the Office of Management and Budget, the Office of Science and Technology Policy (the White House science office), and the National Science Foundation. More broadly, it also included members of the administration and the press because of their influence on the context of budget decisions. This final task required repeated conversations, the presumption of good will on all sides, and a persuasive and unflagging belief in the importance of social science research. Ultimately, however, these conversations were decisive in influencing social science research budgets.

COSSA's initial task was to persuade the Congress to reject or substantially modify the administration's budget proposals. In the United States, the administration proposes a budget, but the Congress has the power to approve or change the President's recommendations. Therefore until the Congress approved the Reagan budget revisions for FY 1982, they remained proposals without the force of law. Because of the critical role Congress would necessarily have in determining the NSF appropriation for FY 1982, COSSA turned for help to social scientists outside Washington to put pressure on their Senators and Representatives to reject the Reagan cuts.

COSSA first established a grassroots network of social scientists in certain key congressional districts. These included the districts of members of the House Budget Committee, those who had large universities in their districts (and would be responsive to the university vote), new Members of Congress, and Representatives selected in an analysis of previous voting records. In this analysis, COSSA staff examined voting records of the two preceding Ashbrook amendments to the NSF budget. Those Representatives who voted with Mr Ashbrook in both years were treated as firm supporters of social science budget reductions and their districts were not included in the network. Those who had opposed Mr Ashbrook on both occasions were assumed to be steadfast in their support of scientific research and, given COSSA's limited time and resources, their districts were also left out of the network. But those

Members of Congress who voted with Mr Ashbrook on one occasion and
against him on another became the focus of COSSA's grassroots political
activities, their inconsistent votes suggesting that they were undecided
but potential supporters of attempts to reject the new budget levels for
social science research.

To create the network, COSSA staff contacted social scientists in over
50 congressional districts in the early summer of 1981. Materials discussing the legislative issues and political strategies involved in preventing
the social science budget cuts were provided and social scientists were
asked to contact their Senators and Representatives. These mailings
were followed up with telephone reminders. The response was encouraging. Congressional mailboxes and telephone logs began to reflect the
concern of the social science community about the Reagan budget policy.
At the Washington level, COSSA staff, frequently in conjunction with
working social scientists, visited virtually every member of the House
and Senate authorising or appropriating subcommittees dealing with the
NSF budget, explaining what social science research encompassed and
why it was important. In many congressional offices, the issue of the
social science budget cuts began to assume a visibility that social science
issues had never previously achieved.

The first political contest

These political efforts, in conjunction with the other activities described
earlier, bore results in the form of decisions taken by the House and
Senate Appropriations Committees to increase the funds available for
social science research in the NSF budget for FY 1982. However the first
and most visible political contest over the social science budget cuts took
place in July 1981, in the House of Representatives debate and vote on
the NSF appropriation. The House Appropriations Committee had
added $70 million to the administration's request for the National
Science Foundation budget, making it clear that some of the added funds
were to be used to increase the budgets of the Foundation's social and
behavioral science research programs. In advance of the consideration of
the bill by the full House, Republican Larry Winn of Kansas, ranking
minority member of the House Subcommittee on Science, Research, and
Technology, announced that he would propose an amendment to bring
the appropriation back down to the level requested by the administration. If passed, the Winn Amendment would have caused significant
damage to the Foundation's social and behavioral science research
programs by upholding the administration's budget cuts and by supporting the administration's budget policy for social science research.

COSSA worked to defeat the amendment in a number of ways. A memo from COSSA was sent to over 4,000 social scientists by their disciplinary associations urging them to contact their Representatives on this issue. Other academic associations also notified their members of the impending vote. Members of the COSSA grassroots network, at this point consisting of over 1,200 social scientists, were sent information about the appropriation and the amendment and were asked to help. In addition, COSSA sent a letter to each of the 435 Members of the House of Representatives asking that they support the Appropriations Committee recommendations to add $70 million to the NSF budget and that they oppose the Winn Amendment. COSSA staff, working with the staff of the American Psychological Association (APA) a member of COSSA, followed up the letters social scientists had sent to their Representatives with visits to congressional offices in Washington, stressing constituents' desire to defeat the amendment. COSSA also worked with friendly Members of Congress to see that 'Dear Colleague' letters from both Republicans and Democrats were sent to all Representatives urging bipartisan opposition to the Winn Amendment.

Through this process, Members of Congress who indicated they were in favor of restoring social science research funds were asked if they would make a statement during the floor debate on the appropriation. COSSA staff, together with APA staff and Dr F. Thomas Juster of the Institute for Social Research at the University of Michigan, then wrote statements for these Congressmen to deliver during the debate. Prior to the vote, COSSA was in frequent contact with both majority (Democratic) and minority (Republican) staff of the House Appropriations Committee to identify and bolster possible opponents of the Winn Amendment. Finally, after the debate, COSSA arranged for supportive Republican and Democratic Congressmen to stand at the doors of the House and encourage opposition to the amendment as their congressional colleagues walked on the floor to vote.

The debate on the Winn Amendment differed appreciably from other recent House debates on the NSF budget. Representative Ashbrook, who had previously led the attack on the social sciences, had died several months earlier and was no longer a participant in the debate. But the difference in 1981 was not the absence of derogatory references to social science research. It was, rather, that the social sciences were at the center of a sustained discussion that was highly supportive of social science research and strongly opposed to the administration's budget cuts in this area. Member after Member rose to discuss why it was necessary to maintain and not to cut social science research budgets. The 'silly research book', a collection of materials put together over the years by congressional staff to defend particular social science research projects from the verbal attacks of Members of Congress, was never needed. Only one Representative criticised the social sciences in the debate, and his remarks were quickly followed by those of another Congressman who complained of the ease with which one could burlesque research and thus avoid dealing with its demonstrated usefulness and importance to the nation. Even Mr Winn, who had proposed his amendment to support the President's budget, made it clear that he was concerned about government spending and was not opposed to social science research.

In the end, the Winn Amendment was defeated by a vote of 264 to 152, the largest vote that year in the House of Representatives in opposition to a Reagan budget measure. Among those voting against the amendment were 69 Republicans who made it clear that they regarded research support – including social science research support – as a bipartisan issue. Since the appropriation affected the total NSF budget, the Winn Amendment would probably have been defeated even without the efforts of the social scientists, but the margin of defeat would have been considerably smaller and the debate quite different in orientation. As it was, the issue of social science research budgets dominated the House debate on the measure. In sharp contrast to earlier congressional debates on NSF budgets, there were, with the single exception mentioned above, no attacks on social science research. Instead, members of the House stressed over and over that it was in the national interest to restore funds for critical research in the social and behavioral sciences. This was remarkable not only because it contradicted the Reagan administration's explicit budget request, but because it was only two years since the House itself had passed an amendment to eliminate NSF's social science budget.

Important as it was politically and symbolically, the defeat of the Winn amendment was merely a battle in the larger effort to restore social science research budgets. The administration subsequently cut the NSF budget for FY 1982 once more – without reference to social science research budgets this time – and the congressional appropriation for NSF had to go through several additional stages before it became law. Once the appropriation for NSF had passed both Houses of Congress and the two bills were reconciled in a conference committee, Foundation officials were responsible for determining the final levels of social and behavioral science research budgets for FY 1982.

Even while the congressional lobbying was taking place, COSSA was attempting to persuade federal officials at NSF, the White House Office of Science and Technology Policy (OSTP), and the Office of Management and Budget (OMB) that without a significant restoration of funding for FY 1982, social science research programs at the Foundation would be seriously curtailed and valuable research data would not be collected. For example, COSSA representatives met repeatedly over the summer and early fall of 1981 with the Director of the Foundation and members of his staff to discuss the issue of social science research budgets. In addition, he and others in the Foundation received visits and letters from academic social scientists about the need to restore the budget cuts.

At the same time as COSSA and the research community exerted pressure from the outside, social scientists within the Foundation were making similar arguments. Formally representatives of the administration, National Science Foundation staff were outside the political process and were expected to support the administration's decisions. However, they were also representatives of the scientific community and were responsible for representing the best interests of their science. Respecting the limits of this ambiguous role, social scientists in the Foundation successfully persuaded the National Science Board, the governing board of the Foundation, to adopt a statement of support for social science research at its June, 1981, meeting.

When the congressional budget process was finally completed, NSF emerged with a lower overall budget than it had expected for FY 1982. Despite this, however, the Director of the Foundation and OMB officials, responding to the arguments of the social scientists and the support they had obtained in the administration and Congress, restored $11 million to the Foundation's social and behavioral science research programs. This was far from a full restoration of the original research budgets, but it was a much better outcome than either the social scientists had feared or their opponents had expected.

Establishing a permanent organisation

The restoration of $11 million to the NSF social and behavioral science research programs marked a victory of sorts, but it was widely recognised that the political problems of the social sciences were not over and that there was a need for a continuing political advocate for social science research in Washington. Despite this, it was not always clear over the summer and fall of 1981 that COSSA's Washington office would be maintained beyond the immediate crisis. There were strong centrifugal forces in the consortium, both in the divergent interests of the member associations and in the great disparities in size among the members. The three months originally allocated for the COSSA effort were stretched twice for six week periods, and then by another three months. Finally, after funds for a full year's budget had been pledged, the ten disciplinary associations decided to make COSSA a formal, permanent advocacy organisation. COSSA was incorporated and its staff registered with the Congress as lobbyists.

Two problems that needed to be worked out for the new organisation were its financial structure and its governing structure. In the last several months of 1981, a new governing structure evolved for the organisation. It consisted of an Executive Committee of ten members, composed of the executive officers of the member organisations (for the American Economic Association, which was located outside of Washington, this meant a local representative of the executive officer) which met monthly to set COSSA policies and priorities. A Board of Directors, meeting once a year, approved the budget and set broad policy guidelines for the organisation. The Board included an elected officer from each of the member associations, the ten executive officers, and four at-large representatives of the research community.

Financial support was obtained from several sources. Despite the budget pressures experienced by a number of COSSA member organisations, each association nonetheless committed financial resources and some autonomy to the new organisation. A tax of $2.00 per 'social scientist' member was levied on each association. Minimum and maximum contributions were established to avoid a situation where one association had an inordinately large or small financial role in the organization. In time, smaller scholarly associations and learned societies were also invited to join the effort by becoming COSSA affiliates. They were asked for considerably lower contributions than the member associations and, in a number of cases, the contribution was set at whatever amount the organization could afford.

A third form of support was obtained through research universities and social science institutions such as the Social Science Research Council (SSRC) and the Center for Advanced Research in the Behavioral Sciences. Dr Harold Shapiro, President of the University of Michigan agreed to help solict COSSA support from leading research universities in the U.S. A letter outlining the importance of such support was signed by Dr Shapiro and by the presidents of Harvard University and Columbia University, and the chancellors of the University of California, Berkeley, and the University of California, Los Angeles (UCLA). Universities were requested to contribute according to a sliding scale based on the total amount of federal social science research funds each had received in the previous year.

The contributions from the three sources – members, affiliates, and institutions – gave COSSA an operating budget large enough to enable the organisation to expand its scope beyond lobbying for NSF social and behavioral science research budgets to include other activities that can be grouped loosely under the categories legislation, education and communication. Each of these areas of COSSA activity during Mr Reagan's first term is discussed below.

Legislation

COSSA's emphasis on the NSF budget gave way after the first year to a more diverse set of legislative issues. Each year, after the President sent his budget to the Congress, the COSSA Executive Committee and staff met to set legislative priorities. These were not confined to the size of research budgets because in some agencies, policy issues took priority. For example, the National Institutes of Health (NIH) generally provided low levels of support for social science research. Rather than seeking congressional appropriations for increasing such expenditures, however, COSSA worked with congressional staff to obtain legislation requiring that each NIH institute appoint a specific number of social and behavioral scientists to its advisory board. This strategy assumed that advisory boards would be more effective than legislative mandate in reorienting NIH research priorities. In another case, COSSA successfully urged the Congress to require a research agency to institute scientific review procedures in place of what appeared to be an arbitrary (and often political) process of selecting research proposals to fund.

Education

The operating assumption behind all COSSA's activites was that opposition to the social sciences was due to ignorance or misinformation about social science research. From this perspective, lobbying was essentially an educational activity and overtly educational activities were viewed as direct contributions to the lobbying effort. COSSA therefore placed a high priority on providing information about social science research to Members of Congress, officials of federal agencies, and the public. To this end, the organisation sponsored a series of congressional seminars. Seminar topics ranged from industrial innovation and productivity, the subject of the first seminar, to health and human behavior and youth unemployment, topics of later seminars. The first several seminars were co-sponsored with the American Association for the Advancement of Science (AAAS) and were further evidence of that organisation's strong support for the social sciences. Later COSSA began to conduct seminars on its own and with other organisations as well. In each case, a topic of national or specifically congressional interest was selected for the seminar and researchers were invited to present their findings.

In addition to the congressional seminars, COSSA representatives met with the heads of federal research agencies to discuss social science research and its relationship to the purposes of each agency. Although the results of these visits were mixed, they served to bring issues of importance to the social sciences to the attention of research agency directors; they also provided COSSA with an opportunity to raise questions about social science research support in the agencies.

COSSA saw its task not only as educating politicians about social science, but also educating social scientists about budget politics. COSSA prepared 'how-to' information sheets on such topics as how to telephone a Member of Congress, how to arrange an appointment with a Member and what to do after the visit, and how to write a Senator or Representative. Members of the grassroots network were informed of legislative issues prior to congressional recesses when Members of Congress would leave Washington to spend time in their districts and meet with constituents. In addition, COSSA representatives spoke at the annual meetings of social science organisations, providing information about the current status of research budgets, COSSA's activities, and ways for individuals to take part in the political effort.

Communication

In addition to its legislative and educational activities, COSSA attempted to provide information about political and policy issues in Washington to the social science community. The principal vehicle for this effort was a newsletter, the *COSSA Washington Update*. First issued weekly, then biweekly, the newsletter contained articles about legislation, research budgets, social science policy issues, sources of research support, and social science news from other nations. Because the newsletter was sent to social scientists in all disciplines, it attempted to establish a common ground of interest and information across the disciplines. Because it was read by university administrators, federal agency research administrators, congressional staff, and reporters for major newspapers, the newsletter also provided current information about social science issues to a diverse and influential audience.

COSSA attempted to improve media coverage of social science research issues in a number of ways. In addition to sending the newsletter to reporters, COSSA sent copies of the papers presented at congressional seminars to those who had attended and to the press. Moreover, in order to encourage social scientists to report their research findings to a broader audience than their academic peers, COSSA circulated materials on how to prepare a press release to members of the research community. The purpose of these activities was to counteract the lingering public distrust of the social sciences that was a legacy of the Golden Fleece awards by providing the public and the media with accurate and useful information on social science research.

At the end of the first term

At the end of Mr Reagan's first term, the social sciences in the United States were both stronger and weaker than they had been at the beginning of the term. The source of weakness was quite simple: overall, federal budgets for social science research were still lower than they had been before Mr Reagan took office. This, at a time when social science research projects and data collection were becoming larger and more expensive, imposed a significant hardship on the research community.

The sources of new strength for the social sciences are more diverse, and over the long term may prove to be more important. First, the Reagan administration was stymied in its attempts to reduce certain social science research budgets. In NSF, for example, the budgets of some of the social and behavioral science programs had been restored to the pre-Reagan levels by the end of the first term and the remainder were approaching that level. In a few agencies, such as the National Institute on Drug Abuse, social science research budgets had actually increased over the FY 1980 levels, although in others, such as the Department of Labor, research programs had almost disappeared. What is significant is not the absolute size of research budgets but the fact that social science research support remained one of the functions of the federal government and that function was no longer seriously questioned.

A second area in which the social science community emerged in a stronger condition at the end of the first term was in the exercise of political power. Social scientists succeeded in building political support in the Congress that prevented the administration from accomplishing its goals for social science budgets and would discourage a repetition of the administration's budget attack of 1981. The political activities of social scientists acting both through COSSA and its member associations and independently provided a classic example of successful interest group politics in the United States.

A third source of strength for the social sciences was their newly acquired political unity. A political crisis, the Reagan budget cuts, created a social science constituency and a social science identification where there had previously been separate disciplines and diverse interests. In addition to the demonstrated political and organisational benefits of unity, the experience of members of many disciplines working together to restore research budgets may assist the research effort as well. Increasingly, the major expenditures for social science research – whether in data bases, instrumentation, or major research endeavors – benefit both intellectually and practically from interdisciplinary participation. That kind of participation is made easier when social scientists have worked together on common problems in other areas.

Paradoxically, it may be that the virulence and depth of the Reagan budget proposals in the first months of 1981 created the conditions necessary for the social sciences to defeat the administration's plans for significant reductions in social science research budgets. If the Reagan administration had been less sweeping in its plans to cut social science research, if the cuts had been more modest or were distributed across all the sciences, or if the administration had been less successful in obtaining congressional approval of its other budget recommendations, then social scientists might have responded differently and less decisively to the budget cuts. However in 1981, the threat posed by the administration was so great that social scientists felt they had little choice but to oppose the budget cuts as actively and as forcefully as possible. Previous reluctance to engage in lobbying disappeared. As a result, by the end of the first term the immediate crisis for social science research funding had subsided, and the social sciences had emerged both with the political experience and unity and with the organisational resources to deal with a similar situation should it arise again.

NOTES

1 For a discussion of congressional attitudes towards social science research before the election of Ronald Reagan, see 'Congressional Budgeting for NSF', by Roberta Balstad Miller, *Public Data Use*, 7(5/6), 1979, pp. 11–13.
2 Those who testified were Reynolds Farley (University of Michigan), Harlan Lane (Northeastern University), Frederick Mosteller (Harvard University), Kenneth Prewitt (Social Science Research Council), Judith Rodin (Yale University), and Herbert A. Simon (Carnegie-Mellon University).
3 *Additional Details on Budget Savings*, Executive Office of the President, Office of Management and Budget, April 1981. Throughout this essay, the term, 'social sciences' is used to encompass those disciplines that are also described by the two terms, social sciences and behavioral sciences.
4 These are discussed more fully in 'Social Science Research in a Conservative Society: The Impact of the Reagan Budget Cuts', unpublished paper by

F. Thomas Juster, presented to the New York Academy of Sciences, January 1982.
5 *Science*, 212, 1 May 1981, p. 497. Mr Carey's editorial is also cited in 'Federal Funding for the Social Sciences: Threats and Responses', by Kenneth Prewitt and David L. Sills, *Items*, 35(3), 1981, p. 43. This article provides a useful summary of the response of social scientists to the budget cuts in the early months of the Reagan administration.
6 In the course of the year, social scientists testified before numerous congressional committees and subcommittees. The first testimony was presented before the House Subcommittee on Science, Research and Technology on 12 March 1981. Zvi Griliches (Harvard University), Lawrence R. Klein (University of Pennsylvania), and Henry W. Riecken (University of Pennsylvania) presented testimony.
7 For further information about the establishment of the Consortium of Social Science Associations, see 'The Institutionalization of COSSA: An Innovative Response to Crisis by American Social Science', by Russell R. Dynes, *Sociological Inquiry*, 54(2), 1984, pp. 211–29; and 'Scientists Beginning to Lobby for More Research Funding', *Congressional Quarterly Weekly Report*, 41(11), 1983, pp. 555–9. Additional information on COSSA's activities during this period can be found in the COSSA Annual Reports for 1982, 1983, and 1984.

Index